THE MAUPEOU REVOLUTION

DURAND ECHEVERRIA

The Maupeou Revolution

A STUDY IN THE HISTORY
OF LIBERTARIANISM

France, 1770–1774

Louisiana State University Press

Baton Rouge and London

Copyright © 1985 by Louisiana State University Press
All rights reserved
Manufactured in the United States of America
Typeface: Linotron Garamond #3
Typesetter: Moran Colorgraphic
Printer and binder: Edwards Brothers, Inc.

Library of Congress Cataloging in Publication Data

Echeverria, Durand.
  The Maupeou Revolution.

  Bibliography: p.
  Includes index.
  1. Prerogative, Royal—France—History—18th century.
  2. Legislative power—France—History—18th century.
  3. France—Politics and government—1715–1774.
  4. Maupeou, René-Nicolas-Charles-Augustin de, 1714–1792.
  5. Political science—France—History—18th century. I. Title.
JN 2369.E26   1985   321.6'0944   84-21327
ISBN 0-8071-1210-0

To B. V. E.

CONTENTS

PREFACE

During the last thirty years of the eighteenth century and the first decades of the nineteenth the civilized countries on both sides of the Atlantic were convulsed by a succession of revolutions. In all of them men used power to change suddenly and radically political or social structures, but they did so by a variety of means, sometimes with fearful bloodshed, sometimes with little violence, and for many different reasons. Urban mobs, peasants, bourgeois, aristocrats, and kings all took their turns at revolution.

The Maupeou revolution, as it was called, which occurred in France from 1770 to 1774, was royalist and (except for some police action in the first stage) nonviolent. It produced immediately a radical but temporary political change and contributed to a profound and lasting transformation in the way the French thought about their government and their society.

The parlements of Paris and the provinces, courts with quasi-legislative functions, had since the Middle Ages shared governmental power with the crown. In the seventeenth century they had attempted unsuccessfully by armed force to make their share dominant, and in the latter half of the eighteenth century they made a second effort, this time by nonviolently eroding the authority of the throne. Louis XV, in a carefully planned coup skillfully managed by his chancellor, René Nicolas Charles Augustin de Maupeou, met the challenge by exiling the magistrates of the Paris Parlement, reforming the provincial parlements, setting up new courts composed of appointees amenable to his royal will, and clearly establishing the absolute power of the crown. The coup succeeded and the new regime lasted until the king's death in 1774, after which the new structure quickly collapsed, for Louis XVI was persuaded by his advisers to dismiss Maupeou and to reinstate the old parlements with their former powers virtually intact.

Thus the Maupeou revolution was ultimately a political failure and accomplished little except to demonstrate that the monarchy could not reform itself. This is not to say, however, that the episode was without consequences. Some historians have speculated that the continuation of Maupeou's reforms might have saved the monarchy, that the French Revolution became inevitable only when his ministry was dismissed by Louis XVI. An equally tenable contrary supposition might be that, under the circumstances that actually existed, a prolongation of this sort of absolutism in France could have hastened the plunge into anti-monarchical revolution. Such unreal hypotheses do not, however, help us to understand what did in fact occur. It seems more productive to attempt to discover what were the actual effects of the actual events.

The thesis of this study is that although Maupeou's political reforms were later reversed or supplanted and so had little historical effect, the crisis of 1770–1774 had ideological consequences of considerable importance. The chancellor's extreme actions provoked intense discussion among the literate classes throughout the nation and aroused both support and passionate opposition. This debate brought to light and subjected to thorough scrutiny the serious political and social problems besetting the nation. The consequence was that many independent-minded persons became newly and acutely aware of the inadequacies of the two alternatives the nation was offered, an absolute monarchy or a monarchy subservient to free-wheeling aristocratic parlements. Creative minds began an active search for a third and better option. This search could not, however, be conducted in an ideological vacuum. Proposals for new political and social structures had to be fashioned from the available cultural inventory by adaptation or rejection of elements found in existing social and political models. The eighteenth-century mind, which habitually thought dialectically, sought to create out of the opposition of the royalist thesis and the parliamentary antithesis a new libertarian synthesis.

Thus neither the *thèse royale* nor the *thèse parlementaire* was barren or wholly anti-libertarian. Both had contained and continued to contain libertarian elements, and independent libertarians, though anti-aristocratic and anti-absolutistic, shared with the aristocrats and absolutists parallel or identical ideas on many points. It is this fact that explains what seem to a modern reader anomalies and contradictions in eighteenth-century thought and politics—that the great libertarian Montesquieu could have been the principal theoretician of the aristocratic parliamentary magistrates and that the great libertarian Voltaire defended the absolutistic Louis XV against aristocrats and Philosophes alike. It is also this peculiar ideological and political context that distinguishes eighteenth-century libertarianism from nineteenth- and twentieth-century liberalism, which has forgotten or renounced its aristocratic and absolutistic origins and has become preoccupied with problems unknown to the eighteenth century.

The interrelations of libertarianism, absolutism, and aristocracy were clearly revealed in the flood of writings and the ferment of ideas occasioned by the events of 1770–1774. It is this intellectual revolution, rather than the political revolution which occasioned it, that is the subject of the following pages. This book is an essay in intellectual history, an attempt to discover and describe, as well as can be done from surviving written evidence, what men and women were thinking during this crisis, both as individuals and as members of groups. It is also an attempt to define the various patterns of this thought, patterns of ideological behavior, one might say, which existed synchronically at the historical moment of the early 1770s. Since these patterns are intelligible only if viewed comprehensively, we must examine, it must be stressed, not merely the ideas related directly to the Maupeou revolution but also all others which were part of the total social, political, and ideological situation in these years, including those already current in December 1770.

Thus this is an examination of the thought of a historical moment, not a history of the development of ideas in time. The description of cultural change, and particularly of the "evolution" of patterns of thinking (to speak metaphorically), is a problem for which there is probably no completely satisfactory solution. Daniel Mornet wrote of his classic work *Les Origines intellectuelles de la Révolution française*, "This study of the diffusion [of ideas] required a complex and cumbersome methodology. It was continually necessary to take chronology into account; the same idea did not have the same significance and implications [*portée*] in 1720, in 1760, and in 1780; yet it was impossible to cut up the century into too many small segments."[1] One might respectfully suggest that while the most practical

---

1. Daniel Mornet, *Les Origines intellectuelles de la Révolution française, 1715–1787* (Paris, 1933), 2.

way to write a study such as Mornet's covering seventy-two years was probably to divide the period into a few segments such as the three he chose, namely 1715–1747, 1748–1770, and 1771–1787, and to treat the thought of each segment more or less synchronically, such an expedient does not solve the dilemma. The significances of ideas may have changed, for instance, as much between 1771 and 1787 as between 1720 and 1760. This present study hopes to explore a solution to this vexing problem by concentrating attention on a brief but important episode in French intellectual history which was long enough to produce describable ideologies but short enough to permit synchronic analysis without excessive distortion. Perhaps such an effort, especially if supplemented by others of a similar nature examining earlier or later limited periods, may lead eventually to a clearer understanding of the progressive changes in French thought during the eighteenth century and of the ideological origins of the French Revolution.

In focusing our attention on the analysis of the ideas current at a certain moment in the course of history we cannot yield to the temptation to give accounts of all the relevant circumstances, for to do so would expand the modest monograph intended to virtually infinite dimensions. We must be concerned, of course, with the political events which immediately caused, stimulated, or modified ideas and also with certain other immediate social circumstances, but it would be beyond our purposes to investigate sociological causes, the relationships, for instance, between class or economic structure and certain ideologies. Similarly we shall note the influence of earlier writers and take into account the previous developments of the principal ideological movements involved—parliamentary, royalist, Physiocratic, and Philosophic; but to retrace in detail these earlier currents or to attempt a systematic history of the ideological origins of the Maupeou revolution would require writing a comprehensive history of French thought to 1774. Though not all the documents examined were written or published during the years 1770 to 1774, they have all been used for the light they cast on French thought during these years. By the same token, to write a fully documented history of the later developments of the ideas of 1770–1774 up to, say, 1789, would be to write a diachronic history of the ideological origins of the French Revolution. In order to illustrate, however, the significance of the thought engendered by the Maupeou revolution, the conclusion does venture a tentative, hypothetical, and undocumented suggestion of how the patterns of thought described synchronically for the years 1770–1774 may have changed and developed diachronically into those ideologies which affected the style and substance of the writings and actions of the French Revolution.

French political and social thought in the eighteenth century, and notably during these crucial years 1770–1774, was so diverse that it resists every taxonomic effort to order it into precise monolithic categories to which every writer or document may be neatly assigned. Yet in order to render comprehensible the chaos of ideas, some sort of order must be imposed in terms of some assumption. In this case the assumption has been that one central issue dominated the political arena during these years, namely whether France was to be ruled by some form of absolute monarchy or whether the governance of the nation was to be in the hands of aristocratic corporations, and that a writer's adoption of one or the other of these propositions, or his refusal to accept either alternative, was, for the moment at least, the best index to his political orientation and a significant determinant of his social philosophy.

The Introduction provides briefly the background of the political events and the state of public opinion. Part I examines the ideas of the self-styled Patriotes, those who supported the original parlements against Maupeou and who produced new versions of what was called the parliamentary or aristocratic thesis. Part II includes analyses of the most significant contemporary exponents of absolutism, first Maupeou's administration and his propagandists, among whom was Voltaire, and then two other examples of absolutistic political philosophy, Linguet and the Physiocrats. Lastly, Part III, "The Third Position," treats the writers who may best be described as "independents," those who, for one reason or another, did not enlist as partisans of either the parlements or Maupeou or did not elaborate theories supportive of either absolutism or of government by aristocratic corporations. These independent thinkers included most, though not all, of the so-called Philosophes but also others who would have rejected that label. As the following pages will show, a good deal of ideological variation is to be found among those adopting any one of these three possible political positions, yet it does seem to turn out that there was within the thought of each group a general coherence which was a function of the writers' positions in the debate between aristocracy and absolutism.

The documentation of a study of such scope could never pretend to completeness. All located primary sources, published or unpublished, which appeared relevant to French social and political thought of the period have been examined, although only those of intrinsic significance or aptly illustrative of prevalent ideas are analyzed or cited. Yet it is well to remember that every scrap of writing influenced by the French experience of 1770–1774 might be to some extent illuminating, and this could be particularly true of unexploited archival materials which might throw needed light on the personalities and motives of the more obscure Patriote and royalist propagandists and on the broader reaches of their thinking beyond the immediate political issues—the sort of information which fortunately is at hand for such well-documented figures as Voltaire and Diderot. Moreover, the horizontal breadth of this inquiry renders virtually every scholarly work related to the directions of modern Western thought to some extent relevant. While acknowledgments have been made of substantial debts—as to Georges Weulersse for his exhaustive studies on the Physiocrats—and interpretations at variance on significant points with those of other scholars have been noted, it would have been otiose to have documented every instance in which my conclusions have paralleled or varied from those of the host of students of the same subjects. It is hoped, for instance, that readers interested in the question of Voltaire's political realism will recognize without assistance the points on which I have differed somewhat from Peter Gay's excellent study.[2]

This book could not have been written without the support provided by a fellowship awarded by the John Simon Guggenheim Memorial Foundation and a Fulbright Postdoctoral Research Grant, which made possible the basic research in the libraries of Paris, or without several stipends for summer research and writing awarded by Brown University. For this assistance, and equally for the guidance during my early investigations by Professors Jean Egret and Ira Wade and for the encouragement and criticism of my colleagues, I am deeply grateful.

2. Peter Gay, *Voltaire's Politics: The Poet as Realist* (Princeton, 1959).

THE MAUPEOU REVOLUTION

The Background of Events

T HE PARLEMENT of Paris had developed out of the King's Court, the *Curia Regis* of the early monarchy. The provincial parlements, possessing smaller jurisdiction and inferior prestige and power, had been created at various dates from 1443 to 1686 and were located in Rennes, Rouen, Toulouse, Dijon, Besançon, Aix, Bordeaux, Grenoble, Douai, Metz, Dombes, and Pau. In addition to being the highest judicial courts, they had developed over the centuries important legislative, investigative, and administrative powers. Since the States General had not met since 1614 and since the provincial states had suffered a decline in power, the parlements had consequently become virtually the only political bodies within the monarchy capable of resisting effectively the royal government and of maintaining a degree of political independence.

Since the Middle Ages the Parlement of Paris had operated in a curiously ambivalent partnership with the king. On the one hand, it never challenged the ultimate authority of the crown, and in fact it was traditionally the most zealous defender of the independence of France from foreign, particularly papal, control. On the other hand, it made throughout its history sporadic efforts to increase its own powers and prerogatives, to limit the constitutional powers of the king, and to maintain the principle of the sovereignty of the French nation.

The Paris Parlement's most serious challenge to the throne had been made during the minority of Louis XIV in the seventeenth century when it led the people of the city in armed revolt and for a time drove the royal court out of the capital. When Louis attained his majority and took over himself the functions of prime minister he made his key internal policy to reduce the political powers of the parlements, and he succeeded so well that he created a monarchy essentially absolute in principle if not in practice. After Louis' death in 1715, however, Philippe d'Orléans, in order to persuade the Parlement of Paris to set aside the royal will and appoint him sole regent during the minority of Louis XV, restored virtually all the court's abolished powers. From this point until the Revolution there ensued between the Parlement of Paris and the crown a continuous political struggle in which the former progressively gained ground until 1770. It did so not by erecting barricades in the streets, as it had during the Fronde Parlementaire of 1648–1649, but by political means, gradually eroding the royal authority and broadening its own powers, both in right and in fact.

These powers consisted mainly of the rights of verification, registration, and remonstrance. By established constitutional theory and practice, the king, acting through his council of ministers, was the source of all legislation, but a law did not have legal force until it had been "verified" and formally registered by the parlements and certain lower courts. By the Declaration of Vincennes of 1715 the Parlement of Paris had regained the right to withhold registration of any law of which it did not approve and to address to the king remonstrances detailing the reasons for its opposition. If the court did not accept the king's justifications of the law in question it could create further delay by iterative remonstrances. The king could then issue *lettres de jussion*, commanding the court to register the law. If these were ignored, he could hold a *lit de justice*, a session of the Parlement at which he or his representative presided and personally ordered the registration. The Parlement could still, however, vote an *arrêt de défense*, forbidding lower courts to recognize the law at issue, to which the king's council could reply by an *arrêt* annulling the *arrêt de défense*. The Parlement's final recourse was to suspend the execution of justice, refusing to hear new cases and bringing to a halt the judicial process within its jurisdiction. The king could then exile the court as a body, as he did in 1720 and 1732, or even take the extreme step of ordering the arrest or exile of the members and replacing the Parlement with a specially appointed court. Usually at some point in this constitutional game one side or the other yielded, but in 1771 the struggle was carried to the ultimate showdown.

The parliamentary magistrates based their right to exercise this form of legislative veto on precedents which, they claimed, had been established in the early monarchy and on the semilegendary powers of the ancient national assemblies, the Comita and the Champ de Mars. Actually their constitutional principles were the creation of a number of brilliant theorists and publicists, of which Montesquieu and Louis Adrien Le Paige, a Jansenistic lawyer, were the brightest lights. These several apologists had drawn inspiration and precedents from the polemics of the parliamentary *Frondeurs* of the seventeenth century, the republican arguments of sixteenth-century Protestant writers and Catholic *Ligueurs*, and even from the doctrines of medieval scholastics.

The magistrates supported their theory of limited monarchy by a number of political principles. The first was called "unity of classes," which meant that the Parlement of Paris was "the chief and metropolitan court of the kingdom," but that all the other parlements were "detachments, or better said, extensions of it. Thus the metropolitan court and all its colonies [were] the various classes of a single and unique Parlement, the various members of a single and unique body, all animated by the same spirit, nourished by the same principles, dedicated to the same purposes." [1]

Second, the parlements asserted the existence of an inviolable French constitution composed of certain "fundamental laws" established by contract between the king and the nation, which the king could not unilaterally abrogate and of which the parlements, acting as a collective supreme court, were the "guardians." Thus they claimed the right to veto laws on grounds not only of policy but also of constitutionality.

This doctrine was based on the third principle that sovereignty resided in the nation, not in the person of the king. By the social contract the nation had delegated certain powers to the crown but had retained the remainder. In the absence of the States General, the parlements claimed to be the constitutional organs and representatives of this national sovereignty.

1. Remonstrances of August 4, 1756. *Les Remontrances du parlement de Paris au 18ᵉ siècle*, ed. Jules Flammermont (Paris, 1895), II, 138.

The parlements' specific functions within this constitution remained, however, uncertain. They frequently referred to themselves as "intermediary powers," a term made current by Montesquieu. Yet since the "constitution" was nowhere set down in a single document but was a composite of historic and legendary precedents, practices, laws, and decrees, variously selected and interpreted according to one constitutional theory or another, the courts' intermediary role could be diversely defined. Did "intermediary powers" imply, as Montesquieu had said, that the parlements were merely "channels" through which monarchical power flowed and was checked, regulated, and "moderated"? Were they impartial arbiters between the two parties to the contract, the king and the nation? Or were they the organs of the national will, the representatives of the nation's inalienable sovereignty, and thus vested with legislative, taxing, and investigative powers as well as judicial authority? It was over these constitutional issues that the Maupeou revolution was waged.

Whatever the claims of the parlements to represent the entire nation, they were in fact composed of members of a single class, the nobility, and they tended to champion aristocratic interests. The office of magistrate in the courts conferred noble status either immediately or after a period of years. It was also venal, that is, originally and still theoretically purchasable by anyone meeting the requirements of age and training. Nevertheless the additional requirements in some parlements of noble birth or of connections with a parliamentary family, the prevalence of intermarriages between parliamentary families, and the frequent practice of passing down an office from one generation to another within a family, all contributed to make the magistracy to a large extent hereditary in fact.

This *noblesse de robe*, as the magistrates and their families were called, was distinct in its predominantly bourgeois origins from the more ancient and prestigious *noblesse d'épée*, but it constituted an *état*, a special functional group within the aristocracy, rather than a separate caste or class. A few magistrates were of the ancient *noblesse chevaleresque*, some descended from parliamentary families that had achieved noble status as early as the fourteenth century, and many belonged to families which had been noble for several generations. It is true that throughout the eighteenth century some *roturiers* continued to make their ways into the magistracy, but the percentage of commoners entering the Paris Parlement from 1715 to 1771 held steady at about a mere 10 percent, which probably was approximately the general rate of accession of wealthy bourgeois into the nobility as a whole by the purchase of *charges* such as *secrétaire du roi* or by other means.[2] Moreover such newly ennobled magistrates were characteristically eager to assimilate themselves to their aristocratic colleagues and zealously exercised their new prerogatives. The *noblesse de robe*, in wealth, in social status, in privileges, and in way of life, were not significantly distinguishable from the nobility as a whole or from the older *noblesse d'épée*.[3] Consequently they acted like nobles politically, working to protect aristocratic privileges, subordinating national to class interests, and enjoying the support of the majority of the upper economic and social classes, from the wealthy bourgeoisie to the Princes of the Blood. Moreover their political power was enhanced by their remarkable esprit de corps, by the cohesiveness produced by intermarriage and common economic and social interests, and by the pride of parliamentary dynasties such as the Lamoignons. The self-esteem and approbativeness of the magistrates was visibly manifested in their magnificent costumes and in the proud traditions of the courts, their claims to ancient origin, their prestige as the most powerful corporations in the kingdom, and the pretension of the premier président of the Paris Parlement to rank above the Princes of the Blood. Finally, it is a fact that their ranks included, along with incompetent and surprisingly many young and inexperienced magistrates, men of great ability, intelligence, and prestige, such as Malesherbes and Maupeou himself, the scion of a notable parliamentary family.

There was no doubt a measure of justification for the accusations of contemporaries such as the Abbé de Véri that the parlements "became

2. François Bluche, *Les Magistrats du parlement de Paris au 18ᵉ siècle, 1715–1771* (Paris, 1960), 82–83, 380; William O. Doyle, *The Parlement of Bordeaux and the End of the Old Regime, 1771–1790* (London, 1974), 12–22.

3. Bluche, *Les Magistrats*, 380 and *passim*. Bluche concedes that his conclusions are valid only for the magistrates of the Parlement of Paris, the largest and most important of the courts, but, while similar studies of the other parlements reveal local variations, there is no reason to suppose that the nationwide picture was significantly different. See also François Bluche, *L'Origine des magistrats du parlement de Paris au 18ᵉ siècle (1715–1771): Dictionnaire généalogique* (Paris, 1956); Albert Colombet, *Les Parlementaires bourguignons à la fin du 18ᵉ siècle* (Dijon, 1937); Jean Egret, "L'Opposition aristocratique en France au 18ᵉ siècle," *Information historique*, November–December, 1949, pp. 181–86; Jean Egret, *Le Parlement de Dauphiné et les affaires publiques dans la deuxième moitié du 18ᵉ siècle* (Grenoble, 1942); Doyle, *The Parlement of Bordeaux*, 127–41.

aroused over trifles which were of no importance to the state, . . . sold to the Court their silence on every issue that concerned taxes, the rights of the people, or the happiness of citizens," and while pretending to be the zealous defenders of the public welfare worked only "to defend their corporative privileges, their personal jurisdictions, and their private feuds."[4] Yet the courts constituted more than an aristocratic opposition to the king and his ministers; they were the only visible constitutional opposition to a government that claimed full responsibility for the condition of the French people. To some extent at least the *noblesse de robe* took seriously their role as leaders of the people. Many, as aristocrats in the best sense, accepted the duty to practice and sponsor the arts and sciences and to administer and support local and national institutions such as hospitals, charitable foundations, schools, universities, and the church.[5] Through their investments in private loans, real estate, and industries they were economically linked with peasants, artisans, and the bourgeoisie.[6] As magistrates they did protest, albeit occasionally, against taxes such as the *taille* that did not affect them directly, and they were active in social legislation and regulation, often of the most detailed kind, as indeed they had been since the fourteenth century.[7]

Their most important national service, however, was ideological. The magistrates and their supporters clearly recognized by the latter half of the eighteenth century, if not earlier, that they could gain their ends only with the support of the Third Estate, and that they could not win this support if their only justification was aristocratic privilege. They therefore based their *thèse parlementaire* on broad principles such as national sovereignty, the contract, law, and representative government. These concepts were republican, and they could—and were to—serve the cause of bourgeois republicanism no less well than the purposes of aristocratic republicanism. The parlements were, it is true, reactionary in the sense that

4. Joseph Alphonse de Véri, *Journal de l'abbé de Véri*, ed. Jehan de Witte (Paris, 1928), I, 64–65.

5. Bluche, *Les Magistrats*, 247–58, 289–96; Colombet, *Les Parlementaires bourguignons*, 189 ff., 258–61; J. H. Shennan, *The Parlement of Paris* (Ithaca, 1968), 123.

6. Egret, "L'Opposition aristocratique," 182; Colombet, *Les Parlementaires bourguignons*, 65 ff.; Bluche, *Les Magistrats*, 143–239; Doyle, *The Parlement of Bordeaux*, 52–115.

7. Shennan, *The Parlement of Paris*, 87–89; Egret, "L'Opposition aristocratique," 185; Colombet, *Les Parlementaires bourguignons*, 300–302.

they sought a return to a system of aristocratic power and privilege. Yet by the principles to which they were compelled to appeal out of political expediency—and which some at least of their partisans sincerely believed—they were radical, nationalistic, and republican. As the Count de Ségur later wrote, "The parlements . . . were giving the signal of revolution, though they believed they were only following the precedents set by their predecessors."[8]

From 1715 to 1770 the parlements had fought a series of intermittent battles against the crown on two great issues, that of Gallicanism and Jansenism and that of taxation.

The Parlement of Paris had been consistently Gallican since the thirteenth century in the sense that it had favored the maximum autonomy of the French church within Catholicism and greater independence for both the clergy and the crown from papal control. On this issue they gained early in the eighteenth century valuable allies in the Jansenists, and they reciprocated by supporting Jansenistic political objectives.

Jansenism, a movement within Catholicism born of the Counterreformation in the first half of the seventeenth century, never had any institutional or corporate existence or formal juridical or legal standing, and was consequently marked by considerable internal diversity and successive modifications. It was of course primarily a religious movement principally defined by its well-known tenets of efficacious grace and predestination, by a belief in the sacred autonomy of the individual conscience, and by moral rigorism, and by the 1770s there were still many who were Jansenists in this religious sense, though it had become increasingly difficult to identify those who did or did not possess the requisite inner convictions and moral austerity to merit the distinction. On the other hand, the Jansenists had from the first been embroiled in both national and ecclesiastical politics in a succession of episodes: first the Abbé de Saint Cyran's opposition to Richelieu's foreign policy in 1635; then the long and bitter conflict with the Jesuits, which began in the 1640s; the papacy's successive condemnations of certain Jansenistic propositions, beginning with Innocent X's bull *Cum occasione* in 1653; the Jansenists' alleged guilt by association with the parliamentary *Fronde*; the hostility of Louis XIV, who regarded the individualistic Jansenists as "républicains," that is, as

8. Louis Philippe, Count de Ségur, *Mémoires, souvenirs, et anecdotes* (Paris, 1827), I, 24.

subversive of his ideal of a unified monarchy, and who finally razed the Jansenists' abbey of Port Royal des Champs in 1711; the Jansenists' adoption of "Richerism," the anti-hierarchical ideas attributed to the theologian Edmond Richer (1559–1631), a movement which championed greater spiritual and ecclesiastical authority for the lower clergy at the expense of the episcopal establishment, who normally enjoyed the support of the throne; and most importantly, Clement XI's bull *Unigenitus* of 1713, solicited by Louis XIV, which besides condemning a long list of Jansenistic propositions contained the famous ninety-first article affirming in effect the right of the pope to excommunicate the king and free French subjects from their obligation to obey him, and which instead of settling the Jansenism problem, as Louis had hoped, made of the Jansenists confirmed Gallicans.

Thus by the second decade of the eighteenth century had developed a politicized Jansenism which was Gallican, anti-Jesuit, and anti-hierarchical, which had continually found itself in opposition to royal authority, and which had discovered natural allies among the magistrates and lawyers of the Paris Parlement. This alliance was cemented by a widespread sympathy to religious Jansenism in parliamentary circles and particularly by the existence of a small but active and influential Parti Janséniste of magistrates and lawyers. This group included some of the leading exponents of the *thèse parlementaire*, most notably the lawyer Louis Adrien Le Paige, and consequently political Jansenism came to incorporate also in its platform the principle of national sovereignty and support of the constitutional rights and powers claimed by the parlements in contradiction to royal absolutism. Thus was Jansenism further politicized, and in contemporary usage the term took on the predominantly political connotations that it no doubt had for the diarist Barbier when he wrote in 1752 that "all Paris is Jansenist."

From 1713 to 1765 the magistrates and lawyers of the Parlement of Paris, with varying support from the provincial parlements, both continued their established Gallican policy and supported the Jansenists against the Jesuits and the episcopacy. In 1714 the Paris Parlement refused to register without qualifications the bull *Unigenitus*. In the early 1730s magistrates and lawyers supported the Jansenistic lower clergy of Paris against their archbishop, Vintimille, in the affair of supposed miracles of Saint Médard. In the 1750s the Paris Parlement formally denied the archbishop of Paris' authority to deny the last sacraments to persons who could not produce *billets de confession* attesting their acceptance of the bull *Unigenitus*, and in its *Grands Remontrances* of 1753 it asserted the necessity of "checking the ambitions and activities of the bishops" and condemned the "continual encroachments by the clergy on the temporal powers and their persistence in claiming . . . independence from all secular jurisdiction and all powers of the sovereign."[9] The king countered by exiling the parlement to Pontoise, but he was eventually obliged to recall it. In 1764 the parlements triumphed again when a protracted campaign led by the Parti Janséniste in the Paris Parlement finally achieved the suppression of the Jesuits in France. And lastly in 1765 the Parti Janséniste engineered the Paris Parlement's declaration nullifying the *Actes* of the General Assembly of the Clergy of France of that year, which had attempted to enlarge the independence of the authority of the church hierarchy from civil power.

Thus by 1770 the Parlement of Paris, seconded by various provincial parlements, had for some fifty-seven years been favoring indirectly religious Jansenism, had supported their own and the Jansenists' Gallicanism, had achieved for the Jansenists their prime objective of the destruction of the Jesuits and a greater subordination of the church hierarchy to civil power, and had received from the Jansenists effective support of their own claims to constitutional powers, with the general result that for a while the parliamentary and Jansenistic parties seemed almost politically synonymous. Yet the main driving force of political Jansenism had been anti-Jesuitism, and once the destruction of the Jesuits had been achieved, with the corollary triumph over the pro-Jesuit bishops and with the consequent fading of the issue of the bull *Unigenitus*, political Jansenism lost its essential motivations and most of its usefulness to the *thèse parlementaire*.

The taxation issue involved all the parlements. The government was

9. *Remontrances du parlement de Paris*, I, 521–609. There is an abundant bibliography on Jansenism but rather fewer studies on political Jansenism in the eighteenth century. See René Taveneaux, *Jansénisme et politique* (Paris, 1965); B. Robert Kreiser, *Miracles, Convulsions, and Ecclesiastical Politics in Early Eighteenth-Century Paris* (Princeton, 1978); and for the decade preceding the Maupeou revolution, Dale Van Kley, *The Jansenists and the Expulsion of the Jesuits from France, 1757–1765* (New Haven, 1975), with the quoted citation of Barbier on p. 27, and "Church, State, and the Ideological Origins of the French Revolution: The Debate over the General Assembly of the Gallican Clergy in 1765," *Journal of Modern History*, LI (1979), 629–66.

confronted with rising expenditures, caused in large part by the Seven Years' War and the extravagance of the court, with continually increasing annual deficits, and with the recurring necessity to float loans at high rates of interest. To meet the crisis it attempted to extract more revenue from the moneyed classes by levying new and higher taxes, correcting abuses in assessments, and preventing the many evasions from which the wealthy profited. These efforts the parlements, of course, vigorously resisted. There were bitter skirmishes in the provinces and in Paris, and the parlements of Pau and Rennes were liquidated and replaced by dummy courts for refusing to accede to the proposed reforms. These royal efforts proved, however, generally unsuccessful, and by the late 1760s the courts seemed to have won the battle and to be in effective control of the nation's tax structure. They failed, however, to use their power to bring order to the financial chaos; deficits continued to mount, the national debt and current obligations rose higher and higher, and the government's credit was so bad that money could be borrowed only at excessive rates. In 1769 Maynon d'Invau, the controller general, reported to the king, "The finances of Your Majesty are in the most frightful state of collapse. . . . The situation is more than terrifying; it can continue no longer. We have reached the moment when it will drive the kingdom into the worst sort of catastrophe, for which there will be no remaining remedy." [10]

In addition to all this, the government faced in the late 1760s the problems of grain shortages, high bread prices, and genuine famine in many areas. In 1763 and 1764 the ministry, persuaded by the arguments of the laissez-faire Economistes, had moved toward a policy of free internal and external trade with the hope of stimulating production and the expectation that prices would stabilize at their natural level. For a while the program seemed to work, but a series of poor harvests starting in 1765 created shortages and high prices. Since the wages of the lowest classes were close to the subsistence level, an increase in the price of bread of even a few sous could constitute a disaster, and one for which the government usually was blamed. A widely spread popular explanation of the grain crisis was the so-called *Pacte de Famine*, according to which the king and his ministers were alleged to have amassed fortunes by creating a monopoly

10. Quoted by Marcel Marion, *Histoire financière de la France depuis 1715* (Paris, 1914), I, 246–47.

in grain and forcing up prices while the people starved. In 1768 and 1770 seditious placards appeared in Paris and troops had to be used to quell rebellious mobs.

Thus there was poverty both at Versailles and in the peasant's cottage. The king could not pay his valets and the peasant could not buy bread. The year 1770 marked a general economic crisis, which was bringing to a close a period of economic expansion that had commenced around 1730. To a century which believed in the feasibility of a rational society, the situation was ironic and absurd.

Finally, the royal government's ability to enlist public opinion in support of constructive reforms was handicapped by the increasing unpopularity of the king. His public image had not been improved by the bad taste he had exhibited in taking as his latest *maîtresse de titre* not someone suitable like Choiseul's sister-in-law, Mme de Gramont, who reportedly aspired to the honor, but instead Jeanne Bécu, who had worked her way up from the ranks of common prostitution through the Parc aux Cerfs to attain the royal bed with the title of Comtesse Du Barry. Louis had acted, as one contemporary remarked, "without respect for the dignity of the throne,"[11] and his amours gave occasion to a stream of anti-royalist pornography and scurrilous doggerel which started in 1770 and became a flood in 1771.

Thus by 1770 the monarchy faced a serious crisis. Its prestige sapped by the unpopularity of Louis XV, its authority insolently challenged by the parlements, the lower classes rebellious because of food shortages and the upper classes because of the threat of tax increases, without effective political support from the church, and faced with imminent bankruptcy, the throne was threatened at its very foundations. The situation demanded the most vigorous, ruthless, and courageous action. It would be difficult to conceive of any alternative at this juncture to Maupeou's absolutistic coup except an aristocratic takeover.

In September 1768 René Nicolas Charles Augustin de Maupeou had taken office as chancellor of France. Fifty-four years old and a member of

11. Pierre Etienne Regnaud, "Histoire des événemens arrivés en France depuis le mois de septembre 1770 concernans les parlemens et les changemens dans l'administration de la justice et dans les loix du royaume" (MS, Bibliothèque Nationale, F.F. 13733–13735), I, 42.

an old parliamentary family, he had been a conseiller of the Parlement of Paris since 1733, président à mortier in 1743, and premier président since 1763. In December 1769 he outmaneuvered Choiseul, who had acted as prime minister since 1758, by bringing into the ministry as controller general the Abbé Terray, also a former conseiller in the Parlement and a man of considerable ability and ambition. These two, with the unwavering support of Louis, who, whatever his faults, understood political realities, engineered the revolution.

The first eleven months of 1770 were used for pre-battle maneuvers. Terray knew that he was not yet able to challenge the parlements on tax reform, so he was forced to meet the crisis in the treasury by a partial bankruptcy in the form of arbitrary reductions of interest on certain government obligations and suspensions of payments on others. These measures caused serious losses to some people (Voltaire claimed he lost 200,000 livres), but since Terray was careful not to touch the *rentes sur l'Hôtel de Ville*, the only kind of government securities in which the magistrates had considerable investments, he met no serious opposition in the Parlement. At the same time, obeying both his own convictions and the pressure of public opinion, Terray reversed the economic policy by reestablishing virtually all the controls on trade in grains. Lastly, Maupeou succeeded in December 1770 in obtaining the virtual prime ministership and the dismissal and exile of his enemy Choiseul by persuading Louis that his foreign minister had been trying to ensure his tenure by embroiling France in a war with England over the Falkland Islands.

Meanwhile, however, the courts had been making equally good progress in their efforts to consolidate and enlarge their own position. There were two notable affairs. The first, which received less public attention but was of considerable political significance, was the case of the unhappy Guillaume Monnerat. This obscure man had been arrested in 1767 by an agent of the Farmers General on the charge of smuggling tobacco and by authority of a *lettre de cachet* had been imprisoned for six weeks in a totally dark underground dungeon with a fifty-pound chain around his neck, held without interrogation for six months, and incarcerated for a total of two years before release. The arrest had resulted from mistaken identity, Monnerat having been charged under the name of another, and the man was obviously innocent. Early in 1770 the Cour des Aides, the court which had jurisdiction over tax cases and of which Malesherbes was the president, authorized Monnerat to bring suit against the Farmers General and awarded him 50,000 livres damages. The royal Council of State immediately issued an *arrêt* voiding the judgment, and there ensued an exchange of *arrêts* and *arrêtés*, of legal moves and countermoves, between the council and the court, which culminated in Malesherbes' eloquent remonstrances "On the Unjust Vexations Exercised against le Sieur Guillaume Monnerat" of September 14. The case was eventually submerged in the crisis of December, but Malesherbes made his points. On the level of principle he pled the causes of liberty of person, fair trial, and protection against arbitrary imprisonment. On the level of politics, he asserted the court's power to supervise, censure, and control the operations of the Farmers General and, more broadly, affirmed the authority of the judiciary over the operations of the executive.

The trial of the Duke d'Aiguillon, the culmination of a long, involved political struggle, was far more spectacular. A confrontation beginning in 1763 between D'Aiguillon, governor of Brittany, and the Parlement of Rennes over new taxes had led to the temporary mass resignation of that court and the arrest of Louis René de La Chalotais (a highly respected magistrate, an enemy of the Jesuits, and a friend of the Philosophes), his son, and four others. Maupeou was conciliatory to an extent, reestablishing the parlement but not (at the king's insistence) freeing the two La Chalotais. The court, seizing on the issue of illegal imprisonment, pushed the case, ordered an inquiry into allegations of briberty of witnesses by D'Aiguillon, and, when this investigation was countermanded by the king's council, referred the charges to the Paris Parlement. The latter court met to consider the case on March 30, 1770, and D'Aiguillon ill-advisedly demanded a trial to clear his honor. Immediately it became apparent that the Parlement had been handed a golden opportunity, for, acting as the Court of Peers and with the acquiescence of the Duke d'Aiguillon, it found itself with full legal power and right to investigate the most secret acts of the royal administration, to interrogate the king's agents, to pass judgment on the conduct of one of the king's favorites, and in general to extend control, as a sort of legislative committee of the whole, over the operations of the executive. With this trial as a precedent, similar charges could be brought against other high officers and the royal government could be harassed into complete subservience. As one of Maupeou's aides later said, "It was not D'Aiguillon who was on trial; it was the government itself."[12]

The king did the only thing he could. By *lettres patentes* registered in a *lit de justice* on June 27 he nullified the entire procedure and dismissed the charges against the duke. This ended the trial but gave the Parlement a moral victory, which it exploited by voting an *arrêt d'indignité* against D'Aiguillon excluding him from all rights of the peerage until he had purged himself of the suspicions staining his honor. The parlements of Bordeaux, Toulouse, Metz, Rouen, and Rennes took similar actions, and Charles Dupaty, a leading magistrate, in an *arrêté* issued by the Parlement of Bordeaux, eloquently made the essential point that if the agents of the executive were above the law and above the authority of the courts, then France was indeed a despotism. The Parlement of Paris was strongly supported by all but one of the Princes of the Blood and was acclaimed by Parisian crowds. It was a signal victory.

Maupeou met this total situation by the edict of December 1770. His motives in precipitating the crisis were complex, and he probably neither foresaw nor planned all the actions he was consequently to take. His ambition was to replace Choiseul as the principal minister, and there is probably some truth in William Doyle's explanation that he hoped that "a confrontation with the parlements would ruin Choiseul's hopes of an easy passage for war taxation" in preparation for an armed conflict with England over the Falkland Islands, that he therefore "attacked the Parlement in order to attack Choiseul," and that once having achieved Choiseul's dismissal he sought to "settle the quarrel with some compromise," but that "increasingly committed despite himself to firm policies, repeatedly he miscalculated the resistance he would meet, and repeatedly was forced to ever greater extremes to overcome it."[13] It may also be true that Maupeou welcomed, as his enemies alleged, the chance to settle some scores with personal enemies among the magistrates. Nevertheless, whatever part such secondary motives may have had, the very real crisis of mo-

---

12. Charles François Lebrun, *Opinions, rapports, et choix d'écrits politiques* (Paris, 1829), 32. See also René Nicolas Charles Augustin de Maupeou, "Mémoire à Louis XVI," in Jules Gustave Flammermont, *Le Chancelier Maupeou et les parlements* (Paris, 1883), 620, 622.

13. William O. Doyle, "The Parlements of France and the Breakdown of the Old Régime, 1771–1778," *French Historical Studies*, VI (1970), 417, 419, 422, 423.

narchical authority and the outrageously provocative and uncompromising language of the edict supports the traditional and most obvious interpretation that the determining purpose of the chancellor, his advisers, and the king was "to take the initiative and crush the opposition of the parlements once and for all," thus clearly and permanently reestablishing the authority of the crown.[14] This basic policy decision seems to have been defined in a memorandum submitted by Maupeou's secretary and adviser Charles François Lebrun, which (as Lebrun later wrote) "proved that it was no longer possible to maintain a government in France, or to establish a sound financial policy, or to put through general legislation, if we persisted in walking blindly in the ruts of the past; and that with all these parlements, divided in their views but united in their opposition, authority could no longer be exercised. . . . We needed taxes, and in the face of existing attitudes we had to expect concerted resistance and strong, active opposition; we resolved to forestall this opposition and to force the parlements to return to the recognized principles of the monarchy, and to erect around them a barrier they could not cross."[15]

The royalist propagandists' device of labeling all of Maupeou's actions as *"réformes"* has perhaps been what has given the illusion of a coherent, preplanned total program which, since it "reformed" the iniquities of the parlements, must have been well intentioned and salutary and which should have been permanent. We can accept the orthodox view of historians that Maupeou did indeed fully intend the basic "reform" of the power coup and at the same time agree with William Doyle's valid points that Maupeou hoped for an easier and less radical victory, that his later "reforms" were improvised, from Lebrun's standing proposals, in order to emasculate the courts and win public approval, and that it does not necessarily follow that because the coup of 1770/1771 was a political necessity dictated by the circumstances, Louis XVI's restoration of the parlements in 1774 was a "fatal mistake," as Cobban and others have said, rather than simply another act of political necessity dictated by new circumstances.[16]

14. Alfred Cobban, *Aspects of the French Revolution* (New York, 1968), 78. Cf. Alfred Cobban, *Old Régime and Revolution, 1715–1799* (London, 1968), 92–93 and *passim*.

15. Lebrun, *Opinions*, 18, 33–34. Cf. Jacob Nicolas Moreau, *Mes Souvenirs* (Paris, 1898), I, 238.

16. See Doyle, "The Parlements of France," 415–16 and *passim*. Cf. Cobban, *Aspects of the French Revolution*, 78–79; Michael John Sydenham, *The French Revolution* (New York, 1965), 18; and other similar interpretations cited by Doyle.

The basic decision of Lebrun's memorandum was implemented by the edict written by Terray during the autumn vacation of the court and presented to the magistrates when they convened for their first full session of December 3. When the court protested, as expected, the decree was registered in a *lit de justice* on December 7.

The *Edit de Décembre* opened with the accusation, nicely calculated to infuriate the magistrates, that the Parlement had been infected by the radical rationalism of the Philosophes: "The *esprit de système*, as unsound in its principles as it is foolhardy in its pretensions, in addition to having done fearful damage to religion and morals, has not respected the deliberations of several of our courts; we have seen them beget one new idea after another and venture principles which, on any other occasion or in any other body, the courts themselves would have condemned as threats to the public order." Next followed a catalog of the magistrates' heresies: their concept of unity of classes and their claims to be "the representatives of the nation, the indispensable interpreters of the official will of the kings, the supervisors of the administration of police powers and of the payments of the debts of the sovereign. . . . Conceding no force to our laws unless they themselves have in free deliberations adopted and consecrated them, they raise their authority to the level of—nay, above—our own, for they reduce our legislative power to the mere faculty of proposing to them our will while they reserve for themselves the right to veto its execution."

The edict unequivocally met the issues of sovereignty and legislative power. It reaffirmed the king's complete and undivided authority by divine right: "We hold our crown from God alone. The right to make laws . . . belongs to us alone, independently and wholly." Consequently the Parlement was not and could not be the representative of the will of the nation and it had no right to share in the power of legislation. It had no rights of "free verification" of the laws or of refusal of registration or of supervision of the executive or financial operations of the government. Its function was purely advisory, and if it was still allowed the privilege of remonstrance, this was granted in order that the sovereign might be assisted, not that his will might be obstructed. Suspensions of service and mass resignations were strictly forbidden.[17]

17. *Recueil général des anciennes lois françaises depuis l'an 420 jusqu'à la révolution de 1789*, ed. François André Isambert *et al.* (Paris, 1821–33), XXII, 501–507.

Obviously a vote to register this document would have amounted to the surrender of all the Parlement's claimed constitutional powers and would have ratified both the principle and practice of absolute monarchism. The Parlement's response was to suspend its judicial operations and go into permanent session as a deliberative body. It sent a series of protests and representations to the king, who replied with *lettres de jussion* written in increasingly stronger language. Maupeou had never expected the edict to be accepted, but he had hoped to provoke its opponents into some violent and ill-considered reaction and thus to divide the magistrates and hold at least a portion of them to form the nucleus of a new court. In mid-January, with his position strengthened by the elimination of the threat of war with England and by Choiseul's dismissal, he decided the time had come for still stronger action.

Between one and four in the morning of Sunday, January 20, each member of the Parlement was awakened by two musketeers beating at his door. He was presented with a *lettre de cachet* ordering him to resume his judicial functions and demanding an immediate written assent or refusal. One hundred and seventeen either replied in the negative, refused to reply, or merely promised to be present at the Palais on Monday morning; only thirty-eight formally submitted. The same day the Parlement met and voted an *arrêté* reaffirming its determination to stand fast. That night every magistrate except the thirty-eight who had yielded was served an *arrêt du conseil* ordering him into exile in some place outside Paris. The thirty-eight who had been spared met in the Palais the next day and voted an *arrêté* expressing their solidarity with their colleagues, and that night they too received orders of exile.

Since the jurisdiction of the Parlement of Paris covered about half of France, the suspension of its services was already causing serious difficulties, and a temporary court had to be established immediately to act in its stead. The chancellor drafted members of the Grand Conseil to serve as the first "Maupeou Parlement," inaugurated January 24 under strong police protection. It was unable, however, to transact any business, for the lawyers, supporting the exiled magistrates, refused to present cases, and whenever the armed protection was relaxed the chambers were turned into chaos by an invading mob, mostly lawyers' clerks, who assailed the new judges with catcalls, insults, and even physical violence.

The provincial parlements and many lower courts, including in Paris the Cour des Aides, the Cour des Comptes, the Châtelet, and the Cour des Monnoies, remained faithful to the principle of unity and protested vigorously in *arrêtés* and in letters and remonstrances to the king. The *Remontrances* of the Cour des Aides, written by Malesherbes, was an eloquent and powerful document, of which over two thousand manuscript copies were said to have been circulated.

Ignoring these protestations, Maupeou proceeded with his plan by revolutionizing the judicial system in all the provinces within the jurisdiction of the Parlement of Paris. By the edict of February 23 he established new courts, named *conseils supérieurs*, in Arras, Blois, Châlons, Clermont-Ferrand, Lyons, and Poitiers, with the power to hear civil and criminal cases which formerly had had to be judged in Paris. Their functions were, however, solely judicial, and the Paris Parlement remained the only court in the area empowered to register new laws. Office in the new *conseils supérieurs* and in the Parlement as well was made appointive instead of venal. Moreover the practice of accepting *épices*, fees paid to the members of a court by the parties in a case, was forbidden and instead the magistrates were to receive salaries from the crown. These reforms, influenced if not conceived by Lebrun, had the asserted purposes of saving provincial litigants the expenses and delays of trials in Paris and of eliminating the professional incompetence resulting from venality and the judicial corruption invited by the payment of *épices*. The crown too stood to profit, for the reduction of the jurisdiction of the Paris Parlement to a modest area around the Ile de France reduced considerably the political leverage the court could exert by suspending its services.

This second edict provoked a new round of loud protests in both Paris and the provinces. Some *bailliages* (lower courts) resigned and the provincial parlements issued more *arrêts* and *remontrances*, fulminating against the new despotism, demanding the convocation of the States General, and even asserting the right of resistance to tyranny. The Princes of the Blood, with the exception of the Count de La Marche and the Duke de Penthièvre, headed the resistance in Paris under the leadership of the Prince de Conti, employing gifted propagandists, setting up a secret press, and issuing in April their famous *Protestation des Princes du Sang*.

Maupeou's next step was a *lit de justice* held on April 13, at which he caused to be registered an edict formally abolishing the offices of the former magistrates in the Paris Parlement, authorizing "liquidation" (reimbursement of the pecuniary value of the offices on condition of voluntary resignation), and establishing a second and permanent "Maupeou Parlement." The new court was duly organized, but Maupeou found it very difficult to persuade competent men to accept appointments to it. Even Moreau, his adviser, later admitted, "All these [new] magistrates seemed to me mediocre, and I was ashamed for the authority of the king." [18] Only a minority of the exiled magistrates ever accepted the offer to liquidate their offices.

The continued, unsubdued, and highly vocal opposition of the other courts required that they too be subjected to reform. Maupeou had originally thought to replace all the provincial parlements with conseils supérieurs, but this plan was opposed by the king and the other ministers on the grounds that it would concentrate too much power in the Paris Parlement. So he chose the alternative of reforming the existing parlements, dismissing all recalcitrant magistrates and subduing the wills of the others. Between August and November 1771 all the parlements underwent purges, except the one at Pau, which had been similarly reformed in 1765. The jurisdiction of the Parlement of Toulouse was reduced, and the parlements of Douai, Metz, Dombes, and Rouen were abolished and their powers transferred to conseils supérieurs or to other courts. The Cour des Aides of Paris and some other lower courts were also abolished. These operations against the provincial parlements proved, however, less effective than the one carried out in Paris, for even after the exile of the most troublesome magistrates the reformed courts, particularly that of Bordeaux, continued to protest against new taxes.

Meanwhile the Parisian lawyers, who had been on strike since January, yielded to economic pressures and agreed on November 6 to return to court and promised Maupeou "passive, blind, and unreserved submission." [19]

As soon as the parliamentary opposition had thus been more or less neutralized, Terray started his revision of the tax structure, for which the

18. Moreau, *Mes Souvenirs*, II, 82.

19. *Journal historique de la révolution opérée dans la constitution de la monarchie française, par M. de Maupeou*, ed. Mathieu François Pidanzat de Mairobert (London, 1774–76), November 11, November 24, December 4, 1771 (II, 239, 265, 279–82).

plans had been ready, it was said, since December. He created a multitude of new taxes on everything from starch to printed matter, increased existing taxes, made the first *vingtième* permanent, extended the second to 1781, and began the long-overdue verification of the rolls on which this tax was based. At the same time he reduced the interest paid on various government obligations. Practically all these measures affected the wealthy, and many the wealthy only. For instance all patents of nobility granted during the current reign were made subject to confirmation at a rate of 10,000 livres, plus a 10 percent surtax. The result of all these various actions was substantial. By the end of his ministry in 1774 Terray had not balanced the budget but he had increased revenues by about 40 million livres, reduced the deficit to 40 or 41 million, and halved the anticipations on future income.[20] This was still not a state of sound financial health, but the government had been given a new lease on life.

On the other hand, while Terray held expenditures stable he did not reduce them, and the extravagance at Versailles continued unabated. Moreover, in his desperate efforts to raise cash, he exploited the broad powers of his office, now unchecked by the parlements, and resorted to what appear to have been unethical and illegal stratagems, not only arbitrarily reducing payments on government annuities and other obligations but even (if we may credit contemporary accusations) recirculating instead of destroying government securities received in payment for annuities and reselling offices the provinces had bought back.[21] Such measures seriously undermined the government's credit.[22]

In its efforts to improve the national economy the ministry met with less success, for after the relative prosperity of the 1760s the country had fallen into a serious recession. Terray broke with the liberal economic policy which the government had followed since 1763 and which had aimed to protect capital investments in property and foster agricultural production by allowing free internal and foreign trade in grains and by subscribing in general to the laissez-faire capitalistic principles of the Economistes. Instead, he purposed to restore political and social stability by

20. Marion, *Histoire financière*, 278.
21. Véri, *Journal*, I, 70, 142–43, 183–84. On Terray's moral reputation with his contemporaries and with modern historians, see Steven L. Kaplan, *Bread, Politics, and Political Economy in the Reign of Louis XV* (The Hague, 1976), II, 648–49, 674.
22. See Douglas Dakin, *Turgot and the Ancien Régime in France* (London, 1939), 115.

bettering the economic security of the lower classes. For instance, he insisted that divided common lands be distributed among all the inhabitants of the locality, not among existing property owners only. "By giving a sort of property to people who have had none," he wrote, "one attaches them to their possessions and forms good family men and good citizens."[23] Most importantly, by the *arrêt* of July 14, 1770, prohibiting exports of grain and by the *arrêt* of December 23, 1770, restoring virtually all the controls over the internal grain trade, Terray went back to the pre-1763 policy of managing the grain economy for the overriding purpose of assuring the subsistence of the consumers. Prices since 1768, he said, "had been maintained at a level far above the means of consumers,"[24] and he wrote Turgot in 1770, "I agree that the system of liberty in trade in grains is infinitely favorable to landowners . . . [but] consumers obviously suffer from a liberty which raises prices to a level that bears no proportion to their means."[25]

In order to make effective his new *dirigiste* policy, Terray attempted to establish an ambitious system for gathering current information on the size, distribution, and movement of the supply of grain, by which he expected to be able to manage the grain market, prevent dearths, and lower prices. He was thwarted, however, by the persistence of mediocre or bad harvests in many parts of the country, by the failure of the intendants to supply the data he needed, by the slowness of his communications, and by the inability of eighteenth-century bureaucracy, despite its sophistication, to deal effectively with the complex and imperfectly understood economic forces at work. The subsistence crisis that had begun in 1765 still continued; bread and wheat prices, despite fluctuations, remained high; and there were serious public disturbances by both rural and urban workers. And despite all his good intentions, the secrecy and inefficacy of his system of controls brought down on Terray's head public suspicion and blame as grievous as that suffered by his liberal predecessors. He com-

23. Quoted in Georges Weulersse, *La Physiocratie à la fin du règne de Louis XV*, 1770–1774 (Paris, 1959), 152.

24. Quoted *ibid.*, 163.

25. Anne Robert Jacques Turgot, *Oeuvres*, ed. Eugène Daire (Paris, 1844), I, 182. Both on the general questions of subsistence and economic policies under Louis XV and on Terray's measures, see Kaplan, *Bread, Politics, and Political Economy*, especially II, 491–702.

plained that the ministry had to maneuver "through a strait full of reefs and shoals," and "in whatever direction it [steered] its course, it [ran] into criticism."[26] He feared that any return to laissez-faire policy might lead to speculation, profiteering, or exportation of needed grain supplies, yet inept and ill-timed controls often destroyed economic incentives and disrupted distribution. For instance, in order to prevent the illegal exportation of grains he imposed complicated restrictions on the coastal trade, which obstructed the normal legitimate flow of goods, which in turn required hastily improvised measures that produced unforeseen bad side effects. As the Abbé Galiani said, "The Controller General, seeing the ship heeled over on one side, tips it over on the other."[27] Terray's policy was not doctrinaire and had the saving quality of pragmatism, but its very lack of abstract theory led to much division of opinion within the government, and provincial intendants were urging every sort of policy from the most rigid *dirigisme* to complete laissez-faire.[28]

Maupeou succeeded even less well in his efforts to control and enlist public opinion. The events of 1771 precipitated a propaganda war probably unequaled in French history until the Revolution. The "Patriotes," as the partisans of the parlements soon began calling themselves, were first off the mark, with the remonstrances, *arrêts, arrêtés*, and letters issued by the various courts in Paris and the provinces. These began to appear soon after the exile of the magistrates. They were theoretically official petitions addressed to the king, but actually they were written to persuade the public, not Louis, and were in fact public statements of position by the various bodies. They were widely circulated both in manuscript and in print, and some, particularly the remonstrances Malesherbes wrote for the Cour des Aides, were well written and effective. These official documents, composed in a traditional dignified and formal style, were soon supplemented by a flood of less restrained propaganda pieces—placards, engravings, satirical poems, jokes, and—principally—pamphlets ranging in length from a few pages to a hundred or more and varying in nature

26. "Circulaire du 28 septembre 1773," quoted by Weulersse, *La Physiocratie à la fin du règne de Louis XV*, 185.

27. Ferdinando Galiani to M. Baudouin, in Galiani, *Lettres de l'abbé Galiani à Madame d'Epinay*, ed. E. Asse (Paris, 1882), 392–93.

28. Weulersse, *La Physiocratie à la fin du règne de Louis XV*, 166–72; Kaplan, *Bread, Politics, and Political Economy*, II, 580–81.

from the crudest libels to sober and reasoned political essays. At least 167 various writings of this sort were printed between 1771 and 1774, in runs of up to 5,000 copies. The most successful was the satirical *Correspondance secrète et familière de M. de Maupeou*, attributed to Jacques Mathieu Augeard, which appeared serially from 1771 to 1773 and was probably printed in the Temple under the protection of the Prince de Conti. It was so popular that its name was given to a new coiffure, "A la Correspondance." The diarist Regnaud called the work "a truly 'national' satire [which] has done and will do more to wreck the establishment of the new Parlement than anything else that can possibly be done."[29] The Patriotes also had their own *nouvelle à la main*, or manuscript newsletter, edited by Pidanzat de Mairobert from December 1770 to April 1775 under the title *Journal historique de la révolution opérée dans la constitution de la monarchie françoise par M. de Maupeou, Chancellier de France*. It was later published in seven printed volumes from 1774 to 1776. But probably the most effective, and certainly the best written, were Beaumarchais' famous *Mémoires* against the magistrate Goëzman of Maupeou's Parlement. The bon mot of the day, "Louis Quinze a détruit le Parlement ancien, et quinze louis détruiront le nouveau," was not far from the truth.[30]

Maupeou reacted with characteristic vigor. He had no scruples about restricting freedom of the press. "I had very severe views on censorship," he later wrote. "I never thought that literature should be considered a branch of commerce, or that one could allow indefinite liberty to a profession which exerts so strong an influence on public morals, on the character of nations, on laws, and on government."[31] He instituted a general policy of rigorous censorship from which many groups, particularly the Physiocrats and the Philosophes, suffered sorely, but of course the Patriotes suffered most of all. He ordered special efforts to discover the author of the *Correspondance* and to prevent its distribution, and *colporteurs* arrested for peddling it were given stiff sentences.

Nevertheless it quickly became apparent that these efforts to stifle the voice of the opposition would not be effective. Should it then be an-

29. Regnaud, "Histoire," II, 209.

30. "Louis the Fifteenth destroyed the old Parlement and fifteen louis will destroy the new one." The reference is to the bribe allegedly demanded of Beaumarchais by a magistrate of the Maupeou Parlement.

31. Maupeou, "Mémoire à Louis XV," in Flammermont, *Le Chancelier Maupeou*, 606.

swered? Some royal advisers argued that to bring the issues into public debate would only make matters worse. But Maupeou decided that silence would be interpreted as weakness or acquiescence. To the question, "Why not ignore the parlements?" he answered: "Had not these ideas become the doctrine of a corps? And if we did not combat them would they not become the doctrine of the public?"[32] So he ordered a counterbarrage of propaganda, which began to appear in April 1771. By mid-June over sixty pieces reportedly had been published, and by early August over one hundred. The latter figure is probably close to the final number of different works, but since many appeared in multiple editions the total of all publications was considerably higher.[33] None, however, seems to have had the popular success achieved by some of the Patriote pieces, even though Maupeou employed the gifted pens of Lebrun, Moreau, and Voltaire.

There is no way of determining quantitatively how effective was the propaganda of either side in changing public opinion or in enlisting partisans. The Patriote effort obviously failed during Louis XV's lifetime to achieve its political objective of returning the former parlements to power. There never had been any possibility, or even any intention, of overthrowing the new regime by a popular uprising; the Patriotes' only hope lay in the pressure of public opinion on Versailles. When by 1772 it became apparent that the Maupeou revolution was a fait accompli and impregnable for the time being to popular protest, the output of Patriote propaganda sharply declined in quantity. But these facts do not in themselves prove a failure to affect the public mind, or Maupeou's success in doing so. Obviously if the Patriotes had not thought their writings could change men's thinking they would not have published them, and if Maupeou had not believed they could do so he would not have tried to suppress their publications and would not have attempted to neutralize them

32. *Ibid.*, 624.

33. François Louis Claude Marin, "Gazette à la main de Marin, 1768–1772" (MS, Bibliothèque de la Ville de Paris), April 22, 1771, fol. 147; *Journal historique*, June 17, August 4, 1771 (I, 364, II, 65). On December 5, 1771, however, the latter source gave the total as 89 (II, 284), and as 87 as of February 13, 1772 (V, 324). Obviously these estimates are not reliable. I have seen a total of 93 different titles and *recueils* in 139 different printings and have found references to additional titles, *recueils*, and editions that I have not been able to locate.

by counterpropaganda. Contemporary comments on the impact of works such as Augeard's *Correspondance* and Beaumarchais' *Mémoires* seem to indicate that Maupeou's judgment was realistic.[34]

There is likewise no hard data which can permit us to say how many French men and women supported one side or the other at any particular moment, for whatever reason. Nevertheless, judging from all that was written by contemporary observers on the state of public opinion and allowing for the impressionistic and anecdotal nature of such evidence and its various biases, one may make the informed guess that a considerable majority of the literate and politically conscious portion of the population was pro-Patriote. It is impossible after reading all the contemporary documents to deny the overall impression of a widespread opposition to the regime. The hostility of the *noblesse de robe* and of the wealthy who suffered from Terray's financial operations was inevitable. As for the others, it seems to have been the style of the revolution that most aroused resentment— the arrogance of the royal words, "The right to make the laws by which our subjects are to be governed belongs to us alone"; the gratuitously vindictive exile of the aged magistrate Guillaume Henri de Lamoignon to a miserable remote mountain village in the dead of winter; Terray's cynical disregard of legality; the intensified censorship; and the efficient, ubiquitous secret police. Diderot complained, "If the Philosophe Denis Diderot went one evening to a house of ill fame, M. de Sartine [lieutenant général de police] would know all about it before he went to bed."[35]

The French people were afraid of what they were calling *"despotisme,"* a word which connoted much more than the parlement's loss of its claimed constitutional powers. There were manifold indications of this pervasive disquietude. The Philosophes (all except Voltaire, and perhaps even he secretly) detested Maupeou even more than they despised the Paris Parlement. Their attitude was mirrored in the audiences at the Comédie Française, which almost halted the performance of Racine's *Les Plaideurs* by

34. For a contrary opinion, see David Carl Hudson, "In Defense of Reform: French Government Propaganda During the Maupeou Crisis," *French Historical Studies*, VIII (1973), 51–76; and his "Maupeou and the Parlements: A Study in Propaganda and Politics" (Ph.D. dissertation, Columbia University, 1967).

35. Denis Diderot, "Observations sur le Nakaz," in Diderot, *Oeuvres politiques*, ed. Paul Vernière (Paris, 1963), 183.

clapping and stamping their feet in applause of the line "Nous n'avons plus d'avocats,"[36] and in the Académie Française, which applauded for half an hour a reference to Malesherbes' great-grandfather. At the other end of the cultural scale were scurrilous anecdotes and verses on the king and Du Barry, such as

> France, tel est donc ton destin,
> D'être soumise à la femelle!
> Ton salut vint de la Pucelle,
> Tu périras par la Catin.[37]

Frederick of Prussia found Maupeou's imitation of his own autocracy ridiculous. "If Providence thought of me in creating the world," he wrote D'Alembert, "it created the French for my amusement."[38]

The most convincing evidence, however, is that supplied by the royalists themselves. Their propaganda pamphlets complained of "the stupid zeal of the people for the parlements" and asked, "Why has this mad idea of despotism been so quickly seized by the multitude and repeated by so many echoes?"[39] Moreau later described what it was like to be a supporter of the chancellor: "Within three weeks I found myself abandoned by a great many people whom I formerly saw constantly." He advised his friend D'Albertas, the first president of the Cour des Aides of Provence, not to accept an appointment in the Maupeou Parlement and expose himself "to the opprobrium with which at that time public opinion covered those who supported the chancellor."[40]

The truly important effect, however, of the passionate debate was not the support it enlisted for one side or the other but the political education

---

36. "We no longer have any lawyers." Siméon Prosper Hardy, *"Mes Loisirs," Journal d'événements tels qu'ils parviennent à ma connaissance, 1764–1789*, ed. Maurice Tourneux and Maurice Vitrac (Paris, 1912), 236–37. Apparently a garbled reference to Act II, Scene 14: "Il faut de part et d'autre avoir un avocat; / Nous n'en avons pas un." ("We must have a lawyer for each party; we have none.")

37. "France, your fate is always ruled by women. You were saved by the Maid, and you will perish by the Whore." *Journal historique*, April 22, 1771 (I, 269).

38. Friedrick II, King of Prussia, to Jean Le Rond d'Alembert, May 7, 1771, in *Oeuvres posthumes de Frédéric II* (Berlin, 1788), XI, 119–20.

39. [Charles, Marquis de Villette], *Réflexions d'un maître perruquier sur les affaires de l'état* (N.p., n.d.), 12; *Le Fin mot de l'affaire* (N.p., n.d. [1771]), 16.

40. Moreau, *Mes Souvenirs*, I, 297, 248.

it gave to the nation. The Maupeou revolution was a profoundly disturbing experience that set the French thinking about fundamental political questions with markedly increased seriousness and concern. The Count de Mercy-Argenteau wrote the Empress Maria Theresa, "Now that everyone has become thoroughly revolted by all that is happening, the public is unrestrained in its discussion. Political questions have become almost the only topics of conversation at the Court, in society, in the city, and indeed in all the kingdom."[41] Mme d'Epinay wrote the Abbé Galiani in April 1771, "Everyone is talking about the nature and constitution of our government. Every sort of mind—female, rustic, philosophic, poetic, prosaic, reasonable, unreasonable—all are busy with these questions and talking about them. The war of the pen is beginning, heads are in ferment, the dictionary is changing, and you hear nothing but big words like 'reasons of state,' 'aristocracy,' and 'despotism.' A danseuse at the Opera was talking the other day about 'anarchy' because she had had to substitute for Mlle. Pelin, who refused to dance unless she had to."[42] And a week later: "Everybody wants to study the foundations of the national constitution. . . . People are questioning principles about which otherwise they would never have dared to think."[43] The Mmes de Mesmes and d'Egmont reported to Gustavus III of Sweden that the naked threat of despotism had awakened the French and was "making them debate the injustice of this power and examine by what right [the king] claims it. The chancellor for the past six months has been teaching the history of France to people who otherwise would have lived all their lives without knowing anything about it."[44] Besenval in his *Mémoires* recalled that "the edict caused the greatest sort of ferment. . . . In conversations and at supper parties no one talked of anything else. These social gatherings became miniature States General in which the ladies, transformed into legisla-

41. *Marie Antoinette. Correspondance secrète entre Marie Thérèse et le comte de Mercy-Argenteau, avec les lettres de Marie Thérèse et de Marie Antoinette*, ed. Alfred d'Arneth and M. A. Geffroy (Paris, 1875), I, 149.

42. Louise Florence Pétronille Tardieu d'Esclavelles, Marquise d'Epinay, *La Signora d'Epinay et l'abate Galiani: Lettere inedite, 1769–1772*, ed. F. Nicolini (Bari, 1929), 165.

43. Ferdinando Galiani, *L'Abbé Galiani: Sa Correspondance*, ed. Lucien Perey and Gaston Maugras (Paris, 1881), 375–76.

44. Auguste Geffroy, ed., *Notices et extraits des manuscrits concernant l'histoire ou la littérature de la France qui sont conservés dans les bibliothèques ou archives de Suède, Danemark, et Norvège* (Paris, 1855), 465.

tors, delivered maxims on public law and historical precedents and enunciated political principles with self-confidence and assertiveness generated by their desire to shine and to attract attention."[45]

Eighteenth-century Paris was continually swept by one fad after another, and such discussions, particularly among the more frivolous, were such a vogue. By the end of 1771 the public was losing interest in the immediate issues, and by 1773 the revolution had long since ceased to dominate social conversations. Yet the intensified interest in politics was more than a passing fashion. "Cours de science politique" were being offered to the public, books on every aspect of politics continued to pour from the presses, the thinking of the Philosophes became increasingly political, and in August 1774 the Grimm-Diderot correspondence noted, "Today there is scarcely a single young man who on leaving his college does not plan to establish a new system of government, scarcely an author who does not feel the obligation to instruct the powers of the globe on the best way to manage their states."[46] This new ideological orientation became permanent. The Maupeou revolution was immediately followed by the American Revolution, which in turn, as the Count de Ségur said, "electrified everyone," and when the Treaty of Versailles was signed in 1783 the Bastille was less than six years away.

The latent power of public opinion was dramatically demonstrated by the events of 1774. At the end of April Louis XV contracted smallpox and died within two weeks. The dependence of the ruling clique on the king's support immediately became apparent. On May 10 the king died; on the eleventh Du Barry was arrested and confined in a convent; on the twelfth the new king, Louis XVI, appointed as his minister of state and confidential adviser the aged Maurepas, who immediately began to maneuver toward the dismissal of Maupeou and the recall of the parlements.

The public reaction to Louis XV's death was a shocking revelation of his personal unpopularity. Six thousand masses were requested at Notre Dame for his recovery when he fell ill at Metz in 1744; six hundred in 1757 after the attempted assassination by Damiens; three in 1774.[47] A

45. Baron Pierre Victor de Besenval, *Mémoires . . . sur la Cour, les ministres, et les règnes de Louis XV et Louis XVI et sur les événements du temps* (Paris, 1805), II, 180–81.

46. *Correspondance littéraire, philosophique, et critique, par Grimm, Diderot, Raynal, Meister, etc. . . .*, ed. Maurice Tourneux (Paris, 1877–82), X, 467.

47. Félix Rocquain, *L'Esprit révolutionnaire avant la Révolution, 1715–1789* (Paris, 1878), 312.

forty-hour vigil of prayer was announced in Paris and the provinces, but the churches remained empty.[48] The story which circulated was that he had caught the smallpox from a pretty young peasant girl (or baker's daughter, or miller's daughter, or the daughter of Du Barry's secretary, depending on the version), whom the king and Du Barry had found gathering grass for her cow near the Trianon and whom for a lark they took back to the palace. The king (who lisped) found her, it was said, "vraiment sarmante," so they gave her a bath, dressed her as a *demoiselle*, got her drunk, and put her in the king's bed.[49] Within hours of his death Louis' already putrifying body was hastily sealed in a lead casket and transported after nightfall to Saint Denis in a hunting carriage accompanied by a scant escort not even dressed in black. This hurried, unceremonious, and almost furtive funeral procession Besenval recalled as "more like a hasty effort to get rid of an unwanted piece of baggage than the rendering of last honors to a monarch." When the escort reached Saint Denis they found the streets and cabarets full of noisy and drunken celebrators. After Louis was buried some jokester scribbled on his tomb, "Hic Iacet. Deo Gratias!" Within a few days so many satirical funeral orations and epitaphs were circulating that one observer said he had given up trying to read them all.[50] Perhaps the least offensive was

> Ci-gît Louis, le pauvre roi;
> Il fut bon, dit-on; mais à quoi?[51]

That the public reaction was against Louis XV personally and not against the crown was demonstrated by the popularity of his grandson

---

48. Véri, *Journal*, I, 85; "Lettres de M. R** à M. M**, concernant ce qui s'est passé d'intéressant à la Cour, depuis la maladie et la mort de Louis XV, jusqu'au rétablissement du parlement de Paris," *Mélanges publiés par la Société des Bibliophiles Français* (Paris, 1826), IV, 9.

49. *E.g.*, Nicolas Baudeau, "Chronique secrète de Paris sous le règne de Louis XVI," *Revue retrospective*, III (1834), 33.

50. Besenval, *Mémoires*, II, 86; *Journal historique*, May 14, 1774 (VI, 8–9); *Mémoires secrets pour servir à l'histoire de la république des lettres en France . . .* , ed. Louis Petit de Bachaumont *et al.* (London, 1777–89), June 15, 1774 (XXVII, 284); "Lettres de M. R**," July 29, 1774 (IV, 73).

51. "Here lies Louis, the poor king. He was good, they say. But for what?" Baudeau, "Chronique secrète," III, 273. Cf. *ibid.*, III, 41–42, 54, 273; Besenval, *Mémoires*, II, 87–88; Moreau, *Mes Souvenirs*, I, 379; *Chansonnier historique du 18ᵉ siècle* (Recueil Clairambault-Maurepas), ed. E. Raunié (Paris, 1879–84), VIII, 314–16, IX, 10.

Louis XVI and the new queen, who when they visited the Chateau de la Muette two weeks after the death were greeted by "an innumerable multitude of people both at the gate of the chateau and at the Porte Maillot and along the avenue leading to La Muette. They passed along this vast space amidst shouts of joy."[52]

Maurepas' efforts to get rid of Maupeou and Terray were actively seconded by the Duke d'Orléans, who reportedly quickly arranged a conference with the new king "on the operations of the chancellor," and were supported by most of the other Princes of the Blood and by Marie Antoinette, who detested all the clique associated with Du Barry. A meeting was held by the Princes of the Blood and the peers of the realm in the *hôtel* of the Duke de La Rochefoucauld to plan concerted action against the chancellor. On June 2 D'Aiguillon's resignation was requested. On June 9 the king canceled Choiseul's exile, probably at the urging of Marie Antoinette, who warmly welcomed the former minister. By the third week in July the king had decided on Maupeou's dismissal and by the end of the month he was admitting, less willingly, that Terray had to go too. Finally, in spite of the opposition of the Dévots and the protests of Mme Adélaïde, the king's aunt, of the Counts de Provence and de La Marche, and of the archbishop of Paris, the dismissals of Maupeou and Terray were announced on August 23 and 24. Turgot, who had joined the government as minister of the navy the month before, took over as controller general.[53]

The reaction to this long-anticipated news and to the subsequent events was a series of celebrations and demonstrations throughout France. As Maupeou drove away from the Chateau de Compiègne, where Louis handed him his dismissal, a crowd assailed him with abuse and threw stones at his carriage, and a second hostile mob waylaid him as he passed through Chantilly. When Terray was crossing the Seine on the ferry at Choisy a crowd gathered on the bank, shouted to the ferryman to throw him in the river, and tried to cut the ferry rope. "Paris was intoxicated with joy," Mme Campan reported.[54] The following Monday morning the inhabi-

---

52. Marin, "Gazette à la main," fol. 203.
53. "Lettres de M. R**," IV, 16, 191, 21–65; Véri, *Journal*, I, 130–82; Moreau, *Mes Souvenirs*, II, 97, 111; Daken, *Turgot and the Ancien Régime*, 121–42.
54. *Journal historique*, August 28 and 30, 1774 (VI, 169, 176); Baudeau, "Chronique secrète," III, 402; Dakin, *Turgot and the Ancien Régime*, 144.

tants of the city awakened to discover in the Place Sainte Geneviève two dummies dressed as Maupeou and Terray, the former hanging from a gallows and the other stretched out on a pile of fagots ready for burning. The next night a crowd reportedly of some twenty thousand persons held a great celebration at the Place Dauphine. A half dozen squadrons of the watch passively stood by as the chancellor was sentenced to death in effigy and his dummy was made to demand forgiveness from the king, the queen, the princes, the magistrates, and the nation, and finally was executed by setting off a charge of gunpowder in the wickerwork body while the onlookers chanted the Salve and danced round the carcass. Then followed a display of fireworks that lasted until five in the morning.[55]

Similar celebrations were later held in provincial cities. In Rouen the chancellor was drawn and quartered in effigy, banquets were given by the Chamber of Commerce and in private mansions, free gin was distributed to the populace, salvos of artillery were fired, masses of thanksgiving were celebrated in the churches, and a lottery was held whose proceeds were distributed to the poor.[56] In Rennes the liberated La Chalotais were greeted four leagues from the city by two hundred young men on horseback and twenty-two carriages filled with nobles and lawyers. The streets were jammed with people shouting "Vive le Roi! Vive M. de La Chalotais," the houses were illuminated, and wreaths and laurel branches were strewn before the carriage of the returning heroes.[57] In Toulouse the celebration of the restoration of the city's parlement lasted a week and a half and included a Te Deum at the cathedral, suspension of classes at the university, parades of students, artisans, and six hundred representatives of the various guilds, free plays, fireworks and illuminations every night, the liberation of prisoners, free bread for the poor, and a special prize offered by the Académie des Jeux Floraux for the best ode commemorating the happy event.[58]

Obviously these celebrations were the results of considerable planning

55. "Lettres de M. R**," IV, 84–85, 87–88; Regnaud, "Histoire," III, 90–98.

56. Regnaud, "Histoire," III, 98; *Journal historique*, November 26, 1774 (VI, 343); Dakin, *Turgot and the Ancien Régime*, 144.

57. *Récit de ce qui a précédé et suivi la rentrée du parlement de Bretagne* (Rennes, n.d. [1774]); Dakin, *Turgot and the Ancien Régime*, 144.

58. *Journal de ce qui s'est passé à l'occasion du rétablissement du parlement de Toulouse dans ses fonctions. Novembre 1774* (N.p., n.d.).

and organization and required large sums of money, but the evidence seems to indicate that though the Patriotes certainly encouraged and exploited popular emotions they did not have to generate them.

The dismissal of Maupeou and the state of public opinion made some sort of reorganization of the parlements inevitable. As the Count d'Allonville later wrote, "The Maupeou Parlement, dragged as it had been through the mud, could no longer endure."[59] The lives of the magistrates were made unbearable; crowds gathered at the Palais morning and evening to jeer and jostle them as they entered or left the court.[60]

The reestablishment of the former parlements was the work of Maurepas, Turgot, and Miromesnil, formerly premier président of the Parlement of Rouen and a conservative Patriote, who had been appointed Garde des Sceaux.[61] They adopted the plan originally conceived by Miromesnil in 1772 for a compromise which would conciliate public opinion by abandoning the prevocative absolutistic formulas and abolishing the Maupeou Parlement but retaining restrictions on the Parlement's powers which, it was hoped, would preserve the gains for the crown that Maupeou had achieved. A new "third parlement" was to be created, free from the vices of the previous ones. The initial plan was reportedly to constitute the new body with magistrates from both the existing and previous courts, but this idea was abandoned as politically impractical.[62]

The decision, it must be understood, was not free. Something had to be done, and once the first step was taken there was no turning back. The ministry could not check the political momentum; to have frustrated the aroused expectations would have set off a reaction too awesome to contemplate. Louis XVI was said to have replied to warnings of the consequences of reestablishing the old parlements, "That may be true. It may be considered politically unwise, but it seems to me that it is the general will, and I wish to be loved."[63] If this was weakness it was also realism.

59. Armand François, Count d'Allonville, *Mémoires secrets, de 1770 à 1830* (Paris, 1838), I, 109.

60. Moreau, *Mes Souvenirs*, II, 100; "Lettres de M. R**," August 31, 1774 (IV, 84).

61. On the complex question of Turgot's role, see Henri Carré, "Turgot et le rappel des parlements," *Institut de France. Académie des Sciences Morales et Politiques. Séances et travaux*, LVIII (1902), 442–58; and Dakin, *Turgot and the Ancien Régime*, 136–43.

62. Armand Thomas Hue de Miromesnil, "Lettres sur l'état de la magistrature, en l'année 1772" (MS, Bibliothèque Nationale, F.F. 10986); *Journal historique*, December 1, 1774 (VI, 356).

63. *Journal historique*, November 8, 1774 (VI, 301).

When the definitive plans leaked out during the final days of October, there was great popular excitement. "You would not believe the joy that reigns here," one observer said, "especially since Sunday, when the secret became known everywhere. . . . The general public is talking about nothing else . . . a sort of intoxication has seized people's minds, and . . . there is not a single citizen who is not going to join the crowd on Saturday and make the heavens ring with his loudest cheers."[64] D'Allonville later made the perceptive comment, "The recall of the exiled parlements, which ought to have been welcomed as a boon, was regarded only as a victory for public opinion, [which] . . . daily was becoming more powerful."[65]

The terms of the settlement were announced at a *lit de justice* on November 12 in the presence of all the notables of the realm, ecclesiastical and secular: Cessation of service and mass resignations were punishable by forfeiture of office, and a Cour Plenière was established to judge magistrates liable to this penalty. The Grand Conseil, abolished by Maupeou, was reconstituted to serve as a standby court should the Parlement refuse to act. The number of magistrates was reduced and the power of the conservative Grand-Chambre was increased by the abolition of two Chambres d'Enquête and the Chambre de Requêtes. (These were chambers within the Parlement with special functions.) On the other hand, Maupeou's conseils supérieurs were abolished and the Cours des Aides of Paris and Clermont-Ferrand were reestablished. Later all the provincial parlements, even that of Pau reformed in 1765, were restored. The ousted magistrates of the Maupeou Parlement were given appointments to the Grand Conseil.

It immediately became apparent that the *lit de justice* was not a compromise but a surrender. The restored Parlement, joined by the Princes of the Blood and the peers of the realm, made its first business to debate and loudly protest the *Ordonnance de Discipline* accompanying the edicts by which the court was reestablished. Vigorous *représentations* were sent on January 8 to the king, who of course rejected them, and the Parlement then passed on January 22 an *arrêté* reaffirming its protests. The edicts and the *Ordonnance* stood, but the general interpretation of events seems to have been that given by the Count de Ségur, who wrote, "The Parlements'

64. "Lettres de M. R**," October 21 and November 9, 1774 (IV, 103, 122).
65. D'Allonville, *Mémoires secrets*, 89. Cf. "Lettres de M. R**," November 13, 1774 (IV, 133); *Journal historique*, November 25, 1774 (VI, 339).

power was unconditionally restored to them; and the spirit of resistance and innovation was emboldened by this victory of the independence of the high magistracy over the government."[66]

Though the magistrates returned unsubdued and still aggressive, they were to some extent chastened by their experience, and they did not henceforth display the overweening arrogance of the years before 1771.[67] Maupeou's experiment in absolutism failed not because there was no need for at least some of his proposed reforms, nor because Louis XVI made a stupid, gratuitous mistake in reestablishing the parlements, but because such a constitution was not viable in the face of the determined opposition of the nobility and the wealthy bourgeoisie and in the absence of active support from any other group except the church. Its philosophy and methods were inadequate to this moment in French history. This did not mean, however, that the traditional constitutional thesis of the parlements was vindicated. The magistrates came out of the years of trial not only bruised but also changed. The prolonged debate had drawn into the ranks of the Patriotes opponents of "*despotisme*" with some pretty radical ideas, and it had also persuaded many that France's future lay neither in the old *thèse parlementaire* nor in the new *thèse royale*, but in some new and better constitutional principles. Some, at least, of the returning magistrates must have perceived the obsolescence of the old arguments and the old causes when they heard the Duke de La Rochefoucauld demand in the very chambers of the newly restored Parlement the necessity to convene "national assemblies, without which everything is irregular and illegal and which neither the Parlement nor even the Princes and the Peers can replace."[68]

66. Ségur, *Mémoires*, I, 38. Cf. "Lettre à M. le comte de Maurepas," in *Journal historique*, VII, 305–306.
67. On the circumspection of the magistrates after 1774 because of the Maupeou revolution, see Jean Egret, *Louis XV et l'opposition parlementaire, 1715–1774* (Paris, 1970), 226; and Doyle, "The Parlements of France," 453.
68. *Journal historique*, January 1, 1775 (VII, 5).

PART I

The Patriotes

ONE

The Patriotes

THE OPPOSITION to Maupeou was composed of different but overlapping groups: first, the *noblesse de robe*; second, the magistrates, incuding members of the lower courts, not all of whom were of noble status; third, the Parti Parlementaire, those actively engaged in organized political resistance to the crown; and fourth, the Patriotes, the broad and inclusive term that was used for all those who favored, or were believed to favor, the restoration of the parlements.

The Parti Parlementaire included in its ranks members from various classes and *états*—magistrates of the courts, lawyers, propagandists from the Third Estate such as Augeard, peers such as the Duke de La Rochefoucauld, and the Princes of the Blood, led by the Prince de Conti. It was a party in the French eighteenth-century sense, more comparable to the American Whigs than to the British Whigs or Tories. United nationally by the spirit and principle of unity of classes and politically by passionate opposition to the existing regime, without formal organization yet well disciplined (*vide* the lawyers' strike), it was politically effective. Like a modern political party it published propaganda, instigated rumors, organized mass demonstrations, and exerted pressure by negotiation, persuasion, and threats.

The Patriotes included these activists but also all other identified sympathizers—the amateur female legislators of Paris supper parties, the cheering crowds of November 1774, and even Philosophes such as Sébas-

tien Mercier. In the eyes of their contemporaries such persons appeared as
clearly distinct politically both from Maupeou's supporters and from those
who opposed both the chancellor and the old parlements. Thus *Patriotes*
is a valid term justified by contemporary usage to designate a historic political group. It is important to understand, however, that membership
was determined only by political orientation, not by any specific comprehensive ideology. As long as one hated Maupeou and cheered the returning magistrates one was a Patriote, whether one was conservative or radical, reactionary or liberal, a defender of aristocracy or a democrat, a devout
Catholic or an anticlerical deist.

A precise sociological analysis of the membership of this opinion group
would be beyond the purposes of this study, and in any case probably would
not be possible from available data. As we have seen in the Introduction,
the evidence seems to indicate that the Patriotes constituted a majority of
the politically conscious and vocal population. Yet even this conclusion
must be qualified. First there is the problem of definition. Are we to count
only the avowed Patriotes, or should we include also those whom Patriote
writers claimed as supporters—for instance such Philosophes as Mercier,
Helvétius, or Raynal? Where do we draw the line in the fuzzy area between partisanship and indifference or neutralism? Second, it must be understood that the Patriotes fluctuated in numbers and in the intensity of
their feelings during the four-year period. If we may judge by the number
of Patriote publications and from contemporary letters, memoirs, and reports of public demonstrations of support, it appears that Patriotisme
reached an initial peak in the spring of 1771, continued vigorous through
the remainder of that year, declined progressively during 1772 and 1773,
was revived in 1774 to reach a new height in November, when the old
Parlement was restored, and then rapidly declined and vanished as a dead
issue.

An additional difficulty is the fact that no social group seems to have
approached unanimity as Patriote or royalist. One Patriote source reported on the division of opinion, "This is a sort of civil war; every family
is divided. Wives despise their husbands, sons avoid fathers, fathers curse
their sons, brothers detest brothers. In short, it is a continuous spectacle
of hatreds and quarrels which perhaps will endure for several generations."[1] Nevertheless it is possible to name some of the active Patriotes

---

1. *Journal historique*, April 23, 1771 (I, 270).

and to distinguish those social groups or classes in which Patriotisme or royalism seems to have been predominant.

Most of the *peuple*, peasants or city workers, too concerned with the problems of day-to-day survival to understand or be interested in the politics of the upper classes, were probably indifferent. This was not true of all, however. Literacy was increasing, and the French peasant was fearful (*vide* Rousseau's *Confessions*) and resentful of any governmental power that affected him personally. This ingrained recalcitrance to authority manifested itself in hostility to the unpopular Louis in the area of Paris and in anti-Parlement feeling in certain provincial capitals, particularly Besançon.[2] After January 1771 the king and Maupeou, as the virtual sole authors and symbols of governmental power, increasingly became the targets of popular resentment caused by worsening economic conditions. The opinions of the lower bourgeoisie, such as artisans and small shopkeepers, are uncertain. They were variously reported as going along with the anti-Parlement resentments of the populace below them and of sharing the anti-royalism of the bourgeois above them.

The ministry received its principal support from the leaders of the church, particularly the pro-Jesuit element (which was strong among the higher clergy and which had not forgiven the Paris Parlement for the expulsion of the Society of Jesus), from the Parti Dévot at Versailles, and from a minority of the nobility. Thus the Patriotes apparently comprised a majority of the nobility and of the wealthy bourgeois, whose interests the parlements had always defended, probably most of the middle bourgeoisie, the Jansenistic clergy, and an uncertain portion of the *peuple* and lower bourgeoisie which varied in size and composition both regionally and in time. Among the nobility, the most active Patriotes were to be found among the Princes of the Blood (with the exception of the Count de La Marche and the Duke de Penthièvre), certain members of the *noblesse d'épée* such as the Duke de La Rochefoucauld, military officers, and of course the *noblesse de robe*, notably Malesherbes and Armand Thomas Hue de Miromesnil, former premier président of the Parlement of Rouen. The bourgeois Patriote activists were mainly magistrates of the lower courts and lawyers and lawyers' clerks, and there seems to have been general support of the parlements by large merchants and bankers, many of whom suf-

2. *Ibid.*, August 10, 1771 (II, 78).

fered from Terray's financial manipulations and who socially and economically blended and identified with the aristocracy.[3]

Patriote books and pamphlets were almost always published anonymously, for good reason, and a large number of the writers on whom we
must rely for a definition of Patriote thought remain unidentified. Of those
whose names we do know, however, virtually all came from the nobility,
the magistrates of the courts, and the lawyers. The individuals or com-
mittees of magistrates who drew up the remonstrances, letters, decrees,
and resolutions issued by the various courts before their suppression remain anonymous, with the exception of Malesherbes, author of the remonstrances published by the Cour des Aides of Paris. Athanase Alexandre Clément de Boissy (1716–1793), author of *Le Maire du Palais* (1771)
was a conseiller of the Cour des Comptes, and Jacques Mathieu Augeard
(1731–1805), the most successful of the Patriote satirists, was the son of
a family of magistrates related to the Lamoignons. Of the nobility there
was Pierre Arnaud Vicomte d'Aubusson (1717–1797), who began his career as a writer on political and economic subjects with his *Profession de foi
politique d'un bon Français* (1771?), and the witty Louis Léon Félicité Duc
de Brancas (Comte de Lauragais) (1733–1824), whose varied writings included his *Extrait du droit public de la France* and his *Tableau de la constitution française*, both published in 1771. The lawyers, the most numerous
group, included André Blonde (1734–1794), an *avocat* who published two
notable works, *Le Parlement justifié par l'Impératrice de Russie* (1771) and *Le
Parlement justifié par l'Impératrice Reine de Hongrie, et par le Roi de Prusse*
(1772); Jean Baptiste Jacques Elie de Beaumont (1732–1786), an *avocat
au Parlement de Paris* and well known jurist, whose *Mémoire pour les Calas*
(1762) had brought him into relations with Voltaire; the Abbé Claude
Mey (1712–1796), also a noted jurist, Jansenist, and *avocat au Parlement
de Paris*, whose lengthy *Maximes du droit public* (1772) was perhaps the most

3. *Au Public abusé: Messieurs, entendons-nous* (N.p., n.d. [1771]), a pro-Maupeou pamphlet and biased against the parlements, is the only contemporary document I have found
which attempts a systematic analysis of public opinion by classes. It describes "le peuple-
peuple" as indifferent to the fate of the parlements and interested mainly in the price of
bread, and "le peuple ouvrier-artisan" as feeling that the parlements would do better to
think about the problems of the people. "Le peuple marchand-bourgeois," "le peuple notable," "le gros peuple financier," "le peuple militaire," "le petit peuple composant la
Robe Courte" (lawyers clerks, etc.), and "les Princes du sang" are all listed as pro-Parlement.

prestigious of all the Patriote works; and Guy Jean Baptiste Target (1733–1806), a third *avocat au Parlement de Paris*, a friend of the Philosophes, and later a member of the French Academy and a leading figure in the Assemblée Nationale Constituante, whose *Lettre d'un homme à un autre homme, sur l'extinction de l'ancien parlement* (1771) was one of the most cogent of the Patriote pieces. Radical Patriote thought was represented by Jacques Claude Martin de Mariveaux (or Marivaux), a brilliant young lawyer who in 1775 sent to every member of the reestablished Parlement of Paris a copy of his *L'Ami des lois*, begun in 1773, which he thought would be welcomed for its attacks on despotism but which the magistrates found too strong for their stomachs and condemned to be burned as "seditious, subversive of the sovereignty of the king, and contrary to the fundamental laws of the realm."[4] Guillaume Saige (whose works have been attributed to his relative Joseph Saige), another lawyer, also published in 1775 a similar work supporting the parlements and attacking absolutism, his *Catéchisme du citoyen*, which was so radical and Rousseauan that it likewise was condemned to burning.[5] A third provocative Patriote writer was Martin Morizot, lawyer, journalist, and pamphleteer, author of the *Inauguration de Pharamond* (1772). To these names must be added of course that of the *nouvelliste* Mathieu François Pidanzat de Mairobert (1727–1779), editor of the *Journal historique*.

Malesherbes inspired a number of these writers, according to Augeard, who served as liaison between the Duke d'Orléans and Malesherbes and other Patriote leaders. Malesherbes aroused Augeard's interest in constitutional questions during a long conversation in which he stressed the points that the power to tax belonged to the States General and that the parlements never should have made an issue of their claim to this function. Augeard decided to make a thorough study of documents relating

4. *Arrêt* of June 30, 1775. See Gabriel Peignot, *Dictionnaire des livres condamnés* (Paris, 1806), I, 298; and Keith Michael Baker, "French Political Thought at the Accession of Louis XVI," *Journal of Modern History,* L (1978), 281–82.

5. Also condemned by the *arrêt* of June 30, 1775. See Peignot, *Dictionnaire*, I, 298, and Baker, "French Political Thought," 281–82, 285, 298–303. Copies of the first 1775 edition are rare but exist in the Bibliothèque de l'Arsenal (Paris) and the Bibliothèque Municipale de Bordeaux. There are three 1788 editions (in the Bibliothèque Nationale), and Elie Carcasonne, *Montesquieu et le problème de la constitution française au XVIIIᵉ siècle* (Paris, 1927), 473, cites two 1787 Geneva editions. On Saige, see also Clarke W. Garrett, "The *Moniteur* of 1788," *French Historical Studies,* V (1968), 263–73.

to the French constitution and he talked with the lawyers Elie de Beaumont, Target, and Blonde, explaining to them Malesherbes' ideas and setting them to reading in the library of M. d'Aguesseau and writing up the results of their research.[6]

Patriote literature may be roughly classed in three types: morale boosters, satirical libels, and works of political philosophy. The morale boosters were written to encourage the lawyers to maintain their strike and to dissuade wavering magistrates from liquidating their offices. They were most numerous in the autumn of 1771, when the majority of the defections occurred, and again in December 1772, when it was feared that the Duke d'Orléans' apparent apostasy in making peace with the Court would set off a wave of liquidations. Such publications, largely appeals to party loyalty and "self-interest," contained little that was politically constructive. The satires and libels ranged from the grossest character assassination, as in the notorious Charles Thévenot de Morande's *Gazetier cuirassé* (1771), a juicy collection of scandalous anecdotes about Du Barry, Maupeou, and Louis XV, to Augeard's witty and devastating *Correspondance secrète*. Some were light and frivolous squibs, some radical outbursts of indignation genuinely revolutionary in intent, such as *Le Propos indiscret*. The chef d'oeuvre of the genre was, of course, Beaumarchais' *Mémoires*. These pieces were often politically effective, but they only occasionally contained serious considerations of principles.

It is in the works of the third type that we find attempts to relate the immediate issues to broad and general political concepts and problems, and it is with these that we shall be mainly concerned in the following pages. One sub-type comprised the remonstrances, letters, decrees, and resolutions of the various courts before their suppression or reformation. Such documents were sometimes eloquent, sometimes presumptuous and bombastic, but they rarely made significant ideological contributions. Outstanding exceptions were Malesherbes' remonstrances of the Cour des Aides of February 1771 and the remonstrances of the Parlement of Besançon of March 11, 1771, a learned and intelligent discussion of such fundamental questions as the nature of property, the origin of government, *raison d'état*, and the necessity of constitutional government. The

6. Jacques Mathieu Augeard, *Mémoires secrets . . . 1760 à 1800, documents inédits*, ed. Evariste Bavoux (Paris, 1886), 38–43.

most original and creative Patriote thought, however, is in the books and pamphlets, some printed, some circulated in manuscript, of whom the most notable identified authors were Aubusson, Blonde, Brancas, Clément de Boissy, Martin de Mariveaux, Mey, Morizot, Saige, and Target.

All these writers, and the many unidentified anonymous authors, were Patriotes in the contemporary sense that they supported the parlements against Maupeou and monarchical absolutism, but they differed among themselves on both principles and applications of principles, and this diversity revealed internal debates within the group on various issues, such as the legislative and taxing powers of the parlements, and produced a progressive blurring of the old *thèses parlementaire* and *nobiliaire*. Yet the clear political objective of all Patriotes did impose definite limits on their ideological spectrum; they characteristically accepted any idea supportive of their immediate purpose, ignored those irrelevant to it, and opposed those dangerous to it. In this broad sense it is possible to perceive in their writings what might be called a Patriote political philosophy dictated by the exigencies of practical politics and by the need for the widest possible public support, but it was not a philosophy one can simplistically categorize as aristocratic or bourgeois, reactionary or liberal.

The diversity and political pragmatism of the Patriotes is perhaps best illustrated by their relationships with individuals and groups of different political orientations. For instance, Choiseul and the Choiseulistes were useful allies against the common enemy Maupeou, but the former minister's position on the reinstatement of the old magistrates remained unclear until late in 1774. Therefore when he returned from exile he was regarded with considerable uncertainty and suspicion until it became clear that he would not be reappointed to the ministry and therefore could pose no threat, whereupon all reserve vanished.[7] Maurepas also was initially seen as a dubious factor, but as soon as the word spread that he was working for the restoration of the parlements he was enthusiastically listed high in the ranks of the Patriotes.[8] On the other hand, Miromesnil, appointed

7. *Journal historique*, June 17, 1774 (VI, 64).

8. *Ibid.*, June 21, 1774 (VI, 70–71); Charles Collé, "Les Revenans," *ibid.*, December 15, 1774 (VI, 391); *Oraison funèbre de très-hauts et très-puissans seigneurs, en leur vivant, les gens tenants les conseils supérieurs de France, prononcée dans la grande salle de l'hôtel-de-ville de C***, le lundi 28 novembre 1774 . . . par M^r D***, avocat en la même ville* (Normandie, 1774).

Garde des Sceaux in August 1774, a staunch supporter of the cause since 1770, came in for hostile criticism as the author of the "third parlement" compromise.[9]

Political considerations similarly governed relations with the Physiocrats and with Turgot, who was identified with that school. The Patriotes as such subscribed to no particular economic theory. The Parlement of Paris, as we have seen, after having gone along with the royal government's free-trade policy inaugurated in 1763/1764, had in December 1768 begun to urge a return to controls and in 1770, in what the diarist Regnaud called a transparent effort "to win the minds of the people," endorsed Terray's restrictive *arrêts* of that year.[10] Laissez-faire economics were still unpopular in 1774 and consequently politically dangerous, so Turgot's accession to the ministry would not in any case have been welcomed, and he had the additional stigma of having served on the special tribunal organized to judge cases during the exile of the Paris Parlement in 1753/1754. He was therefore initially condemned as a man "who has always been a partisan of the authority of the crown [and who] . . . certainly has not changed his way of thinking."[11] But as soon as it became known that he was working for the liquidation of the Maupeou revolution, Patriote opinion about-faced, and he suddenly became "that wise minister who seems to seek only the public good," famous for his "spirit of equity and beneficence" and his active concern for the people.[12] Yet when late in 1774 Turgot proposed the reestablishment of free trade in grains, enthusiasm cooled; there was "division of opinions," and the restored Parlement approached the issue reluctantly and warily.[13]

The ambiguities in the Patriotes' position were most evident in their

9. Collé, "Les Revenans," in *Journal historique*, VI, 390; "Epître à M. le Garde des Sceaux, par un conseiller du parlement de Rouen," *ibid.*, December 18, 1774 (VI, 404–407); "Lettre du chancelier Maupeou à M. de Miromesnil, Garde des Sceaux," *ibid.*, December 28, 1774 (VI, 426–31)—possibly by Beaumarchais; see *ibid.*, December 30, 1774 (VI, 433–34). *Oraison funèbre de très-hauts et très-puissans seigneurs.*

10. Regnaud, "Histoire," I, 26–27. See Kaplan, *Bread, Politics, and Political Economy*, 424–42, 513–27.

11. *Journal historique*, July 25, 1774 (VI, 123).

12. *Ibid.*, August 1 and 31, September 3, 5, 6, 11, 19, 26, October 7, 1774, January 31, 1775 (VI, 130, 177, 184, 187, 188–89, 195, 205, 220, 232, VII, 75–77): *Mes Réflexions sur les idées d'un inamovible et compagnie, octobre 1774* (Paris, n.d. [1774]); *Oraison funèbre de très-hauts et très-puissans seigneurs.*

13. *Journal historique*, December 17, 1774 (VI, 397).

attitudes toward the church and toward the institution of aristocracy. The parliamentary magistrates though Gallicans were nonetheless Catholics, and indeed they had acquired a reputation for rigorous intolerance by their condemnations of irreligious writings (for example Rousseau's *Emile*) and their decisions in cases such as those of Calas and the Chevalier de La Barre. But times were changing, and the Paris Parlement had rehabilitated the name of Calas.

Furthermore, political Jansenism, operating under the aegis of the parlements, while not by intent either anti-monarchical or anti-Catholic, had not only withstood repression by the throne but also in successfully prosecuting its political and religious quarrels within the church had seriously weakened ecclesiastical power and prestige and undermined spiritual authority, and thus unwittingly had collaborated with the deistic or atheistic Philosophes. By 1770, however, political Jansenism's great objective, the destruction of the Jesuits, had been achieved and neither sacerdotal "despotism" nor acceptance of the bull *Unigenitus* forced by *billets de confession* was any longer a live issue, with the result that Jansenism became a party without political objectives of its own and without special usefulness to its parliamentary allies. In the first weeks of the Maupeou revolution Robert de Saint Vincent, a Jansenistic magistrate of the Parlement of Paris, urged that the Parlement accuse the Jesuits of engineering the edict of December 1770 and stigmatize Maupeou as their agent, but his colleagues refused this outdated gambit, inducing Saint Vincent to the "sad reflection that the Jesuits had more protectors in the Parlement in 1771 than in 1761 when they were destroyed."[14] The truth probably was that the Jansenists had far fewer interested collaborators. It may not be literally true that the Jansenists, having defined themselves as anti-Jesuits, by expelling the Jesuits "defined themselves out of existence."[15] Yet it is certainly the fact that, bereft of any vital cause except their support of the *thèse parlementaire*, they saw their political identity rapidly absorbed and lost in the onrushing current of *Patriotisme*, which individual Jansenists such as the Abbé Claude Mey continued to support with increased fervor. The *Journal historique* described the situation thus: "Jansenism, having lost its great merit and true value by the extinction of the Jesuits

14. Quoted by Van Kley, *The Jansenists*, 227.
15. *Ibid.*, 228.

in France, has been transformed into the party of patriotism. Jansenism must be given credit for having always supported the cause of freedom and for having fought against papal despotism with invincible courage. Political despotism is a no less terrible and redoutable monster, and Jansenism today directs against this enemy all its forces, now no longer needed for the other struggle."[16] Jesuitism seemed a vanished threat, but it had been replaced by a moral equivalent in Maupeouism. "State Molinism," one Patriote wrote, "is attempting to establish itself in place of ecclesiastical Molinism."[17]

This identification of Jansenism with *Patriotisme* was reinforced by some notorious incidents, notably the condemnation, allegedly at the instigation of a bishop with Jesuitic sympathies, of members of the Jansenistic faculty of the College of Auxerre to severe punishments, including confinement in the galleys and perpetual exile, for seditious Patriote teachings.[18] Equally notorious was the refusal of the last sacraments to a former attorney general of the Parlement of Aix, Jean Pierre François Ripert de Monclar, until he had both retracted his anti-Jesuitic writings and also disavowed his opposition to the king and Maupeou.[19]

Meanwhile the royalists were similarly politicizing religion. Pro-Jesuits and the Parti Dévot at Versailles, identifying their own brand of religion and their own politics with true Catholicism, denounced the Patriotes as heretics or worse. Reportedly one bishop predicted, "If the [former] Parlement returns, religion is done for"; and "a very devout lady" prophesied that "if the parlements were reestablished, in ten years no masses would be said in all of France."[20] A Jesuitic pamphlet lumped together as the Society's enemies "the Jansenists, the Encyclopedist philos-

16. *Journal historique*, January 20, 1772 (II, 351).

17. *Réflexions sur les affaires présentes* (N.p., n.d. [1771]), 6.

18. *Journal historique*, November 16 and 19, 1773 (V, 59, 62–63).

19. *Ibid.*, July 5, 1773 (IV, 235–36; *Gazette de Cologne*, March 16, 1773; *Journal politique ou Gazette des gazettes*, March 2 and 15, 1773, p. 64; *Lettre d'un gentilhomme du diocèse d'Apt à M.****** (N.p., n.d. [1773]). Voltaire also became involved in this controversy. See François Marie Arouet de Voltaire, *Voltaire's Correspondence*, ed. Theodore Besterman (Geneva, 1953–65), LXXXV, 45, 49–50, 66, 73, 73–74, 236–37. For other anti-Jesuit Patriote publications, see [Charles Thévenot de Morande], *Mélange confus sur des matières fort claires . . .* (N.p., n.d.); *Lettre de M***, conseiller au parlement, à M. le comte de *** . . .* (N.p., n.d. [1771]), 39; *Les Derniers soupirs du soi-disant parlement de Paris . . .* (N.p., 1774), 14. These attacks were seconded by Voltaire in 1774.

20. *Lettre à un duc et pair* (Utrecht, 1774), 4–5.

ophers, and the horde of republican magistrates, enemies of Catholicism, of religion, and of monarchical authority."[21]

These charges were of course extravagant, for there were devout and even bigoted Catholics among the magistrates, but they did serve to identify the Patriote movement with irreligion, and they were not completely unfounded. There is repeated evidence at least of increased religious indifference among the magistrates after 1771.[22] Patriote pamphleteers echoed their enemy Voltaire in urging the secularization of the state and the taxation of church properties.[23] The influential Patriote journalist Pidanzat de Mairobert was openly anticlerical. He described the archbishop of Reims, recently elevated to the cardinalate, as "one of the most ignorant and least intelligent members of the church in France—and that is saying a lot," and he hailed Mercier's attack on religious fanaticism in the play *Jean Hennuyer* as the contribution of "some Patriote writer."[24] Yet certain other Patriote pamphleteers made a special effort to emphasize the parlements' traditional role as "defenders of the precious liberties of the Gallican church."[25] Some reaffirmed the right of the clergy to exist as a privileged order.[26] Others tried to link the clergy's grievances against the crown with their own.[27] Others made the telling argument that Mau-

21. *Journal historique*, July 8, 1773 (IV, 242).

22. Doyle, *The Parlement of Bordeaux*, 136.

23. *Mes Réflexions*, 17–18, *Lettre à un duc et pair*, 24; [Guillaume Saige], *Catéchisme du citoyen, ou Eléméns du droit public français, par demandes et par réponses* (N.p., 1788), 86–87. This work first appeared in 1775; see note 5.

24. *Journal historique*, December 28, 1771, November 7, 1772 (II, 321, III, 335). See also *Supplément à la Gazette de France*, No. 10, November 26, 1772.

25. *Acte de protestation de plusieurs membres du bailliage de Caen, contre l'édit de suppression du parlement de Rouen* (N.p., n.d. [1771]), 2. See also [Jacques Mathieu Augeard], *Oeufs rouges. Première partie. Sorhouet mourant à M. de Maupeou, chancelier de France* (N.p., 1772), 18; "Essai historique sur les droits de la province de Normandie," in *Les Efforts de la liberté et du patriotisme contre le despotisme du sieur Maupeou, ou Recueil des écrits patriotiques publiés pendant le règne du chancelier Maupeou. . . . Ouvrage qui peut servir d'histoire du siècle de Louis XV pendant les années 1770-71-72-73-74* (Paris, 1775), VI, 21–84.

26. E.g., [Saige] *Catéchisme du citoyen*, Chap. 7.

27. E.g., Chambre des Comptes de Paris, "Arrêté de la Chambre des Comptes," February 17, 1771, in *Recueil des réclamations, remontrances, lettres, arrêts, arrêtés, protestations des parlemens, cours des aides, chambres des comptes, bailliages, présidiaux, élections au sujet de l'édit de décembre 1770, de l'érection des conseils supérieurs, de la suppression des parlemens, etc. . . . avec un abrégé historique des principaux faits relatifs à la suppression du parlement de Paris et de tous les parlemens du royaume* (London, 1773), I, 38 ff.; [Guy Jean Baptiste Target], *Lettres d'un homme à un autre homme sur les affaires du temps* (N.p., n.d. [1771]), 91.

peou's kind of statism was anti-theocratic and threatened the church with secular and materialistic absolutism.[28]

There was a similar range in Patriote attitudes toward aristocracy. It is true of course that the magistrates, the core of the Patriotes, had traditionally favored the economic interests of the nobility. But it would be more accurate to say they had favored, first of all, their own personal interests, and after these the interests of the moneyed classes; their policies had been more beneficial, for example, to bourgeois investors than to impoverished provincial *hobereaux*. It is also true that the Parliamentary party was led by the Princes of the Blood, notably the Prince de Conti and the Duke d'Orléans, but these men were unquestionably primarily interested in making political capital out of the crisis, just as the latter's son, the Duke de Chartres, was to do again after 1789 under the name of Philippe Egalité. One already heard expressions of egalitarian sentiments by some nobles, though their sincerity and intentions remain uncertain. The aristocratic applause of *Le Mariage de Figaro* was not to be heard until some ten years later. There may be more significance, however, in the aristocratic participation in French Masonry, reorganized and reinvigorated in 1772/1773, after the Duke de Chartres' election as Grand Master in June 1771. The constitution of the Grand Orient of France, signed June 26, 1773, by both distinguished nobles such as the Duke de Luxembourg (elected Administrateur Général in April 1772) and distinguished commoners such as Lalande and Guillotin, provided the model of a democratic republican government created to give expression to the "general will" under a representative legislature elected by all the members and an independent elected executive.[29] All distinctions of rank, birth, and status disappeared once a Mason entered the door of his lodge, and the vote of a simple artisan counted the same as that of a duke or a *président à mortier*. There is no evidence that the Masonic lodges played any significant part in the opposition to the Maupeou revolution, except perhaps in Bordeaux, where in 1775 the Masons erected a triumphal arch to welcome the restored parlement and the *vénérable* of the lodge delivered an oration

28. [Athanase Alexandre Clément de Boissy], *Le Maire du palais* (N.p., 1771), 11–12.

29. "Circulaire du G∴O∴ [Grand Orient] du 26 juin 1773" and "Circulaire du G∴O∴ du 18 mars 1775," quoted in Gaston Martin, *La Franc-Maçonnerie française et la préparation de la Révolution* (Paris, 1926), 91, 17.

to the premier président returned from exile.[30] Only after 1774 did a significant number of magistrates, lawyers, and members of the Parliamentary party join lodges.[31] Yet the relatively large participation of nobles in
an organization explicitly non-aristocratic in philosophy is an indication
that in these years not all aristocrats defended the theory of aristocracy.

The traditional aristocratic thesis was in fact already badly undermined and was no longer represented in French literature except by rare,
anachronistic, and uninfluential writers such as the Count Du Buat-Nançay, who argued from confused utilitarian and natural-law premises for
the preeminence of a hereditary nobility—and who, incidentally, would
have downgraded the parlements to a subordinate function in the state.[32]
This is not to say that there was any interest, either within or outside the
Patriote movement (excepting a few eccentrics like the Abbé de Mably)
in absolute economic, social, or political egalitarianism. Even liberal
Philosophes such as D'Holbach accepted the necessity of a hierarchically
structured society. The only question for French thinkers was the rationale of the structure, and on this point we find the usual variety of Patriote views.

On one hand, the parlements had always defended not only the financial privileges of the nobility but also their "honneur," and this theme of
the sanctity of aristocratic status Patriote writers continued to support.
The Princes of the Blood asserted in their *Protestations*, "As *gentilhommes*,
we demand the preservation of the rights of the nobility; as peers of France
by birth, we demand the preservation of the rights of the peers and the
peerage."[33] And even the Rousseauistic and democratic Patriote Guil-

30. Martin, *La Franc-Maçonnerie française*, 41–50; Roger A. Priouret, *La Franc-Maçonnerie sous les lys* (Paris, 1953), 102–105; *Récit de ce qui a précédé et suivi la rentrée du parlement de Bordeaux* (1775), cited in *Journal historique*, March 22, 1775 (VII, 217).

31. Alain Le Bihan, *Francs-Maçons parisiens du Grand Orient de France* (Paris, 1966);
Louis Amiable, *La Franc-Maçonnerie et la magistrature en France à la veille de la Révolution*
(Aix, 1894).

32. [Louis Gabriel, Count Du Buat-Nançay], *Les Origines, ou l'Ancien gouvernement de
la France, de l'Allemagne et de l'Italie* (The Hague, 1757); [Du Buat-Nançay], *Eléments de la
politique, ou Recherches des vrais principes de l'économie sociale* (London, 1773); [Du Buat-Nan-
çay], *Les Maximes du gouvernement monarchique, pour servir de suite aux "Eléments de la politique" par le même auteur* (London, 1778).

33. *Protestations des Princes du Sang contre l'édit de décembre 1770, les lettres patentes du 23
janvier, l'édit de février 1771 . . . lues en présence de MM. du Conseil siégeant au Palais, le 12
avril 1771* (N.p., n.d. [Paris, 1771]), 3.

laume Saige conceded that the nobility "enjoy, by virtue of the constitution, an excellence [*illustration*] which is hereditary and inherent in their
persons, whence are derived a very large number of rights and privileges
[specifically including certain tax exemptions], likewise hereditary."[34] The
point that Montesquieu had made was frequently repeated, that in a despotism (which Maupeou was accused of creating) an aristocratic sense of
honor, and even the existence of a true aristocracy, was impossible.
"Whenever titles of dignity or the immunities of the church or the prerogatives of the nobility are found to be inconvenient, all the subjects of
the king will be placed on the same level."[35]

Quantitatively, however, such statements were rare in Patriote literature and were subordinated to the more numerous attacks on absolutism
and to the vindication of "national rights." However dear to the hearts of
Patriote nobles were their aristocratic privileges and *honneur*, the propagandists of the party, we must infer, saw that loud insistence on these
causes was neither politically expedient nor likely to engender broad public support.

Indeed a surprising number of Patriote writings seem to be explicitly
anti-aristocratic in their denunciations of the evils of historic "feudalism." This theme was of course not new to the century (*e.g.*, Du Bos and
D'Argenson), but it had scarcely been part of parliamentary thought. It
was now, however, being effectively restated by the Scottish historian
William Robertson, whose *History of the Reign of the Emperor Charles V*
(1769) appeared in three French editions in 1771. His thesis was that the
feudal system and the excessive power of the nobility in the Middle Ages
had weakened royal power and produced anarchy and the corruption of
religion and morals. The great benefit of the Crusades, he held, had been
to weaken feudalism and bring about the admission of representatives of
the towns into European legislative assemblies, thus tempering aristocratic oppression by an infusion of "liberté populaire."[36] There was the
obvious danger (which royalist writers did in fact attempt to exploit) of
the identification of any infringement on monarchical authority, and spe-

34. [Saige], *Catéchisme du citoyen*, Chap. 8.
35. [Clément de Boissy], *Le Maire du palais*, 11.
36. William Robertson, *Histoire du règne de l'Empereur Charles-Quint* . . . (Amsterdam,
1771), I, 79 and *passim*.

cifically the pretensions of the parlements, with medieval feudalism. This threat the Patriotes tried to meet by turning Robertson's historiography to their own purposes, taking the line that "national liberty" had originally existed in the "general assemblies" of the early French monarchy before the feudal usurpations, that after the Middle Ages the French people had never succeeded in fully regaining their lost liberty, and that the freedom of the nation could be completely restored only if the parlements, successors to the early assemblies, could counter Maupeou's attempt to reduce France once more to feudal slavery.[37]

One finds also in Patriote writings expressions of indignation against the callous indifference of the rich, bourgeois and noble alike, to social injustices. "The powerful unfortunately know nothing of the frightful condition of the poor. They cast cold glances at the peasant's cottage, but they never enter to see the desolation, the hunger, and the despair inside it."[38] The remarkable *Mandement de l'Evêque d'Alais* published by Mairobert described France as a "kingdom divided between two classes. On one hand the provinces are despoiled to provide tribute to the luxury and ostentation of a few families, as contemptible in their origins as in the behavior, who cannot see anything superfluous in their opulence; while in the other class millions of families, earning scarcely enough from their miserable toil to stay alive, seem a living reproach to Providence for this humiliating inequality."[39] Among the more radical Patriotes such feelings seemed to spring from authentically democratic principles: "Man is born free," Mariveaux proclaimed. "No man possesses natural authority over his fellow beings. . . . Laws, kings, nobles, and the clergy in turn

---

37. [Louis Léon Félicité, Duke de Brancas], "Tableau des différents âges de la monarchie française," in *Les Efforts de la liberté*, II, 50–70; Cour des Aides de Paris, "Remontrances de la Cour des Aides relatives aux impôts" (May 6, 1775), in Cour des Aides de Paris, *Mémoires pour servir à l'histoire du droit public de la France en matières d'impôts ou Recueil de ce qui s'est passé de plus intéressant à la Cour des Aides, depuis 1756 jusqu'au mois de juin 1775* . . . (Brussels, 1779), 652; "Essai historique sur les droits de la province de Normandie," in *Les Efforts de la liberté*, V, 73–74; [Claude Mey], *Maximes du droit public françois, tirées des capitulaires, des ordonnances du royaume et des autres monumens de l'histoire de France* (N.p., 1772), and 2nd augmented ed. (Amsterdam, 1775) by [Claude Mey *et al.*]; *Plan d'une conversation entre un avocat et M. le chancelier* (N.p., 1771); [Target] *Lettres d'un homme à un autre homme sur les affaires du temps*, 56. See J. Q. C. Mackrell, *The Attack on "Feudalism" in Eighteenth-Century France* (London, 1973), 17–47, 81.

38. *Maupeou tyran sous le régne de Louis le Bien-Aimé* (N.p., n.d. [1773]), 80.

39. *Journal historique*, September 20, 1774 (VI, 207–208).

have ruled France. The empires of the nobility and of the clergy have been destroyed," and now, in a final turn of the wheel, the rule of law was to be restored.[40] Such sentiments represent one end of the Patriote spectrum, and those of the Princes of the Blood the other.

Opposition to militarism by the Patriotes might seem unlikely because of the general support the parlements seem to have received from the predominantly aristocratic officer corps, but there were reasons for such a bias. Militarism was of course historically associated with the autocracy of Louis XIV, who had "sacrificed twenty million lives to his vain desire for conquest and exhausted the nation's treasury by fifty years of war."[41] More immediate, however, was Maupeou's use of military force to cow parliamentary opposition during the first months of the revolution. Various confrontations, in some of which swords were actually drawn, apparently caused certain Patriotes to give serious thought to the role of the army in the political life of the state, especially a state like the one they thought Maupeou was creating.[42] They recalled Montesquieu's warning that one of the reasons that monarchies tend to degenerate into despotisms is support of the prince by professional soldiers.[43] They described the coup as a plot "to reduce us to a military state" and feared that "the military forces may forget their patriotism . . . and from obedient troops turn into Praetorian Guards. Denmark is today learning the power that can be wielded by a military force uncontrolled by the laws and the courts."[44] The principle fear was not, however, of military dictatorship but of the military as the obedient tool of a dictator. Some Patriotes therefore attempted to undermine military morale by raising the ethical question of the soldier's obligation to obey an illegal or immoral order.[45] One

40. [Jacques Claude Martin de Mariveaux], *L'Ami des loix* (N.p., n.d. [Paris, 1775]), 6, 17.

41. [André Blonde], *Le Parlement justifié par l'Impératrice de Russie, ou Lettre à M****, *dans laquelle on répond aux différents écrits que M. le Ch{ancelier} fait distribuer dans Paris* (N.p., n.d. [1771]), 34.

42. *Journal historique*, January 24, 1771 (I, 70–71).

43. [Blonde], *Le Parlement justifié par l'Impératrice de Russie*, 29. Cf. Montesquieu, *Lettres persanes*, no. 99.

44. "Essai historique sur les droits de la province de Normandie," in *Les Efforts de la liberté*, VI, 70–72.

45. [May *et al.*], *Maximes* (2nd ed.), II, 418–19; [Martin Morizot], *Inauguration de Pharamond ou Exposition des loix fondamentales de la monarchie françoise, avec les preuves de leur exécution, perpétuées sous les trois races de nos rois* (N.p., 1772), 88 ff.

remarkable piece argued that the soldier "must not believe that every order he receives is for the good of society. He cannot abdicate his reason to the extent of accepting as useful or morally right an act which obviously contributes to the total subversion of society. It therefore follows that he cannot, without being guilty of a crime, either give his consent to such an order or collaborate in its execution. For example, no subject has the moral right to obey a prince who seeks to reduce his subjects to slavery, who executes innocent men without legal trial, etc. This would obviously be contrary to the purposes of government. . . . Those who refuse to obey such unjust and harmful use of power condemned by society are not 'rebels' but rather citizens loyal to their country. . . . Virtue is always in the heart of man to tell him when he must obey and when he must resist."[46]

The most complex problem of all is that of the relations between the Patriotes and the Philosophes. We shall examine in Chapter 8 the reactions of the latter to the Maupeou revolution; for the present it suffices to say that Voltaire alone after December 1770 publicly supported the chancellor and attacked the parlements. All others were hostile to Maupeou and his regime but regarded the parlements with varying mixtures of sympathy and contempt.

The accusation in the preamble to the edict of December 1770 that the parlements had been infected by the *esprit de système* was a shrewd stroke. The phrase had various connotations, but to conservatives it meant the rejection of the status quo, contempt for tradition, and the desire to reform the political structure on radical rationalistic principles, specifically those of the Philosophes, or Encyclopedists, as they were usually called. The charge underlined the government's contention that the parlements, despite their historical and traditionalistic arguments, were actually radical and were attempting to subvert the existing political order and erect a new one according to a new rationale that was not unrelated to the rationale of the Philosophes.

Government propagandists made explicit this accusation. One wrote, "It is only too true that the *esprit de système*, which for some time has been producing a flood of writings dangerous to religion and to the govern-

46. "Lettre de M. le comte de***, ancien capitaine au régiment d'***. Sur l'obéissance que les militaires doivent aux commandemens du prince," in *Les Efforts de la liberté*, VI, 330–47.

ment of mankind, has insinuated itself into the deliberations of the sovereign courts of the realm. We could prove by an infinite number of examples that the parlements have adopted its ideas and language in their remonstrances and decrees. To be convinced one needs only to read the articles 'Autorité' and 'Enregistrement' in the *Encyclopédie*."[47]

Conservative Patriotes strongly resented this accusation and tried to retaliate by tarring the royalists with the same brush, saying that the ones really infected by the *esprit de système* were those "who were trying to question principles always accepted as incontestable, to change what has always been considered immutable, and to destroy what has always been respected as necessary to the public welfare. . . . The consistent practise of the magistrates has always been to hold fast to our ancient manners, customs, and laws."[48] Voltaire's public support of the revolution was offered as damning proof of this alleged alliance between the Philosophes and Maupeou.[49] Yet there was in fact little truth in these countercharges. Lebrun said that the chancellor had little or no contact with scholars or intellectuals, and that to a suggestion made in 1769 that he convoke the States General he replied, "If I take this memoir to the council, everyone will . . . accuse me of betraying the throne and being either the accomplice or the dupe of the Philosophes."[50]

There was, on the other hand, substantial truth in the charge that some at least of the Patriotes had caught the philosophic disease. The most notable case is that of the journalist Pidanzat de Mairobert. He had been raised in the house of Mme Doublet and for many years had been a member of her famous salon, where she and her reputed lover, Louis Petit de Bachaumont, had edited with the help of other habitués the famous

47. [Abbé Mary (?)], *Considérations sur l'édit de décembre 1770* (N.p., n.d. [1771]), 6. Cf. *Le Fin mot de l'affaire*, 16–17; *Avis aux dames* (N.p., n.d. [1771], 3; *Dialogue entre un officier françois qui revient de Corse, et son neveu, ci-devant conseiller au parlement de Paris, exilé dans une petite ville* (N.p., n.d.), 13; *Réflexions nationales* (N.p., n.d. [1771]), 15–16; [De Saint Pierre], *Discours d'un pair de France à l'Assemblée des Pairs, sur l'édit de règlement de décembre 1770* (N.p., n.d.), 7.

48. Parlement de Bretagne, "Très humbles et très respectueuses remontrances du parlement de Bretagne au Roi sur la situation actuelle du parlement de Paris, et sur les maux dont l'état est attaqué," in *Recueil des réclamations*, II, 308.

49. *Réflexions générales sur le système projetté par le Maire du Palais, pour changer la constitution de l'état* (N.p., 1771), 4; *Maupeou tyran*, 4–5.

50. Lebrun, *Opinions*, 10, 19.

manuscript newsletter later published as the *Mémoires secrets*. This group, we are told, "were Jansenist, or rather strongly parliamentarian, but not Christian; a believer of a *dévot* was never admitted. . . . They did not flaunt their philosophic freethinking, but they practiced it without talking about it."[51] After Bachaumont's death early in 1771 Mairobert took over the editorship of the *Mémoires secrets* and at the same time started the *Journal historique*. The two *nouvelles à la main* contained many identical items, but the *Mémoires* were edited for subscribers mainly interested in literary and general matters whereas the *Journal* was devoted almost entirely to news on the Maupeou revolution.

The *Mémoires secrets* had always been pro-Parlement.[52] Mairobert's succession to the editorship, however, coinciding with Maupeou's coup, brought a sharp increase in political partisanship. This bias was coupled with a strong and overt sympathy for the Philosophes. The only exception after the edict of December 7 was in the case of Voltaire. Until 1770 the *Mémoires* had repeatedly voiced admiration for the Sage of Ferney; he was almost invariably "that great historian," "that great man," or "that great poet," and the only significant negative criticism was of his biting *Histoire du Parlement de Paris*.[53] But as soon as Voltaire's public support of Maupeou became known early in 1771 this admiration turned into vitriolic enmity. Moreover, Mairobert's attacks were vigorously seconded by other Patriote propagandists. They kept up a running attack from 1771 to 1775, circulating libelous anecdotes, publishing satirical verses, deriding the poet's failing literary powers ("muddy bits of writing, quagmires of stupidity"), and accusing him of disloyalty to his friends and gross self-service, especially of political profiteering by his desertion of his former friend and protector Choiseul to find shelter in the protection of the exiled minister's archenemy, Maupeou.[54] It was even falsely rumored that the resentful Choiseuls had erected atop their château at Chanteloup a weather vane cut in the shape of the Sage's profile.[55] Mairobert's remarks on Pi-

51. *Correspondance littéraire*, IX, 317–18.

52. *Mémoires secrets*, February 4 and March 10, 1770 (V, 73, 91).

53. *Ibid.*, September 15, October 9, 13, 26, 1768, February 4, June 25, July 12 and 17, August 6, 1769 (IV, 119, 132, 134, 143, 227, 302–303, 310, 317, 329).

54. *Ibid.*, March 11, 1771 (V, 256–57).

55. *Ibid.*, November 9, 1771 (VI, 35–36); [Jacques Mathieu Augeard], "Correspon-

galle's statue of the nude and scrawny philosopher were typical of the level of comment: "Those who have seen the Sage of Ferney recently find it a very good likeness. He seems to be gazing out into the distance at all the follies of men and sneering at them with that perfidious smile of his, which less reveals frank gaiety than his evil satisfaction in seeing everywhere men like himself. M. de Voltaire holds in his left hand an unrolled scroll that covers the sad vestiges of his virility."[56] The bitterness of such invective seems to indicate that Voltaire succeeded in doing real damage to the Patriote cause, particularly by citing the execution of Calas and other such miscarriages of justice as reasons for suppressing the parlements.[57]

In contrast, however, Patriote writers either refrained from mentioning the other Philosophes or else claimed them as allies. In 1773 the *Journal historique* said of the Encyclopedists, "Their well-known attachment to the Patriote party is an even greater grievance [of the Dévots] than their so-called irreligion, which is merely a pretext for the campaign being waged against them."[58] And in September 1774 the same periodical saw in the Philosophic affiliations of the new administration a good augury. Of M. de Vennes, the new Premier Commis de Finances, it said, "The philosophy of which he is a partisan will make him amenable and modest. He is well known for having contributed to the *Encyclopédie*, which gives a good idea of his enlightenment and wisdom. M. Turgot is also well known for his attachment to the school, as is M. d'Angivilliers, the Directeur des Bâtiments. All these appointments indicate that justice is being

---

dance secrète et familière de M. de Maupeou," in *Maupeouana ou Recueil complet des écrits patriotiques publiés pendant le règne du chancelier Maupeou. . . . Ouvrage qui peut servir à l'histoire du siècle de Louis XV, pendant les années 1770, 1771, 1772, 1773, et 1774* (Paris, 1775), III, 73; [André Blonde], *Le Parlement justifié par l'Impératrice Reine de Hongrie, et par le Roi de Prusse; ou, Seconde lettre, dans laquelle on continue à répondre aux écrits de M. le Chancelier* (N.p., 1772), 17; *Journal historique*, November 9, 1771 (II, 231–32); [François Métra, ed.], *Correspondance secrète, politique et littéraire, ou Mémoires pour servir à l'histoire des cours, des sociétés et de la littérature en France depuis la mort de Louis XV* (London, 1787–90), January 28, 1775 (I, 176). The story was a canard, but it was true that the German artist Jean Huber made silhouettes of Voltaire in the form of a weather vane, some of which were sent to the Choiseuls by friends.

56. *Mémoires secrets*, August 4, 1772 (VI, 204). Other attacks on Voltaire, too numerous to cite, can be found frequently in both the *Mémoires secrets* and the *Journal historique* from March 11, 1771, to January 27, 1775.

57. E.g., [Blonde], *Le Parlement justifié par l'Impératrice Reine de Hongrie*, 17.

58. *Journal historique*, January 8, 1773 (IV, 20).

rendered to that sect which was so besmirched in the mind of the late king by persons who painted it in the most fearsome colors."[59] Individual Philosophes were singled out. D'Holbach's description of despotism in his *Système de la nature* was interpreted as a portrait of Maupeou.[60] The Chevalier de Chastellux, "one of the leaders of the Encyclopedic party," was praised for withdrawing his candidacy to the Académie Française in favor of the Patriote Malesherbes.[61] When Raynal's *Histoire des deux Indes*, dated 1770, finally appeared in 1772, the *Journal historique* predicted accurately that Maupeou's Parlement would suppress it, "for one finds in it reflections so vigorous, so bold, so true, and so contrary to the principles on which the present despotism is established that its public sale cannot be tolerated for long."[62] Frederick's letter to D'Alembert that called France the laughing stock of Europe was gleefully quoted.[63] Mairobert wrote an enthusiastic review of Helvétius' posthumous *De l'Homme*, which had been banned, he said, "not only because of its irreligion but also because of its patriotism. [M. Helvétius] before his death was already in bad repute with the ministry for having expressed too freely his views on the chancellor's revolution. The affectionate eulogy [Saint Lambert] printed as an introduction to [Helvétius'] *Poème sur les bonheur*, which insinuates that the distress this revolution caused M. Helvétius poisoned his remaining days and perhaps hastened his death, has not helped to make his works better received by the government. But what [Helvétius] wrote in the preface to his latest work will put the seal on the ministry's disapproval: 'My country,' he cries in grief, 'has finally passed under the yoke of despotism. . . . The names of French authors will never again bring honor to our people; this degraded nation is now despised by all Europe.' "[64]

These opposite attitudes to Voltaire on one hand and to the rest of the Philosophes on the other constitute a further example of the influence of political considerations on Patriote ideology. Yet the alliance between the two groups was based on more than expediency. Among the leaders of the parliamentary party were men who were as much Philosophes as Patri-

59. *Ibid.*, September 5, 1774 (VI, 187–88).

60. [Blonde], *Le Parlement justifié par l'Impératrice de Russie*, 56.

61. *Journal historique*, December 21, 1774 (VI, 413).

62. *Ibid.*, May 22, 1772 (III, 125–26).

63. *Réflexions sur ce qui s'est passé à Besançon le 5 et 6 août 1771* (N.p., n.d.), 20–21.

64. *Journal historique*, January 8, 1774 (V, 115–16).

otes. Malesherbes when Directeur de la Librairie (chief government censor) had followed a deliberately lenient policy toward the Philosophes, with many of whom he had close personal ties. The Duke de La Rochefoucauld d'Enville, in whose *hôtel* the Peers and the Princes of the Blood plotted Maupeou's overthrow and who played a dominant part in the first sessions of the restored Parlement in 1774, was to be a close friend of Benjamin Franklin, an enthusiastic Americanist, and fellow Mason with Voltaire, Franklin, Condorcet, and Brissot. The Prince de Beauvau, who protested vigorously at the *lit de justice* of April 13, 1771, and who was replaced as commandant of Languedoc for his reluctance to use military force against the rebellious parlement of that province, was an intimate of Mme d'Houdetot's circle, as was the lawyer Target, one of the best of the Patriote propagandists.[65]

Patriotes and Philosophes, fellow victims of Maupeou's repression, frequently found themselves talking the same political and philosophic language. They laughed together when the Sorbonne proposed a prize for the best essay in defense of a proposition worded to signify the opposite of the meaning intended: *Non magis Deo quam Regibus infensa est ista quae vocatur hodie Philosophia.*[66] They likewise shared the joke when the official *Gazette de France* was reproved by the *Gazette Ecclésiastique* for being "too philosophic" in copying from an English paper the report that the British colonies had "an innate taste for liberty."[67] In the Académie Française the two parties made common cause against the Dévots. When in 1771 the eulogies of Fénelon by Laharpe and the Abbé Maury were crowned by the Academy but condemned by the government, at the request of the bishop of Paris, for "religious reasons," Patriotes and Philosophes joined in protesting this gag on the most august intellectual body in Europe.[68] And when the Abbé de Voisenon, an Academy Dévot, composed for Mme de Valentinois a fete to be staged at Versailles which contained a line that

65. *Ibid.*, August 29, 1771 (II, 108).
66. *Ibid.*, January 8, 1773 (IV, 20). "What is today called philosophy is no more [!] offensive to God than it is to kings."
67. *Ibid.*, May 5, 1774 (V, 305).
68. *Ibid.*, October 7, 1771 (II, 181–82); *Mémoires secrets*, October 1, 1771 (VI, 3). Cf. Voltaire's letters to Jean François de Laharpe, September 26, 1771; to Jean Le Rond d'Alembert, September 28, 1771; and to D'Argental, October 11, 1771, in Voltaire, *Corrrespondence*, LXXX, 66, 67, 75.

seemed to flatter Maupeou, he was treated with glacial disapproval by the philosophic Academicians. To his protest that "On lui avait prêté beaucoup de sottises," D'Alembert replied, "Tant pis, M. l'abbé. On ne prête qu'aux riches."[69]

An amusing example of the interweaving of the Philosophic and Patriotic strands in the politics and ideologies of the day is the story of Le Blanc de Guillet's tragedy *Les Druides*, on which Condorcet and others collaborated.[70] A Gallic king, Indumar, consecrates his daughter Erimène to the gods, preventing her from marrying the prince she loves, Clodomir. Around these central characters move a number of Druids, good or bad depending on whether they oppose or sanction the sacrifice of natural love to religious superstition. Cynodax, an enlightened Druid, declaims against "an odious religion," "fanaticism," and "holy tyrants" (priests) and appeals to "the law of reason" and to "humanity." The whole work was a transparent Philosophic attack on Catholicism employing the Voltairian gambit of putting the Dévots in the dilemma of either espousing paganism or approving an attack on religious bigotry. Fortunately, however, an obtuse censor approved the play, which opened March 7, 1772. Within a few days the Grimm-Diderot correspondence was commenting, "The acclamation with which the audience greeted [lines in the play] is an ill omen for the reputation and authority of the clergy. . . . Everyone says the Grand Druid is the Archbishop of Lyons and the Chief Druid the Archbishop of Paris."[71] Cynodax, the good Druid, was taken to be Voltaire, Erimème was Madame Louise, Louis XV's daughter, who had recently taken vows as a Carmelite, and of course "le roi bonasse," the dupe of the fanatical priests, was Louis himself.[72]

Augeard's Patriote pamphlet, *A M. Jacques Vergès, et aux donneurs d'avis,* published about April 1, contained the following lines:

I go frequently to plays, and a short time ago I saw two which made me happy as a king. One, not new, was *Arlequin voleur, prévôt et juge.*

69. *Journal historique,* December 7, 1771 (II, 289–90). The pun is untranslatable, but the sense is: "[He protested that] people had attributed (prêté) to him a lot of stupidities." "Too bad. People lend (prête) only to those that have."

70. See Condorcet to Voltaire, April 14, 1772, in Voltaire, *Correspondence,* LXXXI, 185–86.

71. *Correspondance littéraire,* March 15, 1772 (IX, 471).

72. *Journal historique,* July 4, 1772 (III, 184–85).

. . . The other was *Les Druides*. . . . It is about a high priest who persuades a king's daughter to take religious vows in order to increase the power of his clerical clique through the influence the princess will gain over her father by her remarkable action. And I said to myself, "C'est tout comme chez nous." Ah, in those days and in these days, the ambitions of priests have always been the same.[73]

Some time later, according to the story, Marie Antoinette, who kept herself au courant of Patriote propaganda, "was playing twenty-one with the king, and every time she made the same number of points as His Majesty she said, 'C'est tout comme chez nous.' The king asked the dauphine why she kept repeating this phrase, and to answer him she gave him to read the pamphlet from which it came."[74] The phrase "C'est tout comme chez nous" quickly became the bon mot of the day, and another Patriote propagandist used it as the title of a pamphlet drawing a parallel between Maupeou's revolution and the absolutistic revolution in Denmark, engineered by Count de Struensee, who had been overthrown and beheaded in January 1772. The Dévots were furious, and according to the Grimm-Diderot correspondence "spouted fire and flames against the author and the play" which had occasioned the whole affair; the Cardinal de La Roche-Aimon personally complained to Louis.[75] The result of course was that everyone rushed to see the "sermon-tragedy" and applaud "the humanity" of the good Druid. The consequence was inevitable, for the allusion to Mme Louise and the ministry's need for a generous *don gratuit* from the Assemblée du Clergé meeting in June made it easy for the archbishop and the Dévots to persuade the king and the ministry to close down the play.

It would be difficult to say whether the Patriotes or the Philosophes derived more amusement and political advantage from this trivial but typical episode. It must be remembered, of course, that this congruence of political interests was the accidental result of common enmity to the Dévots and the ministry. There were plenty of pious and conservative Patriotes who would have been insulted to be identified with the Ency-

73. [Jacques Mathieu Augeard], "A M. Jacques Vergès, et aux donneurs d'avis," in *Les Efforts de la liberté*, III, 70–71. "C'est tout comme chez nous": "That's just like the way we do things" or freely: "We too."

74. *Journal historique*, July 4, 1772 (III, 184–85).

75. *Correspondance littéraire*, April 1, 1772 (IX, 480).

clopedists, and the great majority of the Philosophes despised the political record of the parlements. But at the same time, all the opposition groups tended to be drawn together by their very opposition.

Such coalitions were particularly fostered by the general policy of rigorous censorship, of which the Patriotes were by no means the only victims. Speeches in the French Academy were placed under the censorship of the Sorbonne, the Physiocrats were virtually silenced, and the Philosophes came under increased pressure. Not only were Raynal's *Histoire des deux Indes* and Helvétius' *De l'Homme* banned, and Panckoucke's entire edition of the *Supplément à l'Encyclopédie* walled up in the Bastille, but even Voltaire, despite his services, found to his chagrin that he could not smuggle a single copy of his recently printed *Questions sur l'Encyclopédie* into France. Censorship of newspapers seems to have been particularly vigorous. Copies of the *Courrier du Bas Rhin*, the *Gazette de Berne*, and the *Gazette de Bruxelles* were seized at the border, the *Journal de Verdun* and the *Journal encyclopédique* were forbidden to print any political news, and Maupeou's Parlement at Rennes ordered the *Gazette des Gazettes* lacerated and burned for having dared to print a piece entitled "Requête des pauvres, du Diocèse de Rennes," condemned as a seditious libel "tending to inculpate the Parlement in the eyes of the people."[76]

The former parlements had of course themselves been harsh censors on occasion, yet an increasing number of Patriotes, adopting Malesherbes' liberal views, were saying that freedom of the press was a fundamental law of any just government.[77] Indeed censorship not only converted men to liberalism; it also fomented radicalism. Since all Patriote writings had to be published clandestinely in any case, many writers decided they might as well be hanged for a sheep as a lamb, wrote what they pleased, and ventured into ideas they otherwise never would have dreamed of publishing. Thus censorship paradoxically created intellectual diversity and openness.

Nevertheless this diversity and openness operated only within certain limits. Patriote political philosophy, perhaps partly because of Males-

76. *Journal historique*, April 15, October 15, 1771, October 16, 1772, July 19, 1774 (I, 252, II, 194, III, 305, VI, 110–11).

77. [Pierre Arnaud, Vicomte d'Aubusson], *Profession de foi politique d'un bon François* (N.p., n.d. [1771]), 18.

herbes' influence but mainly because it was largely the work of lawyers and magistrates, was principally based on the traditions of French law and parliamentary constitutional theory and was relatively little affected by political thought outside these traditions. As Elie Carcasonne has shown, an influential source was Montesquieu, a former *président à mortier* of the Parlement of Bordeaux, who provided the Patriotes with their political vocabulary.[78] He was repeatedly cited on a number of points—the distinction between monarchy and despotism, the degeneration of governments, intermediary powers and bodies, the necessity of a depository of the law, the protection of liberty and property afforded by the principle and formalities of law, and of course his famous definition of liberty.[79] Nevertheless one gets the strong impression that the Patriotes quoted Montesquieu more to give authority to their arguments than because he was the direct source of their operative ideas. During the twenty years since the publication of the *Esprit des lois* the essential problem had changed from the creation of a political structure which could moderate monarchical power and prevent despotism to the choice between what now seemed the only remaining alternatives, despotism or aristocratic republicanism. New issues such as the recall of the States General tended to supplant those central to the *Esprit des lois*.

Indeed for the radical Patriotes Rousseau was more relevant than Montesquieu. The *Contrat social* may have had during these years more readers than has been supposed, as I have suggested elsewhere.[80] In any case it was timely, for its essential political concepts—the contract itself, national sovereignty, the general will, and the conditional delegation of authority by the nation to the government—were all ideas which Patriote writers were studying and discussing at length. The more conservative did not cite Rousseau by name, which is perhaps understandable after the Paris Parlement's condemnation of *Emile*, but important passages in the works of De Brancas, Mey, and Morizot do remarkably parallel Rousseau's thinking, though positive evidence of direct influence is lacking. We have indications that the *Contrat social* was frequently quoted during the heated

78. Carcasonne, *Montesquieu et le problème de la constitution française*, Chap. 9.

79. Montesquieu, *De l'Esprit des lois*, Book XI, Chap. 3.

80. Durand Echeverria, "The Pre-Revolutionary Influence of Rousseau's *Contrat Social*," *Journal of the History of Ideas*, XXXIII (1972), 543–560.

political supper parties in 1771.[81] The radical Patriotes Mariveaux and Saige borrowed Rousseau's ideas freely and buttressed their arguments with long quotations from the *Contrat social*.[82]

Other major political philosophers seem to have had, at the most, minor influence. Patriotes cited Massillon, Fénelon, and Bossuet, particularly Bossuet's distinction between absolute and arbitrary power. Only Mey, Morizot, the Besançon remonstrances, and the author of the pamphlet *Nous y pensons* revealed any acquaintance with important foreign thinkers. Mey, Morizot, and the Besançon author had read Hobbes, whose ideas they discussed; Mey quoted Locke and Burlamaqui; and Grotius, Vattel, and Pufendorf were also mentioned by these writers. Contemporary foreign writers who today seem far less significant were better known: Robertson; Jean Louis Delolme, whose *Constitution de l'Angleterre* (1771), the first extensive study in French of the British constitution since Montesquieu, was banned by the government and hailed by the Patriote press; and Catherine of Russia, whose *Instruction pour la commission chargée de dresser le projet d'un nouveau code des lois* (1769), largely plagiarized from Montesquieu (and likewise banned by Maupeou's government, to Voltaire's acute embarrassment), was praised by Mey and Target and used by Blonde as the basis for his *Le Parlement justifié par l'Impératrice de Russie*.[83] Indeed the Patriotes seem to have found contemporary European politics more relevant to the issues under debate than the theories of earlier political philosophers. There is no evidence, it is true, in support of the royalists' charges that the Patriotes were trying to introduce the British constitution into France and that they were willfully confusing the French parlements with the British Parliament, yet they did indeed study the Revolution of 1688 and the British constitution, which seemed to achieve limitations on royal power that corresponded generally with Patriote objectives and which had, some said, made England "the only place where truth and liberty can still speak."[84] At the same time, the Patriotes were deeply disturbed by their perception of the Maupeou revolution as part of

---

81. *Avis aux dames*, 4–6.

82. [Mariveaux], *L'Ami des loix*, 6–9; [Saige], *Catéchisme du citoyen*, 12, 16, 54, 166.

83. On Delolme, see *Journal historique*, November 11, 1771 (II, 237–39).

84. *Ibid.*, September 10, 1772 (III, 273). Cf. [Thévenot de Morande], *Mélange confus sur des matières fort claires*, 8; [Blonde], *Le Parlement justifié pas l'Impératrice Reine de Hongrie*, 31, 120; *Supplément à la Gazette de France*, No. 8, p. 5.

a general European trend toward "enlightened despotism," exemplified
by Frederick of Prussia, Count de Struensee's regime in Denmark, and
Gustavus III's coup in Sweden in 1772.[85]

Thus Patriote thought had its main roots deep in French legal and constitutional tradition rather than in the broad ground of European speculative philosophy, and it strove to defend what it believed were the traditional liberties of the French people against the wave of autocracy that
seemed to be inundating continental Europe. In this respect the movement was strongly nationalistic. Yet it also saw itself as a local response
to this general European crisis, which was being supported by plausible
theories justifying enlightened despotism and statism. To this threat the
Patriotes offered the alternative of republican corporatism. This was, it is
true, a corporatism which to many seemed vitiated by its too frequent ob-
session with preserving antique forms, structures, and privileges and
linked with a reactionary concept of aristocracy that could not survive in
the rapidly changing new society, already on the verge of industrialism
and "providential democracy." Yet this alternative did contain the clearly
viable proposition that only if effective political power were vested in some
sort of national corporation or set of corporations could the liberties and
rights of all classes, including those of the nobility, be preserved.

85. On Frederick see "Essai historique sur les droits de la province de Normandie,"
in *Les Efforts de la liberté*, VI, 70–71; [Blonde], *Le Parlement justifié pas l'Impératrice Reine
de Hongrie*, 9. On Struensee, see *C'est tout comme chez nous. . . . Sentence sur la cause (de la
nation française) d'une part, accusateur contre (Ch.-Aug.-Nic.-René de Maupeou) d'une autre part*
(N.p., n.d. [1772]). On Gustavus III, see *Supplément à la Gazette de France*, No. 8, pp.
3–5; *Journal historique*, September 6 and October 30, 1772 (III, 268, 322).

TWO

Patriote Constitutionalism

T HE TWO most significant contributions the Patriotes made to the development of French eighteenth-century thought were their concepts of liberty and of constitutionalism. It is an indication of the thorough secularization of French thought that by 1770 there was a broad acceptance of the propositions that the summum bonum for the individual was not his spiritual salvation as the church taught, but his freedom to pursue happiness in this world, and that this freedom could be assured only by the proper constitution of his society and government. Though these principles were openly and explicitly championed only by materialistic Philosophes such as D'Holbach and Diderot, they were tacitly assumed not only by all the Philosophes but also by the Patriotes and royalists as well. The two propositions were complementary: Individual and collective freedom and happiness depended on the right constitution of society, and the purpose of the constitution was to guarantee the freedom and promote the happiness of the individual.

The word *constitution* was a learned and legal term which entered the French political lexicon during the Renaissance and in the eighteenth century was still developing various new meanings. It still retained its early sense of established law or ordinance, as in the denomination of the bull *Unigenitus* as *la Constitution*. In political usage it was thus applied to the supposed historic legal act by which the French government had originally been constituted; in this sense it was virtually synonymous with the contract and its provisions. By extension it also signified the original, essential elements constituting the French government, and hence the right nature of the state. In the 1770s, by a further metonymy, it was coming to designate a specific (though still variously defined) sacred structure of fundamental laws and principles which protected the rights and liberties of citizens and according to which the French government was organized and should operate. This was the modern political sense of the word adopted by the Americans in 1787 (substituting "Constitution" for "Articles of Confederation") and by the French in 1789.

The Patriote constitution, in this latter sense, was justified by three authorities—tradition, natural law, and public utility. Here lay a possible though not necessary source of basic inconsistency and confusion, for what was sanctified by long usage might not be just in the eyes of reason, and what was for the good of the French people either might be without precedent or might stand as unjust before the tribunals of humanity and reason.

Justification by precedent had been the "official" doctrine of French constitutional theory since the Renaissance and was essential to the legal mode of thought in which the magistrates had been professionally trained. Precedents could be established by ancient custom (the traditionalistic school) or by historical or quasi-historical events or documents (the historical school), but in either case the principle was that constitutionality was created by the usage of centuries. This was the orthodox line, the one followed by conservative Patriotes, and probably the most prevalent. Its greatest recent exponent was Louis Adrien Le Paige, whose *Lettres historiques* (1753) demonstrated that the Paris Parlement had had a continuous history from the "General Parlements" of Germanic times down through the Middle Ages and the Renaissance to the eighteenth century and had always kept its corporative identity and its same essential composition, functions, and powers.[1] Blonde was being wholly traditionalistic when he wrote, "Tradition alone has taught us our mutual obligations and has informed us to what extent the prince can extend his authority and where the subject's duty to obey ends and his duty to resist begins." And so was the Duke de Brancas when he proudly avowed, "I have found the public

1. [Louis Adrien Le Paige], *Lettres historiques sur les fonctions essentielles du Parlement, sur le droit des pairs, et sur les loix fondamentales du royaume* (Amsterdam, 1753–54).

law of France in the laws made by the French. . . . I have walked only on the ground of history."[2] On the same assumptions the ultraconservative author of the *Réflexions générales*, on one hand, inveighed against the Philosophic *esprit de système*, the spirit of impetuous enterprise which "without regard for what exists, without respect for tradition . . . thinks it can by itself regenerate and renovate everything," and on the other hand with equal fervor denounced Maupeou for trying to replace the unalterable constitution of France with the concept of an evolving political structure according to the heinous principle "that there is no law which is essential and cannot be abrogated."[3]

Natural law philosophy, the second authority invoked to justify the Patriote constitution, can be traced at least as far back as the Stoics. It had been Christianized by the scholastics of the Middle Ages, secularized by Grotius, Sidney, Pufendorf, and other Protestant thinkers of the sixteenth and seventeenth centuries, and further developed by Jurieu, Locke, Burlamaqui, Vattel, Rousseau, and others. Its essence was belief in a rational moral order of the universe which any man endowed with common reason could perceive without the aid of either divine or human authority. This order could be defined in terms of universal—and therefore "natural"—normative moral rights and laws, to which all human behavior and specifically all positive laws, constitutional or statutory, should conform. Perhaps the foremost Patriote natural-law philosopher was Claude Mey, who wrote that the purpose of his *Maximes* was to study "the primal law, the natural law which is the source of all other laws. The original law engraved in the hearts of all men has taught them to know the nature of government and the fundamental motive of its institution." Even scriptural authority, he said, did not always apply, for "the Holy Scripture has not always existed; yet in all times men have needed a way of knowing the intentions of the Creator for men living in society. . . . Therefore men have had to seek in nature and in their present condition proofs of His will," and thus learn their rights and duties.[4] The Count d'Aubusson in his *Profession de foi politique* stressed the uniformitarianism of the doctrine,

2. [Blonde], *Le Parlement justifié par l'Impératrice de Russie*, 3. Louis Léon Félicité, Duke de Brancas, *Extrait du droit public de la France* (N.p., 1771), i, iii.

3. *Réflexions générales sur le système projetté par le Maire du Palais*, 4, 105.

4. [Mey *et al.*], *Maximes* (2nd ed.), I, 7, 9, II, 27, 28 ff.

arguing that natural law "is of all ages, of all places, and of all kinds of government whatsoever—the invariable code whose principles are constant, incontestable, simple, and clear in the eyes of right reason," and which therefore is the only possible basis of just government.[5] Parallel statements are found in the writings of Miromesnil and Malesherbes, in the remonstrances of the Parlement of Besançon, and elsewhere.

Natural law arguments were sometimes Cartesian in their rationalism, as in the recommendation to the French people by the pamphlet *C'est tout comme chez nous* that they practice "methodical doubt" in making their political judgments. Other writers followed Rousseau in advocating reliance on "conscience" or moral intuition for the perception of natural law and the moral fitness of particular political institutions. The *Lettre d'un ancien magistrat* asserted, "The king has no subject who does not possess a conscience and who must not have the inflexible resolution to obey God rather than men. If the king orders him to commit an injustice, should he obey? Certainly not. He must resist, that is, refuse to obey."[6] Natural law was the philosophic basis of the Patriote doctrines of the sovereignty of the nation, the contract, and natural rights.

The third basis of Patriote constitutionalism, the principle of public utility—"utilité publique"—was logically merely an inference from natural law, a statement of the self-evident principle that the only rational and moral purpose of government is the welfare of the governed. Indeed, it was no more than a modern version of the old Roman natural-law dictum, *Salus populi suprema lex esto*, which Patriote writers repeatedly cited. "It is natural law," Mey wrote, "that gives as the supreme law the welfare and happiness of the nation."[7] Moreover it was natural law that a priori defined the right nature of public "happiness" and "welfare." Thus "utilité publique" was a doctrine quite distinct from the utilitarianism of the day, derived from Hobbes and expounded principally by D'Holbach, a materialistic, empirical, and individualistic philosophy which equated the good with individual pleasure and defined the social good as that which produced the greatest such good for the greatest number. Of this sort of utilitarianism not a trace can be found in Patriote writers.

5. [D'Aubusson], *Profession de foi politique*, 1–2.
6. *C'est tout comme chez nous*, 1–2; *Lettre d'un ancien magistrat à un duc et pair sur le discours de M. le chancelier au lit de justice du vendredi*, 7 *décembre* 1770 (N.p., n.d. [1771]), 53.
7. [Mey *et al.*], *Maximes* (2nd ed.), I, 45.

Though public utility was a logical and historical corollary of natural law, in practice there was a tendency to regard it as a distinct though parallel philosophical premise. Thus Morizot wrote that laws must be based on the principle of "public utility" but *also* be in accord with justice and equity, and that social law derived from an instinctive sense of social justice, "a disposition of the soul which, preferring the common good to private interest, safeguards the rights of society and preserves for those who compose society what is due them."[8] This philosophy, it is clear, was far from the individualistic, empirical, and hedonistic utilitarianism of D'Holbach.

Though each of these three arguments, tradition, natural law, and public utility, had its special advocates, we must not suppose that they gave form to distinct schools or movements within Patriote thought. There seems to have been little or no awareness of the danger of philosophical inconsistency in appealing to all three simultaneously, as did Brancas, for instance, when, after developing at length and in detail the historical and traditionalistic justifications of the parlements, he wrote, "The motive and effect of the law must be utility, the happiness and prosperity of all citizens. Natural reason confirms in all minds the necessity of the essential characteristics of law."[9]

The French constitution was not inscribed in any single document, but neither was it in the strict sense unwritten, for it was composed of the "fundamental laws" of the nation, which were in fact recorded in ancient charters, in treaties, in the express conditions of union of certain provinces with the crown, in the coronation oath, in royal edicts, in dissertations by learned authorities, and in the annals of the nation. All of these laws were held to be consecrated not only by tradition but also by reason and public utility. This general concept of a constitution of fundamental laws was freely accepted by the royalists and was not a point of debate. The expression "lois fondamentales" had been in use since the second half of the sixteenth century, and the fundamental-law theory can be traced in French history at least to the thirteenth century.[10] The Patriotes fre-

8. [Morizot], *Inauguration de Pharamond*, 113, [Martin Morizot], *Le Sacre royal, ou les Droits de la nation françoise, reconnus et confirmés par cette cérémonie* (Amsterdam, 1776), Chap. 1.

9. [Louis Léon Félicité, Duke de Brancas], *Tableau de la constitution françoise, ou Autorité des rois de France, dans les différens âges de la monarchie* (N.p., 1771), 52.

10. See André Lemaire, *Les Lois fondamentales de la monarchie française d'après les théoriciens de l'ancien régime* (Paris, 1907).

quently quoted Bossuet's dictum that "there are fundamental laws that cannot be changed," and Louis XV acknowledged in his edict of February 1771 that there were certain laws which he was in "l'heureuse impuissance de changer."[11]

The issue between the Patriotes and the royalists was not the existence of fundamental laws, but rather their definition, their sources, and their susceptibility to amendment. It is impossible to give a single list of all the fundamental laws cited by Patriotes to which all Patriotes would have subscribed, for though certain propositions were acceptable to all, the label "fundamental law" could be and was affixed to any political principle a particular writer might believe essential—even freedom of the press. Nevertheless we can derive from the analysis of the great number of Patriote writings a rough consensus, a general and widely supported constitutional position. Mey probably gives us the best summary. There were, he said, two basic kinds of fundamental laws: first, "les lois fondamentales naturelles et essentielles" established by natural law and the principle of public utility. Among these were the law of the supreme good of the public welfare, *salus populi supreme lex esto*, and the rights of the citizen to life, liberty, property, estate, and honor, including such specific rights as taxation by consent and protection from imprisonment without fair trial. These laws, dictated by reason and nature, were common to all governments and were the basis of the social contract. Second, there were "les lois du royaume," which were also fundamental laws of the French monarchy but were arbitrary conventions peculiar to France, clauses in the national synallagmatic contract between the French prince and the French people. Though not specifically or necessarily derived from the universal nature of sovereignty, they could not be in contradiction to natural law and hence could not include any grant of absolute royal power over the life, liberty, or property of the people. Their function was to establish the special and unique constitution of the French monarchy and to define the limitations on the powers of the French king. Examples were the Salic Law governing succession to the crown, the inalienability of the royal domain, and the various constitutional powers of the parlements and the States General. These two kinds of fundamental laws stood in distinction from "les lois du roi," positive laws which could be modified or repealed

11. *Recueil général des anciennes lois françaises*, XXII, 513.

according to the demands of new circumstances, and which therefore were "mortal like the king."[12]

This constitutionalism might be considered a sort of political analogue of the scientific Cartesian naturalism of the century. It began by positing a priori certain fundamental laws or principles from which all proper operations of the government could be deduced, just as the necessary operations of the physical universe could be deduced from Descartes' hypotheses of matter and extension. These fundamental principles, whether inherent in the traditional nature of the French state or in the moral order of the universe, could be directly intuited, and their logical applications were deducible by common reason. Therefore there could be only one true French constitution, and it was by hypothesis immutable. Consequently the Patriotes saw no need to incorporate in this constitution any mechanism for its own amendment, adaption, or evolution in time. Their political "Cartesianism" contrasts with the empiricism of Maupeou and the Anglo Saxons, who both, their other differences notwithstanding, believed that the best constitution relative to the existing conditions of society could be determined by observation and experience and who both provided for constitutional change and evolution, the former by royal fiat, the latter by legislation, amendment, or judicial interpretation.

The basis of Patriote constitutionalism was formed by three fundamental assumptions or articles of faith: the sovereignty of the French nation; the existence of a national general will; and the existence of a contract. From these axioms were derived the corollaries of the inherent illegitimacy of royal absolutism and the right of the general will of the sovereign nation to be represented by a constitutional corporation.

Although the parlements were accused by their opponents of proposing to arrogate to themselves sovereign power, and although some Patriotes such as Miromesnil conceded that in fact the courts had sometimes behaved as though this were their intention, the truth is that not even their most radical partisans, and certainly none of the parlements themselves in any official document, ever explicitly made such a claim.[13] The real issue was whether sovereignty resided in the person of the king or in the nation as a whole.

12. [Mey *et al.*], *Maximes* (2nd ed.), I, 225–86.
13. Miromesnil, "Lettres sur l'état de la magistrature," 20, 21, 32–33.

The Patriote concept of national sovereignty affirmed that political authority rightfully and permanently belong to the whole nation as a moral entity. It stood in direct contradiction to the theory of divine right developed in the seventeenth century, which placed in the prince as a person ultimate secular authority, conferred by God absolutely though with certain moral obligations.

National sovereignty was by no means a new idea, for it derived from a long philosophic tradition which can be traced as far back as the Stoics, and expressions of it were current in the seventeenth and earlier eighteenth centuries. Massillon had preached to the young Louis XV that he had received his authority from the nation. Yet he had added the all-important qualification that the grant was irrevocable and absolute, which of course relegated the sovereignty of the nation, like the sovereignty of God, to the realms of political theory and left the actual absolute authority of the reigning prince unimpaired.

Prior to their dissolution and reform in 1771, the parlements had never formally or explicitly denied effective absolute royal authority (though they had challenged it often enough in practice), and even after the coup the more conservative Patriotes continued to accept the thesis. Miromesnil categorically asserted that "there is no human power with the right to constrain the monarch to the observation of the laws and fundamental principles of the monarchy." True, it was "the duty of the monarch to judge himself according to the laws of natural equity, . . . to temper the effects of his own authority, . . . and to conform to the constitutional principles of his state and to the laws established by his predecessors and those he has himself enacted."[14] But these moral obligations, for which the king was answerable to his own conscience and to God—not to the nation—in no way detracted from his own effective sovereign authority.

In the course of the Maupeou revolution, however, this traditional concept of national sovereignty was displaced by a quite different idea, implicitly in the writings of conservative Patriotes but more clearly and explicitly in those of their more radical supporters. More and more frequently was voiced the principle that "it is the nation that is sovereign."[15]

14. *Ibid.*, 71.
15. [Mariveaux], *L'Ami des loix*, 21; Brancas, *Extrait du droit public*, 45; [Mey *et al.*], *Maximes* (2nd ed.), II, 23; [Morizot], *Inauguration de Pharamond*; *Nous y pensons; ou Réponse*

Moreover, the new qualifications were added that the nation *remained* permanently "sovereign and legislator," and that the king was merely "the first minister and agent of the sovereign," serving under a conditional contract.[16] The author of *L'Avocat national*, arguing from the principle of public utility, said that government and society were justified only by their contributions to the common welfare and by their protection of the citizens' natural rights of life, liberty, and property. Government, whether by one man or by many, should be "the meeting place and center of all individual wills." This was to deny to the king any justified existence or power except as an instrument of the national welfare. His interest was not separate from and coequal with those of the people, as the defenders of Louis XV were claiming; it was subordinate to the interests of the people. "The power of the head of the state . . . cannot exist whole and perfect except by the closest union with the body over which it presides and of which it is a part. The nobles and orders of the kingdom are not intermediary powers which intercept the [power of] sovereignty; they are very members and sinews of sovereignty."[17] Sometimes this denial of any autonomous authority to the king could sound like revolutionary egalitarianism in the protests of radicals such as Morizot, who wrote, "God did not place one man under the yoke of servitude and raise up another to have the authority of master; God created all men in the same equality."[18]

Yet the intent was not to reject monarchism but rather to subordinate the king to the absolute sovereignty of the nation, to replace at the top of the political structure the *roi* by the *patrie*. This is why the advocates of the new constitutionalism chose the name "Patriotes" and proudly called themselves, some twenty years before the Revolution, "citoyens," in the sense of members of the sovereign nation. The king of France was already becoming the king of the French. The nation was becoming "the king, the nobles, and the people" all together, all members of the state and all

---

de MM. les avocats de Paris à l'auteur de l'avis: Pensez y bien (N.p., n.d. [1771]), 12; *Principes de la législation françoise, prouvées par les monuments de l'histoire de cette nation, relatifs aux affaires du temps* (N.p., 1771); *Réponse aux trois articles de l'édit enregistré au lit de justice du 7 décembre 1770* (N.p., n.d. [1771]).

16. [Mariveaux], *L'Ami des loix*, 21.

17. "L'Avocat national, ou Lettre d'un patriote au sieur Bouquet . . . ," in *Les Efforts de la liberté*, VI, 194, 252.

18. [Morizot], *Le Sacre royal*, Chap. 1.

enjoying the common quality of citizenship. Soldiers should not say they "served the king" but that they "served their country." The "king's officers" should be called the "nation's officers." [19] Propagandists appealed to the "sentiments patriotiques" of the lawyers to maintain their boycott of the Maupeou Parlement. [20] Augeard described himself as neither a Jesuit nor a Jansenist, a parliamentarian nor an anti-parliamentarian, but simply a "citoyen," a man who loved his *patrie* and was grieved to see it oppressed. M. de Bretignières, a magistrate of the Grand-Chambre exiled and critically ill, refused to yield to Maupeou, saying, "It is no great misfortune to die for one's country." Target, in words reminiscent of a passage in Rousseau's *Contrat social*, wrote, "I should like to see only one nation, one family of brothers who have essentially the same interests and the same rights—the interests and rights to preserve what we all hold in common: as men, our lives and our liberty; as citizens, our honor, our estates, and our properties; and as subjects, our government and our prince." [21] Thus the new national sovereignty was more than an idea; it was at the same time a new sentiment of common nationality and of patriotism.

It did not, however, imply anything approaching democracy in either the modern or the eighteenth-century senses. The *peuple* (in these contexts never equivalent to the laboring class) were the nation as an organic whole. It was assumed that all citizens could participate through a hierarchy of functions within the class-structured society—like the various parts of a body—in a collective sovereignty, and that each could enjoy virtual representation in the aristocratic corporations and in the prince. There was certainly no thought of universal franchise or of active, positive liberty for all. Yet in the increasing ferment of Western thought, which had recently produced Rousseau's *Contrat social* and was soon to bring forth the American Declaration of Independence, this new concept of national sover-

19. [Mariveaux], *L'Ami des loix*, 21; "Lettre de M. le comte de***," in *Les Efforts de la liberté*, VI, 343; [Blonde], *Le Parlement justifié par l'Impératrice Reine de Hongrie*, 52.

20. *Nous y pensons*, 17. Also *Lettre des habitans de Rouen au corps des avocats, resté fidèle aux lois et à la province.—Detail de la conduite tenue depuis la Saint-Martin 1771, par les avocats du Conseil Supérieur, et par le corps dont ils sont détachés* (N.p., n.d. [1772]); *Plan d'une conversation entre un avocat et M. le chancelier* (N.p., 1771).

21. [Augeard], "A M. Jacques Vergès," in *Les Efforts de la liberté*, III, 68; *Supplément à la Gazette de France*, No. 6, May 1, 1772; [Target], *Lettres d'un homme à un autre homme sur les affaires du temps*, 1.

eignty inevitably acquired modern implications, and the more radical Patriotes, to the horror of the conservative magistrates they supported, were writing, "The people governed by the law must be the authors of the law. It is the right of those who associate themselves together to regulate the conditions of their own society." And, "A nation is an assembly of free men . . . who hold authority over themselves."[22]

Even the most conservative supporters of the parlements subscribed to the idea that the nation as a living collective entity possessed a general will, which was usually called "le voeu de la nation." This concept, like that of national sovereignty, was an ancient idea with religious sanction, as in the often quoted dictum, *Vox populi, vox Dei*. It was far from revolutionary when taken to mean, as it most frequently was, that the king was the "natural organ" of "the voice of the people." This concept imposed on him a moral obligation to attune his own will to the "unanimous will of the people."[23] Yet the alternative phrase *volonté générale*, which was also frequently used, suggested rightful independent initiative and was given this Rousseauistic significance by radicals like Mariveaux, who wrote, "Laws . . . are acts of the general will. . . . The legislative power belongs to the people. . . . The effective will of the prince or the magistrate is or should be simply the general will, that is, the law."[24]

Thus, although the magistrates and their supporters conceded to the crown extensive constitutional powers, and some acknowledged that these powers might be in fact or theory absolute, the general position was that ultimately sovereignty resided in the nation and that the nation had the right to will its own welfare. This meant—and on this point there was virtual unanimity—that the relationship between the king and the nation was contractual.

The contract was usually conceived as a two-step process: first the union of naturally free men in a society in order to safeguard their individual rights and liberties, to make secure their persons and properties, and to permit cooperation; and second, the delegation of their collective authority to a prince under a conditional agreement. It was the conditional

22. [Mariveaux], *L'Ami des loix*, 6; "Les Propos indiscrets," in *Journal historique* (new ed.; London, 1776), III, 308.

23. [Morizot], *Inauguration de Pharamond*, 116; *Les Derniers soupirs*, 36.

24. [Mariveaux], *L'Ami des loix*, 6–8.

nature of the second contract that distinguished the theory of the Patriotes from that of Hobbes and aligned them with Locke and Rousseau.

Prior to the first agreement, Mey said, men possessed natural liberty
and the natural right to property, and the purpose of the first contract was
the preservation of these rights. He conceded that by the act of association
men voluntarily sacrificed a portion of their rights and liberties, but they
gave up only as much as was necessary to ensure the ultimate purposes of
society, peace and security; and whatever rights and liberties they had not
relinquished they continued to hold and enjoy.[25]

The second contract, the one between the people and the prince, was
the important one in the current debate, for it determined the specific form
of any government; by it the people chose the kind of republic they wished,
a democracy, an aristocracy, or a monarchy.[26] "It is obvious," Morizot
wrote, "that any people in establishing themselves as a social body, that
is, as a nation, are free to choose between these three forms of government, and consequently the one which they adopt, having no basis other
than this act of election by the people, can continue to exist, rationally,
only by virtue of a contract. Thus it is the contract that determines the
center of public authority."[27] The terms of this contract, the laws "which
form the constitution and by which the entire body of the nation determines the form of government, . . . the laws which regulate the manner
in which the ruler is to govern and which prescribe the limits of his authority," were then the "fundamental laws of the state."[28]

The contract was by no means a mere hypothetical theory. In the first
place, certain provinces with a strong sense of autonomy, particularly
Normandy, insistently asserted the existence of historical written legal
contracts embodied in the agreements and charters under which they had
joined the realm.[29] In the second place, the theory of the contract was a
working principle with important practical applications and consequences.

25. [Mey *et al.*], *Maximes* (2nd ed.), I, 39, 211, 238.
26. Brancas, *Extrait du droit public.*
27. [Morizot], *Le Sacre royal*, 50.
28. [Brancas], *Tableau de la constitution françoise*, 53.
29. *Manifeste aux Normands* (N.p., n.d. [1771]). Also, Cour Souveraine de Lorraine
et Barrois, "Lettre . . . au Roi du 23 mars 1771," in *Recueil des réclamations*, II, 539; *Manifeste aux Bretons* (N.p., 1772).

The first of these was that any authority delegated to the crown was limited, conditional, and revocable. The Parlement of Besançon argued, "A desire to protect themselves from dangers brought men together in societies. Out of this union was formed a protective authority clothed with all the power necessary to assure the public safety. It would be most strange to suppose that the act of consent which at that time created a prince and subjects would have had as its purpose to submit the latter to the arbitrary and unlimited will of the former." "The people," said the pamphlet *Nous y pensons*, "in accepting a monarch never consented to abandon to him arbitrary and absolute authority, for they never intended that they could be arbitrarily reduced to a state of slavery."[30]

Second, "men having united in society with the sole purpose of promoting the public welfare, it is a truth of natural law that a people who have given themselves a king never intended to elect him for his own personal benefit but rather for the benefit of the nation he was to govern." From this it followed that "kings . . . have full power to promote the welfare of their subjects but no power to oppose their welfare. . . . Every act that tends to . . . alter the rights of the nation or to infringe on any legitimate property is null by lack of power."[31]

Third, the contract was synallagmatic; as Mey said, all the fundamental laws of the constitution were the "effects of pacts or conventions and could not be altered except by the joint consent of the contracting parties."[32] This theory was maintained in order to deny the king any right to modify unilaterally the constitution. But a truly synallagmatic contract (that is, one with completely reciprocal rights and obligations) would have been a flaw in the Patriote thesis, for it would have meant that the nation had no more right than the prince to change unilaterally the terms of the agreement, and thus it would have ceased to be truly sovereign. Therefore the synallagmatic second contract was often tacitly abandoned and replaced by what Rousseau had called the "commission." The "commission" was not a true contract at all, but merely the act by which the prince was hired as a sort of high public servant on terms which the em-

30. Parlement de Besançon, "Remontrances du parlement de Besançon," March 11, 1771, in *Recueil des réclamations*, II, 396–97; *Nous y pensons*, 9.

31. [Morizot], *Inauguration de Pharamond*, 1; *Lettre de M. ***, conseiller au parlement*, 34.

32. [Mey *et al.*], *Maximes* (2nd ed.), I, 347.

ployer, the sovereign nation, could change at will. It was this concept of
the "commission" that the Parlement of Brittany was upholding when it
asserted, "Only the nation can possess the power to change the conditions
of the contract between the prince and the subjects found in the fundamental laws."[33] Mey discussed the problem at length, and though he believed that "the king and the people together can change the form of government by establishing new constitutional laws," he maintained, citing
Sidney and Locke, that since the people consulted only their own best interests in selecting one form of government rather than another, "it follows that this rule which alone controlled the establishment of the government must likewise alone control its maintenance and continuation.
. . . [Therefore] those who established a government cannot bind their
heirs. . . . It would be absurd to force a people to remain under a government imperfect in its origin and susceptible to improvement in the
light of new knowledge and experience." He even claimed that "the nation can change the order of succession."[34] Morizot likewise gave to the
nation the unlimited right to change the constitution and the prerogatives of the king.[35] *Le Propos indiscret* forthrightly defined the state as "an
assembly of free men who have given themselves a king to act in their
name, and to exercise the authority they hold over themselves. Let it be
clear that they hold the monarch to certain conditions, the infraction of
which abrogates both the contract and the authority of the king."[36]

These philosophic concepts of national sovereignty, the general will,
and the contract were principles directly applicable to concrete issues in
the practical politics of the day, yet they were too abstract in themselves
to have great popular appeal or polemical effect. What rallied the Patriotes and their many supporters was the war cry of *despotisme*. *Despotisme*
and its antonym *liberté* were the two most frequent words in French politics from the edict of December 1770 to the Bastille. Montesquieu had
described despotism as the one form of government that is invariably evil—
evil in its *principe*, fear; evil in its nature; evil in its effects. On this judgment there was agreement by all parties. No one except an intellectual

33. Parlement de Bretagne, "Arrêté du parlement séant à Rennes. Du 16 mars 1771,"
in *Recueil des réclamations*, II, 294.
34. [Mey *et al.*], *Maximes* (2nd ed.), I, 207, 273, 286.
35. [Morizot], *Inauguration de Pharamond*, 115.
36. "Les Propos indiscrets," in *Journal historique* (new ed.; London, 1776), III, 308.

enfant terrible like Simon Linguet dreamed of defending outright despotism.

Yet it was not easy to draw the line where despotism ended and legitimate monarchy began. Montesquieu had said in his *Esprit des lois* that the distinguishing characteristic of monarchy, which he classed as a "gouvernement modéré," was the existence of political laws that checked and moderated the power of the king, either by the separation of powers as in England, or, as in France, by "intermediary powers"—the nobility, the clergy, and the parlements. As he was careful to stress, however, and as the Patriotes had learned from experience, the existence of such constitutional checks made a government moderate in theory only. They did not necessarily make it moderate in fact.

Bossuet in his *Politique tirée de l'Ecriture sainte* had made the quite different distinction between arbitrary power, which was despotic, and legitimate absolute power, which voluntarily accepted and obeyed those laws which it was morally obligated to respect. This concept of benign self-moderating absolutism was adopted, under the name of "enlightened despotism," by certain Philosophes, notably Voltaire, who proposed, however, as royal guidelines not Catholic ethics or national tradition but the dictates of enlightened reason, and it was also championed under the name of "despotisme légal" by the Economistes, who would have substituted the dictates of economic laws as the regulating principles.

The theory of self-moderating or self-regulating absolutism was attractive to conservative Patriotes, for it offered the possibility of a compromise which might avert a constitutional crisis. It seemed possible to acknowledge the theoretically absolute power of the king but to conceive of him as a head of state divinely appointed to represent the nation's will who would freely consent to act only according to the dictates of natural law, public utility, and the traditions of the French constitution, and who would voluntarily submit to the admonitions of the parlements whenever his will was temporarily "deceived" by evil ministers like Maupeou. That is, he was to be absolute in theory but limited in fact. This was the position of Miromesnil and of the Parlement of Paris in its *arrêté* of January 16, 1771.[37] This theory did not, of course, abridge the right—or indeed the obligation—of the courts and of individual citizens to protest and re-

37. *Journal historique* (London, 1774–76), I, 32.

sist the "deceived" will of the king, for such resistance was true fidelity
to the crown and to the principle of justice.

Since these Patriotes reserved the right to define the legitimate or illegitimate acts of the throne, this proposition to accept absolutism in theory but deny it in practice was an obvious sophistry which Maupeou never
thought of accepting and which the majority of the Patriotes disavowed.
The *Journal historique* reported that "a few parlements" had unfortunately
admitted "this absurd and revolting proposition [of divine right]," which
"never should have been advanced in a century as enlightened and as
philosophic as our own," but it was happy to note that such exceptions
were rare.[38]

The proposition was "absurd" for two reasons. First, what for many
was intolerable was the very justification of absolutism in theory, the bla-
tant intent of the edict of December "to establish despotism legally," not
any particular despotic actions by the administration.[39] The diarist Regnaud's comment was typical of this sort of reaction: "Though the nation
had for long been forced to bend its neck beneath the yoke imposed upon
her, since this yoke had not been established as a law and existed only as
a fact, France had always acquiesced out of love for her kings. But in this
affair [of the edict of December 1770], ashamed to find herself treated like
a slave and to see despotism legalized, she raised up her head and announced that she was a free nation."[40]

Second, many asserted that legitimate absolutism was a logical absurdity, a contradiction in terms. All absolute power, Morizot said, is by
definition unlimited and hence necessarily arbitrary and illegitimate.
"Absolute authority is by its very nature the opposite of legitimate authority." Arbitrary authority exists, another Patriote wrote, "whenever
any will whatsoever is law and necessarily the law."[41]

Since the apologists of the crown made no use of Hobbes's contract
theory and since their argument of the efficiency of absolutism was scarcely
supported by the record, the only serious thesis the Patriotes had to refute

38. *Ibid.*, June 17 and August 4, 1771 (I, 365, II, 66).
39. *{Deuxième} Lettre d'un bourgeois de Paris à un provincial, sur l'édit de décembre 1770,
et ses suites funestes* (N.p., n.d. [1771]), 2.
40. Regnaud, "Histoire," I, 30.
41. [Morizot], *Le Sacre royal*, 76; *Plan d'une conversation entre un avocat et M. le chancelier*,
11.

was divine right. This they did in three ways: The first was simply to assert that divine right was a heretical and revolting notion, "not merely idolatry of the creature" but "idolatry of the crime."[42] The second was to empty the theory of all force by extending divine sanction to all human authority that served social justice. "A servant," Blonde said, "is obliged to obey his master; the law of God requires him to do so. But the servant must first consent to recognize the master as his master." Or as Malesherbes wrote, "Divine power is the origin of all legitimate power; but . . . the end and object of power is always the greatest happiness of the people."[43] The third answer was to transfer divine right from the king to the people, according to the dictum *Vox populi, vox Dei*. "The king and the law," Morizot wrote, "receive their authority from the same source, that is, from the unanimous will of the people, or rather from the will of God himself, Who when He told Samuel to 'listen to all that the voice of the people told him' made manifest that He deigned to establish this means to make known His will regarding human societies under His protection."[44]

Thus the initial willingness of conservative Patriotes that the French monarchy remain absolute in name provided it voluntarily cease to be so in fact was soon overwhelmed by a general and unqualified condemnation of all absolutism. The code word for every form of absolutism was *despotisme*, and the evils of *despotisme* became the dominant theme not only of the political literature of 1771 but also of political discussions in the salons, in the city streets, and in the provinces, if we may credit contemporary observers. A character in one of Maupeou's propaganda pieces complained, "Since I have set foot in France, along all the roads I have traveled and in all the inns, I have heard talk of nothing but *despotisme*."[45]

Despotisme was denounced as contrary to divine law, to reason, to nature, to the purposes of government, to the constitution, and to the his-

42. "L'Accomplissement des prophéties, pour servir de suite à l'ouvrage intitulé Le Point de vue; Ecrit intéressant pour la maison de Bourbon," in *Les Efforts de la liberté*, VI, 175.

43. [Blonde], *Le Parlement justifié par l'Impératrice de Russie*, 60; Cour des Aides de Paris, *Remontrances de la Cour des Aides de Paris, délibérées dans le mois de janvier 1771. Touchant l'édit de règlement du mois de décembre 1770* (N.p., 1771), 10.

44. [Morizot], *Inauguration de Pharamond*, 103.

45. *Dialogue entre un officier françois qui revient de Corse et son neveu*, 21.

toric traditions of France. It was called a conspiracy "to deprive all classes within the state of their rights, their privileges, their liberties, their property, and even their lives." The Patriotes cited Helvétius' words, "Despotism stifles the thoughts in men's minds and the virtue in their hearts."[46] They also recalled Montesquieu's description of despotism as the most egalitarian of all forms of government, for it reduced all men to equal servitude. The fear, real or feigned, was voiced that the king might abolish all "distinctions of rank under the pretext that all subjects must be equal in the eyes of the sovereign."[47] The preamble of the edict of December 1770 had spoken of "the principles which determine our actions and which reasons of state often do not permit us to reveal." This was taken to mean that *raison d'état* was to be the governing principle of the new despotism, that the collective and individual welfare of the citizens was to be sacrificed to the so-called good of the state, and that this statism was to be a cloak for personal despotism. "Reasons of state," the Parlement of Besançon protested, "being by their nature nothing more than the reasons of the prince, leave everything to his personal will" and provide him with "a thousand excuses to abuse as he may please all the rights of citizens by concealing behind the curtain of some pretended interest of the state . . . any unjust or illegal act [he] may wish to commit."[48]

Perhaps the most interesting indictment of the absolute authority of the executive was Malesherbes' analysis of the evils of bureaucratic and administrative despotism unchecked by an independent judiciary. In his *Remontrances au sujet des vexations injustes exercées contre le sieur Guillaume Monnerat* he reported that the investigations of his court had "revealed a deliberate system of despotism operating outside the law, a plot . . . to substitute arbitrary authority for legal procedures." This scheme, the work "of a few men in government finances" who freely admitted their purposes, had, he said, already been put into execution, and its chief weapons were the *lettre de cachet* and imprisonment without proper judicial hearing, as the Monnerat case proved.[49] In the more famous remonstrances of the

46. [Blonde], *Le Parlement justifié par l'Impératrice de Russie*, 38; *Journal historique* (London, 1774–76), January 8, 1774 (V, 116).

47. [Clément de Boissy], *Le Maire du palais*, 37.

48. Parlement de Besançon, "Arrêté du parlement de Besançon du 26 février," in *Recueil de toutes les pièces concernant les affaires du tems* (N.p., 1771), 177–78.

49. Cour des Aides de Paris, "Remontrances au sujet des vexations injustes exercés contre le sieur Guillaume Monnerat, 14 september 1770," in Cour des Aides de Paris, *Mémoires pour servir à l'histoire du droit public*, 505.

Cour des Aides of 1775 Malesherbes resumed his attack on this "oriental despotism" operating on the lower administrative levels—the tyranny of the obscure, anonymous bureaucrat. The centralized system of the regime had a constant tendency, he said, to pass accountability upward to the next higher level in the bureaucracy so that it was impossible for the helpless citizen to fix the responsibility for any administrative act on any particular functionary, and all appeals against injustice or error were frustrated. This was the despotism of "the petty functionary, the man who is absolutely unknown within the state and yet who, speaking and writing in the name of the ministers, has like them absolute, irresistible power, and who is even more secure than they from any investigation simply because he is so inconspicuous."[50]

The fact that the first of these remonstrances was written just before Maupeou's coup and the second the year after his fall reveals that bureaucratic despotism was not peculiar only to Maupeou's regime. In fact it had been under active investigation and debate since about 1761.[51] Though the Maupeou revolution intensified attention to the issue of abuse of power by the executive on all administrative levels, the problem was the object of increasing concern by all politically conscious groups in France from the bankruptcy of John Law to the execution of Louis XVI. This strong, cumulative reaction against royal, ministerial, and bureaucratic malfeasance explains not only the Patriotes' search for a constitution that would prevent such abuses but also the inevitable failure of any effort such as Maupeou's to increase even more the power and independence of the royal executive machine.

It was much easier, however, to denounce monarchical absolutism than it was to find a practical alternative. Yet the Patriotes were morally and politically obligated to propose some specific constitutional structure better than the one established by Maupeou. For centuries the French state had been a system of dynamic equilibrium between the king and the Paris Parlement, the power of each constantly expanding or contracting in relation to the other. Both the crown and the courts had hitherto always accepted this fluid and unstable power system as the essential and permanent nature of the French monarchy. The *thèse parlementaire* had always

50. Cour des Aides, "Remontrances de la Cour des Aides relatives aux impôts" (May 6, 1775), *ibid.*, 629, 633, 656, 658.
51. See Egret, *Louis XV et l'opposition parlementaire*, 116–17.

been an ideology designed to defend parliamentary power but never a program to abolish the partnership of crown and court within the monarchy.
With Maupeou, however, this adversary form of government seemed to
have ended. The avowed intent of the coup was to put an end to dual government and place total power in the crown. The survival of the parlements, which of course was the purpose of the whole Patriote operation,
consequently seemed to demand the opposite resolution, the creation of
an absolute corporation.

This was at least the logical objective, and some of the Patriotes saw
it clearly and tried to achieve it. The effort was doomed to failure, however, for many reasons. The principal political function of the parlements
was to defend the interests of the nobility, and the nobility since Richelieu had been existing in a sort of symbiotic relationship with the crown.
It was therefore really impossible to divorce entirely the political interests
of the king and the aristocracy. Second, the parlements, for all their elaborate arguments drawn from ancient precedents, possessed at the most only
problematic and limited constitutional powers on which even their supporters were not in agreement. Furthermore the popular support they enjoyed at the moment was more the product of resentment against Maupeou and the king than of inveterate loyalty, and it was far from
unanimous. Third, the magistrates were by training and instinct conservative, and though they were ready to defend what they believed were their
legal powers and rights, they were not disposed to undertake revolutionary innovations. Fourth, the exile of the Parisian magistrates to all corners
of France and the purges of the provincial courts had deprived the Parti
Parlementaire of any forum in which to debate and fashion a new constitution. And finally, Maupeou's efficient police were able to prevent any
sort of revolutionary action. There was therefore absolutely no way the
suppressed magistrates could have met together in a sort of aristocratic
Convention Nationale, and hence there was never any possibility of their
putting together and enforcing a practical constitution. Consequently,
since Patriote aristocratic constitutionalism could never be effected and
since Maupeou's absolutistic formula was in fact fated to collapse, the only
possible outcome was that which occurred, an uneasy return by the settlement of 1774 to the status quo ante to await the solution of 1789.

Thus Patriote constitutionalism, in the sense of a new plan of government, existed only inferentially in the set of specific proposals found in the courts' remonstrances, decrees, and letters of 1771 and in the writings of Patriote theorists and pamphleteers. It was barren of immediate political results but not necessarily without significance in the development of French political philosophy.

No one denied the obvious fact that the parlements, even if granted all they were demanding, would lack both the constitutional authority and the real political leverage necessary to make them the supreme rulers of France. Therefore the essential demand of the Patriotes was for the reconstitution of the States General (which had not met for a hundred and fifty-seven years), with the assumption that the courts would retain their claimed traditional functions. "The parlements of France," Target wrote, reflecting Malesherbes' thesis, "possess only very limited powers. They do not compensate for the loss of the States General, which they do not represent. They cannot in any sense replace them in the matter of taxes, which they have acquired the power to register, though without any right that I know of." Other writers concurred. Mey ascribed to the States General the powers to give the necessary consent of the people to taxes, to initiate legislation, and to collaborate with the king in the enactment of new constitutional "lois du royaume."[52] Morizot proposed the convocation not of the traditional three estates but of what he called "the General Diet of the nation," a more broadly constituted body representing the people, the intellectuals, and the magistrates, and possessing full and exclusive power to enact legislation and impose taxes. "Nothing," he wrote, "can replace the National Diet in questions involving the interests of the entire kingdom or in the enactment of new laws. Nothing can be a substitute for the always necessary will of the true representatives of the nation. . . . Even the parlements, which are only 'verifiers of the law,' that is, judges of the conformity of administrative acts with the ancient laws of which they are the custodians, are never competent to deliberate on a new law. Nor are they competent to deliberate on the creation or extension of a tax, for no tax can be created or extended except by a law recognized by the nation to be in the public interest."[53] Saige was even more radical, for he ac-

52. [Target], *Lettres d'un homme à un autre homme sur les affaires du temps*, 93; [Mey et al.], *Maximes* (2nd ed.), I, 109, 136, 251, 307, II, 1 ff., 124, 267, 342, 343, 345.
53. [Morizot], *Inauguration de Pharamond*, 139.

cepted Rousseau's principle that the general will, and hence the powers
to legislate and tax, were inalienable and could not be represented, but
he gave to the States General the authority to act as the "organs" of the
general will, a formula that brought him in effect to the same position as
the others.[54]

This call for the reestablishment of the States General came from all
quarters of the Patriote movement—from Malesherbes, the chief insti-
gator of the idea, from his disciples Augeard and Blonde, from Pidanzat
de Mairobert, from Clément de Boissy, from various anonymous pamphleteers, from nobles, and from the parlements of Normandy, Brittany,
Dijon, and Toulouse.[55] Indeed the preface to the *Recueil des réclamations*, a
compilation of the protests issued by the various courts, said, "The entire
magistracy demands the convocation of the States General, in order to
return to them the precious powers with which they have been entrusted."[56]

Maupeou, of course, never considered acquiescing to this demand. He
had rejected the suggestion without a moment's hesitation when Lebrun
had made it in 1769, for he foresaw that to assemble the States General
would be to open a Pandora's box of demands and problems, as indeed
was to happen in 1789, and that the parlements would remain no less hos-

54. [Saige], *Catéchisme du citoyen*, 54, 64–65, 116 and *passim*.
55. Cour des Aides de Paris, "Remontrances . . . relatives aux impôts" (May 6, 1775),
in Cour des Aides de Paris, *Mémoires pour servir à l'histoire du droit public*, 687; [Jacques
Mathieu Augeard], *Correspondance secrète et familière de M. de Maupeou avec M. de Sor****
{Sorhouet}, conseiller du nouveau parlement (N.p., n.d. [1771]), I, 85, II, 93–94; [Blonde],
Le Parlement justifié par l'Impératrice Reine de Hongrie, 5; *Journal historique* (London, 1774–
76), III, 352–53 and *passim*; [Clément de Boissy], *Le Maire du palais*, 109; *Réponse aux
trois articles*, 3; *Lettre écrite au nom de la noblesse de France, à chacun des princes séparément* (N.p.,
n.d. [1771]); "Lettre de la noblesse de Normandie au duc d'Orléans," in *Supplément à la
Gazette de France*, No. 9, p. 1; Parlement de Normandie, "Lettre du parlement de Normandie au Roi, sur l'état actuel du parlement de Paris, du premier février 1771," in *Second
receuil de divers arrêtés et lettres au Roi de différens parlemens du royaume sur l'état actuel du parlement de Paris* (N.p., 1771), 23; Parlement de Normandie, "Lettre du parlement de Rouen
au Roi. Du 8 février 1771," in *Recueil des réclamations*, I, 210; Parlement de Normandie,
"Arrêté du parlement de Rouen du 5 février 1771," *ibid.*, II, 192; Parlement de Bretagne,
"Protestation du parlement de Bretagne contre sa suppression. Du 23 octobre 1771," *ibid.*,
II, 568; Parlement de Dijon, "Arrêté du parlement de Dijon. Du 1 mai [1771]," *ibid.*,
II, 463–75; Parlement de Toulouse, "Remontrances du parlement de Toulouse. Du 6 avril
1771," *ibid.*, II, 356–57.
56. *Recueil des réclamations*, I, iv.

tile to the reforms he thought necessary.[57] Since he was not under the pressure of a financial crisis as Necker was to be in 1789, he could ignore the issue. This was fortunate, for except for a few vague proposals such as that of Morizot, few Patriotes of these years seem to have perceived that the ancient and obsolete States General could not be resurrected in its old form, and that any new national assembly would have to be given a wholly new constitution.

If, then, the States General could not be restored, all that the Patriotes could debate was the constitutional function of the parlements. Their specific proposals had no historic consequences, but the discussions reveal interesting developments in Patriote constitutional thought.

Montesquieu had called the courts "intermediary powers." There was a significant range of opinions on what this phrase meant. The most conservative position, the one held by those who still clung to the hope of a self-moderating absolutism and best exemplified by Hue de Miromesnil's compromise proposal of 1772, saw the courts as defenders of the throne against attempts to erode or pervert its powers.[58] This had indeed been the historic function of the Paris Parlement in its adamant opposition to any encroachment by the papacy on the king's authority, a consistent policy from the magistrates' championship of the Pragmatic Sanction of Bourges of 1438 down to their eighteenth-century Gallicanism. Rome had not been the only threat however. The Paris Parlement, it was claimed, had defended the throne against "les grands vassaux," against "certain orders in the States General," and "unfortunately sometimes even . . . against the clergy."[59] In the present juncture it was defending the king against "his minister [Maupeou]," who was trying to make himself "the master of the throne and tyrant over the people," and was maintaining the "stability of the law" against Louis' own "momentarily deceived will."[60] By this theory the magistrates were "representatives of the nation" only in that they were specifically charged to "define the national interests, . . . to alert the prince, to inform him of the sufferings of the

57. Lebrun, *Opinions*, 19.
58. Miromesnil, "Lettres sur l'état de la magistrature," 5, 8.
59. *Lettre d'un ancien magistrat à un duc et pair*, 15, 18.
60. [*Deuxième*] *Lettre d'un bourgeois de Paris*, 11; Parlement de Normandie, "Lettre du parlement de Normandie au Roi. Du 26 février 1771," in *Recueil des réclamations*, II, 215–16.

people, to call his attention to the activities of his ministers," and "to prevent attempts . . . to surprise and deceive his will."[61]

This thesis was the oldest and was far more conservative than Montesquieu's concept, which had been (ostensibly at least) adopted by Catherine of Russia, who gave it further currency in her *Instructions* to her own states general and in turn influenced Blonde. Montesquieu had concurred to an extent in seeing the parlements as passive obstacles against political pressure, but he had not pictured them as bulwarks facing downward and outward against pressures on the throne. Instead his "intermediary powers" faced upward and were erected to resist the downward force of royal authority and thus serve as checks or channels ("canaux") to retard and moderate monarchical power, "so that [as Blonde said] it may never be said that the nation is without a protector against royal power."[62]

A third concept was more dynamic. It pictured the magistrates as umpires or liaisons between the king and the nation, protecting one against the other and providing a needed means of communication between the two. According to this thesis the Parlement defended "equally the people against abuses of power and the sovereign against excesses of liberty." The court was "by its nature and purpose the organ of the sovereign to the nation and of the nation to the sovereign." Its duty was to "serve the king in his subjects and the subjects in their king, . . . to be constantly the respected channel of this double interest."[63]

The most radical and probably the most frequent interpretation was that the parlements neither had a special obligation to safeguard royal authority nor were neutral intermediaries, but rather were responsible to and for the nation as a whole. As Augeard said, they were either the immediate "representatives of the people" or else they represented them indirectly as "the representatives of the States General." To use a current metaphor, they were "the voice of the people." "If the Parlement is deprived

61. *Lettre de M.***, conseiller au Parlement*, 12; [*Deuxième*] *Lettre d'un bourgeois de Paris*, 3, 11.

62. [Blonde], *Le Parlement justifié par l'Impératrice Reine de Hongrie*, 6.

63. Cour des Comptes, Aides et Finances de Normandie, "Remontrances de la Cour des Comptes, Aides et Finances de Normandie, 18 avril 1771, in *Recueil des réclamations*, II, 255. *Lettre de M.***, conseiller au parlement*, 41; Guy Jean Baptiste Target, *Discours prononcés en la Grand'Chambre, par M. Target, avocat, le 28 novembre 1774, à la rentrée du parlement* (N.p., n.d. [1774]), 2–3.

of its right to represent the truth," Augeard asked, "what national body is left to defend us against the ministers and to protest respectfully to the king that he rules over subjects, not over slaves?"[64]

These four interpretations of the phrase "intermediary powers" were not distinguished or debated by the Patriotes; a writer might shift from one to another without being conscious of any inconsistency. Yet they were clearly distinguishable positions, and the discernible movement during the early 1770s from the conservative and traditional interpretation to the most radical theory is a significant indication of the growth of the idea, even in aristocratic and conservative circles, that some sort of national corporation had to be created independent of the crown and deriving its authority from the nation itself.

The theory that the Paris Parlement represented the nation rested mainly on the claim that the States General at their meeting at Blois in 1576 had authorized the court to act in their absence as "a sort of miniature States General [*une sorte de trois états en raccourci au petit pied*] with the power to suspend, modify, or refuse edicts."[65] The provincial parlements, especially that of Normandy, claimed similar authority as temporary "representatives of the provincial estates and the bond uniting all the orders of which the province is composed."[66] This authority delegated by the States General and the provincial estates to the parlements was taken to include the powers to legislate and to tax, but the Patriotes were far from unanimous agreement on the extent of these powers.

The parlements' rights of verification, registration, and remonstrance implied that the legislative initiative was vested in the king under the French constitution, and indeed the Paris Parlement in January 1771 conceded to Louis XV that "the power to make laws belongs to you alone, without qualification or division."[67] Yet these parliamentary rights, which were not contested by the crown, also clearly implied the collaboration of the courts in the legislative process. This collaboration was held to be a fundamental law, expressed in the famous and frequently cited dictum of the Edict of Pistes (**A.D.** 864), *Lex consensu populi et constitutione regis fit.*

64. [Augeard], *Correspondance secrète*, I, 174, 131, II, 89.
65. [Mey, *et al.*], *Maximes* (2nd ed.), I, 130.
66. *Acte de protestation de plusieurs membres du bailliage de Caen*, 2.
67. Parlement de Paris, "Arrêté du 16 janvier 1771," in *Journal historique* (London, 1774–76), I, 32.

But what did "consensu populi" mean? Here again we find a range of interpretations.

The most conservative theory was that the Parlement was, first, the depository, the place of official registration of the laws, and, second, a supreme court charged with preserving inviolate the constitution by reviewing all new laws and "preventing those which are contrary to justice and to the fundamental laws of the state." Its role by this interpretation was that of "a purely passive resistance which limits itself to inaction."[68] Nevertheless a law, though initiated and willed by the king, did not have legal force until it had been duly registered by the courts. Moreover, it was contended, the magistrates as "priests of the law" had the moral obligation to withhold their approval of any law they judged unjust or unconstitutional and to force the executive to remain in the "happy incapacity to touch the rights of citizens."[69] Thus "the king, although legislator, cannot force the magistrates to submit to a law which they believe to be unjust."[70]

This was obviously a contradiction in terms and an unworkable constitutional principle, as experience had repeatedly shown, for it posited an absolute legislative power subject to an absolute veto. It was precisely this absurdity in the constitution that the edict of December 1770 was intended to eliminate by the king's denial of any moral or legal obligation to accept parliamentary vetoes. Yet if the magistrates had accepted this amendment they would have been reduced to a purely advisory body without real power. Consequently some Patriotes felt forced to adopt a far more radical and republican theory, namely, that the monarch had a constitutional obligation to bow to the parlements' vetoes. This interpretation rested on the proposition that "the essential form that renders legal the will of the monarch . . . is the consent of the nation."[71] The Parlement had, or should have, it was argued, the power to exercise "the inalienable right which [the nation] has always had to participate in [con-

68. [Blonde], *Le Parlement justifié par l'Impératrice Reine de Hongrie*, 11; *Lettre de M.****, *conseiller au Parlement*, 29.
69. *Journal de ce qui s'est passé à l'occasion du rétablissement du parlement de Toulouse*, 64; [Blonde], *Le Parlement justifié par l'Impératrice Reine de Hongrie*, 17.
70. [Mey et al.], *Maximes* (2nd ed.), II, 402.
71. Parlement de Bretagne, "Remontrances du parlement de Bretagne. Du 24 juillet 1771," in *Recueil des réclamations*, II, 309.

courir à] the political administration of the kingdom and in the legislative power, a right which the nation holds from itself and which is not derived from any royal grant."[72]

This doctrine would have made the Parlement, or rather the parlements (by the principle of unity of classes), a national legislature coequal with the king-legislator. There was of course no historical precedent in France for such a constitutional structure. Moreover the more radical Patriotes did not like either the division of legislative power between two branches of the government or the proposal that the magistrates alone form the national legislature. They wished to give the authority to enact laws to a quite distinct and nationally representative body. Morizot proposed his "National Diet." Saige would have made the States General the legislative "organs" of the general will and would have deprived the parlements of any legislative function. In compensation he suggested that the Paris Parlement together with its provincial "emanations" form a "senate" serving simultaneously as a "second branch of the executive," the supreme court of justice, the depository of the law, and a sort of "perpetual council of the nation" authorized to speak for the people whenever the nation was not assembled.[73]

The parlements' constitutional control over taxation was an even more vexing problem. Since the death of Louis XIV the parlements had in fact repeatedly succeeded in blocking new taxes and preventing fiscal reforms that would have increased the taxes on the nobility and the wealthy. As we know, Maupeou's and Terray's principal immediate objective was to put an end to this roadblock, which was starving the government into bankruptcy.

Yet there were good constitutional and historical grounds for the Patriote contention that the power of taxation did not belong to the king. The imposition of taxes had always been regarded as a political act of a nature quite different from the enactment of civil or political laws, and there did not exist the modern assumption that legislative and taxing powers must be vested in the same authority. In the Middle Ages the kings of France had generally met their normal governmental expenses with the

72. [Brancas], "Tableau des différens âges de la monarchie françoise," in *Les Efforts de la liberté*, IV, 63.

73. [Saige], *Catéchisme du citoyen*, Chaps. 2–5.

income from their own domains; the extra monies contributed in emergencies by the free cities and feudal lords and authorized by the States General had been, in theory at least, voluntary gifts, as still were in the eighteenth century the *dons gratuits* voted by the Assemblées du Clergé and the provincial estates. Moreover it was a principle of natural law that taxation without consent was arbitrary confiscation and "an explicit infringement of the right of property."[74] Thus the Patriotes generally agreed that the nation had the right to authorize in some way or another the taxes it paid. The difficulty was in finding the way by which this consent should be formally given.

Malesherbes was convinced, as we have seen, that the power to tax belonged to the States General alone and that the parlements never should have claimed it, and he convinced Augeard and Target of the correctness of this position. Brancas too concurred.[75] In the indefinite absence of the States General, however, this was not a theory of much practical use. Consequently most Patriotes took the position (which incidentally justified the parlements' past actions) that the States General held the original power to tax, but that until they were reconvened this power was constitutionally delegated to the parlements.[76]

Another important constitutional issue was federalism. The Patriotes do not seem to have foreseen the probability that a single national legislature (the States General) would have diminished or destroyed provincial autonomy, as it was to do in 1789. This was a curious blindness, for they all, and especially the provincial magistrates and their supporters, strongly supported parliamentary federalism and maximum governmental decentralization. The principle of unity of classes, the doctrine that all the parlements were "classes" of a single body or "emanations" of a single

74. [Guy Jean Baptiste Target], *Lettre d'un homme à un autre homme, sur l'extinction de l'ancien parlement, et la création du nouveau* (N.p., n.d. [1771]), 2.

75. [Augeard], *Correspondance secrète*, I, 46–63, 85; [Target], *Lettres d'un homme à un autre homme sur les affaires du temps*, 93–94; [Brancas], "Tableau des différens âges de la monarchie françoise," in *Les Efforts de la liberté*, IV, 75–76.

76. [Mey *et al.*], *Maximes* (2nd ed.), I, 130; [Blonde], *Le Parlement justifié par l'Impératrice Reine de Hongrie*, 19; *Plan d'une conversation entre un avocat et M. le chancelier*, 29–30; *Recueil des réclamations*, preface, I, ii; Parlement de Besançon, "Remontrances du parlement de Besançon" (March 11, 1771), in *Recueil des réclamations*, II, 403; Cour des Comptes, Aides et Finances de Normandie, "Arrêté de la Cour des Comptes, Aides et Finances de Normandie, du 27 septembre," *ibid*, II, 571.

parlement with the right to consult and act together, was really merely a claim to the right to cooperate in opposing the crown. The magistrates had no desire to establish "the right to assemble in a single place, or to extend their authority over one another's jurisdictions, or to hold themselves all bound by the decrees of any one court."[77] On the contrary, their purpose was to defend the autonomy of the separate parlements and the separate provinces, which Maupeou was attacking. By abolishing the Parlement of Rouen he had enlarged the jurisdiction within which the Paris Parlement had the sole power to verify laws, and it was reported that he intended to make his new Paris Parlement the only court in the realm authorized to register new laws. This would have been a means of realizing his intention, announced on February 23, 1771, "to reunite France as much as possible under the empire of the same laws just as it has been united under the empire of the same prince."[78] To this threat, which in fact was never executed, the provinces reacted vigorously. The well-written and violent *Manifeste aux Normands* said that these proposed reforms and the destruction of the Parlement of Rouen violated the "contract of union" by which the Duchy of Normandy had been joined to the French crown in 1204 and which guaranteed the "laws, customs, freedoms, and liberties" of Normans and gave to the estates of Normandy (or in their absence to the Parlement of Normandy) the right to consent to taxation. "Differences of origins, customs, and tribunals are what separate provinces and nations from one another. These immemorial boundaries perpetuate patriotism, different ways of life, and the memory of great deeds, which all help to create an *esprit de corps* without which everything falls into impotence." The author even hinted that Normandy should reestablish its ancient bonds with England, "our fatherland." Norman lower courts joined in the chorus of protests, and they were echoed by similar objections from Franche Comté and Brittany.[79] The Parlement of Besançon denounced the proposed unification of the legal code as an infringement on provincial autonomy. "It would not be possible," it protested, "to proclaim more clearly the intent to abolish all the rights, liberties,

77. *{Deuxième} Lettre d'un bourgeois de Paris*, 5.
78. Quoted by Flammermont, *Le Chancelier Maupeou et les parlements*, 375.
79. *Manifeste aux Normands*, 1–2; Parlement de Bretagne, "Remontrances du parlement de Bretagne, 11 mars 1771," in *Recueil des réclamations*, II, 388.

franchises, and privileges of the various provinces, to abrogate all acts, treaties, and capitulations under whose guaranties the provinces were united to the crown. This is an act of universal subversion."[80]

Thus the provincial Patriotes tried to resist the trend toward increasing governmental and administrative centralization which, as Tocqueville later showed, had characterized the history of modern France especially since Richelieu, and which Maupeou was doing his best to accelerate. Tocqueville's warnings that centralization was ultimately inefficient and that it destroyed individual liberty were anticipated by a fellow Norman who wrote, "A single parlement . . . charged with verifying and maintaining [all] the laws could neither discover all the disadvantages that a given law might have for each different province nor provide sufficiently prompt remedies against violations in places distant from the capital. Moreover it would become dangerously powerful." Such centralization, another writer warned, would leave citizens with no way of opposing the multiplication of taxes; "our liberties, our properties, our dignities, and our prerogatives would be at the mercy of the king's minister," and this would be "the most absolute despotism."[81] For all their self-serving opposition to tax reform and their reactionism, these provincial Patriotes saw clearly the threat to individual freedom posed by Maupeou's dream of a centralized, uniform, efficient, monolithic state and thus anticipated certain aspects of the liberalism of John Stuart Mill and Alexis de Tocqueville.

Patriote resistance to centralization and to the concentration of power in the executive was also expressed in their writings on the issues of judicial tenure and the law. During the early months of the Maupeou revolution and again in 1774 and 1775 during the celebrations of the restoration of the parlements, there was a great deal of talk about the "honor," dignity, prerogatives, and privileges of the magistrates. These words denoted, first of all, the honorific status of the *noblesse de robe* and the mag-

80. Parlement de Besançon, "Remontrances du parlement de Besançon, 11 mars 1771," in *Recueil des réclamations*, II, 388. See also Parlement de Provence, "Arrêté du parlement de Provence, du 18 mars 1771," *ibid.*, II, 497 ff.

81. "Essai historique sur les droits de la province de Normandie," in *Les Efforts de la liberté*, VI, 66; "Lettre aux officiers de justice des provinces sur les dangers du projet des conseils supérieurs dans le ressort du parlement de Paris," in *Les Efforts de la liberté*, IV, 1–6.

istracy. For instance one pamphleteer warned the magistrates, "The voluntary liquidation of your offices would be regarded in the present juncture as an explicit renunciation of the position which you have chosen to fill and in which Providence has placed you. What other place henceforth could you occupy with honor? . . . Your position in society must be the most precious, the most sacred thing in the world for you."[82] Removal from judicial office was thus seen as arbitrary derogation of social status. But the dismissals could also be resisted on somewhat higher ethical grounds as confiscation of property without due process of law, since the offices were venal and the right of tenure could be construed as a form of property. The next higher step was to defend the irremovability of the judiciary on constitutional grounds. Target argued that the magistrate's right to tenure of office was not merely a "titre de propriété" but was more fundamentally a "titre d'état et de fonction" and as such had preceded the institution of venality of office. That is, it had been a constitutional right before becoming a property right.[83]

Finally, on the highest level was the principle that liberty could not exist without an independent and irremovable judiciary. The Princes of the Blood declared that "of the rights of Frenchmen, one of the most useful to the monarch and most precious to his subjects [was] the right to have perpetual and irremovable bodies of citizens" who represented the people's right to invoke the law and were responsible for the enforcement of old laws and the verification of new ones. In order to fulfill these duties, the Princes argued, the courts had to be secure from punitive action. "This security," they said, "cannot exist without the irremovability of those to whom are entrusted such important duties. The functions [of the judiciary] have always been regarded as one of the principal safeguards of public liberty against abuses of arbitrary power, and they are as much integral parts of the constitution as any other fundamental law of the monarchy." Similarly Target argued that "it is a completely absurd proposition that a body [the Parlement] whose essential function is legal resistance to the seduced will of authority may be destroyed by that same authority."[84] All

82. *Lettre d'un François aux victimes d'Ebroïn* (N.p., 1771), 6–7.
83. [Target], *Lettres d'un homme à un autre homme sur les affaires du temps*, 68.
84. *Protestations des Princes du Sang*, 2; [Guy Jean Baptiste Target], *Réflexions sur la destitution de l'universalité des offices du parlement de Paris par voie de suppression* (N.p., n.d. [1771]), 17.

these assertions of the irremovability of the judiciary were merely restatements of Montesquieu's principle that the separation of the executive and judicial powers is essential to political liberty. As Blonde stressed, if judges were removable without cause at the convenience of the king and his ministers, then the prince was in effect given authority to condemn the innocent, and no man was safe.[85]

The Patriotes generally did not distinguish clearly between political (or constitutional) law and civil law, for they were charging the ministry with violations of both, and in many instances, such as the confiscations of venal offices, it was not always clear which kind of law was at issue. In either case, however, they emphasized three essential qualities of law: first, that its source must be corporative, not personal; second, that it must be unalterable except by the legislation of a constitutional corporation and safe from subversion by the executive; and third, that it must apply to all citizens equally.

The first quality was basic and central to the struggle between Maupeou and the parlements. "The law," Morizot wrote, "can never be an arbitrary action willed by an absolute power or the expression of the personal desires or private interests of the prince."[86] Capricious, private authority was contradictory to the nature and purpose of law, for it abolished security of property, security of estate, and security of civil liberty.[87] The Parlement of Provence cited the king's intervention in the D'Aiguillon trial as an example of violation by the arbitrary will of the executive of the unalterability and impartiality of the law: "If by such means one individual can gain impunity, then there is no security for anyone; the powerful will be free to exploit the weak, who will vainly invoke the protection of the law. Every criminal with credit in the government or who enjoys political favor can evade trial by the courts."[88] Such fears were not groundless, for there seemed to be plentiful evidence of ministerial inter-

85. [Blonde], *Le Parlement justifié par l'Impératrice Reine de Hongrie*, 72–73.
86. [Morizot], *Inauguration de Pharamond*, 112.
87. [Target], *Lettres d'un homme à un autre homme sur les affaires du temps*, 22–23; *Plan d'une conversation entre un avocat et M. le chancelier*, 11; Cour des Comptes, Aides et Finances de Normandie, "Remontrances de la Cour des Comptes, Aides et Finances de Normandie, 18 avril 1771," in *Recueil des réclamations*, II, 253; Parlement de Dijon, "Lettre du parlement de Dijon au Roi, 6 février 1771," *ibid.*, II, 454; Regnaud, "Histoire," I, 23.
88. Parlement de Provence, "Remontrances du parlement de Provence. Du 18 février 1771," in *Recueil des réclamations*, II, 483.

ference in due legal process—not only in the D'Aiguillon and Monnerat cases, but also in the large losses suffered by many, as Voltaire could testify, from Terray's illegal financial operations, for which no legal recourse was permitted. It was reported that Maupeou himself resolved an embroiled lawsuit over a sum of 20,000 livres which one of his henchmen claimed under his father's will, by the simple expedient of writing an *arrêt de conseil* ordering the notary entrusted with the money to hand over the entire sum and sending a sergeant and a locksmith to collect it. Blonde reported that of sixty decisions rendered by the Cour des Aides fifty had been reversed by the king's council. This, he said, not only made the work of the courts useless; "it meant that the king, or rather the controller general and the tax farmers, are the judges as well as the parties in these cases."[89] Not all these allegations have been documented, but there is little doubt that circumvention of criminal and civil law by the executive was a valid constitutional issue.

The integrity of political law required that the king and the agents of the executive act in accord with the constitution and registered statutes. "The liberty which princes owe their peoples," Clément de Boissy wrote, citing Massillon, "is the liberty of law. You are the master of the lives and fortunes of your subjects, but you can dispose of them only according to law. . . . The law must have more authority than you." Or as Mey said, "In monarchical states, it is not the sovereign but the law which should reign."[90] The most obvious application of this principle was to the bureaucracy and the tax farmers, who were acting without judicial constraints and often in contravention of the law. Many Patriotes echoed Malesherbes' protests against misuse of *lettres de cachet*, by which agents of the government and the tax farmers were imprisoning citizens indefinitely without trial.[91]

The Patriote concept of civil law was founded on the principles of natural law and natural rights: "The primary law, which is that of nature and

89. *Journal historique* (London, 1774–76), November 23, 1771 (II, 263–64); [Blonde], *Le Parlement justifié par l'Impératrice Reine de Hongrie*, 73–74.

90. [Clément de Boissy], *Le Maire du palais*, 27. Cf. Jean Baptiste Massillon, *Sermons* (Paris, 1768), 148, 149; [Mey *et al.*] *Maximes* (2nd ed.), I, 70.

91. Cour des Aides de Paris, "Remontrances au sujet des vexations injustes exercées contre le sieur Guillaume Monnerat," in Cour des Aides de Paris, *Mémoires pour servir à l'histoire du droit public*, 505–509.

which applies to all persons . . . assures every man his constant rights to property, liberty, and life." The phrase "to every man" was an essential and frequently stressed qualification. "The first principle of law," Brancas wrote, "should be that the law speaks in all cases, to all persons, and concerning all."[92] Secondly, the purpose of civil law was to assure liberty in the broadest sense, both by assuring the citizen, in accordance with Montesquieu's definition, the power to do all he should will to do and protecting him against being forced to do what he should not will, and also, in accordance with Montesquieu's other definition, by assuring him of a sense of security.[93] Many Patriote writers applied liberty under the law particularly to the guaranty of the right of property.[94] Mey, however, advanced a broader concept. "The right of property," he wrote, "however precious it may be, yields first place to the power to do all that one may legitimately will and to be master of one's own will in all that is not contrary to the law."[95]

Nevertheless, while the courts and their supporters spoke thus in terms of broad principles, they tended for the most part to ignore injustices caused by the antiquated and chaotic state of French law and to excuse miscarriages of justice such as the Calas case. They refused, as we have seen, to support the plan conceived by Lebrun for a uniform national code of laws, which Maupeou approved and announced on February 23, 1771. Moreover, they refused to support or endorse Maupeou's abolition of *épices* and of venality of judicial office and his establishment of courts more convenient to litigants (the conseils supérieurs). All the Patriotes acknowledged implicitly or explicitly that these reforms were desirable in principle and that they were generally approved by public opinion, yet they argued that they were really political diversions, or that they had failed to achieve their purposes, or that they were not worth the subversion of

92. "L'Avocat national," in *Les Efforts de la linberté*, VI, 193; Brancas, *Extrait du droit public*, 61.

93. [Mey *et al.*], *Maximes* (2nd ed.), I, 70; Parlement de Toulouse, "Remontrances du parlement de Toulouse, du 6 avril 1771," in *Recueil des réclamations*, II, 336.

94. *E.g., Protestations des Princes du Sang*, 1; Parlement de Normandie, "Lettre du parlement de Normandie au Roi. Du 26 février 1771," in *Recueil des réclamations*, II, 215; Parlement de Bretagne, "Remontrances du parlement à Rennes, 19 février 1771," *ibid.*, II, 281; Parlement de Besançon, "Remontrances du parlement de Besançon, 11 mars 1771," *ibid.*, II, 386.

95. [Mey *et al.*], *Maximes* (2nd ed.), I, 161.

the principle of law, the constitution, the right of private property, and the parlements.

This is not to say that some Patriotes did not make specific recommendations for reform. They urged that the laws should be fixed and stable; that they should be clearly written products of careful reflection; that they should be in accord with the constitution; that they should be published and available for examination by any citizen; and that they should be applied by enlightened, independent judges in strict conformity to judicial procedure and with careful observance of all the traditional formalities.[96] "Many people," Blonde wrote (quoting the *Journal encyclopédique*), "complain of the delays and formalities which assure the citizen of a free state the security of his property and liberty."[97] These excellent proposals produced, however, no tangible results. Even if they had had broad, sincere, and active support among the Patriotes, which is doubtful, the dismissal of the magistrates prevented any possible reforms until 1774, and after that date the unresolved constitutional issues distracted attention from such problems.

The refusal to support Lebrun's plan for a uniform legal code is understandable: it was not politically expedient to endorse a proposal by the opposition; the Patriote magistrates and lawyers were conservative and predisposed against radical innovations; and there were plausible arguments for preserving at least some special provincial laws in a nation still socially and culturally fragmented. Yet the absurd inconsistencies and injustices of the chaotic legal system were too notorious to be denied, and it is significant that Lebrun's proposal was a part of Maupeou's program about which Patriote writers made few comments.

Despite this weakness in the area of legal and judicial reform, Patriote writers did at least achieve a clear formulation of the ideal of society under law: a government operating within the framework of a fixed constitution; constitutional guaranties of specific individual rights and liberties; equality of all citizens before the law; an independent judiciary; the in-

---

96. *Ibid.*, II, 1 ff.; Cour des Aides de Paris, "Remontrances de la Cour des Aides relatives aux impôts, 6 mai 1775," in Cour des Aides de Paris, *Mémoires pour servir à l'histoire du droit public,* 635; *Observations sur l'édit du mois de février 1771, portant création de conseils supérieurs* (N.p., n.d. [1771]); [Blonde], *Le Parlement justifié par l'Impératrice Reine de Hongrie,* 44, 72–73.

97. [Blonde], *Le Parlement justifié par l'Impératrice de Russie,* 12.

violability of the law by any private will, especially by the will of the executive or his agents; and impartial administration of justice by courts under fair, exhaustive, and proper procedures. Especially they must be given credit for affirming as vigorously as any of their contemporaries the Lockean precept that there can be no liberty without law.

On the other hand, the simplistic proposal to recall the States General and return to the parlements all the powers they claimed was historically regressive and was not likely to be any more successful in 1771 than it would prove to be in 1789. Despite Montesquieu, separation of powers was an Anglo-Saxon principle that never was fully integrated into the parliamentary thesis, and the Patriote theoreticians do not seem to have perceived the need for some mechanism for coordinating the judicial functions of the parlements, the legislative functions of the States General, and the executive functions of the crown, and for eliminating the destructive conflicts that plagued the existing constitution. Thus in sum it may be said that Patriote constitutionalism appears in retrospect rich in ideals and principles, but poor in practical political solutions.

THREE

Patriote Libertarianism

I N MODERN political thought the idea of liberty is closely associated with the idea of equality. This was not generally so before 1789.
In fact, as we shall see in later chapters, aside from a few utopian
communists, notably the Abbés Mably and Morelly, who knew they were
not suggesting practical forms of government, virtually no French thinker
before the Revolution made the assumption that liberty could not exist
without equality. Rousseau, it is true, postulated the interdependence of
liberty and equality, but he did not mean economic equality, and he conceded in his *Contrat social* that it might well be true that in the modern
world a society of free and politically equal men could exist only on the
shoulders of a disenfranchised proletariat. Diderot advised Catherine to
grant the right to vote only to "grands propriétaires," and D'Holbach
projected a society of classes structured on utilitarian principles. Voltaire,
despite his early admiration for the British Parliament, believed that a
representative legislature would be an impractical absurdity in France.
Condorcet as late as 1786 was saying that the right to vote was the least
important of the fundamental rights and that it probably should not be
granted to all citizens in a large modern state. Indeed few of the Philosophes, fewer still of the Patriotes, and none of the royalists would have
disagreed with Montesquieu's statement that "the power of the people has
been confused with the liberty of the people," or with his judgment that
the most egalitarian states, excessive democracies and despotisms, were

the least free. Until the Revolution democracy was generally regarded as an antique curiosity among the theoretically possible forms of government; few doubted that in a modern society inequalities of not only wealth and social status but also privilege and political power were both inevitable and proper. The bourgeoisie was far more interested in upward social movement and penetration if possible into the nobility than in the abolition of the institution of aristocracy. The tyranny of the majority was a danger still far out of sight, but Tocqueville's principle that liberty and equality were distinct political phenomena more likely to be mutually destructive than mutually supportive was a seldom-questioned truism in the eighteenth century.

Broad, comprehensive, total equality was not under discussion. The issues were specific kinds of equality, equitable inequality, and the proper distribution of inequality. These problems were only sometimes related to liberty. On such questions the parlements, as the immediate representatives of the nobility and of privileged persons of wealth, were the most conservative group in France, and their supporters generally followed their lead, though not without exceptions.

The Patriotes, it is true, did strongly support equality before the law, but as a necessary means to safeguard personal liberty and private property, not as a self-evident principle of justice. The principles of national sovereignty, the general will, and the contract seemed to imply political equality for all, but the assumption of virtual representation rather than universal franchise made this equality theoretical, not effective. On the other hand, we find frequent defenses by the Patriotes of special privilege and status, under the names of *honneur* and *état*, which were elevated to the dignity of natural rights. We also find a general silence on the questions of equal taxation and equality of wealth. A number of Patriote writers did call on the king "to look down with compassion from the eminence of his throne over the far reaches of his provinces, where the wretched inhabitants are without bread, or moisten what bread they can find with bitter tears."[1] "Too far removed from the poor," he knew "nothing of . . . their desolation, hunger, and despair." These expressions of commiseration led up, however, to the rhetorical question: "From whom will he learn

---

1. "Mandement de l'Evêque d'Alais," in *Journal historique* (London, 1774–76), September 20, 1774 (VI, 207).

if he stops the mouths of his magistrates?"[2] This was merely an obvious gambit, like the pamphlets slanted to lower-class readers, to identify the parlements with the animosity of the poor against the royal government.[3] It is also true that Malesherbes as president of the Cour des Aides of Paris did make his court the "defender of the people" against the "monstrous administrative system."[4] But these efforts, which had general parliamentary and Patriote support, were made more in the cause of justice than of equality. In short, no political group of the time was characteristically less egalitarian than the Patriotes.

Nonetheless *liberté* was the great slogan. After 1770 the word was on the lips of all men and women of every political persuasion—even the royalists; in 1776 it would become the catchword of the popular enthusiasm for the American *Insurgents*; and it was to be finally enshrined in the sacred formula of the Revolution, *Liberté, Egalité, Fraternité.*

But *liberté* was only a word, and it would be a great error to assume that in every usage it had an invariable one-to-one relationship with a single clearly defined idea. As Montesquieu observed in his *Esprit des lois*, no word was used with more different meanings. Liberty was not a single idea; it was a category of ideas whose only necessarily shared attribute was that they were all denoted by the same verbal symbol, by the same cluster of phonemes.

The word *liberté* had long existed in the French language. In the 1770s it still retained the meaning it had possessed since early times of specific special powers enjoyed by certain individuals or groups, as in such phrases as "la liberté absolue du roi," with the sense of unlimited royal authority, or "la liberté de l'église,"[5] with the sense of special ecclesiastical political powers such as those exercised by church courts, or special immunities, as from taxation. Similarly the term designated the special powers, privileges, and immunities of the parlements, as in the phrases, "la liberté des

2. *Maupeou tyran*, 80–81. See also [Clément de Boissy], *Le Maire du palais*, 101–102.

3. E.g., *Les Etrennes supérieures de Normandie pour l'année bissextile 1772* . . . (N.p., n.d. [Rouen, 1772]).

4. Cour des Aides de Paris, *Très-humbles et très-respectueuses remontrances que présentent au Roi notre très-honoré souverain et seigneur, les gens tenant sa Cour des Aides à Paris* (May 6, 1775) (N.p., n.d.), 33–34. See also Cour des Aides de Paris, *Remontrances de la Cour des Aides de Paris, délibérées dans le mois de janvier 1771*, 7.

5. *Lettre d'un bourgeois de Paris*, 17; *Lettre à un duc et pair*, 23.

fonctions de la magistrature" and "liberté d'enregistrement."[6]

While this usage persisted, an important semantic shift was taking place, probably under the influence of the natural-law and natural-rights theories, from this original meaning of special powers and privileges enjoyed by particular persons and groups to a second meaning, the powers and privileges enjoyed by the nation as a whole. Patriote writers were clearly conscious that they were using the word in this later and different sense when they underlined the distinction by qualifiers, as in the phrases "liberté publique," "liberté générale," and "liberté nationale." The significant contrast between the two meanings is felt, for instance, in Mercier's phrase "liberté publique et particulière" and in the sentence of a writer who said the magistrates would refuse liquidation of their offices because they were "trop généreux pour accepter une liberté personelle; c'est la liberté générale qu'ils demandent."[7]

"Liberté nationale" signified the collective political power of the sovereign nation, that is, its general will expressed and realized through the parlements or the States General in opposition to the claimed absolute power of the throne, *despotisme*. An example is the sentence, "L'édit du mois de décembre dernier . . . est un système réfléchi tendant à substituer la servitude à la liberté nationale et à consacrer par une loi le pouvoir national [du roi]."[8] The parlements constantly claimed that in defending their powers of remonstrance, free verification, and registration they were "défenseurs de la liberté nationale."[9] By synecdoche the word *liberté* was also extended to mean the sentiments which inspired defense of national sovereignty and opposition to *despotisme*, and it thus became synonymous with "esprit patriotique," as when Augeard wrote, "Je veux vous montrer, monsieur, ce qu'est un citoyen français, avec quel noble liberté il sait braver un injuste ministre."[10]

6. *Lettre d'un ancien magistrat à un duc et pair*, 50; Cour des Aides de Paris, *Remontrances de la Cour des Aides de Paris, délibérées dans le mois de janvier 1771*, 10.
7. [Louis Sébastien Mercier], *Jean Hennuyer, évêque de Lisieux, drame en trois actes* (London, 1772), 14; *Les Filets de Monseigneuer de Maupeou* (N.p., n.d. [1772]), 8.
8. Parlement de Normandie, "Lettre du parlement de Rouen au Roi, du 8 février 1771," in *Recueil des réclamations*, II, 198.
9. Parlement de Normandie, "Remontrances du parlement séant à Rouen, 19 mars 1771," in *Recueil des réclamations*, II, 224.
10. [Augeard], *Correspondance secrète*, 61.

These significations of the word *liberté* fall within the general sense of what Isaiah Berlin has called "positive liberty."[11] The liberty of the king, the liberty of the church, the liberty of the parlements, and the liberty of the nation, all meant unrestricted exercise of political power. But, as we have seen, the Patriotes never abandoned the concept of a dualistic monarchical constitution and they therefore could not envisage simply a head-on collision of the absolute positive liberties of the throne and the nation or the total triumph of the positive liberty of either. Obviously in a pluralistic system any positive liberty had to be less than perfect. Consequently, under the influence of Montesquieu and the British example, they sought the limitation of the positive liberty of the king by the establishment of the "negative liberty" (again Berlin's phrase) of citizens, that is, constitutional protections against the exercise of power, specifically against the unjust and arbitrary exercise of royal power—for instance by guaranties against imprisonment without trial and illegal confiscation of property.

It was negative liberty that Montesquieu was describing when he wrote, "In a state, that is, in a society under law, liberty can consist only in being able to do what one should will to do, and in not being forced to do what one should not will. . . . Liberty is the right to do all that the laws permit." His second definition described negative liberty in its psychological effects: "Political liberty [liberty in a state] is that tranquillity of mind which is produced by the opinion that each man has of his own security. . . . It consists in security, or at least in the conviction one has of one's security."[12] Both these definitions were quoted and paraphrased literally hundreds of times by Patriote writers.

Negative liberty was thus simply the denial of the exercise of absolute power—of *despotisme*, under which, as Morizot wrote, by the very nature of this form of government the people are in effect serfs or slaves, their lives at the disposition of the ruler, with no right to property and under no law except the prince's will.[13] "If arbitrary power can commit offenses,

11. Isaiah Berlin, *Two Concepts of Liberty: An Inaugural Lecture Delivered Before the University of Oxford on 31 October, 1958* (Oxford, 1958).

12. Montesquieu, *De l'esprit des lois*, Book XI, Chaps. 2 and 3; Book XI, Chap. 6; Book XII, Chap. 2.

13. [Morizot], *Le Sacre royal*.

abolish offices, and confiscate property," the Parlement of Normandy said, "then this is the end of the liberty of the people."[14] The *Réflexions succinctes*, quoting Bossuet, summed up the idea: "Government is established to free all men from all oppression and violence. This is what constitutes a state of perfect liberty."[15]

Patriote championship of the principle of negative liberty was immediately occasioned by the edict of December 1770, by the dismissal and exile of the Paris magistrates, and by the fear of new taxes which the courts could no longer thwart, all of which were denounced as despotic infringements on property and freedom of person. Yet however narrow the initial provocation, the Patriotes, seeking broad public support, deliberately widened the debate to embrace the negative liberties of all classes. Typically the Parlement of Brittany declared that if the king had the right to confiscate for his own advantage any office he chose to declare vacant, then "nothing will prevent the same right from being exercised against the properties of all his subjects, and henceforth no property will be safe from the hand of arbitrary power."[16]

The negative liberty of the individual, like the positive liberties of the parlements and the nation, was often asserted on traditionalistic and historical grounds, usually in claims that the French since the Frankish kingdom had always been "hommes libres." The essential justification, however, was the Lockean doctrine of natural rights. "Natural liberty," Mey wrote, "is the right which nature has given all men to dispose of their persons and property in whatever way they judge most conducive to their happiness." Since all men were born equal, no one had a natural right to command another, and hence all men were born free. From this axiom followed the usual corollaries: "The right to have sole power over oneself and one's actions, or in other words the right to preserve one's liberty, entails the duty of every man to respect the liberty of his fellows, and consequently the right of anyone who suffers injury . . . to defend his liberty."[17] Target argued that all the various individual rights comprised by

14. Parlement de Normandie, "Lettre du parlement de Normandie au Roi, du premier février 1771," in *Second recueil de divers arrêtés et lettres au Roi*, 22.

15. *Réflexions succinctes sur ce qui s'est passé au parlement de Paris depuis le mois de décembre 1770* (N.p., n.d.), 3.

16. Parlement de Bretagne, "Remontrances du parlement de Rennes, du 23 janvier 1771," in *Recueil des réclamations*, II, 281.

17. [Mey *et al.*], *Maximes* (2nd ed.), I, 212, II, 28.

the term *liberty*, such as the right to fair trial, were likewise self-evident. [18] Mariveaux's ideas were obviously directly derived from Rousseau's *Contrat social*. "Man is born free," he wrote. "No man has natural authority over his fellows. Force creates no right. . . . To renounce one's liberty is to renounce one's quality as a man, the rights of humanity, and even one's duties." Liberty is therefore inalienable. "To say that a man gives himself freely is an absurd and inconceivable statement. Such an act is illegitimate and null by the simple fact that anyone committing such an act would not be in his right mind. To suppose the same act by a whole people is to suppose a nation of madmen." Consequently the only legitimate society is that created by the social contract, by which "a man can be both free and subject to the law, since the laws are no more than the expression of our wills." [19]

This doctrine of natural liberty and natural rights was epitomized in the Patriote slogan *Vie, Liberté et Propriété*, which was repeated literally hundreds of times, but with interesting and significant variations. One was the addition or substitution of the words *honneur* or *état*, by which was meant the enjoyment of the various special rights proper to an individual's social, professional, or political position. Also important as an echo of Montesquieu was the use of the word *sûreté* either alone or with a qualifier, as in the phrases "sûreté de vie," "sûreté des personnes," "sûreté de la liberté," "sûreté des biens," and "sûreté d'honneur." Fairly frequently the terms *fortune* or *biens* were used in place of *propriété*. These variations are significant, for they indicate that the slogan was not a cliché and that these writers, working more or less independently and severally thinking along similar but not identical lines, were all attempting to formulate in brief and effective form what they believed to be the basic natural rights of man.

Analysis of the elements of the slogan reveals the anatomy of Patriote libertarianism. Though *propriété* was sometimes a synonym for *biens* or *fortune* (money, tangible possessions, or real property), it was generally used (as was the English equivalent *property* by Locke) in its broader original sense to denote whatever a person might legitimately claim for his exclusive enjoyment or possession—his life, his goods, his person, or his so-

18. [Target], *Lettres d'un homme à un autre homme sur les affaires du temps*, 17.
19. [Mariveaux], *L'Ami des loix*, 6, 23–24, 26.

cial, professional, or political and civil privileges. Thus we find in general currency the phrases "propriété des personnes" in distinction from "propriété des biens," and also "propriété des offices," "propriété d'état [status]," and even "propriété universelle." The Parlement of Besançon gave a good definition: "Property . . . includes all that is necessarily dear and precious to man: his customs, his liberty, his life, and his possessions."[20]

On the other hand, *liberté* (the "negative" liberty of individuals) had equally broad denotations comprising the right and power to enjoy in security and without restriction one's life, person, profession, social privileges, and goods—in short, one's *propriété*. Thus it is correct that in the eighteenth-century lexicon liberty meant the right to property, but it must be understood that property did not mean only tangible possessions such as money, invested capital, or land. Liberty was simply the power to enjoy whatever one had the right to enjoy, and property was all the things one should have the right to enjoy. Each term defined the other.

It should be noted that this concept of liberty which appears in Patriote writings is broader than Montesquieu's. Montesquieu had defined liberty as the unrestricted power to *act* ethically ("pouvoir faire ce que l'on doit vouloir"), but the Patriote definition was the unrestricted power to *possess* property (in the broad sense of all ethically proper attributes of the person), plus the power to *enjoy actively* these rightful attributes.

Thus the problem is to identify these rightful attributes. Here we find a curious tactic in Patriote thought. To the eighteenth-century mind there was no traditional or logical reason that every right had to be universal; rights had always been attached to all sorts of special status or office. There were the rights and immunities of the clergy, the rights and immunities of the judiciary, and the rights and immunities of the nobility. All these were forms of negative liberty. Yet under natural law all these rights were precarious and contingent, for no man could rationally claim the inherent (that is, natural) right to be a cleric or a judge or a noble. He could, however, base his right to the enjoyment of the prerequisites of any special status on the universal natural right of property. Therefore the Patriotes, in order to gain their immediate objective of buttressing special private or group rights found it most expedient to concentrate on defend-

---

20. Parlement de Besançon, "Remontrances du parlement de Besançon, 11 mars 1771," in *Recueil des réclamations*, II, 384.

ing universal rights enjoyed by all. In so doing, they perforce democratized their political philosophy.

The first of these universal attributes was the right to property in the restricted sense of tangible possessions—money, goods, land, or invested capital. This was asserted to be a fundamental law of the French constitution.[21] Yet it was also justified as a pre-political and pre-social natural right. It formed, Mey said, "an essential and imprescriptible attribute of the subject. . . . When the people joined together to create a state and when they chose a king, they were free and were the proprietors of their lives and possessions."[22] The Parlement of Besançon declared, "The land, which was common to all in the beginning, was later divided, and . . . this division compensated each proprietor for the right which he previously held to the whole. Thus ownership of property is derived . . . from nature and gives to men an inalienable title founded on the human condition and on the necessity to provide for one's subsistence." Saige and Aubusson took similar positions, adopting Locke's labor theory of the origin of the right of property.[23]

The right to life was less stressed, for Maupeou was not being accused of extrajudicial executions. Nevertheless it was obviously a fundamental natural right. "The primary effect of the liberty of the citizen," Mey said, "is that he is sure of his existence, that he peacefully enjoys the days accorded to him by Providence, and that his life is not the sport of violence and caprice."[24] And Saige wrote: "The preservation of the individual being the principal purpose of the social institution, and liberty itself, both natural and civil, being only a means to provide for this preservation, any attempt against the life of a citizen by a magistrate, except in the case when the laws have pronounced the penalty of capital punishment for some offense . . . [is] a violent infraction of the original contract . . . [and] an atrocious crime."[25]

21. *Protestations des Princes du Sang*, 1; Parlement de Normandie, "Lettre du parlement de Normandie au Roi. Du 26 février 1771," in *Recueil des réclamations*, II, 213.

22. [Mey *et al.*], *Maximes* (2nd ed.), I, 39, 70.

23. Parlement de Besançon, "Remontrances du parlement de Besançon, 11 mars 1771," in *Recueil des réclamations*, II, 385; [Saige], *Catéchisme du citoyen*, 60; [Aubusson], *Profession de foi politique, passim*.

24. [Mey *et al.*], *Maximes* (2nd ed.), I, 171.

25. [Saige], *Catéchisme du citoyen*, 58.

Of far greater immediate concern was the right of freedom of person, which indeed was repeatedly being violated by forced exiles without judicial hearing and imprisonments under *lettres de cachet* without due process of law and fair trial. These penalties the Patriotes condemned as violations both of the fundamental laws of the realm and of the natural laws of reason and humanity. Target said that all citizens had the self-evident rights to be protected from arbitrary imprisonment, to be allowed to defend themselves within twenty-four hours of their arrest, and to be judged by their natural judges. "No member of society," Saige wrote, "can be deprived of . . . the protection of the laws of his country . . . except by the law when he has been guilty of some offense against a citizen or against all the citizens as a body."[26]

The Patriotes had plenty of occasions for accusing Maupeou and the king of violating this fundamental right—the detention and exile without trial of the La Chalotais, which the Parlement of Brittany vigorously protested as a violation of "the right of every citizen to be judged by his natural judges"; the exile without trial of the magistrates of the Paris Parlement; and the many other imprisonments and forced exiles under *lettres de cachet* for political crimes and even for the private convenience of influential persons.[27] The *Journal historique*, for instance, reported that Goëzman, Beaumarchais' enemy, and another conseiller of Maupeou's Parlement while walking in the Tuilleries overheard one Blanchard, a *procureur* of the old Parlement, make some uncomplimentary remarks about his successors, so they reported the conversation to the police and obtained a *lettre de cachet* ordering Blanchard's exile. Another alleged case was that of the Dame Mallard, a former nurse of the Dauphin, who was imprisoned by a *lettre de cachet* on false accusations made by relatives who were trying to get possession of her fortune.[28] Mey, Augeard, and even the cautious Miromesnil joined the general Patriote protestation against such vi-

26. [Target], *Lettres d'un homme à un autre homme sur les affaires du temps*, 17; [Saige], *Catéchisme du citoyen*, 58.

27. Parlement de Bretagne, "Lettre du parlement de Bretagne au Roi du 25 mars 1771," in *Recueil des réclamations*, II, 299; "Requête d'une partie de la noblesse de Normandie au Roi" (October, 1772), *ibid.*, II, 262.

28. *Journal historique* (London, 1774–76), July 26, 1772 (III, 219); August 18, 1773 (IV, 291–92).

olations of personal liberty.[29] No one, however, was more eloquent than Malesherbes, who was the author of the Cour des Aides' *Remontrances au sujet des vexations injustes contre le sieur Guillaume Monnerat*:

> Formerly [*lettres de cachet*] were reserved for state business, and under these circumstances, Sire, justice was obliged to respect the confidentiality of your administration. Next they were issued on a few occasions when they seemed justified, as when the Sovereign was touched by the tears of a family who feared disgrace. Today they are considered necessary whenever a commoner has failed to show proper respect for a person of standing, as though the powerful did not already have sufficient advantages.
>
> They have become the normal punishment for indiscreet talk, without any more proof than the accusation of some informer, evidence which is always unreliable since an informer is always a suspect witness. . . . It is notorious that they are granted in any case involving the interests of any private person with a modicum of influence, even though his interests may in no way concern either Your Majesty personally or the public welfare. The practice has become so prevalent that any man of any standing at all would think it beneath his dignity to seek reparation for an injury through the regular channels of justice.
>
> These orders signed by Your Majesty are often filled in with the names of obscure persons of whom Your Majesty could not under any circumstances have knowledge. They are at the disposal of your ministers, and therefore at the disposal of your ministers' clerks, by reason of the great number that are issued. They are entrusted to the administrators of the capital and of the provinces, who may issue them merely on the recommendations of their subdelegates or other subordinate officials. There is no doubt that they find their way into many other hands, since we have seen in this case that they are freely given at the request of a mere Farmer General. Indeed, we can say that they are often issued at the request of the employees of the tax farmers, for only the petty clerks can discover and identify a person accused of fraud.
>
> The result of all this, Sire, is that no citizen in your realm can be

29. [Mey *et al.*], *Maximes* (2nd ed.), I, 162; [Augeard], *Correspondance secrète*, II, 143; Miromesnil, "Lettres sur l'état de la magistrature," 123.

sure that his liberty will not be sacrificed to the vengeance of someone. For no one is big enough to be safe from the enmity of a minister, and no one is small enough not to be the object of the spite of some tax clerk.[30]

Negative liberty for all citizens was a principle susceptible to extension to a large number of specific rights—freedom of action, freedom of movement, freedom of profession, and freedom of domicile. Mey, as we have seen, regarded this broad concept of individual liberty as more important than the specific right to the free enjoyment of tangible property. "One is rightly more jealous," he wrote, "of one's freedom of action, of one's freedom to govern one's own conduct and one's own destiny, of one's protection against restrictions and constraints on one's way of life, except insofar as public order may require or the law may rule. . . . Liberty gives to the citizen free choice of his domicile, of his friends, of his daily occupations, etc. . . . These are possessions . . . derived from natural law and . . . they form the happiness of men in this world."[31] Saige stressed the right of every man either to dwell on his native soil or to travel as he willed, and Target added the freedom to travel outside the state.[32] The Parlement of Brittany addressed to the king a forceful letter on the sanctity of the citizen's home and immunity from illegal search, occasioned by the king's officers' forcible entry into the dwelling of a *substitut du procureur général* of Rennes.[33]

An inevitable conclusion from this broad interpretation of negative liberty was that the citizen's conscience is also part of his "property," that he rightfully possesses freedom to act in accordance with his conscience both as a natural right and also as a necessary means to fulfill his obligations to God, and that these obligations override his duty to any secular authority. This principle, moreover, was consonant with the Jansenistic belief in the sanctity of the individual conscience. The author of the *Lettre*

30. Cour des Aides de Paris, "Remontrances au sujet des vexations injustes exercées contre le sieur Guillaume Monnerat," in Cour des Aides de Paris, *Mémoires pour servir à l'histoire du droit public*, 512. Malesherbes repeated his protests in Cour des Aides de Paris, "Remontrances de la Cour des Aides relatives aux impôts, 6 mai 1775," *ibid.*, 646–47.

31. [Mey *et al.*], *Maximes* (2nd ed.), I, 161.

32. [Saige], *Catéchisme du citoyen*, 58; [Target], *Lettre d'un homme à un autre homme sur l'extinction de l'ancien parlement*, 2.

33. *Journal historique* (London, 1774–76), June 9, 1771 (I, 357–58).

d'un ancien magistrat wrote, we recall, "The king has no subjects who have not the right to a conscience, and who must not be inflexibly resolved to obey God rather than men."[34] The parlements before 1771 certainly had not been known as defenders of freedom of thought, speech, press, or religion, but the tactical decision of the Patriotes to support the cause of the magistrates on broad ethical grounds led to statements far more libertarian than the past record of the courts. "Man," an anonymous pamphleteer wrote, "as a being endowed with reason, cannot deny his own nature and renounce the use of this reason. . . . When reason indicates to him the true and the good, no power exists which has the right to make him say the contrary; consequently no power has the right to make him act against the dictates of his conscience."[35] "The slave does not reason," Target wrote. "The free man thinks, and thought is always fatal to despotism."[36] The Cour des Comptes, Aides, et Finances of Normandy told the king, "Happy is the empire in which fear does not stifle men's talents, and in which terror does not enchain the faculties of the soul."[37]

The principles of freedom of conscience and of freedom of expression were challenged and defended in a multitude of incidents. One M. Lambert, a Jansenist who had resigned in protest from the Grand Conseil, had the courage to defy a *lettre de cachet* ordering him to resume his duties by saying, "His Majesty . . . could not be the master of his honor and his conscience."[38] The arrests of the Jansenistic faculty of the College of Auxerre for making anti-government statements was denounced as a violation of what today would be called academic freedom.[39] A journalist connected with the *Gazette de France* who had the temerity to speak against the chancellor in private conversations was condemned to the Bastille.[40] And as we have seen, the government made vigorous efforts to suppress the printing and distribution of Patriote writings and imposed heavy sentences on the *colporteurs* it succeeded in arresting.

34. *Lettre d'un ancien magistrat à un duc et pair*, 53.
35. "Lettre de M. le comte de ***," in *Les Efforts de la libertè*, VI, 331.
36. [Target], *Lettres d'un homme à un autre homme sur les affaires du temps*, 56.
37. Cour des Comptes, Aides et Finances de Normandie, "Remontrances de la Cour des Comptes, Aides et Finances de Normandie, 18 avril 1771," in *Recueil des rèclamations*, II, 225.
38. *Journal historique* (London, 1774–76), April 21, 1771 (I, 266).
39. *Ibid.*, November 16, 1773, October 10, 1774 (V, 59–61, VI, 236–37).
40. *Ibid.*, August 19, 1771 (II, 92–93).

The Parlement of Paris was one of the official censoring bodies in the French government and it had exercised its powers vigorously if not always consistently. But now its supporters were those whose ox was being gored. Moreover, it must be remembered that there were among the Patriotes men who had always had liberal views on freedom of the press. Malesherbes, the most enlightened and tolerant directeur de la librairie of the Ancien Régime, had in 1758 adhered to his libertarian principles to the extent of rejecting D'Alembert's demands that he suppress the attacks being made on the Philosophes by the Jesuit *Journal de Trevoux* and by the anti-Philosophes Fréron, Moreau, and Palisot. He wrote the angry Encyclopedist:

> I am very sorry about the distress which the criticisms of Fréron and the others have caused you. It would certainly be my wish that nothing might detract from the satisfaction which your success has won for you and that you might enjoy in peace your high reputation, the only reward befitting your talents. I regret even more that some lines imprudently scattered here and there in the work of which you have been one of the editors [the *Encyclopédie*] have given rise to accusations which must have unpleasant consequences. But I draw a sharp distinction between what displeases me, or even what I disapprove as a private individual, and what I must prevent as a public official.
>
> My principles are that in general literary criticism is permissible, and that all criticism which is directed solely at the book criticized and in which the author is judged only on his work is literary criticism.

If a work were libelous, Malesherbes continued, recourse to the courts was always possible. But it was not the function of a censor to prevent such libels, he said, for to attempt to do so would stifle all criticism.[41]

Malesherbes in 1758 was defending freedom of the press only for literary criticism, and he acknowledged his official duty to censor political criticism of the government and attacks on the Catholic Church. By 1771, however, some of his fellow Patriotes wished to liberate political criticism as well. Aubusson described freedom of the press as a right necessary to implement the principles of natural law. He argued that all men had the

41. André Morellet, *Mémoires inédites . . . sur le dix-huitième siècle et sur la Révolution* (Paris, 1821), I, 49–50.

need to understand the natural laws on which their rights were based. Therefore it was the prince's duty to permit the free publication of "this useful knowledge" and to allow "freedom of the press" to all works not offensive to religion, morals, or the reputation of a citizen. This liberty, he said, was "a fundamental law of all just governments," and it was "in truth a crime of *lèse humanité*" to "try to arrest the progress of the Enlightenment. . . . Such an infringement on legitimate freedom to think and write always and inevitably leads to arbitrary despotism and to anarchy."[42]

Pidanzat de Mairobert did more than catalog in his newsletters all the restrictions the government was imposing on the press; he also clearly made his own views known. For instance in September 1771 he included in the *Journal historique* the text of "Les Huit péchés capitaux," which extolled "freedom of the press" as "that vigilant guardian of civil liberty and of property which brings happiness to the peoples of England, Holland, Switzerland, and Germany."[43] The following month he wrote, "The publication of the uncompromising condemnation of the two discourses crowned by the French Academy [Laharpe's and Maury's eulogies of Fénelon] . . . contributes considerably to confirm the belief that the policy of the government is to extend its despotism even over our minds."[44] And when in 1774 the ministry decided to require the submission of new works to the censor both before and after publication, he charged that the new regulation had the secret purpose of "destroying literature and of gradually bringing back the age of ignorance, in accord with the principles of despotism."[45]

The strongest statements came of course from the radical Patriotes. Saige wrote, "We must consider as an essential part of the liberty of the citizen his freedom to reason either in writing or verbally about public affairs and the conduct of the administration." To deprive a citizen of this right, he said, was an act of despotism. Only the concentration of the attention of all men on the public welfare could create the "patriotism . . . and social enlightenment necessary to guide the understanding of the leg-

42. [Aubusson], *Profession de foi politique*, 18–19.

43. "Les Huit péchés capitaux," in *Journal historique* (London, 1774–76), September 16, 1771 (II, 144).

44. *Journal historique* (London, 1774–76), October 7, 1771 (II, 181).

45. *Ibid.*, April 3, 1774 (V, 261).

islative body. Therefore to be able to communicate to one's nation the ideas
that one believes advantageous to her, and to be able to warn her of the
dangers she faces and enlighten her on the defects of her constitution constitute both a right and a duty inherent in every individual in the state."[46]

Religious freedom is the last liberty one would expect the parlements
or their supporters to advocate, for the La Barre and Calas cases were still
fresh in the public mind. Certainly no parlement supported the principle
in any offical paper, and it is significant that Aubusson carefully excluded
"works offensive to religion" from protection of freedom of the press. Yet
by the 1770s the spirit of irreligion was prevalent among all literate
Frenchmen, from valets to nobles and even the clergy, and the Protestants
in many parts of France were enjoying de facto toleration. This new attitude was found among Patriotes as well as among others. So while religious freedom certainly was not a recognized tenet of the parliamentary
ideology, it is nevertheless true that Patriotes could support religious liberty without feeling it was inconsistent with support of the parlements.
Pidanzat de Mairobert was notable for his advocacy of toleration; he compared the exile of the magistrates to "Saint Bartholomew's Day and the
expulsion of the Protestants." He also published a notice of a "Mémoire
présenté au Roi par les Protestants de Guyenne le 3 du mois dernier [Feb-
ruary 1775], pour supplier S. M. de leur accorder la liberté de conscience." "This," he commented, "is the title of a publication in which
these unhappy subjects employ every means humanity can suggest to touch
our august monarch and to obtain this grace which Nature solicits and
which wise statemanship suggests as the means to keep in the realm these
loyal subjects and bring back to France those whom the error of former
times so cruelly proscribed."[47] Similarly Blonde condemned Louis XIV's
"cruel and unjust persecution of the Protestants." Target cited as a prime
example of *despotisme* the exile of 500,000 Huguenots "driven from France
by fanaticism" and the persecution of "two million more . . . subjected
to insults and harassment by an unrestrained soldiery."[48]

Achievement of these various kinds of negative liberty was not sup-

46. [Saige], *Catéchisme du citoyen*, 59–60.
47. *Journal historique* (London, 1774–76), October 28, 1771 (II, 205–206); March 8,
1775 (VII, 162).
48. [Blonde], *Le Parlement justifié par l'Impératrice de Russie*, 34; [Target], *Lettre d'un
homme à un autre homme sur l'extinction de l'ancien parlement*, 2.

posed to require equality of wealth, equality of social status, or equality of political power. No Patriote—not even the radical Saige—made such an assumption. One could persuasively argue, as Voltaire did, that these freedoms could be better assured by an enlightened despot than by unruly and irresponsible aristocratic corporations, just as one could conversely and with equal plausibility argue that liberty would be better assured by patriotic aristocratic courts than by arbitrary despotism. Neither argument required the condition of equality.

Yet the concept of negative liberty did inescapably point to political equality. The doctrine of natural rights was juridically egalitarian, both because these rights by definition pertained to all men equally, and because their protection required equality before the law. Moreover, to advocate simultaneously "national" positive liberty and the negative liberty of natural rights inevitably suggested an interdependence between the two. Blonde made this explicit when he wrote, "The power [of the parlements] to refuse registration of a law contrary to the maintenance of these various rights [of life, liberty, and property] is the only way to preserve them."[49] This was to say that positive liberty was the essential means of safeguarding negative liberties.

The obvious next logical step was to reason that equality of rights required equality of positive liberty, that is, universal representation in a national legislature or the States General, which because it would speak for all would assure the rights of all. The anti-aristocratic, or at least anti-feudal, element in this idea may have been partly suggested by the thesis of William Robertson's *History of the Reign of the Emperor Charles V* (translated in 1771) that the admission of free cities into the various European national legislatures had "tempered the rigor of aristocratic oppression by an admixture of popular liberty."[50] In the same year Brancas described the original French constitution as one by which the people as a whole had ruled through general national assemblies and under which they had enjoyed political liberty until with the rise of feudalism the nobles usurped the power of the nation and reduced "a free people to veritable servitude."[51] The democratic implications of such historical interpretations

---

49. [Blonde], *Le Parlement justifié par l'Impératrice de Russie*, 15.
50. Robertson, *L'Histoire du règne de l'Empereur Charles-Quint*, I, 79.
51. [Brancas], *Tableau de la constitution françoise*, 20.

were clear, and Saige, influenced by Rousseau, made them explicit when he stated that the essential condition of (negative) liberty was that the "nation," not the prince, hold the legislative power. "Civil liberty," he said, is "the personal independence of each of the members of the social body from any other power than the legislative power." As long as the citizen is subject only to the legislative power residing in the "political body," Saige continued, "his person will enjoy the most perfect security that can be morally imagined," for since the "political body" cannot seek its own harm, it must seek its own good. Therefore "civil liberty, and consequently personal security, can exist only in states in which the legislative power resides in the very body of the citizens."[52]

This democratic conclusion was of course antithetical to the defense of aristocratic privilege, the parlements' initial political purpose. It is therefore quite understandable that the Paris Parlement in 1775 ordered Saige's book lacerated and burned after he had proudly sent a copy to every magistrate. Nevertheless, democracy was logically implicit in the theses the Patriotes developed to defend the parlements, and particularly in their call for the reestablishment of the States General.

The distance between the initial practical purposes of the parlements in resisting the edict of December 1770 and the principles with which their apologists concluded is one reason that it is impossible to categorize simply and neatly the parlements and their supporters under general rubrics supplied by nineteenth- or twentieth-century politics. They were Burkean conservatives in that they believed that French liberty could be assured only by the preservation of the traditional national constitution; for this reason they opposed the revolution Maupeou had engineered. The magistrates and the many lawyers among their active supporters were by profession conservative in their ingrained respect for precedent and tradition and their instinctive distrust of innovation. The Patriotes were conservative in their concept of an unalterable constitution without provision for evolution or amendment, in their opposition to the historic trend toward governmental and administrative centralization, in their defense of established aristocratic privileges and immunities, and in their efforts to consolidate the gains the nobility had made since the Regency. They were unconstructively conservative in raising such a din of protests against

52. [Saige], *Catéchisme du citoyen*, 54–55.

new taxes, increases in rates, cancellations of exemptions, stricter collections, the extensions of the first and second *vingtièmes*, and revisions of the rolls on which these taxes were based—all the while refusing to make any useful suggestions for the resolution of the government's financial crisis other than the reduction of the extravagance at Versailles and the dismissal of Maupeou and Terray.[53] They even may be called conservative for their general refusal to consider a truly democratic constitution, though it is difficult to see how in this respect they were more conservative than any other group. On the other hand, they were fighting reactionism when they opposed Maupeou's attempt to revive the obsolete absolutism of Louis XIV. They were precursors of the liberalism of Tocqueville, Malesherbes' great-grandson, in their opposition to autocratic administrative centralization.[54] And they were constitutional "liberals" in their demands for a limited monarchy based on the principles of the sovereignty of the nation and the contract, and in their championship of negative liberty and a bill of rights. Yet there was certainly nothing socialistically "liberal" in their real indifference—despite their professed commiseration with the poor—to the manifold and pressing social problems, particularly that of feudal and seignorial rights.

The question of whether the Patriotes were revolutionary is, however, valid. Were the parlements indeed, as the Count de Ségur later said, "giving the signal for revolution"?[55] Maupeou's coup was called "la révolution Maupeou." Was there an attempt to counter with a "révolution parlementaire" or a "révolution patriotique"?

53. Jean Baptiste Jacques Élie de Beaumont's "Lettre sur l'état du crédit du gouvernement en France, en date du 20 juin 1771," in *Les Efforts de la liberté*, IV, 13–94, was an intelligent study of the problem but the only solution it suggested was the dismissal of Maupeou. Miromesnil in his "Lettres sur l'état de la magistrature," 1–5, 26, recognized that the government's financial problems were deep-rooted and could not be blamed entirely on Maupeou and Terray, and Mey (*Maximes* [2nd ed.], I, 54) laid down some sound financial principles, but neither made a constructive proposal. Malesherbes seems to have been alone in suggesting specific reforms (abolition of the *corvée*, public inspection of the rolls of the *vingtième*, etc.) but not until 1775 in the *Remontrances relatives aux impôts*, issued by the Cour des Aides of Paris. (See Cour des Aides de Paris, *Mémoires pour servir à l'histoire du droit public*, 628–96.) Of course the parlements themselves had made various fiscal proposals.

54. See J. P. Mayer, "Avant propos," in Alexis de Tocqueville, *De la démocratie en Amérique: Les Grands thèmes* (Paris, 1968), 17.

55. Ségur, *Mémoires*, I, 24.

In answering this question we must bear in mind that to the pre-1789 European mind (especially before 1776) the word *révolution* did not yet have the denotations and connotations it later acquired. Locke's theories of natural rights and the contract had intended to justify the British revolution of 1688, and the Patriotes' adaptations of this political philosophy may thus be said to have revolutionary roots. It is true that the direct influence of Locke was limited, yet there were obvious parallels with Lockean revolutionism. The *Journal historique*, for instance, defined the contract as "a reciprocal act by which a people says to a man: 'You will be king on such and such conditions, and we shall be loyal to you. If you violate these conditions, we the people will be your judge.'"[56] But how was this judgment to be enforced? The *Manifeste aux Bretons* answered, "The law and the precedents of society agree with natural law in authorizing legal resistance, which only the guilty partisans of tyranny could have reason to call rebellion."[57] But then what was "legal resistance"? The majority of the Patriotes seem to have defined it as "passive resistance," which Blonde said "must always be . . . limited to the non-execution of orders and other arbitrary demands incompatible with the consciences and legitimate rights of subjects." Such resistance, it was claimed, was not rebellion but devotion to the true interests of the crown and hence "actually an act of obedience."[58]

Yet the right to violent resistance was occasionally defended; some Patriote writings certainly sounded like calls to armed revolt. The *Journal historique* cited Delolme's *Constitution de l'Angleterre*, which said that the Revolution of 1688 had "confirmed beyond a doubt . . . the doctrine of resistance, the final resource of an oppressed people."[59] Mey conceded that when the conditions of the contract had been violated the subject was freed from the obligation of obedience, and active resistance was justified. Clément de Boissy wrote, "All men tremble before despots; no man loves them. . . . When the people think they are the stronger, they revolt; if not, they grumble and curse the tyrant."[60] The highly inflammatory *Le*

56. *Journal historique* (London, 1774–76), July 6, 1771 (II, 21).
57. *Manifeste aux Bretons*, 20.
58. [Blonde], *Le Parlement justifié par l'Impératrice de Russie*, 3. See also [Morizot], *Inauguration de Pharamond*, 109; *Les Derniers soupirs*, 38.
59. *Journal historique* (London, 1774–76), November 11, 1771 (II, 238–39).
60. [Mey *et al.*], *Maximes* (2nd ed.), II, 227; [Clément de Boissy], *Le Maire du palais*, 12.

Propos indiscret, written in 1772 but not printed until 1776, urged active resistance, "for it is certain that twenty million men were not created for one man. They are stronger than he."[61] Pidanzat de Mairobert quoted Georg von Holland's *Réflexions philosophiques*: "A people who attempt to overthrow a despot risk nothing, for slavery is the worst of all evils. Not only do a people have the right to refuse to accept such a form of government; they have an equal right to destroy it."[62] And the *Manifeste aux Normands* declared, "If in a free nation there arises a despot . . . accuse not the laws. Accuse the cowardice of those who did not resist tyranny. Accuse those who accepted despotism, knowing that nowhere on earth is a single man stronger than a number of men who have the will to break their chains and be free. . . . Slaves are sometimes as guilty as tyrants, and . . . it is difficult to tell whether liberty suffers more from those who violate her or from those who will not defend her."[63]

This was certainly the rhetoric of revolution, but the evidence of events seems to prove that it was in fact no more than rhetoric. After the scuffles in the Palais de Justice during the first days, all active resistance ceased. There is absolutely no indication of any concerted plans for armed revolt. Maupeou successfully called the parlements' bluff, and the Patriotes' only option was to maintain as best they could the support of public opinion and of their powerful adherents, particularly the Princes of the Blood, and to wait for an opportunity to regain the initiative by political means, as they finally did after the death of Louis XV. The Patriote counterrevolution of 1774, like the Maupeou revolution of 1770–1771, was a revolution only in the French pre-1789 sense—a political coup, a palace revolution.

Yet the Count de Ségur, writing retrospectively after 1789, was in a sense correct in saying that the parlements "gave the signal for revolution"—revolution in the modern sense. They did not achieve a revolution themselves, nor were they able to offer to France an alternative constitution that had any chance of working in the modern world that was taking shape. Yet they did at least convince the French that the theocratic ab-

61. "Le Propos indiscret," in *Journal historique* (new ed.; London, 1776), III, 308–309.
62. *Journal historique* (London, 1774–76), January 25, 1773 (IV, 42).
63. *Manifeste aux Normands*, 24.

solutism of Louis XIV was an absurd anachronism in the 1770s and that the nation must be granted greater positive liberty through some sort of national legislature and assured negative liberty by a constitutional bill of rights. In so doing they decreed their own doom. The parlements vanished forever in the holocaust of 1789, and Malesherbes, the greatest of the Patriotes, died under the guillotine after courageously and vainly defending Louis XVI before the Convention.

It seems futile to attempt to second-guess history by speculating on the consequences of what would have happened if Louis XVI had not made the "mistake" of reestablishing the parlements. Maupeou's coup in 1770 was the obvious—and apparently in hindsight, the only—way to assure the immediate continuation of the existing monarchy, to which the alternative would not have been revolution but chaos. And Louis XVI's dismissal of Maupeou in 1774 appears in hindsight the inevitable liquidation of an exhausted expedient. The succession of these two events revealed the inadequacy of both the parliamentary thesis and the royalist antithesis, and by the dialectic of history produced a synthesis of the two, a new thesis which also was inevitable, because it happened.

PART II

The Absolutists

FOUR

The Royalists

THE FRENCH eighteenth-century theory of absolutism may be simply stated as the antithesis of the parliamentary thesis that national political power should be exercised by corporations such as the parlements or the States General. In contradiction, it posited that all governmental authority was and should be vested absolutely in a single will, embodied in a hereditary prince. The principle had been effectively realized by Louis XIV and was being demonstrated with equal effectiveness by Frederick of Prussia and Catherine of Russia, despite these two monarchs' Philosophic dialogues. It was expounded in the early 1770s by Maupeou himself, by his perceptive secretary Charles François Lebrun, by the gifted publicist Jacob Nicolas Moreau, best known for his famous satire against the Philosophes, the *Mémoire pour servir à l'histoire des Cacouacs*, and by lesser propagandists. Outside the government the general theory was variously modified, notably in the writings of Simon Linguet and Voltaire.

The *thèse royale*, that is, the theory of absolutism as it appeared in the writings of spokesmen for the regime—probably over one hundred titles in all—had original and prophetic features as a working concept of government, but it was remarkably thin as a political philosophy. In both these respects it reflected the character of Maupeou, who was an intelligent, ambitious, hard-working, and eminently practical politician. "His life was completely devoted to his work," Lebrun later recalled, and he had no interest in literature or time for abstract philosophy. "It was by pure chance if he had any contact with a scholar or a Philosophe. I scarcely knew any myself except through their works. . . . Even vacations were devoted to work."[1]

One finds in only a handful of the royal apologists a few citations of earlier theorists of absolutism—a single reference to Hobbes, one to Du Bos, a couple to D'Argenson, and that is all.[2] In fact the royalists were more likely to quote the Patriotes' favorite authorities—Massillon, the *Iudicium Francorum*, Le Paige, and especially Montesquieu, who with only one exception was always cited with approbation.[3] Of contemporary authors only Mably, Rousseau, and Voltaire appear to have had some minor influence. Lebrun, who knew Mably personally, admired his *Phocion*, to which with Maupeou's approval he extended protection, and the abbé's *Histoire de France* was quoted on the danger to liberty and property from the union of judicial and legislative functions in a single body.[4] Rousseau's *Contrat social* was quoted on the need for the French to achieve an authentic national character.[5] Voltaire was himself publishing pamphlets in support of Maupeou but he was only occasionally cited by government apologists. His denunciations of the parlements' role in the Calas affair could be used effectively, as could his article "Tyrannie" in the *Questions sur l'Encyclopédie*, and his name could be thrown in the face of Philosophic supporters of the parlements, but he was also an embarrassment, for the

1. Lebrun, *Opinions*, 10.
2. On Hobbes, see [Charles François Lebrun], *Observations sur l'écrit intitulé: Protestations des Princes* (N.p., n.d. [1771]), 6–7. On Du Bos, see [Pierre Bouquet], *Lettres provinciales, ou Examen impartiale de l'origine, de la constitution, et des révolutions de la monarchie françoise, par un avocat de province à un avocat de Paris* (The Hague, 1772), 14. On D'Argenson, see "Réflexions d'un citoyen sur l'édit de décembre 1770," in *Le Code des François. Recueil de toutes les pièces intéressantes publiées en France, relativement aux troubles des parlements, avec des observations critiques et historiques, des pièces nouvelles et une table raisonnée* (Brussels, 1771), II, 272, 293, and *Nouvelles réflexions d'un citoyen sur l'édit de décembre 1770* (N.p., n.d. [1771]), 48.
3. On Massillon, see "Réflexions d'un citoyen," in *Le Code des François*, II, 267. On the *Iudicium Francorum*, see [Bouquet], *Lettres provinciales*, letter 8, and *Observations d'un ancien magistrat* (N.p., n.d. [1771]). On Le Paige, see [Bouquet], *Lettres provinciales*, 15, 122, and *passim*. For the negative criticism of Montesquieu, see *Lettre d'un officier du régiment de *** à Monsieur de ***, son frère, conseiller au parlement de **** (N.p., n.d.).
4. "Réflexions d'un citoyen," in *Le Code des François*, II, 265.
5. "Observations avec les réponses, sur l'écrit qui a pour titre: Réponse au citoyen qui a publié ses Réflexions," in *Le Code des François*, II, 407.

ministry had no wish to be tarred with the brush of Philosophic irreligion.[6]

Similarly the royalists showed little interest in political developments abroad. The Philosophes could be taunted with their friendships with Frederick, and the contemporary governments of Sweden, Poland, Geneva, and England could serve as examples of the dangers of republicanism, but the only significant attention to foreign politics was that which Lebrun gave to the British constitution, of which more will be said presently.[7] In short, the apologists of royalism were interested not in political theory or foreign models, but in political practice in France. Except for the luminaries Lebrun, Moreau, and Voltaire, royalist authors appear less inclined to theoretical political philosophy than the Patriote propagandists.

It was of course necessary to justify monarchical absolutism, but the several arguments used scarcely added up to a philosophy. The first was justification by tradition: "The authority of our kings is consecrated by the passage of time and by a prescription established by many centuries." An abundance of *arrêts*, edicts, and other documents were assembled to support this claim.[8] The second was the seventeenth-century theory of divine right, reasserted but not reexamined: The French monarchy was the rule "of one king alone, independent and absolute, who holds from God alone a power for which he is responsible to Him alone."[9] The third and most important argument was pragmatic, an adaptation of the principle of public utility; it simply asserted that it could be empirically demonstrated that the *salus populi* was best assured by royal absolutism. "If an entire people could be happy . . . it would be under the rule of *one* man

6. On the Calas affair, see *Lettre de M. C*** à M. de St ***, à Rouen. Servant de réponse à la Lettre du parlement de Normandie au Roy, en date du 8 février, sur l'état actuel du parlement de Paris* (N.p., n.d. [1771]), 35, and [Saint Pierre], *Discours d'un pair de France*. On Voltaire's article "Tyrannie," see "Observations avec les réponses, sur l'écrit qui a pour titre: Réponse au citoyen qui a publié ses Réflexions," in *Le Code des François*, II, 428. On Voltaire and the Philosophes, see *Avis aux dames*, 3.

7. On Frederick, see *Réflexions nationales*, 16. On foreign "republicanism," see *Dialogue entre un officier françois . . . et son neveu*, 41, and "Réflexions d'un citoyen," in *Le Code des François*, II, 293.

8. "Réflexions d'un citoyen," in *Le Code des François*, II, 293; *Monumens précieux de la sagesse et de la fermeté de nos rois, pour le maintien de leur autorité* (N.p., 1771).

9. *La Tête leur tourne* (N.p., n.d. [1771]), 14.

[italics *sic*], for petty passions have less hold on the soul of a sovereign king than on private individuals given power to govern. Under a king there is more uniformity, more coherence, and more continuity in the principles and policies of government." Lebrun put the idea more succinctly: "The public welfare is inseparable from the maintenance of authority."[10]

The only significant attempt to justify monarchical absolutism by natural law was that made by Moreau in a work written in 1764 but published in 1773. He started with the traditional assumption that the universe is governed by immutable physical and moral laws given by God for the governance of the material universe and human society. Moreau then posited that in order to assure a just moral order God had created two "authorities" or moral powers, the power of property and the power of government. "Legitimate government" protected liberty and property and regulated men's lives according to God's divine plan, conciliating differences, pacifying disturbances, protecting the unfortunate, and avenging the oppressed. By its nature such government required obedience from all, and "it is never possible to deny its legitimacy." Lastly, shifting to the argument from history, Moreau purported to prove that only absolute monarchism fitted these specifications of legitimate government. "It is by the laws of nature," he wrote, "that I shall prove that there is no government unless property and liberty are protected, and it is by history that I shall prove that property has been precarious whenever our kings have ceased to be powerful and absolute; . . . that those who under the feudal regime oppressed the people were the same tyrants who divided among themselves the debris of royal authority; and that the crown had to regain its rights for slavery to disappear."[11]

This argument, which two other writers touched on but failed to de-

10. *Réflexions nationales*, 21; [Lebrun], *Observations sur l'écrit intitulé: Protestations des Princes*, 24.
11. [Jacob Nicolas Moreau], *Leçons de morale, de politique et de droit public, puisées dans l'histoire de notre monarchie, ou Nouveau plan d'étude de l'histoire de France, rédigé par les ordres et d'après les vues de Monseigneur le Dauphin, pour l'instruction des princes ses enfants* (Versailles, 1773), 173–201. See also Moreau's "Des Différences de la monarchie et du despotisme, ou Lettre de M. M. [Moreau] à M. D. L. C. [de La Condamine]," written in 1773 and dated January 2, 1774, in his *Principes de morale, de politique et de droit public, puisés dans l'histoire de notre monarchie, ou Discours sur l'histoire de France, dédiés au Roi* (Paris, 1777), I, 1–109.

velop, is interesting, for it ascribes the origin of government to natural law itself rather than to the contract, as was usual in contemporary natural-law political theory.[12] But since Moreau justified the peculiar form of government under debate, monarchical absolutism, by the empirical evidence of its historical efficacy, he was really repeating the familiar public-utility argument behind a natural-law façade.

The thinness of these abstract philosophic arguments contrasts sharply with the solid logic of royalist reasoning on practical issues, particularly on the realities of political power. Louis' defenders maintained that a truly limited monarchy, either one checked by Montesquieu's intermediary powers or one operating under the British doctrine of separation of powers, would be in practice impossible. There were really only two choices, they said, an absolute monarchy or a republic, for supreme authority was by definition indivisible and total; it resided in one place or another. The real issue was whether the king or the parlements were to hold this supreme authority. Lebrun wrote:

> If the sovereign power were limited, it could be limited only by an equal power or by a greater one. In the first case we should have two masters; in the second, there is a contradiction in terms. This check which is so difficult to imagine will be, they say, the law itself. Vain sophistry! The law alone is inert and without life; there must be a power to apply it, a foresight to direct it, a wisdom to interpret and modify it. Shall this power be the parlements? Then the supreme authority is placed in their hands, and that is the end of the monarchy.[13]

This logic exposed, the royalists stressed, the concealed contradiction in the attempts by the more conservative Patriotes to avoid denying the sovereignty of the throne while ascribing sovereign constitutional powers to the parlements and the States General: "On one hand the power of resistance, and on the other a throne in fact absolute; magistrates with legislative power, and an independent king; national sovereignty, and indivisible [royal] authority; . . . in short, a republican system and a state

12. Cf. [Bouquet], *Lettres provinciales,*67; and *Entretien d'un ancien magistrat et d'un abbé, sur le discours de M. Séguier, au lit de justice du* 13 *avril* 1771 (N.p., n.d.). Bouquet said the sovereign's power is limited by "the rules of natural and non-positive justice" and the *Entretien* admitted the validity of the principle of natural law sustained by Patriote writers.

13. [Lebrun], *Observations sur l'écrit intitulé: Protestations des Princes,* 9.

operating as a pure monarchy. That is what you are trying to conciliate." [14] "Do the parlements share sovereignty with the prince, or do they
not? That is the question. Your writers would like to imply an affirmative
answer without making it explicit." [15]

There was no such ambiguity in the royalist positions on any issue raised
by the Patriotes involving the exercise of real political power. Maupeou's
flat refusal to convene the States General was correct, it was asserted, for
the Estates possessed no powers except of remonstrance and petition and
they would only cause dissension, confusion, and delay, or at best could
only approve the king's decisions. [16] Legislative power belonged to the king
alone; it never had been granted to the States General and therefore could
not be exercised in their absence by the parlements. The only representative of the people was the king. It was absurd to ascribe such a function
to the courts: "You see Monseigneur Jacques, who the day before yesterday was selling cloth in his father's shop? Yesterday he gave forty thousand francs to have the right to judge cases. Today Monseigneur Jacques
is the representative of the Archbishop of Lyons, of the Baron de Mont-
morency, and of all the bourgeois of Paris." [17] The parlements were simply the agents and organs of royal power, and as such they properly examined the laws before publication, registered them, served as their
depository, enlightened the king with advice, and could even voice objections, but always as "officers of the king [*gens du roi*]." [18] The contention that freedom of verification was a fundamental law had no historical
basis. Remonstrance was not a right but "un pur effet de la bonté de nos
rois." [19] Under the influence of Montesquieu it was conceded that the courts
were intermediary powers, but only in that they served as "the channel
[*canal*] which the [king] uses to make known . . . his will, his laws, and
the tributes he imposes." They "could retard a sudden and arbitrary ex-

14. *Réflexions nationales, 11,*

15. *Lettre d'un avocat de Paris, aux magistrats du parlement de Rouen, au sujet de l'arrêt de
cette cour du 15 avril 1771* (N.p., n.d. [1771]), 6.

16. *Entretien d'un militaire et d'un aocat sur les affaires présentes* (N.p., n.d.), 20; *Recherches
sur les Etats Généraux* (N.p., n.d.), 6, 32; *Entretien d'un ancien magistrat et d'un abbé*, 32.

17. "Lettre du public, à Messeiurs les ci-devant officiers du parlement de Paris," in *Le
Code des François*, II, 56.

18. "Réflexions d'un citoyen," in *Le Code des François,*, II, 255 ff.; *Lettre de Saint Louis
aux Princes du Sang* (N.p., n.d.), 7.

19. *Entretien d'un ancien magistrat et d'un abbé*, 11; *Le Fin mot de l'affaire*, 13.

ercise of authority" and thus prevent the too hasty enactment of an unwise law, but they should be only a "delaying obstacle," not "an impassable wall" like that erected by the *liberum veto* of the Polish constitution, which would make the French king "no more than the image of a phantom monarch."[20] They had no right to investigate or censure the operations of the executive, as Louis made clear by quashing the trial of D'Aiguillon. The doctrine of unity of classes, specifically forbidden by the edict of December 1770, was a new idea, Maupeou said, which had not existed before about 1750 and had been invented to wrest sovereignty from the king and introduce "Anglicism" into France by federating all the parlements into an imitation of the British House of Commons.[21] Cessation of service, also forbidden by the edict of December 1770, was not only disobedience to the king but also an anarchical act that inflicted great hardship on the citizens of the nation.[22]

Only the issue of judicial tenure seems to have given the royalists some difficulty. It could be maintained that the king as absolute sovereign could revoke any delegation of authority.[23] This argument, however, cut the ground under Maupeou's promise that his newly appointed magistrates would be "inamovibles." Moreover the offer to "liquidate" the confiscated venal offices, compensating the dismissed magistrates with substantial sums, clearly acknowledged that tenure of office was a property right. Consequently the royalists kept multiplying the justifications—that there was a distinction between "biens naturels," which the king guaranteed, and "biens politiques," whose enjoyment was contingent on "submissive, obedient, and faithful performance"; that mass dismissal was the only possible punishment for mass disobedience; that tenure of office was not a constitutional principle; etc.[24]

The theory of the sovereignty of the people was not even mentioned.

---

20. *Dialogue entre un officier françois . . . et son neveu*, 38; *La Tête leur tourne*, 18, 20, 22.

21. Maupeou, "Mémoire," in Flammermont, *Le Chancelier Maupeou et les parlements*, 636; *La Folie de bien des gens dans les affaires du temps* (N.p., n.d. [1771]), 4; *Le Songe d'un jeune Parisien* (N.p., n.d.).

22. E.g. [Abbé Mary (?)], *Considérations sur l'édit de décembre 1771*, 37–38.

23. "Réflexions d'un citoyen," in *Le Code des François*, II, 255–94.

24. [Charles François Lebrun], "Remontrances d'un citoyen aux parlemens de France," in *Le Code des François*, I, 423; *Au Public abusé; Entretien d'un militaire et d'un avocat; Lettre d'un avocat de Paris; Lettre de Saint Louis aux Princes du Sang; Nouveau catéchisme françois* (N.p., n.d.); *Nouvelles réflexions d'un citoyen*, 37; *La Raison gagne* (N.p., 1771).

The idea of the general will (*volonté générale*) or the will of the nation (*voeu de la nation*), however, could be accommodated within the absolutist thesis, but only by positing the identity of the national will with the personal will of the prince: "The king is the person of the state . . . the center where come together all its forces, all its wills. . . . He is the universal organ of the faculties of every individual, the soul, so to speak, by which each man exists." Similarly the royalists could admit a social contract in the sense that the universal and unanimous will of the nation, consecrated by its experience of more than twelve hundred years, rejected any other form of government.[25] But this was the only admissible meaning, for the king's power came from God and in human terms was unconditional and irrevocable.[26] There was no historical basis for the belief in a compact between the monarch and the people, and if at his coronation the king swore to render justice and defend the Catholic religion, he made these promises to God, not to the people.[27]

All these rebuttals of the various clauses in the parliamentary thesis were merely restatements, in the form of negative corollaries, of the absoluteness of absolutism. The positive and constructive contributions of the *thèse royale* are found in the proposals for implementing this basic principle.

Lebrun had gone to England in 1762 and had returned a year later speaking English and well acquainted with British law and politics.[28] He was greatly impressed by the security of the British throne, the easy and effective operation of the machinery of government, the centralization and unity of the state, and the freedom from obstruction by the nobility or corporations like the French parlements. "France," he told Maupeou, "would be happy under such a constitution." The essential reason for the good order in the British state, Lebrun believed, was the working alliance between the commonality and the government, and he saw no reason why a similar partnership could not be made to work equally well in France now that, as he believed, all classes were better educated in the principles of politics. "The Third Estate," he was sure, "would support the govern-

25. *Nouveau catéchisme françois*, 5, 1–5.

26. *Dialogue entre un officier françois . . . et son neveu*, 33.

27. *Examen analytique et raisonné d'un écrit qui a pour titre: Protestations des Princes du Sang* (N.p., n.d. [1771]), 5–6; *Dialogue entre un officier françois . . . et son neveu*, 33.

28. Lebrun, *Opinions*, 5–6.

ment against the views and interests of the nobility, the clergy, and the parlements."[29] Lebrun seems to have understood that there was a relationship between the political behavior of British commoners and their participation in the government, and it was probably this perception that prompted him to suggest to Maupeou the convocation of the States General and the formulation of specific plans for inculcating in the French people a sense of civic duty.

Maupeou adopted Lebrun's strategy of attempting to enlist the support of the Third Estate against the Second and the First, but he does not seem to have envisaged the political education and the radical constitutional changes which would have been necessary to make the strategy work. His rejection of the proposal to reconstitute the States General was consistent with his general policy of refusing to extend to any group or class positive political liberty or share in the administration of the state. In fact it was precisely for attempting to so "republicanize" the French government that the royalist propagandists attacked the Patriotes, accusing them of wishing "to introduce the English system of government into France" and of trying to inflict on the French the fearful aristocratic despotism of England's "mixed government," under which it was possible for "a Wilkes insolently to flout all the orders of the state and violate all its laws by invoking the principle of liberty."[30]

Lebrun also hoped that the ministry could enlist the support of the Philosophes. "It seemed to me," he later wrote, "that the government could make them useful allies in matters of administration and internal political affairs, directing their attacks against the barriers that separated province from province, the [fiscal] privileges which burdened the people with an unequal share of the taxes, the innumerable conflicting *coutumes* [local common law], the various systems of jurisprudence, the impractical distances between courts and litigants, and the usurped jurisdictions."[31] This plan seemed to have a better chance of success, for both the reforms themselves and the neat rationalism of administrative centralization and unification were indeed likely to appeal to the *esprit de système* of the Philosophes, who in any case had no liking or respect for the parle-

29. *Ibid.*, 18.
30. *La Folie de bien des gens*, 4; *La Tête leur tourne*, 17.
31. Lebrun, *Opinions*, 13.

ments. Nevertheless Lebrun's hopes were realized only in the case of Voltaire, and then for rather special reasons. Neither Lebrun nor Maupeou trusted or understood the Philosophes, and because of their commitment to statist absolutism and their reliance on the Dévots for political support they could make no concessions to Philosophic libertarianism, particularly on the issues of freedom of press and religion.

Thus the basic principle of absolutism itself prevented the radical accommodations which would have been necessary to create a populist-Philosophic monarchy. Consequently the ministry was left with only two lines to pursue—offer administrative reforms as tangible evidence of the advantages of absolutism and discredit as much as possible by word and action the aristocracy.

Lebrun saw clearly the political advantages of administrative reform. "When we exercise authority," he wrote in 1769 in a memoir to Maupeou, "we show the hand that established it, preserves it, and avenges it. We should also demonstrate that authority is beneficial, that it serves as a center uniting the interests of all and is a rampart defending the interests of all." [32] He therefore proposed plans for the improvement of the administration of social welfare, education, and the judicial and legal systems. First he suggested the establishment in each diocese of a government "bureau" to provide social services for the poor. Second, he proposed a system of national education which by employing such means as games, student government, and student teachers would not only instruct the mind but also "create citizens" and teach the young "to practice public virtues." Third, his plans for judicial and legal reform involved the improvement of legal education, the requirement of proof of high professional competence for appointment to judgeships, prohibition of venality of judicial offfice, abolition of *justice seigneurial*, revision of the criminal laws, provision of counsel to the accused, review of all capital sentences by the sovereign, changes in the jurisdictions of the parlements, the creation of conseils supérieurs, and the establishment of a conseil des parties to act as a sort of national supreme court. [33] To these original recommendations he later added the abolition of *épices* and the writing of a uniform national code of laws. All these suggestions Maupeou approved at least in principle, and, as we know, some he put into effect.

32. *Ibid.*, 173.
33. *Ibid.*, 172 ff.

These plans for social, educational, legal, and judicial reform were complemented by Terray's economic policies, which made substantial progress in eliminating the tax privileges of the nobility, produced some real though not very effective efforts to aid the impoverished by holding down prices, and favored the poorer peasants in the distribution of common lands.

Some of the government's propagandists, ignoring questions of political principle, concentrated on praising and explaining these reforms. This line did not, however, prove very effective, first, because many of the plans were never realized, and second, because those that were implemented did not produce all the predicted benefits. As the Patriotes said and modern scholars have agreed, the so-called "free justice" probably cost the average Frenchman more than the old justice had, and the corruption and incompetence of the new courts, made notorious by Beaumarchais, was acknowledged even by the royalists.[34] And while the fiscal reforms alleviated the government's financial problems they placed added burdens on wealthy bourgeois without lightening those on the poor. Thus on the whole the argument of reform does not seem to have had much political success.

Consequently in order to gain the support of the Third Estate Maupeou's propagandists had to make their dominant themes the evils of aristocracy and the dangers of republicanism. Both could be amply documented with true or alleged examples of the parlements' misgovernment, irresponsibility, hostility to the church, and indifference to the public welfare.[35] The most frequent line, however, was the lesson of history: In

34. Doyle, *The Parlement of Bordeaux*, 149.

35. The charges included failure to improve the hospitals, refusal to reform the laws and the judicial system, miscarriages of justice, professional incompetence, collaboration with monopolists to drive up the price of bread, oppression of the clergy, and even conspiracy to destroy the nobility and abase the Peers of the Realm. *E.g.*, *Au public abusé; Discours de M. le premier président de la Chambre des Communes du Caffé de Dubuisson, successeur de Procope, sur les affaires actuelles de l'état* . . . (N.p., n.d. [1771]), 19, 21; *Entretien d'un militaire et d'un avocat*, 31; *Examen analytique et raisonné*; *Le Fin mot de l'affaire*, 19; *Ils reviendront; ils ne reviendront pas; ou le Pour et le contre* (N.p., n.d.), 33–37; *Lettre de M. C*** à M. de St ****, 10–11, 35; *Lettre de Saint Louis aux Princes du Sang*, 12; "Lettre du public," in *Le Code des François*, II, 67; *Lettres américaines sur les parlemens, 1770 et 1771* (N.p., n.d. [1771]), 25; *Mémoire sur le droit des pairs de France d'être jugés par leurs pairs* (N.p., 1771); *Ménippe ressuscité, ou l'Assemblée tumultueuse* . . . (N.p., n.d.), 43; *Ode sur la rentrée du parlement de Paris* (N.p., n.d.); *Pensez-y bien ou Avis à MM. les avocats de Paris* (N.p., n.d.); *La Raison gagne; Réflexions d'un vieux patriote sur les affaires présentes* (N.p., n.d. [1771]), 9; *Réflexions nationales*, 5; *Réponse au libelle intitulé: Le Parlement justifié* (N.p., n.d. [1771]), 5;

the Middle Ages "the supreme power [of the king] was attacked by the ambitions of the great nobles. The nation at that time was too blind to see and defend its own true interests. It allowed itself to be divided, and soon France became a nation composed of a horde of petty tyrants and a thousand herds of slaves, *gentes de corpore et potestate*, whom their lords gave away, bought, or sold as they saw fit, pitiful scraps of humanity bound to the soil, like beasts of the field. . . . The weaker were our kings, the heavier were the chains that enslaved the people; the measure of royal authority was the measure of the liberty of the people. . . . Finally the feudal regime came to an end. Our kings regained their full power, and France her full liberty."[36] Maupeou's mission was to preserve this great victory.

> Si le grand Richelieu, pour sauver la Patrie,
> Sut abaisser les Grands et dompter l'Hérésie,
> Maupeou, plus grand encore, sans glaive ni combat,
> Sauva, par un Edit, le Monarque et l'Etat.[37]

The dragon of feudalism, still alive, was again attacking with renewed ferocity. The parlements were attempting to subject the nation to "a monstrous hereditary aristocracy" and "bring disorder, weakness, and anarchy to all branches of the government."[38] Under "parliamentary despotism," the new feudalism, "the citizen, stripped of all distinctions of rank and quality, would be constantly under the eyes of his masters or their agents, whose caprices he would have to respect and whose will he would have to fear."[39] This "feudalism" was of course that of the royalist historians, the identification of aristocratic infringements on monarchical power with medieval anarchy. Except for Lebrun's plan to abolish *justice seigeuriale*, Maupeou's apologists were virtually silent on the issue of existing feudal and seignorial rights.

Some of these writers were truly prophetic in their warnings to the nobility not to use the slogan of liberty to stir up the people against their

---

[Saint Pierre], *Discours d'un Pair de France*; [Villette], *Réflexions d'un maître perruquier*, 12; [Charles, Marquis de Villette], *Le Soufflet du maître perruquier à sa femme* (N.p., n.d.).

36. *Nouveau catéchisme françois*, 5–6.

37. *Ils reviendront*, 41.

38. *Nouvelles réflexions d'un citoyen*, 24; *Lettres américaines*, 34.

39. *Idées d'un patriote* (N.p., n.d. [1771]), 13–14; "Réflexions d'un citoyen," in *Le Code des François*, II, 273.

king. Liberty, they cautioned, was a two-edged sword that could be turned against nobles as easily as against the throne:

> From all the chains that weigh down all [other] classes in the nation [the nobility] are free. All the exemptions, all the favors they enjoy, are paid for by the humble citizen. It is dangerous to tell a people that legitimate authority infringes on their rights, for this is to tell them they can attack privileges which have always been violations of common law. What will the nobles do when the cry of liberty that they have taught is shouted back at them, when protests are brought to their bar of justice against their prerogatives of rank and birth, when they are told that a Frenchman is a free man, that the right to ravage the fields of the poor is an inhuman right, more destructive than all the edicts ever issued of the fundamental laws of the nation? . . . When you demand justice in the name of the nation, begin by treating the nation justly.[40]

And the anonymous *La Tête leur tourne* advised the people,

> If you wish to overthrow the throne, at least raise up the entire nation on its ruins. Blood will flow, the present generation will know the most terrible sort of suffering, France will perhaps be destroyed forever. But at least you will not be accused of the stupidity of having got rid of one master in order to subjugate yourselves to two thousand despots. And if you tear the crown from the head of your legitimate king, you will not have done so to place it on the head of the first rascal that came along with 10,000 écus to buy himself a magistracy.[41]

The second great danger was republicanism, the new weapon of aristocratic despotism. "Under the pretext of reforming the state" the parlements would "reduce the people to the most base form of servitude while holding before their eyes the specious image of liberty":[42]

> We shall witness the cruelty that the senates of republics inflict on their citizens, who have no share in the government. . . . Let us not be dazzled by the flattering descriptions of other governments, or by the de-

40. *Réflexions nationales*, 24–25.
41. *La Tête leur tourne*, 21–22.
42. *Le Confiteor d'un ci-devant avocat, qui n'étoit pas du commun* (N.p., n.d. [1771]), 5.

ceptive image of an ill-understood liberty. We know that in a democracy wisdom does not determine the laws dictated by the blind mob
. . . and that in an aristocracy family loyalties, private interests, and personal quarrels always divide the body of the sovereign. . . . Our fatherland is our monarch. . . . Our patriotism the proud republican calls base homage to despotism. Slave to his fellow equals, he accuses us of being the slaves of our king. He does not see that his legislators are his tyrants.[43]

This thesis of the common interests of the Third Estate and the crown did not, however, imply any revival of D'Argenson's idea of democratic monarchism or any disposition to grant the people a share in sovereignty. "If every citizen," Pierre Bouquet wrote, "held an equally responsible share in the sovereignty and the administration of the state, our government would be so republican that not only would public power be vested in all the citizens as a body, but also each citizen would share in the exercise of this power and in the administration of the state. But if all the members of a society exercised sovereign authority, over whom would they exercise it?"[44]

Since the immediate danger was supposed to be aristocratic, not popular rule it is difficult to understand the vehemence with which these royalists denounced democratic power. "The most terrible license of all," Moreau said, "is that of the mob, and if you entrust the law to their hands you make the law useless. . . . When the people are aroused they turn into mad beasts, and if by misfortune they gain the upper hand . . . that is the end of liberty and security."[45] "The people," another royalist wrote, "shout whenever they take it into their heads to shout, against good sense just as often as against a bad prince. They almost always mistake the shadow for substance, illusion for reality, lies for truth. When seized by violent emotions they turn into vile creatures . . . ferocious beasts blinded even against their own interests. Have the people ever supported any faction and not ended by falling that faction's first victims?"[46]

43. [Abbé Mary (?)], *Considérations sur l'édit de décembre* 1770, 74, 81–82.
44. [Bouquet], *Lettres provinciales*, 123.
45. Moreau, "Lettre à M. de La Condamine," in *Principes de morale*, I, 47, 51.
46. *Nouvelles réflexions d'un citoyen*, 48. See also *La Raison gagne*, 7; *Entretien d'un militaire et d'un avocat*, 34–35.

Perhaps the explanation is that despite all the talk of aristocratic despotism what the royalists really feared was that the aristocrats would precipitate a popular revolution. "Is not the natural tendency of all great corporations to create revolutions?" Parliamentary principles were "not merely republican but anarchical."[47] "They say that everything must be changed, they wish to reshape all our thinking, proscribe all accepted principles, deny all traditions, in short, give a new form and a new impulse to the entire body politic."[48] "And do not say that because our manners are more urbane than our ancestors' there is no cause for alarm. The spirit of rebellion is capable of anything. The people obey whatever ideas are put in their heads. They become a torrent rushing into the maelstrom toward which they are drawn by their true or false interests, or even by mere caprice. Dark days are often the prelude to violent storms. Factious minds are taking advantage of these troubled and overcast times to weave plots, to contrive intrigues, to conspire secretly."[49] "Does the idea of a revolution astonish you?" the magistrates were asked. "You are rushing toward one; you are carrying with you the whole nation. From your tribunals rise malignant vapors that infect with revolt. Your letters, your decrees sow seeds of rebellion in every mind and . . . plant in men's hearts the desire for revolution."[50] "You have formed a plan . . . to incite the people to revolt."[51]

As the alternative to these horrors, the royalists offered the French people the security of absolutism. It is possible to discern two quite distinct images of the new France that they proposed. One was only slightly to the right of the ideal of the more conservative Patriotes. The king was seen as paternal figure, "master in his kingdom as you are master in your own house . . . a father in the midst of his children, [who] punishes them, rewards them, and pardons them when they deserve his forgiveness, consulting only his own paternal love."[52] Under such self-regulating abso-

47. *Le Confiteor d'un ci-devant avocat*, 5; *Entretien d'un ancien magistrat et d'un abbé*, 8.
48. *Réflexions nationales*, 15–16.
49. *Recherches sur les Etats Généraux*, 55.
50. [Lebrun], "Remontrances d'un citoyen," in *Le Code des François*, I, 402–403.
51. *A l'auteur de la Correspondance entre M. le chancelier et M. de Sorhouet* (N.p., n.d. [1771]), 3.
52. *Les Bons citoyens, ou Lettres des sénatographes, écrites par des gens respectables* (Rouen, 1771), 5–6.

lute power, France would conform to Montesquieu's concept of a "gouvernement modéré." Though the king's power was absolute and bound by no contractual obligations, France did have a constitution in that the king, in order to be a monarch and not a despot, perforce had to act in accord with the essential nature of monarchism, whose principles could be called, if one wished, "fundamental laws." He had to permit for his own enlightenment "remonstrances and representations" from his officers, keep inviolate "the liberty and property of his subjects," and govern by the laws he himself wrote and enforced through his courts.[53] These were principles descriptive of the true nature of monarchy, not normative prescriptions, but in certain writers they sounded very much like the binding fundamental laws of the Patriotes. Thus Pierre Bouquet wrote—and as a consequence had his work suppressed by Maupeou, whom he thought he was supporting—that the sovereign's power was limited by the laws of God, "the rules of natural and nonpositive justice," and also by "the fundamental laws of the state, which require that the prince exercise his sovereignty according to its proper nature and in the form and under the conditions by which this sovereignty was established." Another writer specified these conditions: "The prince cannot change the nature of the government or the order of succession to the crown. The liberty and property of his citizens are inviolable. Whatever is contrary to these laws is legally null and void." "The inalienable rights of humanity," Moreau said, "are the fundamental principles of all societies."[54] This sort of thinking amounted in effect to promising Locke's natural rights and society under law and Montesquieu's liberty under law—but without conceding their premises, for the royalists always kept the reservation that "monarchical authority in France can . . . be moderated only by itself."[55]

Yet when we look closely at the royalists' "inviolable" rights to property and liberty we find that these concepts were considerably narrower than in the Patriote ideology. Only Moreau among the royalists derived

53. "Réflexions d'un citoyen," in *Le Code des François*, II, 260.

54. [Bouquet], *Lettres provinciales*, 67–68; *Nouvelles réflexions d'un citoyen*, 9; Moreau, "Lettre à M. de La Condamine," in *Principes de morale*, I, 5.

55. [Lebrun], "Remontrances d'un citoyen," in *Le Code des François*, I, 380. See *Au public abusé*, 14; [Lebrun], "Remontrances d'un citoyen," in *Le Code des François*, I, 378; Moreau, "Lettre à M. de La Condamine," in *Principes de morale*, I, 55; "Réflexions d'un citoyen," in *Le Code des François*, II, 260–62.

the right of property from natural law. Moreover *propriété* did not have the broad meaning given to the word by Locke and the Patriotes; it meant only tangible possessions. Consequently it was an inviolable right but not an absolute one. "Government," Moreau wrote, "may diminish the subject's enjoyment of his property in order to assure it, just as it may abridge his liberty to preserve it." Since taxation did not require consent, the distinction between legitimate and confiscatory taxes was, Moreau acknowledged, "very difficult to define."[56] So was legitimate appropriation of property, as the problem of the liquidation of offices made clear.

Liberty also had a narrower meaning in the royalist lexicon. In the positive sense of exercise of political power by anyone other than the king it was invariably rejected with pejorative epithets—"l'esprit d'indépendance," "liberté d'opposition," "votre liberté indéfinie," or "votre liberté imaginée"—and denounced as both a chimerical right and a source of anarchy and rebellion. "What do you mean," one royalist asked, "by your *'nation libre'*? That France has the right to choose her own sovereigns as she pleases? That she can abolish the monarchy if she sees fit? That she can despoil the sovereign of the eminent prerogatives attached to his crown? Restrict or divide his power? Prescribe how he shall use it? Summon him before a tribunal? Demand of him an accounting of his administration? Punish him for misuse of his authority?"[57]

The only true liberty for the royalists was negative liberty, security from unjust or abusive power. It was variously designated as "liberté nationale," "liberté politique," "liberté civile," or "liberté publique." This was the liberty that had been violated by the feudal lords and was now being threatened by aristocratic republicanism. It meant the protection of *le peuple*, of the little man, from oppressive aristocratic corporations and privileged individuals by a benevolent central power. It was a populist, egalitarian, anti-aristocratic liberty that could survive only under the protection of authority. "True civil liberty can exist only in a state in which the sovereign is powerful enough to subjugate without distinction all the members of the body politic to the empire of his laws."[58]

It was clear what this liberty gave freedom from, but it was not so clear

56. [Moreau], *Leçons de morale*, 104–106.
57. *La Tête leur tourne*, 9–10.
58. [Abbé Mary (?)], *Considérations sur l'édit de décembre* 1770, 82.

what it gave freedom to do. Presumably it included freedom to live, though this right was never mentioned; none of the royalist propagandists spoke of the right to live in Linguet's sense of freedom from starvation. It obviously did not mean the right to enjoy special privileges, the rights of *honneur* and *état* so dear to the Patriotes. It meant the right to possess and enjoy tangible property only with qualifications. It had no implication of freedom of expression or freedom of religion, and there was no mention of the right to fair trial or of guaranties against arbitrary imprisonment, or of freedom from bureaucratic despotism. Moreau alone gave something of a definition when he described liberty as the right to the fruits of one's labor, the right to marry whom one chose, to raise children, to transmit to them one's property, and to make enforceable contracts.[59] At the most it seems to have meant the assurance (but not as an absolute right) of the enjoyment of one's property and the promise of just, benevolent paternalistic rule and good order.

Nevertheless this concept of liberty contained a historically important principle. It was not only a liberty less extensive than the Patriotes'; it was also a liberty different in kind. The Patriotes were in the Montesquieu-Tocqueville tradition, which advocated protection of the negative liberty of the individual against *despotic governmental power* by such devices as the separation of powers, intermediary powers, corporations, decentralization, and federalism. The royalists were in the Rousseau-Marx tradition, which advocated protection of the negative liberty of the individual against *oppressive individuals, classes, and corporations* by creating a benevolent dictatorship vested in the majority or the king or the proletariat. The ideal was a society in which "the humblest citizen can . . . defend his property and honor against the most powerful." This is why Lebrun said, "The happiness and welfare of the people are inseparable from the maintenance of authority."[60]

Upon this ideal of the protective, paternalistic, and essentially passive state Maupeou and Lebrun projected a second far more dynamic image which did not deny the first concept but rather overrode it. This was a statism, and like all statisms it could not admit any notion of constitu-

59. Moreau, "Lettre à M. de La Condamine," in *Principes de morale*, I, 45.

60. *Au public abusé*, 14; [Lebrun], *Observations sur l'écrit intitulé: Protestations des Princes*, 24.

tionalism. The king, Maupeou wrote, is not bound by law, and the parlements were properly judged guilty of defiance of royal authority and violation of the one fundamental and primary law of all "civilized" states, the prohibition of resistance to "the power of the state [*la puissance publique*]." "Such rigor," he conceded, "would perhaps not be proper in a republic or in a government in which all considerations must yield to the demands of the constitution. In countries of that sort invariable laws rule and the executive power never has the right to modify or temper them. But in a monarchy . . . to attempt to confine public authority to judicial forms is to denature the character of monarchical government."[61]

The primary principle of this statism was unity—absolute, undivided, centralized unity of authority, whether legislative, administrative, or judicial—"unity of government, unity of obedience, and unity of nation." "In unity of government we find the joining of all powers, all wills, all interests. The prince and the state in our eyes are one. We locate the fatherland in the monarch; in serving one we serve the other."[62] "The will of the king is the will of the state."[63] "The monarch is the only representative, the one juridical organ of the nation, the sovereign arbiter, the unique interpreter of the national will. . . . He is the only repository of public power, and in a true sense the people and the monarch are one. The nation is considered to reside wholly and entirely in the person of the monarch, who . . . proposes in his edicts no less than the general will for our obedience."[64] Thus the king was not really above the law, for he was the law. The sovereignty of the nation and the general will were affirmed, but they existed only as they were unified in the person of the monarch.

In such a state the supreme and indeed the only duty of the subject to his sovereign was "full and entire obedience to his will. . . . From obedience flows as a necessary consequence order and tranquillity. It is the principle of all good, the mainspring of the public welfare." Pamphlets addressed to the populace iterated and reiterated this lesson of obedience to "not' bon roi."[65]

61. Maupeou, "Mémoire," in Flammermont, *Le Chancelier Maupeou et les parlements*, 630.

62. [Abbé Mary (?)], *Considérations sur l'édit de décembre 1770*, 58, 82.

63. *Le Songe d'un jeune Parisien*, 22.

64. *Lettre de M. C*** à M. de St ****, 15–16.

65. *Nouveau catéchism françois*, 8; e.g., *Ah! Les Grands Sots! ou Réflexions de F. M. A. D. V. {François Marie Arouet de Voltaire} décrotteur, sur les affaires du temps* (N.p., n.d. [1771]).

The justification of this sort of statism was neither divine sanction nor
tradition but public utility and *raison d'état*. France and the king were one
and they were their own reason for being, and since France and the people
were likewise one, there was a complete identity of self-interest. "The most
advantageous [law] for the people . . . is without contradiction the maintenance of the supreme power."[66]

As in Rousseau's *Contrat social*, this monolithic concept of the state left
no place for semiautonomous or supranational groups, and all subordinate
organizations had to be absorbed into the unity of the state. For instance
Moreau wrote, "The power of the military, which is by nature destructive, cannot be too firmly controlled." And as for the church: "Though
kings owe respect, protection, and liberty to the pastoral powers representing Jesus Christ, God never entrusted to the church the scepter that
governs empires."[67] This then was no theocratic monarchism. By the same
token and *a fortiori*, the divisiveness inherent in the parlements and the
States General was absolutely unacceptable. "If [sovereignty] is divided
the nation is under several wills, and a multiplicity of wills inevitably in-
flicts suffering and enslavement on the people."[68]

This concept of the state as an organic entity motivated and justified
entirely by its own self-interest gave complete freedom for adaptation and
growth—in perfect antithesis to the static constitutionalism of the Patriotes. Lebrun was strongly influenced by Montesquieu's *Esprit des lois*,
which he said had early "taken possession of all my thinking."[69] Perhaps
for this reason he had an especially keen sense of the rapid sociological
changes in progress in France and of the necessity to modify continuously
the government to adapt to new conditions. "In politics," he wrote, "what
is truth at one time may become error at another. The antiquity of civil
laws does not give them a title to irrevocability. The forms of monarchical
government therefore do not possess an absolute consistency, for the same
laws do not always produce the same effects, and the alteration of the
principle and character of a nation inevitably brings new needs and requires new measures. If political authority did not move as the people

66. *Nouveau catéchisme françois*, 5.
67. [Moureau], *Leçons de morale*, 61–62, 97.
68. *Nouveau catéchisme françois*, 5.
69. Lebrun, *Opinions*, 5.

move, such an immobile and static monarchy would collapse and fall to pieces."[70] He believed "that most laws are as variable as manners, customs, and political interests. I can accept as sacred no institutions except those which are of the essence of the government, those without which it would lose its form and nature. . . . Almost all our good laws are new laws; the ancient ones are abuses of justice. May a bold and wise hand finish the task of destroying what is left of this barbarous Gothic structure and give to France the uniformity it needs."[71] Similarly Moreau wrote, "The political constitution of one country is not that of another. Everything changes with the passage of centuries, and there is not a single nation in Europe today whose government is what is was four hundred years ago." And the author of the *Entretien d'un militaire et d'un avocat*: "Laws must be relative to the needs of the men for whom they are written, to their varying mores, to economic change."[72] The great practical value of the absolutistic state was its complete freedom to alter itself immediately in response to new circumstance, for the "king" (the central power) alone had the right and power to decide political necessity.

Maupeouan politics conceived the state as a living creature at the center of which was the "king," its "universal soul, which communicated to the vast body warmth and life and by whose influence everything moved, accelerated, or stopped"—like Diderot's spider at the center of its web—perfectly equipped to adapt, evolve, and survive in new social environments.[73] This was an excellent application of eighteenth-century naturalism to politics. It perceived already Tocqueville's wave of "providential democracy," the obsolescence of the French aristocracy, and the whole social and economic revolution already in process, and it proposed for the nation's future governance the logical structure of the authoritarian, unified, centralized, egalitarian, benevolent welfare state—the very eventuality Tocqueville later so dreaded.

It is difficult to imagine how this modern ideal of secular statism could have been realized in France in the 1770s. In the first place it was ob-

---

70. [Lebrun], *Observations sur l'écrit intitulé: Protestations des Princes*, 12–13.

71. [Lebrun], *Lettre de l'auteur des Observations sur les Protestations des Princes, à M. Dupaty, avocat général de Bordeaux* (N.p., n.d.), 9–10.

72. Moreau, "Lettre à M. de La Condamine," in *Principes de morale*, I, 4; *Entretien d'un militaire et d'un avocat*, 22.

73. [Lebrun], *Observations sur l'écrit intitulé: Protestations des Princes*, 12.

scured as an idea by the traditional image of the theocratic patriarchal monarchy that royal apologists felt constrained to maintain. In the second place it could not break entirely with the past, as logic demanded, but was forced to carry on the entire inefficient, corrupt, and tradition-ridden apparatus of the French monarchy. Magistrates could be exiled but the parlements as institutions could not be. It was not practical to renounce the political alliance with the church. Thus a very modern idea came through merely as an inept revival of Louis XIV's theocratic absolute monarchism. This obviously would not do.

FIVE

Voltaire

V OLTAIRE'S many writings, public and private, relating to the Maupeou revolution and his personal involvement in the political crisis are of particular interest for two reasons. First, the abundant documentation accumulated by two centuries of Voltaire studies reveals clearly in his case what is less obvious and easily forgotten in other cases—that behind every statement of political philosophy or public policy stood the man who made it, his personality, his prejudices, and his special purposes, avowed or unavowed, selfish or altruistic. Second, Voltaire distinguished perhaps more sharply than anyone at the time between positive and negative liberty and stated even more explicitly than the other royalists the proposition that personal freedom could be assured only by the denial of political power to corporations representing either the aristocracy or the Third Estate.

Voltaire had personal reasons for his decision to support Maupeou. Established in his chateau at Ferney a few miles from the Swiss border, he was busy exercising his leadership of the Philosophes—indeed of the intellectual life of all Europe—and at the same time conducting various lucrative businesses, his colony of Swiss watchmakers, his plans to develop at Versoix a lake port in French territory to rival Geneva, and other enterprises. Though forbidden to return to Paris, as he longed to do, and obliged to publish his writings in Switzerland or elsewhere outside France, he was nevertheless in correspondence with French ministers and politi-

cians who officially or unofficially extended to him a wide variety of favors, particularly special privileges for his commercial enterprises, whose
continued prosperity depended, he claimed, on this support. He had enjoyed an especially cordial relationship with Choiseul, virtual prime minister until 1771, who had backed the Versoix project and had even allowed the French ambassador to Spain to serve as a sort of *commis voyageur*
for Voltaire's watches.[1]

Consequently Choiseul's fall from power in December 1770 created for
Voltaire the danger of serious financial losses. Though he continued to
express his undying loyalty and gratitude to the exiled minister, he wasted
no time in making overtures to Maupeou.[2] On January 27 he wrote Marin,
one of the chancellor's henchmen, "If I had access, as you do, to the chancellor, I should like, my dear correspondent, to learn if it is indeed true
that the poor people of the provinces will no longer be obliged to travel
a hundred and fifty leagues from their homes to plead their cases in court,
and that a new legal code, which we so badly need, is indeed being written. We must on this occasion prepare a civic crown for the chancellor."[3]
Marin showed this signal of support to Maupeou, as Voltaire expected,
and also took pains to circulate manuscript copies.[4] This overture having
been accepted, the Philosophe proceeded immediately to supplement it
by publishing anonymously between March and May 1771 eight pamphlets written in defense of Maupeou, praising his reforms and satirizing
the parlements.[5] Furthermore he reaffirmed his position publicly in the

1. Léon Kozminski, *Voltaire financier* (Paris, 1929), 278–79.

2. The chief source for the history of Voltaire's private reactions to the Maupeou revolution is François Marie Arouet de Voltaire, *Voltaire's Correspondence*, ed. Theodore Besterman (Geneva, 1953–65), vols LXXVIII–LXXXIX.

3. Voltaire to François Louis Claude Marin, January 27, 1771, *ibid.*, LXXVIII, 59.

4. Mme Du Deffand obtained a copy which she sent to the Choiseuls. See note and
letter from Etienne François, Duke de Choiseul to Marie Anne de Vichy-Chamrond, Marquise Du Deffand, March 11, 1771, *ibid.*, LXXVIII, 60, 151.

5. *Avis important d'un gentilhomme à toute la noblesse du royaume* (N.p., n.d. [Geneva,
1771]), published before March 18; *Fragment d'une lettre écrite de Genève 19 mars 1771, par
un bourgeois de cette ville, à un bourgeois de L*** {Lyon}* (Geneva, 1771), before March 30;
Sentiments des six conseils établis par le Roi, et de tous les bons citoyens (N.p., n.d. [Paris, 1771]),
between March 18 and April 9; *Réponse aux Remontrances de la Cour des Aides, par un membre
des nouveaux conseils souverains* (N.p., n.d. [Geneva (?), 1771]), between March 13 and April
9; *Très-humbles et très-respectueuses remontrances du Grenier à Sel* (N.p., n.d. [Geneva, 1771]),
before April 16; *Lettre d'un jeune abbé* (N.p., n.d. [Geneva (?), 1771]), before April 17; *Les*

article "Parlement de France" in the *Questions sur l'Encyclopédie* and privately in letters to his friends and in flattering verses addressed to Maupeou and to Du Barry.[6]

This shift in political allegiance from Choiseul to Maupeou was not really the volte-face that it appeared, for Voltaire had had since 1717 relations with Maupeou's family, to which he boasted in 1767 deep attachment.[7] He had indeed reason to be grateful, for in 1767 he was saved from a sticky involvement in the smuggling of banned books by the intervention of Maupeou's father, then vice chancellor.[8] When the son became chancellor in 1768 Voltaire transferred to him his attentions, soliciting various favors and sending a handsome copy of the *Précis du siècle de Louis XV* "en beau maroquin, à filet d'or," which was acknowledged by "a charming letter" from the chancellor.[9] In 1770 he presented a copy of the first edition of the *Questions sur l'Encyclopédie*. "We are fortunate," he wrote D'Alembert in 1769, "in having a chancellor of great intelligence, reason, and indulgence. He is a treasure sent to us by God in our misfortunes."[10] Moreover Voltaire's *Histoire du Parlement de Paris*, published in May 1769, through not "instigated" by Maupeou or written to support the chancellor's still-unformulated "program," as has been said, had skillfully satirized the courts, refuted their constitutional claims, and clearly committed Voltaire in advance to support of Maupeou's revolution.[11] Indeed Voltaire's inveterate, intense, and even vindictive hostility

Peuples aux parlements (N.p., n.d, [Geneva (?), 1771]), April or early May; *L'Equivoque* (N.p., n.d. [Paris (?), 1771]), probably early May. There were other 1771 editions. See Durand Echeverria, "Some Unknown Eighteenth-Century Editions of Voltaire's Political Pamphlets of 1771," *Studies on Voltaire and the Eighteenth Century*, CXXVII (1974), 61–64.

6. Voltaire, "Eloge de Maupeou," in Voltaire, *Oeuvres complètes*, ed. Louis Molland (Paris, 1877–85), X, 588; Voltaire's letter in verse and prose to Jeanne Bécu, Countess Du Barry, *ca.* July 5, 1773, in Voltaire, *Correspondence*, LXXXV, 157–58.

7. Voltaire to Jean Amédée Honoré de Rochefort d'Ally, February 4, 1767, in Voltaire, *Correspondence*, LXIV, 168.

8. See Voltaire to Count d'Argental, February 8, 1767, and to Armand de Vignerot Du Plessis, Duke de Richelieu, February 9, 1767, *ibid.*, LXIV, 169–70, 183–84.

9. "Bound in fine morocco ornamented in gold." Voltaire to Charles Joseph Panckoucke, October or November, 1768, and to Count d'Argental, November 18, 1768, *ibid.*, LXX, 128, 170–72.

10. Voltaire to René Nicolas Charles Augustin de Maupeou, August 22, 1770, and to Jean Le Rond d'Alembert, June 4, 1769, *ibid.*, LXXVI, 127, and LXXII, 61.

11. See J. H. Brumfitt, *Voltaire Historian* (Oxford, 1958), 70; Gustave L. Desnoires-

to the parliamentary magistrates, exacerbated but not caused by the Calas and La Barre cases, made it impossible that he would not have applauded the purge of the courts, even if it had not also been good business to do so. The Sage of Ferney was indeed, as he indignantly protested, only being consistent with his principles.

Nevertheless Voltaire's public support of the chancellor infuriated the Duke and Duchess de Choiseul, for in being driven from office by Maupeou and exiled to Chanteloup they had suffered serious financial losses as well as deprivation of political eminence.[12] They contemptuously dismissed Voltaire's protestations of continued fidelity and his excuses that he supported Maupeou only because he so hated the "assassins of La Barre."[13] If they did not erect atop their chateau a weather vane in the shape of Voltaire's profile they might well have done so, and their resentment received sympathy not only from the Patriotes but even from Philosophes such as Diderot and Condorcet, who joined in the general censure of Voltaire's seeming willingness to veer with the winds of political expediency.[14]

---

terres, *Voltaire et la société au 18ᵉ siècle: Voltaire et Genève* (Paris, 1875), VII, 382; Gay, *Voltaire's Politics*, 317; Robert R. Palmer, *The Age of Democratic Revolution: A Political History of Europe and America, 1760–1800* (Princeton, 1959), I, 98. Voltaire had been working on the *Histoire* since January 1768 (see Voltaire to Servan, January 13, 1768, in Voltaire, *Correspondence*, LXVIII, 39–42), when Maupeou was still premier président of the Parlement. Maupeou had been chancellor for only eight months when the *Histoire* was published in May 1769, and he did not formulate his "program" until the following year. There may be some truth in Bachaumont's report that Maupeou "provided material for its composition" (*Mémoires secrets*, July 17, 1769 [IV, 317]), but Voltaire obtained documentation from other sources as well (*e.g.*, Voltaire to D'Hornoy, February 6, 1769, in Voltaire, *Correspondence*, LXXI, 85).

12. On the Choiseuls' losses, see Voltaire, *Correspondence*, LXXVIII, 37–38.

13. See the letter of the Duchess de Choiseul to Mme Du Deffand, April 26, 1771: "How despicable that man Voltaire is! What a coward! He makes excuses, he accuses himself, he makes a tremendous to-do over things he has no need to say [Il se noie dans son crachat pour avoir craché sans besoin]. He makes recantations, he blows hot and cold, he doesn't realize what he is saying. He is disgusting and pitiful." Marie Anne de Vichy-Chamrond, Marquise Du Deffand, *Correspondance complète . . . avec la duchesse de Choiseul, l'abbé Barthélemy et M. Craufort . . .* (New ed.; Paris, 1866), I, 408.

14. See note 55, Chap. I, herein. Also Marie Jean Antoine de Caritat, Marquis de Condorcet to Anne Robert Jacques Turgot, spring 1771, in Condorcet, *Correspondance inédite de Condorcet et de Turgot*, ed. Charles Henry (Paris, 1883), 48; *Correspondance littéraire*, August 1 and October 15, 1772 (X, 40, 81); Denis Diderot, "Le Neveu de Rameau," in Diderot, *Oeuvres romanesques*, ed. Henri Bénac (Paris, 1951), 405–406; Diderot to Naigeon, *ca.* June 1772, in Voltaire, *Correspondence*, LXXXII, 68–69; "Epître à Fréron contre Voltaire," in *Journal historique* (London, 1774–76), II, 104.

Though the hectic press of politics during the spring and summer of
1771 prevented the new ministry from making prompt payment for support received, Voltaire was eventually rewarded. He did not, it is true,
get back his 200,000 francs, despite a direct appeal to Terray.[15] Moreover
the ministry decided to discontinue or greatly reduce the government's
contributions to the Versoix project.[16] In October he did however receive
from D'Aiguillon an official commitment of support of his watch manu-
factory, and immediately the problems he had been having since April
with the tax, postal, and customs officials vanished.[17] During Maupeou's
regime his "colony" expanded from twelve buildings to ninety-four, and
by 1774 he was manufacturing and selling more than 4,000 watches an-
nually, with a market value of about 450,000 livres.[18] Furthermore he
benefited from a number of other favors from the ministry. Some were for
himself, such as the suppression of Clément's *Quatrième lettre à monsieur de
Voltaire* (which had libeled Voltaire's nephew Mignot and the poet himself by alleging they were the grandson and nephew of the *pâtissier* Mignot
satirized by Boileau).[19] Others were for his friends and acquaintances.[20]
Yet in a number of ways Voltaire was disappointed. He was unable to persuade the ministry to do anything for the serfs of Saint Claude, whom he
was trying to have freed from the feudal rights held over them by the Benedictines; he did not succeed in rehabilitating D'Etallonde, who had fled
France to escape the fate of his friend the Chevalier de La Barre, drawn
and quartered for impiety; he did not obtain, as he confidently hoped,
relaxation of the prohibition on importation of his publications into France;

15. Voltaire to Joseph Marie Terray, *ca*. November 20, 1772, in Voltaire, *Correspondence*, LXXXIII, 152–53.

16. See Count d'Argental to Voltaire, October 20, 1771, and Armand de Vignerot
Du Plessis, Duke de Richelieu to Voltaire, February 20, 1772, *ibid.*, LXXX, 96, and
LXXXI, 84.

17. Emmanuel Armand de Vignerot Du Plessis de Richelieu, Duke d'Aiguillon to
Voltaire, October 9, 1771, *ibid.*, LXXX, 74.

18. Kozminski, *Voltaire financier*, 278.

19. Voltaire to René Nicolas Charles Augustin de Maupeou, December 20, 1773, and
Maupeou to Voltaire, January 7, 1774, in Voltaire, *Correspondence*, LXXXVI, 175–76,
and LXXXVII, 15.

20. *E.g.*, a pension for his nephew Mignot and a letter of apology from the Lieutenant
of Police for an insult to a friend of Mignot's (*ibid.*, LXXXIII, 150–51, 196; LXXXVI,
99–100, 126), and some positive action toward the complete rehabilitation of Sirven (*ibid.*,
LXXXI, 82). He courageously supported Laharpe, whose *Eloge de Fénelon* was condemned
by the king's council (*ibid.*, LXXX, 66).

and perhaps the most bitter disappointment of all was that he did not receive permission to return to his beloved Paris. Voltaire had needed political patronage as much for his humanitarian purposes as for his own private interests; on the whole, Maupeou satisfied his latter needs more amply than he did the former.

Like the Philosophes generally, Voltaire became increasingly concerned with politics after 1770, as is graphically indicated by the number of political articles inserted in the various editions of the *Questions sur l'Encyclopédie* from 1770 to 1774. And at no time in his long career did he speak out more eloquently or in more specific terms in defense of the negative liberties than he did during the Maupeou revolution. The English example was prominent in his mind. "Liberty and property—that is the English cry," he wrote. "It is the cry of nature."[21] From the British constitution he drew up his definitive list of natural rights: "Complete freedom of person and freedom of property; the right to speak to the nation by one's pen; the right to be judged in a criminal case only by a jury of free men; the right to be judged in any case only according to the precise terms of the law; the right to profess any religion one wishes."[22] He wrote an *épître* to Christian VII of Denmark praising him for establishing freedom of the press, and he took credit for the spread of the same liberty to Geneva, where, he wrote, "freedom of thought is gradually becoming established as it exists in England. There are those who accuse me of this change. I should like to deserve the same reproach from Constantinople to Dalecarlia."[23] Freedom of religion and the secularization of the state had long been Voltaire's great causes and formed the principal themes of his *Dictionnaire philosophique* and now of his *Questions sur l'Encyclopédie*,[24] but his main concerns during the 1770s seem to have been the right of property and freedom of person.

Voltaire's defense of the right of property was concentrated on his at-

21. Voltaire, "Propriété," in *Questions sur l'Encyclopédie*, in *Oeuvres*, XX, 291.

22. Voltaire, "Gouvernement" (1771, 1774), *ibid.*, XIX, 296. This passage was added in 1774.

23. Voltaire, "Epître au roi de Danemark Christian VII. Sur la liberté de la presse accordée dans tous ses états" (January, 1771), in *Oeuvres*, X, 421–27; Voltaire to Duvernet, May 4, 1772, in Voltaire, *Correspondence*, LXXXII, 8.

24. *E.g.*, Voltaire, "Eglise" (mainly 1771), "Tolérance" (1764, 1765, 1772), and "Droit canonique" (1771), in *Questions sur l'Encyclopédie*.

tempt to persuade Louis XV and his Conseil d'Etat to abrogate the right
of mortmain held by the Benedictines of Saint Claude over the peasants
of Franche Comté, who dwelt in the mountains behind Ferney. He argued
that this seignorial right, which prevented the transmission of ownership
except to heirs continuously on the land, was an infringement of the natural right of property: "You adduce a prescription, but we cite to you a
more authoritative prescription, that of the law of nations, that of nature.
It is not our obligation to prove that we were born with the rights of all
men; it is your obligation to prove that we have lost these rights."[25] As
spokesman for the peasant communities he told the king, "They entreat
Your Majesty to grant them emancipation of their persons and their possessions, to restore them to the condition of citizens, of free subjects, and
to restrain the alien hands that reach out to seize the fruit of their patri-
mony." Mortmain, Voltaire asserted, was "contrary . . . to the most precious principles of liberty held by the French nation. To be French is to
be free; the very name of Frenchman stands as a symbol of property of person. . . . France knows no slaves; it is the asylum and sanctuary of liberty.
In France liberty is indestructible."[26]

At the same time and like Malesherbes and other Patriotes, Voltaire
was protesting against abuses of *lettres de cachet* and demanding the reform
of judicial procedures to safeguard the rights of the accused—specifically
the abolition of torture and of convictions on insufficient evidence and the
guaranties of open trials, public examination of witnesses, and judgments
by juries.[27] He worked hard to rehabilitate D'Etallonde, Sirven, and others who had been the victims of miscarriages of justice. On all these issues
his position was identical with that of Montesquieu, and like Montes-

25. [François Marie Arouet de Voltaire], *Au Roi en son conseil. Pour les sujets du Roi qui
réclament la liberté de la France. Contre des moines bénédictins devenus chanoines de Saint Claude
en Franche-Comté* (N.p., n.d. [Geneva, 1770]), 19.

26. [François Marie Arouet de Voltaire], "Second requête au Roi," in [Voltaire], *Collection des mémoires présentés au Conseil du Roi par les habitants du Mont-Jura et le chapitre de
S. Claude, avec l'arrêt rendu par ce tribunal* (N.p., 1772), 18; Voltaire, *Coutume de Franche-
Comté sur l'esclavage imposé à des citoyens par une vieille coutume,* in *Oeuvres,* XXVIII, 372, 378–
79. See Mackrell, *The Attack on 'Feudalism' in Eighteenth-Century France,* 107–109, 113–
14, and *passim.*

27. Voltaire, "Arrêts notables" (1770), "Crimes ou délits de temps et de lieu" (1771),
and "Criminel" (1771), in *Questions sur l'Encyclopédie,* in *Oeuvres,* XVII, 388; XVIII, 273–
78, 278–84.

quieu he wrote, "To be free is to be subject only to the law."[28]

Voltaire's own experiences under the Maupeou regime gave him good reasons for defending the negative liberties. He had suffered illegal confiscation of property in his loss of 200,000 livres. He was equally bitter about the government's continued refusal to allow the importation from Geneva of the *Questions sur l'Encyclopédie.* In March 1771 he had written his printer, Cramer, "I still expect much from the chancellor." By October, however, he had given up all hope that he would be an exception to Maupeou's strict censorship. "All we can do now," he wrote Marmontel, "is adore in silence the hand of the god who chastises us. The Jesuits have been abolished; the parlements have been reformed; now it is the writers' turn. . . . There is no way now to send a single book to Paris. . . . Can you imagine that all the volumes of the *Questions sur l'Encyclopédie* so far have been printed in Geneva, in Neuchâtel, in Avignon, and in Amsterdam; that all Europe is full of them, and not a single copy can get into Paris? Once belles-lettres were protected in France; times have somewhat changed."[29] But it was not only for himself that Voltaire was concerned. He was deeply disturbed by the censorship of the French Academy and particularly by the suppression of Laharpe's *éloge* before that body.[30] To a Protestant friend he wrote, "The ministry is too busy with the parlements to think about persecuting the French Protestants. . . . They are coming down harder on the Philosophes than on the Protestants, but if neither speak too loudly they will be allowed to breathe in peace. This is all we can hope for in the present situation." And to D'Alembert: "A conspiracy has been organized against *bon sens,* as well as against liberty. What consolation have we left? A small number of friends to whom we can say what we think—when the doors are closed."[31]

Nevertheless and in spite of these principles, this disappointment, and this pessimism, Voltaire supported the Maupeou regime to its final hours.

---

28. Voltaire, "Gouvernement" (1771, 1774), *ibid.,* XIX, 295.

29. Voltaire to G. Cramer, March 1771, and to Jean François Marmontel, October 21, 1771, Voltaire, *Corrrespondence,* LXXVIII, 170, and LXXX, 99.

30. Voltaire to Jean François de Laharpe, September 26, 1771, to Jean Le Rond d'Alembert, September 28, 1771, and to Count d'Argental, October 11, 1771, *ibid.,* LXXX, 66, 67, 75.

31. Voltaire to Jean Gal-Pomaret, October 14, 1771, and to Jean Le Rond d'Alembert, October 19, 1771, *ibid.,* LXXX, 79 and 89–90.

His essential reason was that, however discouraging were some of the ministry's policies and actions, he remained convinced that Maupeou was fundamentally right in holding that France's salvation lay in a strong, centralized, absolute government and that the Patriotes and his fellow Philosophes were wrong in advocating republican government by corporations, whether aristocratic or not. He saw clearly that the essential issue was sovereignty and the exercise of positive liberty. Who was to rule France, to manage the national debt, control taxation, spend the money, and make and execute the laws—the king and his ministers, or some sort of corporation, the parlements, the States General, or a new national assembly? Only the first answer was for Voltaire possible, for the dangers in absolute power seemed to him much less than the dangers of republican anarchy. The parlements, he said, were attempting "to raise a hundred democratic thrones on the ruins of a throne that has endured for nearly fourteen centuries. . . . You seem to fear a tyranny which may someday supplant the moderate exercise of power. But let us be much more afraid of anarchy, which is tyranny by a tumultuous mob [*une tyrannie tumultueuse*]."[32]

There were also positive advantages in autocracy. Voltaire was persuaded by the argument of the efficiency of centralization. In defending the preeminence of the royal Conseil d' Etat he wrote, "The difference between this supreme tribunal and yours [the Parlement] is that this council, which is the only body in the government that is as old as the monarchy itself, by being located next to the throne functions as a center where comes together all the business of the kingdom. It is cognizant of all the various workings of the government, of which you see only a portion."[33] In his pamphlets Voltaire concentrated on the practical value of the reforms achieved by Maupeou's unfettered authority—the savings in time and money to litigants from the new conseils supérieurs, the abolition of venality and *épices*, and the expectation of cheaper justice.[34] Moreover, a single central authority could be more easily moderated and manipulated

---

32. [Voltaire], *L'Equivoque*, 13.
33. [Voltaire], *Les Peuples aux parlements*, 6.
34. [Voltaire], *Avis important d'un gentilhomme*; [Voltaire], *L'Equivoque*; [Voltaire], *Fragment d'une lettre écrite de Genève*; [Voltaire], *Les Peuples aux parlements;* [Voltaire], *Réponse aux Remontrances de la Cour des Aides*; [Voltaire], *Sentiments des six conseils*; [Voltaire] *Trés-humbles et trés-respectueuses remontrances du Grenier à Sel.*

by the individual citizen than could the manifold and dispersed authorities of corporations. An omnipotent prince or prime minister could be cajoled by a flattering letter or a well-turned poem, but how could one reach free-wheeling, irresponsible parlements? *Vide* the Calas case. This was what Voltaire meant when he kept writing his friends, "I prefer to obey a magnificent lion that was born much stronger than I rather than two hundred rats of my own kind."[35]

Voltaire's objection to government by corporations was fundamental. The principle of the second contract or *commission*, that the prince received his authority conditionally from the people, was utterly unacceptable to him. One of the reasons he worked so hard in 1774 to deny the authorship of the *Lettre d'un théologien* was that the author, Condorcet, had written, "Princes have received their authority from the people."[36] But regardless of theory, Voltaire was convinced that, in France at least, corporations were incapable of governing. "We are not worthy of being free," he wrote his nephew D'Hornoy. "Read carefully the history of France, and you will find that corporations [*compagnies*], starting with the Sorbonne and ending with the Jesuits, have never achieved anything but absurdities. We are pretty children who have to be led by the hand." To Richelieu: "Our nation has always been frivolous, and sometimes very cruel, and it has never been able to govern itself, and it is not worthy of being free. I shall add too that I should prefer, in spite of my great love of liberty, to live under the paw of a lion than to be continually exposed to the teeth of a thousand rats like myself." And to the Marquis de Florian: "I don't know how this affair of the parlements will end, but I should dare to say that corporations [*compagnies*] make greater mistakes than individuals do, for, since no one [in such a body] is individually responsible, everyone does as he pleases."[37] Of Claude Mey's *Maximes* he wrote, "I have been told it is a powerful book, but is it a good one? Do we Welches [French] have a public law? It seems

35. Voltaire to Jean François de Saint Lambert, April 7, 1771, in Voltaire, *Correspondence*, LXXIX, 12.

36. See Voltaire to Marie Antoine Jean de Caritat, Marquis de Condorcet, August 20, 1774, and to Claude Henri de Fuzée, abbé de Voisenon, August 20, 1774, *ibid.*, LXXXVIII, 174–75.

37. Voltaire to D'Hornoy, April 29, 1771, to Armand de Vignerot Du Plessis, Duke de Richelieu, May 20, 1771, and to the Marquis de Florian, February 25, 1771, *ibid.*, LXXIX, 42, 81, and LXXVIII, 113.

to me that the nation assembles only in the pit of a theater. If it showed as much bad judgment in the infamous States General as it does in the infamous Comédie Française [*Si elle jugeait aussi mal dans le tripot des états généraux que dans celui de la Comédie*], it was no mistake to abolish the States General."[38]

Voltaire's image of absolute monarchy often seemed to coincide with the patriarchal, idyllic, benevolent monarchism projected by certain royalists and conservative Patriotes. He liked to see the king not as the titular head of the Versailles bureaucracy but as a kindly shepherd:

> Je laisse au roi mon maître, en pauvre citoyen,
> Le soin de son royaume, où je ne prétends rien.[39]

His "Epître au Roi de Suède" (1772) reiterated this theme of the humble subject's peaceful contentment under a benign master:

> Un état divisé fut toujours malheureux.
> De sa liberté vaine il vante le prestige;
> Dans son illusion sa misère l'afflige:
> Sans force, sans projets pour la gloire entrepris,
> De l'Europe étonné il devient le mépris.
> Qu'un roi ferme et prudent prenne en ses mains les rênes,
> Le peuple avec plaisir reçoit ses douces chaînes.[40]

At the same time Voltaire was sympathetic to some of the tenets of the new statism. Like Lebrun he believed that the modern state could not have an irrevocable constitution but rather must be capable of continuous organic growth and adaptation, and that political evolution was possible only in an absolute monarchy. This was one of the key points of his *Lois de Minos*, a political tragedy written between December 18, 1771, and January 12, 1772, which he hoped Louis would reward by permitting the author's

38. Voltaire to Jean Le Rond d'Alembert, September 4, 1772, *ibid.*, LXXXIII, 4.

39. Voltaire, "Les Cabales" (1772), in *Oeuvres*, X, 176. "As a humble citizen I leave to my king the responsibility for his kingdom, in which I claim no share."

40. Voltaire, "Epître au Roi de Suède," *ibid.*, X, 448. "A divided state has always been an unhappy state. It boasts of the glory of its empty liberty, and suffers in its illusion. Without power and without hope of glory, it becomes the scorn of an astonished Europe. But once a firm and prudent king takes the reins in his hands, then the people gladly submit to his gentle chains."

return to Paris, but which he was unable to persuade the Comédie Française to produce. King Teucer, in order to prevent the sacrifice of his daughter as decreed by the ancient and superstitious irrevocable laws of Minos, overrides the adamant opposition of his reactionary senate by staging a coup d'état with the aid of his army, makes himself absolute ruler, and abolishes the evil laws. The lesson was obvious: The Enlightenment required the drastic revision of the antiquated and iniquitous political system that reactionary corporatism was trying to preserve, and this political revolution could be achieved only by an absolute ruler. "The laws must be changed," Teucer proclaims. "You must have a master." Lest the reader possibly miss the point, Voltaire added a footnote: "The purpose of this tragedy is to prove that it is necessary to abolish a law when it is unjust."[41]

By "law" Voltaire meant any law; injustice was not to be allowed sanctuary in constitutionality. There were no "fundamental laws" that the head of state could not change. "The fundamental law of every country," Voltaire wrote, "is that a man must sow wheat if he wishes to have bread and raise flax and hemp if he wishes to have cloth, that every man is master in his own field. . . . But the idea of a fundamental law created by the fluctuating wills of men and at the same time irrevocable is a contradiction in terms, an abstraction, a chimera, an absurdity."[42] Thus he supported Maupeou's denial of the principle of constitutionalism.

To the Patriote objection that all absolute power is by definition arbitrary and therefore unjust, Voltaire replied with the stock answer of self-regulating absolutism. He vigorously denied that he was advocating like Linguet oriental despotism:

> On m'a trop accusé d'aimer peu Moustapha,
> Ses vizirs, ses divans, son mufti, ses fetfa.[43]

And in the *Lois de Minos* he had King Teucer tell his daughter,

> Le peuple, en apprenant de qui vous êtes née,

41. Voltaire, *Les Lois de Minos*, *ibid.*, VII, 225, 180.
42. Voltaire, "Loi salique" (1771), in *Questions sur l'Encyclopédie*, in *Oeuvres*, XIX, 608.
43. Voltaire, "Epître à l'Impératrice de Russie" (1771), *ibid.*, X, 435. "I have been too often accused of having little love for Mustapha, his viziers, his divans, his mufti, his fetfa [*lettres de cachet*]."

En détestant la loi qui vous a condamnée,
Eperdu, consterné, rentre dans son devoir,
Abandonne à son prince un suprême pouvoir.[44]

To these lines Voltaire affixed an often-quoted footnote: "We do not mean here by supreme power that sort of arbitrary authority, that tyranny which the young Gustavus III . . . has recently abjured and solemnly proscribed by reestablishing concord and causing the laws to reign with him. By supreme power we mean reasonable authority based on the laws and tempered by them, that just and moderate authority which cannot sacrifice the liberty or life of a citizen to the malevolence of a sycophant, which submits itself to justice, which links together inseparably the good of the state and the good of the throne, which makes of a kingdom one great family governed by a father. Whoever proposes any other idea of what a monarchy is sins against the human race."[45]

This was the essence of Voltaire's political faith—that the enlightened, moderate, self-regulating exercise of absolute power was a reasonable expectation and was the form of government most capable of assuring the tranquillity and security of its citizens and of protecting their negative liberties, and that drastic action if necessary should be taken to create such absolute power. It has often been noted that Voltaire predicted revolution, but the revolutions he foresaw were like those staged by King Teucer, by Gustavus III, and by Maupeou, revolutions supplanting aristocratic corporatism with enlightened absolutism. "Does not this century seem to you, my dear philosopher," he wrote D'Argental "to be the century of revolutions, beginning with the anti-Jesuit revolution and ending with the revolution in Sweden, and perhaps not ending there?" The day before he had written Frederick II of Hesse-Cassel, "The noble revolution in Sweden carried out with such firmness and prudence by your cousin the king gives one the desire to live. The prince is like you; he makes himself loved by his subjects."[46]

44. Voltaire, *Les Lois de Minos, ibid.*, VII, 232. "The people, having learned your true birth and the law that has condemned you, dismayed and filled with consternation, become again dutiful subjects and concede to their prince his supreme power."

45. *Ibid.* The reference was to the king of Sweden's Maupeou-like coup d'état of August 1772.

46. Voltaire to Count d'Argental, September 16, 1772, and to Frederick II, September 15, 1772, *ibid.*, LXXXIII, 20, 17.

Thus Voltaire believed that benevolent enlightened absolutism was the wave of the future. It appeared to him not only the most practical and hopeful political formula but indeed the only possible one. The other options were aristocratic or democratic republicanism, and both he rejected as impractical and anarchic. They were impractical because he believed that on the record the French people were incapable of exercising positive liberty, of governing themselves through any sort of representative body, that they were "a nation of unruly children who have to be either spanked or coaxed with sweets."[47] The judgment seems harsh, even accepting the examples he adduced, but it is understandable if we take him to mean that the habit of self-government was not part of the pattern of French culture, as it was, for instance, of Anglo-Saxon culture. On the other hand, Voltaire's belief that republicanism in France would be anarchic merits some analysis, for evidently he foresaw that those whom a republic would bring to power, the nobles or the people, would prove to be disruptive and dangerous forces. It is possible, therefore, that his attitudes to these two social classes, the nobility and *le peuple*, may be relevant to his politics.

M. de Voltaire, né Arouet, like many other upwardly mobile bourgeois, had not hesitated to assume the aristocratic particle, and during his lifetime he acquired many friends in the nobility, for some of whom he undoubtedly felt sincere affection. Yet he had long held, as was early evidenced in his *Lettres philosophiques*, that aristocracy was a vicious political institution in the modern world. He echoed other apologists of Maupeou in describing the *thèse nobiliaire* as a modern continuation of the oppressive and anarchical feudalism of the Middle Ages, and he blamed the eighteenth-century survivals of feudal and seignorial rights as much on the parlements as on the church.[48] Aristocracy he saw as a force inherently inimical to both enlightened reform and enlightened government. This was the second thesis of the *Lois de Minos*:

47. Voltaire to Armand de Vignerot Du Plessis, Duke de Richelieu, April 20, 1771, *ibid.*, LXXIX, 14.
48. Voltaire, "Gouvernement" (1771, 1774), in *Questions sur l'Encyclopédie*, in *Oeuvres*, XIX, 287–90; Voltaire, *Extrait d'un mémoire pour l'entière abolition de la servitude en France* (1775), *ibid.*, XXIX, 403; Voltaire, *Lettre du révérend père Polycarpe, prieur des Bernardins de Chézery, à M. l'avocat général Séguier* (1776), *ibid.*, XXX, 337; Voltaire, *Lettre d'un jeune abbé* (1771), *ibid.*, XXVIII, 381–83; Voltaire, *Nouvelle requête au Roi en son conseil* (1770), *ibid.*, XXVIII, 369; etc.

Tel est l'esprit des grands depuis que la naissance
A cessé de donner la suprême puissance.
Jaloux d'un vain honneur, mais qu'on peut partager,
Ils n'ont choisi des rois que pour les outrager.

. . . .

Tout noble, dans notre île, a le droit respecté
De s'opposer d'un mot à toute nouveauté.[49]

The same position was reiterated throughout the *Questions sur l'Encyclopédie.*

On the other hand, Voltaire was equally convinced that the lower classes, "the fickle, riotous, misguided people," were incapable of exercising responsible political power.[50] Though he was quick to come to their defense against aristocratic or clerical oppression and though he conceded that the vices of the multitude were preferable to the vices of the privileged, democracy was to him a monstrous form of government. "The multitude of heads devour themselves."[51] Contradicting the Physiocrats, he saw no benefit in the education of the populace. "Some people," he wrote, "have set up schools on their estates, and I have done so myself, but I am afraid of them. I believe it is fitting that a few children learn to read, write, and cipher, but the majority, especially the children of agricultural workers, should know nothing but farming, for we need only one pen for every two or three hundred arms. Tilling the earth requires only a very common intelligence. . . . We must therefore employ as many men as we can at this simple sort of work and make them dependent on it."[52]

Despite his dislike of aristocracy, Voltaire was no egalitarian. He granted that all men have the same digestive systems and that if all lived in a state of nature in which every need was satisfied they would indeed

49. Voltaire, *Les Lois de Minos, ibid.,* VII, 175, 201–202. "This has been the essential motive of nobles ever since birth ceased to confer supreme power. Jealous of a sort of honor which is empty but which they can all share, they have chosen kings only to outrage them. . . . Every noble on our island has the sacred right to voice his opposition to every new reform."

50. *Ibid.,* VII, 176.

51. Voltaire, "Démocratie" (1771), in *Questions sur l'Encyclopédie,* in *Oeuvres,* XVIII, 333.

52. Voltaire, "Fertilisation" (1771), *ibid.,* XIX, 111.

all be equal. But in the state of society, in which every man is dependent on others, equality can never be more than a philosophic dream. Equality as a political ideal, equality of positive liberty, was a dangerous absurdity. "I know scarcely anyone," he wrote, "except Jean Jacques Rousseau whom one can reproach with believing in these ideas of equality and political liberty [*indépendance*] and all those other fantasies, which are merely absurd."[53]

Voltaire was a political realist in that he exercised the political power of his pen and prestige for the achievement of specific and concrete goals, whether the prosperity of his colony of watchmakers or the liberation of the peasants of Saint Claude, and in that his political theory was designed both to further these ends and to be consonant with the actualities of French national character and French society as he saw them. Yet this preoccupation with visible immediate objectives and situations sometimes led him to ignore fundamental inconsistencies in his general political strategy and philosophy, and these basic contradictions had a way of surfacing as practical dilemmas in the world of real politics.

It is true that isolation from the political arena in Paris, despite his voluminous correspondence, was a handicap. As he wrote Mme Du Deffand in 1774, after he had fumbled an opportunity to reinstate himself in the good graces of the Choiseuls, "You must realize . . . that when one is a hundred leagues away one cannot sense what is apropos to every occasion [*Il ne faut pas s'imaginer . . . qu'on puisse deviner à cent lieues l'à-propos du moment*]." Especially striking was his failure to recognize the political significance of the edict of December 1770, which as late as January he thought would be forgotten in six weeks.[54] Yet distance does not explain all of Voltaire's practical difficulties.

First, there was a fundamental inconsistency in the continuation of his campaign to "écraser l'infâme"—which, whatever its other implications, certainly meant the destruction of the Catholic Church in France—and his support of a regime whose main political bulwark was the church. As Daniel Mornet wrote in analyzing the period after 1750, "Political au-

53. Voltaire, "Egalité" (1764, 1770–1772), *ibid.*, XVIII, 473–77; Voltaire to Armand de Vignerot Du Plessis, Duke de Richelieu, February 15, 1771, in Voltaire, *Correspondence*, LXXVIII, 93.
54. Voltaire to Marie Anne de Vichy-Chamrond, Marquise Du Deffand, *ca.* December 15, 1774, and January 6, 1771, *ibid.*, LXXXIX, 166, and LXXVIII, 12.

thority never ceased to operate in close partnership with religious authority. It never opposed the demands of the clergy, before the Edict of Toleration, either in principle or by action. . . . The battle against fanaticism was by the nature of the situation in fact a battle against existing political authority, against the state. It was the state that was fanatical; it was the state that was resented; it was the state that was weakened to its foundations by the defeat of fanaticism."[55] Voltaire was working at cross purposes. The government he backed banned his antireligious writings and politely refused to inconvenience the Benedictines of Saint Claude. And in addition he suffered the embarrassments of finding himself the political ally of the anti-Philosophe Moreau and the Parti Dévot.

Second, Voltaire had to pretend to shut his eyes to the fact that Maupeou's regime was less enlightened and less efficient in practice than its proposed reforms had led him to expect. He soon was disenchanted with Terray's handling of the nation's finances. "Is it possible," he wrote D'Argental in 1771, "that after nine years of peace we are worse off than we were during a disastrous war!"[56] The tax on new titles of nobility he could treat with ironical humor, but the taxes on paper and books and the new regulations on the sale of grain were not so funny.[57] "The plague is not in Moscow" (as had been reported), he wrote Hennin. "The plague is in the royal treasury in Paris."[58] Worse still, Maupeou's enlightened absolutism, instead of protecting negative liberties, was still further restricting them. Censorship was tighter than ever. Voltaire did not dare allow his nephew D'Hornoy, a former magistrate, to visit him at Ferney. He had to fear that his "Epître au Roi de Danemark" on freedom of the press had come out at a very inopportune moment.[59] D'Alembert and Condorcet finally convinced him that the reestablishment of the Jesuits was a very real possibility.[60]

55. Mornet, *Les Origines intellectuelles de la Révolution française*, 471.

56. Voltaire to Count d'Argental, July 17, 1771, in Voltaire, *Correspondence*, LXXIX, 187.

57. Voltaire to Joseph Vasselier, August 9, 1771, to G. Cramer, September 26 and October ?, 1771, and to Jean Le Rond d'Alembert, October 19, 1771, *ibid.*, LXXX, 10, 64–65, 82–83, 89–90.

58. Voltaire to Pierre Michel Hennin, November 17 or 18, 1771, *ibid.*, LXXX, 131.

59. Voltaire to D'Hornoy (in disguised handwriting), February 18, 1771, and to Jean Le Rond d'Alembert, February 13, 1771, *ibid.*, LXXVIII, 100–101, 88.

60. Voltaire to Jean Gal-Pomeret, May 22, 1771, Jean Le Rond d'Alembert to Vol-

Voltaire was well aware that his continued apparent support of the oppressive aspects of Maupeou's regime was alienating a large section of public opinion, including that of Philosophes with no love for the parlements, and he could justify himself only by harping on the past inequities of the courts. For instance he once rather plaintively wrote Mme Du Deffand, "I know well that party spirit, the personal interests of a large number of families, and the fear of new taxes and of arbitrary government have caused some people in Paris to desire the return of the old Parlement, but for my part, madame, I avow that I could not regard except with horror those bourgeois [the exiled magistrates] who set themselves up as tyrants over all other citizens and who were at the same time ridiculous and bloodthirsty."[61]

Privately, however, Voltaire felt frustrated and depressed. Beaumarchais' *Mémoires* finally convinced him that the Maupeou Parlement was as corrupt and incompetent as the Patriotes had been saying. "I am afraid," he wrote D'Argental, "that brilliant madcap may be right after all, and everyone else wrong. What knavery, dear God! What a shocking business!"[62] Chronically ill and a semi-invalid, he had moments of deep pessimism, as when he wrote D'Alembert in May 1773, "It would be much better to correct oneself than to get angry. It very often happens that what ought to produce good produces only evil. . . . The only thing to do is to cultivate freely letters and one's own garden. . . . I laugh at the follies of men, and at my own follies." And to the same friend a month later: "Once again I say, one must cultivate one's own garden. This world is a chaos of absurdities and horrors. I have proof enough. At least I have tried not to contradict myself in my thinking." And in July: "There is no more communication, no more trust, no more consolation. All is lost; we are in the hands of barbarians."[63]

taire, February 26, and March 22, 1774, and Marie Jean Antoine de Caritat, Marquis de Condorcet to Voltaire, March 6 and March or April, 1774, *ibid.*, LXXIX, 84, and LXXXVII, 89–91, 139–40, 105–107, 153–54. The result was Voltaire's *Lettre d'un ecclésiastique sur le prétendu rétablissement des Jésuites dans Paris, 20 mars, 1774* (N.p., n.d. [Geneva, 1774]).

61. Voltaire to Marie Anne de Vichy-Chamrond, Marquise Du Deffand, March 29, 1773, in Voltaire, *Correspondence*, LXXXIV, 178. Cf. Voltaire to Jean François Marmontel, January 6 and 26, 1772, *ibid.*, LXXXI, 7, 40.

62. Voltaire to Count d'Argental, December 30, 1773, *ibid.*, LXXXVI, 190.

63. Voltaire to Jean Le Rond d'Alembert, May 20, June 7, and July 14, 1773, *ibid.*, LXXXV, 95, 126, 170.

Voltaire's discouragement from the failure of the French experiment in enlightened absolutism is indicated by his reactions to the end of the regime. The news of Louis XV's death filled him with dismay, for he was well aware of the new king's "dull hatred" of him.[64] He knew too that Maurepas was not his friend, and he feared the return to power of Choiseul, of whose continuing enmity he was now fully conscious.[65] Realistically he began to accommodate to the turn of events. His *Eloge de Louis XV*, rushed through Cramer's press in Geneva, was, despite its title, an implicit acknowledgment of the failures of the past reign.[66] He kept assuring Maupeou of his support, asking new favors of him and welcoming any indication that the minister might survive.[67] Yet when the bad news came he carefully kept silent about it, if we may judge from his extant correspondence. He did, however, both publicly and privately hasten to announce his enthusiasm for the new ministry. "I expect great things of M. Turgot," he wrote D'Argental. "Never did a man enter the ministry with stronger popular support. . . . I shall ask of him only some small protection for my colony."[68] Indeed he did request his "small protection."[69] Voltaire was gratified to find Turgot as amenable as Choiseul and

64. Besterman's phrase, *ibid.*, LXXXVIII, xxv.

65. On Maurepas, see Voltaire to Count d'Argental, June 15 and October 24, 1774, *ibid.*, LXXXVIII, 56 and LXXXIX, 68. On Choiseul, see Voltaire to Count d'Argental, May 18 and June 18, 1774, to François Louis Claude Marin, May 22, 1774, to Marie Anne de Vichy-Chamrond, Marquise Du Deffand, June 25 and September 7, 1774, and to De Lisle, July 1 and 4, 1774, *ibid.*, LXXXVIII, 21–22, 27, 64, 67–68, 77–78, 79, and LXXXIX, 11.

66. Voltaire apparently learned of Louis' death on May 16 and sent the manuscript to Cramer about the 20th. The piece was printed before the end of the month, with the date May 25, 1774. See *ibid.*, LXXXVIII, 19, 26, 36, 38.

67. Voltaire to François Louis Claude Marin, May 22 and 27, 1774, to Count d'Argental, June 3, July 28, and August 12, 1774, and to René Nicolas Charles Augustin de Maupeou, August 14, 1774, *ibid.*, LXXXVIII, 27, 35, 42, 124–25, 151–53, 157–58.

68. Voltaire to Count d'Argental, September 23, 1774, *ibid.*, LXXXIX, 23. Already in August Voltaire had publicized his support of the new ministry by publishing his *Au Révérend père en Dieu, Messire Jean de Beauvais, créé par le feu roi, Louis XV, évêque de Senez*, followed in the fall by his *Petit écrit sur l'arrêt de conseil du 13 septembre 1774*.

69. Voltaire, *Au Roi en son conseil*, in *Oeuvres*, XXIX, 305–308. Voltaire to Marie Jean Antoine de Caritat, Marquis de Condorcet, August 18 and September 28, 1774, to Count d'Argental, October 10 and 24, 1774, to Armand de Vignerot Du Plessis, Duke de Richelieu, October 14, 1774, and to Anne Robert Jacques Turgot, October 10, November 21, and December 7 and 9, 1774, in Voltaire, *Correspondence*, LXXXVIII, 170–71 and LXXXIX, 29–30, 43–44, 45, 51–52, 67–68, 112–13, 141, 150.

Maupeou.[70] His admiration for Turgot was certainly sincere, but the same cannot be said of his encomiums of Louis XVI. His prediction to D'Argental, "The dawn of this reign heralds the most beautiful of days" was neither ingenuous nor prophetic.[71]

Voltaire's response to the restoration of the old parlements was even more equivocal. Until November 1774 he expressed strong opposition to the "third Parlement" plans of Maurepas, Turgot, and the Princes of the Blood, of which he had reports.[72] Yet once the royal edicts were published he quickly made known his approval. "I like what M. de Maurepas is doing to settle this difficult problem," he wrote D'Argental on November 24. "He has met the wishes of the people, and in reestablishing the Parlement he has not diminished in any way the authority of the king. This is certainly the dawn of a new reign." The same day he also wrote Mme Du Deffand praising the "noble and wise behavior of the ministry in this difficult affair."[73] These letters make it likely that the "Excerpt from a Letter Received from Ferney, Dated December 10" published in the *Mémoires secrets* was inspired if not written by Voltaire. It read:

> We have received the report of the *Lit de Justice*. The edicts were read to M. de Voltaire. He admired everything, and especially the edict reestablishing the Parlement of Paris, the articles of which seemed to him well conceived to keep a proper check on that body. He praises M. de

70. Voltaire to Anne Robert Jacques Turgot, November 21 and December 30, 1774, and Pierre Michel Hennin to Charles Gravier, Count de Vergennes, December 26, 1774, *ibid.*, LXXXIX, 113, 194, 186; Gay, *Voltaire's Politics*, 332 note.

71. Voltaire to Count d'Argental, July 6, 1774, in Voltaire, *Correspondence*, LXXXVIII, 83. See also Voltaire to Marie Jean Antoine de Caritat, Marquis de Condorcet, August 12, 1774, *ibid.*, LXXXVIII, 154 and Voltaire, *Epître à Henri IV sur l'avènement de Louis XVI* (Paris, 1774).

72. Voltaire to Count d'Argental, June 18 and September 5, 1774, to De Lisle, July 1 and 15, 1774, to Marie Anne de Vichy-Chamrond, Marquise Du Deffand, June 25, July 28, and September 7, 1774, to Paul Claude Moultou, August 6, 1774, to D'Hornoy, August 10, September 5, and October 2, 1774, to Marquis de Florian, September 19, 1774, to Marie Jean Antoine de Caritat, Marquis de Condorcet, September 28, 1774, to De Lalande, November 4, 1774, to Joseph Vasselier, November 7, 1774, in Voltaire, *Correspondence*, LXXXVIII, 64, 67–68, 77–78, 98, 126, 142, 147, and LXXXIX, 6, 8, 10, 19, 29, 32–33, 84, 92.

73. Voltaire to Count d'Argental, November 24, 1774, and to Marie Anne de Vichy-Chamrond, Marquise Du Deffand, November 24, 1774, *ibid.*, LXXXIX, 119, 120. See also Voltaire to D'Hornoy, November 20, 1774, and Voltaire to Thibouville, November 28, 1774, *ibid.*, LXXXIX, 108–109, 129.

Maurepas in the highest terms. As for M. Turgot, his loyalty to him is its own reward; he is an old friend and supporter. He recently received from M. Turgot a four-page letter that filled him with joy.[74]

Nevertheless, on the last day of the year he wrote Mme Du Deffand, "I should like to eat the hearts of the judicial murderers of the Chevalier de La Barre."[75] Was Voltaire temporarily deceived by the language of the edicts into believing that the magistrates would be effectively subdued and controlled, and was he later disillusioned by the restored Parlement's defiant remonstrances against the attempted limitations on its powers?[76] Or had he, as a political realist, merely been accommodating himself to a fait accompli?

In reading Voltaire's letters and publications of the year 1774 one receives the impression that he felt far less personal involvement and interest in this political crisis than he had in that of 1771. There was no repetition of the anguished complaints of imminent financial ruin, for the change in ministry never posed a serious threat to his "colony." He esteemed Turgot as a man, but only the edict of September 13 restoring free internal trade in grains drew his public endorsement, and this was not a measure for which he could feel the same strong enthusiasm he had had for Maupeou's reforms. During the last months of the year, if we may judge by the correspondence, Voltaire was far more concerned with persuading everyone he did not write Condorcet's indiscreet *Lettres d'un théologien* and with rehabilitating D'Etallonde than he was with politics in the capital. His unwonted silence on political issues was so obvious that it caused general surprise. The *Ligue découverte*, a Patriote pamphlet published in October or November 1774, ironically reproached Voltaire for his failure to speak out, and Pidanzat de Mairobert snidely commented, "His silence . . . is indeed all the more extraordinary because he has always been quick to seize opportunities to express himself. But he has so loudly proclaimed his views that now he is greatly embarrassed to find a way to retract

74. *Mémoires secrets*, December 23, 1774 (VII, 289). Also in *Journal historique* (London, 1774–76), December 24, 1774 (VI, 417–18).

75. Voltaire to Marie Anne de Vichy-Chamrond, Marquise Du Deffand, December 31, 1774, in Voltaire, *Correspondence*, LXXXIX, 196.

76. See Voltaire to Dominique Audibert, December 19, 1774, to Joseph Vasselier, *ca*. December 19, 1774, and to Hermanches, December 20, 1774, *ibid*., LXXXIX, 170, 173, 174.

them."[77] Disillusioned with political activism, the Sage of Ferney had returned, at least for a while, to his own garden.

Despite his eminence, Voltaire was not the mind or the voice of France, and we must be careful in generalizing from one man's experience. Yet the failure of the Maupeou revolution for Voltaire may cast some light on the reasons why it failed for France. The royalists had advanced some highly reasonable propositions, most of which the future was to justify: that the French government urgently needed drastic reform of its fiscal, judicial, legal, and administrative structure; that the form of the government must be susceptible to modification and adaptation; that aristocracy, despite its late vigor, was an obsolete institution incapable of meeting the problems of the modern state; that the political future of France lay in the Third Estate; that the government had to move to alleviate the economic and social needs of the lower classes; that the negative liberty of citizens should be protected; and finally that the only practical way to achieve these ends was by creating a strong, centralized, unified government. All these propositions Voltaire accepted, and he saw no reason why such a state could not be completely secularized and why Maupeou's narrow concept of negative liberty could not be broadened to include all the individual rights he was championing.

These last two addenda were of course the sticking point. The French state could not be secularized without getting rid of the traditionally theocratic monarchy. And as both the Patriotes and the other Philosophes clearly saw, negative liberty could not exist without positive liberty. If the French people, and particularly the bourgeoisie, were to enjoy all the freedoms Voltaire and his friends were demanding, they could be sure of doing so only by holding in their own hands political power. The measure of the liberty of the people was the power of the people. The function of the Maupeou revolution was to demonstrate conclusively to the French— and apparently to Voltaire too—that the ideal of an enlightened, benevolent, libertarian absolutism could not be realized.

77. *Journal historique* (London, 1774–76), December 16, 1774 (VI, 394).

SIX

Linguet

T HE LAWYER Simon Nicolas Henri Linguet (1736–1794) deserves a few pages, though he represents no school of thought.[1] He was a free-wheeling, paradoxical iconoclast who kept insisting on what he believed were the economic and political realities of modern society; and in ridiculing all the *thèses*—parliamentary, royalist, Physiocratic, and Philosophic alike—as hypocritical cloaks of self-interest he cast considerable light on the issues. He had an embarrassing way of agreeing on at least some points with every group, but always for the wrong reasons. Though he was the most arrant absolutist of all, the ministry could not dare use him as a propagandist.[2] Voltaire, who admired the brilliance

1. For the most recent general study of Linguet, see Darline Gay Levy, *The Ideas and Careers of Simon-Nicolas-Henri Linguet: A Study in Eighteenth-Century French Politics* (Urbana, 1980).

2. As an absolute monarchist, an opponent of the Physiocrats, Philosophes, and *parlementaires*, and lawyer for D'Aiguillon, Linguet considered himself—and was considered—generally supportive of the Maupeou-Terray-D'Aiguillon regime, under which he apparently enjoyed, until his disbarment, some special favors. Maupeou had, however, no wish to be identified with advocacy of Asiatic despotism or with Linguet's other shocking paradoxes. There is no evidence that the chancellor instigated or subsidized any of Linguet's publications between December 1770 and November 1774, and in fact none of Linguet's writings of this period focused on the essential issues stressed by Maupeou's propagandists. Consequently, while Linguet was certainly a propagandist for his own quite special, radical, and populist *thèse royale*, I believe it is misleading to call him a "pro-government propagandist . . . and star advocate . . . of the Maupeou parlement." See *ibid.*, 94 and 192.

of his mind and sympathized with him on many questions, could not be his apologist.[3] He was detested by the parliamentary lawyers and magistrates, who succeeded in having him disbarred. He was feared by the Physiocrats, whose premises he lambasted and whose "despotisme" he endorsed.[4] And he was an inveterate enemy of the Philosophes, though he too preached the imperative need for social reform.[5] His major political work, the *Théorie des lois civiles*, antedated the Maupeou revolution, but his *Lettres sur la théorie des lois civiles, Réponse aux docteurs modernes*, and *Du plus heureux gouvernement* appeared in 1770, 1771, and 1774 respectively.[6]

Linguet's starting point was the premise that all political powers, laws, and titles to rights are in truth derived from the exercise of force, from violence and usurpation, and can have no moral sanction from either divine or human authority. "Sovereigns possess and exercise power because they possess it. Their exercise of power is their title to power. . . . They are justiciable before no tribunal." "Our first legislators were conquering robbers, their first ordinances were merely devices for dividing up the

3. *E.g.*, Voltaire to N. C. Thieriot, March 4, 1769, in Voltaire's *Correspondence*, LXXI, 136: "I have a high opinion of M. Linguet. He has ideas and he can express them."

4. Simon Nicolas Henri Linguet, *Canaux navigables, ou Développement des avantages qui résulteraient de l'exécution de plusieurs projets en ce genre pour la Picardie, l'Artois, la Bourgogne, la Champagne, la Bretagne, et toute la France en général. Avec l'examen de quelques-unes des raisons qui s'y opposent, etc.* (Amsterdam 1769); Linguet, *Réponse aux docteurs modernes, ou Apologie pour l'auteur de la "Théorie des loix" et des "Lettres sur cette théorie." Avec la réfutation du système des philosophes économistes . . .* (N.p., 1771); Linguet, *Du Pain et du bled* (London, 1774); Linguet, "Lettre de M. Linguet [à l'abbé Roubaud]," in *Journal de politique et de littérature*, November 15 and December 5 and 15, 1774; [Linguet], *Lettre à l'auteur des "Observations sur le commerce des grains"* (Amsterdam, 1775); [Linguet], *Théorie du libelle, ou l'Art de calomnier avec fruit. Dialogue philosophique, pour servir de supplément à la "Théorie du paradoxe"* (Amsterdam, 1775) (a reply to Morellet's *Théorie du paradoxe*). See Weulersse, *La Physiocratie à la fin du règne de Louis XV*, 154–56, 196, 197, 200, 204, 207–208, 219, 221–22.

5. [Simon Nicolas Henri Linguet], *Le Fanatisme des philosophes* (London, 1764); [Linguet], *La Cacomonade: Histoire politique et morale, traduite de l'allemand du docteur Pangloss, par le docteur lui-même depuis son retour de Constantinople* (Cologne, 1766).

6. [Simon Nicolas Henri Linguet], *Théorie des loix civiles, ou Principes fondamentaux de la société* (London, 1767); Linguet, *Théorie des lois civiles* (rev. ed.; London, 1774); [Linguet], *Lettres sur la "Théorie des loix civiles, etc." Où l'on examine, entr'autres choses, s'il est bien vrai que les Anglois soient libres, et que les François doivent, ou imiter leurs opérations, ou porter envie à leur gouvernement . . .* (Amsterdam, 1770); Linguet, *Du plus heureux gouvernement, ou Parallèle des constitutions politiques de l'Asie avec celles de l'Europe; servant d'introduction à la "Théorie des loix civiles"* (London, 1774).

booty," and all present laws descend from these origins. "Our titles to property are . . . power and primitive violence later legitimized by prescription."[7] Thus the theories of natural law and the contract were absurdities.

His second premise was that in society "liberty and power [*empire*] are synonymous. The only ones who can be free are those for whom society procures advantages, and these are, no one can deny, those who are in command. The more absolute their power, the greater the advantages they enjoy in society, and consequently the more they are free."[8]

Linguet's logical conclusion, which was also Locke's, was that liberty and government are by definition contradictory; the nature of government is to command, and the nature of liberty is to not obey.[9] The "liberty" that all the parties of the time were offering to the people was worse than an illusion; it was a dreadful deceit. It could not be real liberty, for the people were not being offered real power; it was merely unprotected independence, the right to survive as best one could at the bottom of the free-enterprise melee. A horse, Linguet reminded his readers, never starved to death; its master fed it even if he had to sacrifice his own needs to do so, or else he sold it to someone who could. The same protection was given a slave. "But the day laborer, who belongs to no one, whose poverty is unknown and ignored, of whom one is quit as soon as he is paid off, whose death is no one's loss and whose well-being is no one's concern, he can languish and die in his hovel and no one gives him a thought."[10] In the state of nature men had been free and equal, but, just as Voltaire was saying that the inherent economic dependency of the individual in the state of society made equality impossible, so Linguet said it made liberty impossible:

> O men of all nations, of all ranks, of all ages, listen to me! You are being deceived. You were born free, and they are trying to persuade you that you can still be free. This is a fantasy. Whatever could help to realize this dream would only increase your suffering. Liberty had, like all things, its advantages and disadvantages. Now a new kind of

7. [Linguet], *Théorie des loix civiles* (1767), I, 73, 35, 63.
8. Linguet, *Réponse aux docteurs modernes*, I, 252.
9. [Linguet], *Lettres sur la "Théorie des loix civiles*," 104.
10. Linguet, *Réponse aux docteurs modernes*, II, 111–12.

life has been created for you, likewise with its advantages and disadvantages, and you cannot escape it. It requires that you be divided into two groups; one, small and idle, which on the pretext of governing and maintaining order devours the fruits of the labor of the other larger group, which remains subjugated and without hope of freedom. This situation is called society and government. . . . It is the true and only natural order of political societies.[11]

It is impossible to doubt the sincerity of Linguet's compassion for the common people. Well-heeled philosophers who shut their eyes to the anguish of the poor revolted him. A line in Saint Lambert's *Saisons*, "O Mortels fortunés, vos travaux sont des fêtes!" aroused his furious indignation. It was "either a blood-stained irony or a revolting lie. . . . When I first read this horrible verse I was moved to tears. 'Poor, unhappy wretches,' I cried, 'who eat ashes soaked with tears, whose birth has been blighted by poverty, whose every moment is a prey to despair, whose life is one prolonged death, who can hope for rest only after your last breath, it is you who have been painted in the gay picture!'"[12]

If there was anything in society under government that could deserve the name of liberty it would be the freedom of the poor from economic oppression by the rich and powerful. It would be the liberty to live. "What is liberty?" Linguet asked. "There is no doubt that the freest people are those in that society in which each individual enjoys the most respect, in which the most numerous and strongest barriers have been erected against oppression, and in which the whole government acts to protect its citizens."[13] The only possible meaningful liberty was the protection, tranquillity, and security of the weak.

Therefore the people's greatest need was the assurance of their right to property, by which Linguet meant assurance of their means to subsist. Even though all property had its origin in violence, "it is clear that it must be respected and that whoever violates it sins against society. . . . Everything is derived from property; there is nothing in the world that is not related to it." It was true that an absolute prince enjoyed a sort of possession of the totality of all his subjects' properties, but "his title was no

11. *Ibid.*, I, 245–46.
12. [Linguet], *Lettres sur la "Théorie des loix civiles,"* 166–67.
13. *Ibid.*, 101.

more valid than theirs." His welfare depended on the welfare of his people, and this common welfare of prince and people depended in turn on
the security of each subject's right to subsist. "The most glorious governments are soon overthrown if the property of the people is not secure."[14]
Pufendorf's dictum that "the prince, in case of pressing need, may appropriate either by force or with consent a subject's property" was "an
abominable principle . . . directly contrary to the very nature of monarchy."[15]

But the right to property did not mean for Linguet, as it did for the
Physiocrats, the individual's right to use his possessions for his own exclusive benefit irrespective of the consequences to others. It meant the right
of the humblest subject to possess property adequate for his subsistence.
"The partial property right of a master to a few sacks of grain is subordinate to the universal property right of the whole people to the territory
they occupy and to the products it grows. . . . By right, every living being
has the authority to demand food. His teeth and his stomach are his patents. He holds these rights from nature. . . . The first of his duties, the
most sacred, is self-preservation."[16] "The supreme law is the welfare of
the people. The first of all properties is the right to live."[17]

This supreme right could be guaranteed only by the enforcement of a
measure of economic equality—not an equal sharing of property, but a
firm policing of the rich and assurance to the poor of at least a necessary
minimum, "the establishment of the greatest possible equilibrium between the two classes, which will procure for the inferior class the greatest
possible sum of liberty and enjoyment that their degradation permits, and
at the same time will keep the superior class in the most violent possible
state of fear and repression, so that they may be prevented from abusing
their power." This control could be exercised only by an absolute prince
with unlimited and unconditional power. "If [the people] ever will be able
to be happy that they are alive it will be . . . when a strong arm extends
equally over all parts of the state and keeps all subjects constantly in their
places."[18] "The interest of the majority is that the state be peaceful and

14. [Linguet], *Théorie des loix civiles* (1767), I, 61–65, 78–80.
15. [Linguet], *Lettres sur la "Théorie des loix civiles,"* 72–73.
16. Linguet, *Résponse aux docteurs modernes*, II, 63, 54–55.
17. Linguet, "Lettre de M. Linguet," in *Journal de politique et de littérature*, December
15, 1774, p. 232.
18. Linguet, *Réponse aux docteurs modernes*, I, 246–50.

that the authority of the prince be recognized beyond dispute, and that his authority not be dependent on a crowd of petty tyrants who seek to destroy and usurp it and who under the pretext of protecting the people ravage them and agree among themselves only on dividing up the plunder."[19]

Thus Linguet arrived at his famous paradoxical conclusion that the only truly free monarchy was an oriental absolutism. "True political liberty exists in Asia, and it exists only there. . . . Europe is the one area in the world where the powerful enjoy the privilege of being unjust with impunity."[20]

This conclusion explains his infuriating condemnations of libertarian "philosophic declamations" as "meaningless, useless, and even dangerous." The self-appointed apostles of freedom had not liberated a single Negro from slavery or raised a single day laborer's pay by a sou.[21] Their theory of "a sort of fictitious liberty" by which citizens surrendered a part of their liberty to preserve the remainder and under which they were to have "the happiness to live under the law" and in obeying the law remain free and thus "obey freely" was a cruel sophistry that "made liberty consist in slavery." Obedience to anything, even the law, was the denial of liberty, and civil liberty was a contradiction in terms.[22]

The theory that monarchical power had been voluntarily granted under a conditional contract was worse than an ahistorical "fantasy"; it was dangerous. Its proponents "have claimed that this theory is the only barrier against oppression; they have failed to see that it leaves them helpless."[23] Linguet saw no difference under the contractual argument between a eunuch in a harem and a citizen of Sparta.[24]

Montesquieu's and the other Anglophiles' ideal of a limited, moderate, constitutional monarchy was, Linguet said, in principle deceptive and in practice tyrannical. "Fundamental laws," if the phrase meant anything more than the reaffirmation of absolute power and the right of succession, were a myth.[25] He concurred with the royalists' rebuttal that sovereignty

19. [Linguet], *Théorie des loix civiles* (1767), I, 73.
20. Linguet, *Réponse aux docteurs modernes*, I, 251, 254.
21. [Linguet], *Théorie des loix civiles* (1767), II, 511–12.
22. [Linguet], *Lettres sur la "Théorie des loix civiles,"* 105–106.
23. [Linguet], *Théorie des loix civiles* (1767), I, 66–67.
24. [Linguet], *Lettres sur la "Théorie des loix civiles,"* 102.
25. Linguet, *Réponse aux docteurs modernes*, I, 263.

was indivisible. "There is no monarchy," he said, "if the king is forced to abide by fixed and established laws. The essence of monarchy is the right to legislate. If there is a superior power possessing this right, [the king] is under the command of that power, and then he is no longer the sovereign but only a magistrate representing the sovereign."[26] Representative legislatures, separation of powers, and intermediary powers, as in England and as advocated by Montesquieu, served only to create political instability, weaken the king, and expose the people to exploitation; proponents of these institutions "have never been interested in the good of the people, only in their own interests, advantages, and . . . privileges."[27]

Locke's theory of inalienable rights and liberties was only another excuse for license by the powerful and another threat to royal power. The freedom of expression preached by the Physiocrats with the arguments that "the truth can stand examination" and that free discussion makes the people rational and submissive was a dangerous absurdity. No government in the world could be completely reasonable; this idea was "capable of overturning all thrones and subverting all empires."[28]

The Physiocrats' advocacy of general public education was equally dangerous and for the same reason, that it threatened public order and the stability of the autocracy. Peasants taught to read and write would become "beaux esprits contemplateurs" and refuse their proper tasks. Who then would do their work? "In society everyone has his proper place, and he should stay in it." To start the common man thinking would only discourage him and cause trouble. He is "docile only as long as his head is empty. . . . A man destined by his social class and birth to useful but hard labor must not be allowed to give free flight to his mind. . . . The best educated peasants are generally the most quarrelsome and most litigious. . . . For three-quarters of mankind, it is enough that they know how to obey."[29]

Obviously Linguet was in complete agreement with the royalists' rejection of democracy. Theoretically, he admitted, the citizens of a perfect

26. [Linguet], *Lettres sur la "Théorie des loix civiles,"* 37.
27. Linguet, *Réponse aux docteurs modernes*, I, 257–58. Also, [Linguet], *Lettres sur la "Théorie des loix civiles,"* 94–108 and *passim*.
28. Linguet, *Réponse aux docteurs modernes*, II, 35–36.
29. *Ibid.*, II, 39–45.

democracy would all be free, for all would be sovereign.[30] In practice, however, the people would be corrupted by demagogues; there would be no way to determine their will; the principle of majority rule would lead to endless disputes; the inevitable result would be chaos; and eventually the majority would be subjugated by a minority of "liberators."[31]

Most dangerous of all was the Physiocrats' idea of economic liberty, for a free market in truth meant complete license for the rich to exploit the poor by keeping wages at a minimum and letting prices rise freely. Thus the poor would be driven down to the level of bare subsistence or worse, and they could expect no help from the generosity of the rich landowners, as the theory predicted. All Linguet could find in the writings of the Physiocrats was, he said, the idea "that the rich and noble [*les grands*] are everything and the people are nothing. They publish collections of precepts written for the education of tigers to teach them how to sharpen their claws and strengthen their teeth."[32]

In this jungle that society inevitably was, there would always be tigers and sheep. The only truly compassionate solutions were, first, to put in charge Voltaire's "beau lion," whose self-interest would be served by the preservation of the common right of all the animals to "property," that is, to their means of subsistence; and, second, to fight to limit the so-called "liberty" of the tigers, which only increased their license and made it more difficult for the lion to maintain a measure of order and equality in mankind's struggle to exist.

It is significant that Linguet agreed with the royalists Maupeou, Lebrun, and Voltaire (and also with Diderot) in conceiving of society as an organism in a constant process of growth, development, and transformation, and in insisting on the need for constant revision of the political and legal structure. He liked to compare social change to the growth of the human body, and he said that trying to govern France by the obsolete laws of past centuries was like dressing a thirty-year-old man in the clothes he wore when he was a child of four. It might suffice temporarily for the legislator to "agitate from time to time" the laws, "as a spider shakes its web to free it from the dust that weighs it down. . . . One must contin-

30. *Ibid.*, I, 253.
31. [Linguet], *Théorie des loix civiles* (1767), I, 72.
32. Linguet, *Réponse aux docteurs modernes*, I, 113; II, 150 and *passim*.

ually pass one's hand over [the laws] and brush off the dust accummulated during the daily operations of the bar." But eventually such remedies become inadequate. "Soon the task is not to clean the fabric but to weave a new piece of cloth." [33] Linguet cited in particular the urgent need to revise the laws on property, because of the tremendous increase in the trading of investments, and also the laws on debtors and usury, which were indeed causing absurd judicial problems. This proposal of a complete revision of the French legal code was of course precisely what Lebrun recommended to Maupeou and later finally helped to carry out under Napoleon. The need for governmental reform extended beyond the laws, however, and Linguet prophetically warned that a general restructuring was overdue. "If the rulers of empires fail to use these precious years, revolutions will soon do for them the task they have refused. But reform by violence can only destroy the state." [34]

It is not possible to dismiss Linguet as an absurd eccentric; he was a highly intelligent man and a brilliant lawyer. His proposal to turn France into an oriental despotism was merely a rhetorical gambit designed to *épater* the bourgeois libertarians and shake them out of their smug pharisaism. He did not, it is true, meet the objection of the Patriotes and the Philosophes that although the self-interest of a despot should in theory produce benevolence in practice it does not. Yet he was in the French tradition extending from Richelieu through Louis XIV and Napoleon I to De Gaulle that posited that social order and justice require a strong executive. He anticipated the Marxists by asserting that economic justice for the masses is more important than liberty for the bourgeoisie, and he anticipated Harold Laski's accusation that the "liberalism" of the eighteenth century was the ideology of capitalistic free enterprise. And most particularly, he underlined the apparent inherent contradiction in the thesis of his principal enemies, the Physiocrats, who claimed to reconcile libertarianism with absolutism, in what they called "despotisme légal."

33. [Linguet], *Théorie des loix civiles* (1767), I, 44.
34. *Ibid.*, I, 38.

SEVEN

The Physiocrats

THE PHYSIOCRATS, or Economistes as they were first known as, offered a fourth kind of absolutism, which they called "despotisme légal." Their doctrine was antithetical to the oriental despotism of Linguet on the issue of liberty, for they preached not the right to live under the protection of maximum authority but the freedom to act under minimum regulation. In contradiction to Maupeou they gave primacy to the individual, not to the state. They were closest to Voltaire in that they held that negative liberty could exist without positive liberty, yet they differed from him on a number of important points such as general public education.

The beginning of the Maupeou revolution coincided with the Physiocrats' loss of political influence and an abrupt decline in the prestige of their ideology.[1] During the period from Controller General Bertin's declaration of May 1763 abolishing restrictions on the internal grain trade to the dismissal of Maynon d'Invau in December 1769, Physiocratic principles had controlled the government's economic policy. But whether because of bad harvests, excessive exports, or dislocations caused by abuses of the new liberty, or a combination of all three, high bread prices and shortages of grain grew progressively worse from 1765 to 1770, except

1. Georges Weulersse, *Le Mouvement physiocratique en France, de 1756 à 1770* (Paris, 1910), I, 241. Throughout this chapter I am obviously deeply indebted to Weulersse's exhaustive studies, as well as to Kaplan's *Bread, Politics, and Political Economy.*

for a brief respite in 1769. This apparently decisive refutation of Physiocratic theory by bitter experience convinced both the public and the government. Terray formally terminated the ministry's free-trade policy by the *arrêt* of December 23, 1770, which the Paris Parlement endorsed and indeed had anticipated by its own *arrêts* of December 1768, January 1769, and August 1770.

The Philosophes too had declared war against the Physiocrats. Their opening gun was Grimm's "Sermon philosophique prononcé le jour de l'an 1770."[2] The Abbé Galiani was jubilant over its success and followed it up by the massive volley of his *Dialogues sur le commerce des blés* (1770).[3] Mme d'Epinay wrote him triumphantly in November, "Everybody is making fun of their writings. . . . You are victorious."[4] When the Abbé Morellet tried to reply with his *Réfutation* of the *Dialogues*, Galiani, Grimm, and Mme d'Epinay, with the approval of Terray and the support of Sartine, lieutenant général de police, managed to have the already printed edition locked up in the Bastille, where it remained until 1774.[5] Diderot too abandoned the Physiocrats.[6] In 1773 the Academy gave a kind of official blessing to the general repudiation by crowning Necker's *Eloge de Colbert*. The ministry cooperated with the Philosophes' feud not only by preventing the Physiocrats from publishing their writings but also by censoring their principal journal, the *Ephémérides du citoyen*, so strictly that the editor, Du Pont de Nemours, finally ceased publication in 1772. Only after Turgot's appointment in 1774 were the Philosophes and the Physiocrats briefly reconciled, but they later broke permanently. All this opposition by the ministry, the Parlement, and the Philosophes was supported—and certainly to a degree occasioned—by the apparently widespread hostility of the public, which blamed the grain shortages and the high price of bread in 1770 on the Physiocratic policies of the Choiseul ministry. "Whole provinces crying for bread," Bachaumont re-

2. *Correspondance littéraire*, VIII, 414–41.
3. Ferdinando Galiani to Louise F. M. Tardieu d'Esclavelles, Marquise d'Epinay, May 5, 1770, in Galiani, *Sa Correspondance* (3rd ed.; Paris, 1890), 138.
4. Louise F. M. Tardieu d'Esclavelles, Marquise d'Epinay to Ferdinando Galiani, November 7, 1770, in Epinay, *La Signora d'Epinay et l'abate Galiani. Lettere inedite*, 115.
5. Weulersse, *Le Mouvement physiocratique*, I, 239.
6. See Denis Diderot to Antoine de Sartine, March 10, 1770, in Diderot, *Correspondance*, ed. Georges Roth (Paris, 1963), X, 32–35.

ported in May 1770, "bear the strongest witness against [the Physiocrats'] spirit of innovation. . . . [The people in the provinces] blame them, perhaps unjustly, for their misfortunes, but the weight of circumstances makes a strong argument, especially in the mouth of a poor wretch dying of hunger."[7] An index of the loss of public support is the decline after 1770 of the provincial agricultural societies, which had been an important base of the Physiocrats' strength.[8]

Nevertheless, Physiocracy was one of the important ideologies of the eighteenth century, and it continued to influence the thought of the 1770s despite the school's fall from favor. Mme d'Epinay's statement in April 1771 that the Physiocrats had dropped "into the most perfect oblivion" is not to be taken literally.[9] Effective leadership had passed from the aging Dr. Quesnay to Victor Riqueti Marquis de Mirabeau, at whose home the group held *assemblées* every Tuesday. The demise of the *Ephémérides*, which Diderot said by 1772 "nobody was reading," was perhaps as much due to Du Pont's incompatibility with the tasks of editorship as to difficulties with the censor.[10] The Abbé Nicolas Baudeau was to revive the journal in December 1774 under the title of *Nouvelles Ephémérides économiques*, and in the interim the Abbé Pierre Joseph André Roubaud, the workhorse of the group, kept the flag flying from 1770 to 1774 by editing the *Journal de l'agriculture, du commerce, des arts et des finances* and the *Gazette d'agriculture, commerce, arts et finances*. Raynal supported the Physiocratic thesis in his phenomenally successful *Histoire des deux Indes*, as did D'Holbach, a Physiocrat on economic questions, in his *Système social* (1773). Chastellux adopted the term *physiocratie* (though giving it his own meaning) in his *De la Félicité* (1772), a book which contained much the Physiocrats could approve.[11] Even within the government a measure of support continued; Moreau's economic ideas, for instance, were not dissimilar. A minority of the original provincial parlements, those of Grenoble, Aix, Toulouse, and

7. *Mémoires secrets*, additions of May 29, 1770 (XIX, 220).

8. Weulersse, *La Physiocratie à la fin du règne de Louis XV*, 24, 157.

9. Louise F. M. Tardieu d'Esclavelles, Marquise d'Epinay, to Ferdinando Galiani, April 5, 1771, in Epinay, *La Signora d'Epinay et l'abate Galiani. Lettere inedite*, 165.

10. *Correspondance littéraire*, IX, 460.

11. Du Pont de Nemours found in *De la Félicité* "a host of very sound ideas." Carl Knies (ed.), *Carls Friedrichs von Badens brieflicher Verkehr mit Mirabeau und Du Pont* (Heidelberg, 1892), II, 39.

Bordeaux, refused to register the *dirigiste* decree of December 23, 1770, and later the reformed parlements of Aix, Toulouse, and Bordeaux under the pressure of local opinion continued until 1773 to stand for Physiocratic principles.[12] Even some of Maupeou's provincial intendants favored a free-trade policy.[13] Moreover, though the Physiocrats were careful not to become involved in the struggle between the Patriotes and the ministry, they had been sympathetic to the parlements' constitutional position, and their covert detestation of the chancellor gave them many allies.[14] Thus the Physiocrats remained an ideological power that cannot be discounted. They temporarily regained political influence after the appointment of their ally Turgot in 1774 and continued as an organized group into the 1780s.[15] Even after their dissolution their ideas lived on and diffused during the nineteenth and twentieth centuries in such movements as laissez-faire economics, free trade, Negro emancipation, scientific agriculture, public education, anticolonialism, and world peace.

12. Weulersse, *Le Mouvement physiocratique*, I, 236: Weulersse, *La Physiocratie à la fin du règne de Louis XV*, 6, 170–71, 175, 179; Georges Weulersse, *La Physiocratie sous les ministères de Turgot et de Necker, 1774–1781* (Paris, 1950), 28; Kaplan, *Bread, Politics, and Political Economy*, 457–71, 565–66, 579.

13. Weulersse, *La Physiocratie à la fin du règne de Louis XV*, 166–72.

14. Quesnay and Mirabeau remained silent before 1770 on the independence of the judiciary and on the parlements' rights of remonstrance, verification, and registration, but they apparently never took exception to the strong support on these issues voiced by Du Pont de Nemours and Mercier de La Rivière. See Pierre Samuel Du Pont de Nemours, "De l'Origine et des progrès d'une science nouvelle" (1768), in François Albert and Albert Bayet (eds.), *Les Ecrivains politiques du 18ᵉ siècle: Extraits, avec une introduction et notes* (Paris, 1904), 336–38; *Ephémérides du citoyen, ou Bibliothèque raisonnée des sciences morales et politiques*, 1769, No. 5. See also Pierre François Joachim Henri Mercier de La Rivière, *L'Ordre naturel et essentiel des sociétés politiques* (1767), quoted by A. Mathiez, "Les Doctines politiques des Physiocrates," *Annales historiques de la Révolution française*, XIII (1936), 198; Pierre François Joachim Henri Mercier de La Rivière, *De l'Instruction publique, ou Considérations morales et politiques sur la nécessité, la nature et la source de cette instruction . . .* (Stockholm, 1775), as republished in *Nouvelles éphémérides économiques, ou Bibliothèque raisonnée de l'histoire, de la morale et de la politique*, 1775, No. 10, pp. 116 ff. The Abbé Baudeau wrote in his diary, "Paris and the majority of the provinces will never accept being ruled by Maupeou, whom everyone hates, which is to say a lot, and whom everyone despises, which is even more." Baudeau, "Chronique secrète," III, 81. See also *ibid.*, III, 31, 64, 405, etc. Even Mirabeau made oblique references in his *assemblées* to the sufferings of a people living under "arbitrary authority." Victor Riqueti, Marquis de Mirabeau, "Discours pour l'ouverture des assemblées économiques, prononcé par M. le marquis de Mirabeau au mois de novembre 1774," in Knies (ed.), *Carls Friedrichs von Badens brieflicher Verkehr*, II, 317.

15. See Weulersse, *La Physiocratie sous les ministères de Turgot et de Necker*, 235–47.

The decline of the Physiocrats was due to the rejection of their economic theories, not of their political philosophy. Yet their politics, our main concern here, derived from their economics. Their basic premise was that nature's gratuitous contributions of rain, sun, and soil were the only true source of the wealth of nations, and that all occupations other than agriculture were "sterile" and merely changed the forms of wealth without increasing its amount. This principle dictated a social and political structure designed with one sole purpose, to increase the national wealth by promoting agricultural production. They advocated greater capital investment in agriculture and minimum investment in industry; the creation of a rural as opposed to urbanized society by reversing the demographic movement to the cities; scientific agronomy; higher agricultural prices and lower industrial prices; minimal agricultural labor costs, but the education of the peasants; the abolition of feudal and seignorial rights; improvement of roads and canals; large-scale farming; extended tenure for tenant farmers; the transfer of common lands to more productive private ownership; and, most fundamentally, maximum liberty for all private economic enterprise and absolute freedom of internal and external trade, particularly in grain.

Two fundamental political policies followed from this socio-economic program. The first was to propose, like Terray, a general reform of taxation, but of a very different sort. Since agriculture was the only source of new wealth, only income from agricultural production should be taxed, and existing taxes should be abolished—import and export duties, of course, and also the *taille* (direct tax on commoners), *capitation* (head tax), the *gabelle* (salt tax), and especially the *corvée*, which was so harmful to agricultural productivity—keeping only the *vingtième* on income from land, which the Physiocrats approved as at least in theory "just, natural, and proportionate." [16] Second, the political constitution of the state had to be designed to satisfy the requirements for maximum agricultural production.

The hallmark of the Physiocrats was their complete trust in reason. They were Cartesian rationalists, not Newtonian empiricists; their thinking was characteristically deductive and mathematical, not inductive or experimental. They would start with a hypothesis, such as their basic

16. Baudeau, "Chronique secrète," III, 40.

premise that the soil is the sole source of wealth, which they had intuited immediately and directly, and from such an axiom they would then deduce by mathematical logic all the necessary conclusions. Physiocracy, Du Pont de Nemours said, was "the true science of political arithmetic."[17] The word *nécessairement* recurred like a refrain in their expositions. Politics, economics, and morality were merely mathematically logical deductions from the "natural laws" that they had discovered. The universe of the Physiocrats had a beautiful mathematical order to which man had only to conform by using his reason. "The first lesson of our school," Mirabeau taught his disciples, "is to proceed step by step and believe only one's intelligence."[18] "There exists in the physical world and in the moral world," Paul Boesnier de L'Orme wrote, "a certain order of causes and effects which man can discover and follow in order to arrive at a certain end."[19]

Thus the Physiocrats were rationalists also in their complete faith in the power of enlightened human reason to control individual and social behavior in man's best interests. "In all ages," Boesnier de L'Orme continued, "man has been governed by his emotions. But the misuse of the emotions is only the result of human ignorance. The ignorant man can be enlightened, and the enlightened man can make a better use of his emotions. His will, guided by better laws, can follow more closely the order of nature." Consequently he subscribed to Turgot's theory of progress through enlightenment. "If man were unable to improve his lot, what good to him would be his intelligence, which distinguishes him from the brutes?"[20]

The assumption that there was only one order of nature and that all normal men when enlightened possessed sufficient reason to perceive its laws inevitably led the Physiocrats to uniformitarianism and the denial of Montesquieu's relativism, which had described each society as the unique result of its own special climate, terrain, customs, and so forth. They confidently enunciated universal economic and political truths valid for all

17. Quoted by Mathiez, "Les Doctrines politiques des Physiocrates," 193.
18. Victor Riqueti, Marquis de Mirabeau, quoted by Weulersse, *La Physiocratie à la fin du règne de Louis XV*, 17.
19. Paul Boesnier de L'Orme, *De l'Esprit du gouvernement économique* (Paris, 1775), 21. The date of the censor's approval indicates that this work was written prior to November 1774.
20. *Ibid.*, 22–23.

mankind; they spoke of "the moral world" and "the physical world," not of France in distinction from England. It is true that they cited the examples of China and the British colonies in North America, but this was precisely because they claimed that in these lands the successful application of Physiocratic principles had demonstrated their universal validity.

From this uniformitarianism came their philosophic idealism. They created, by the use of reason alone and not on any empirical grounds or from historical evidence, an ideal social model, and then strove to make phenomena conform to it. In fact, their dogmatic determination to realize this ideal made their rationalism only a sort of pseudo-Cartesianism, for, according to Cartesian physics, theory could and should be verified by the observation of measurable data. The Physiocrats made few if any attempts at experimental verification. Instead they tried by social reform to force experience to vindicate their ideal. The Abbé Morellet acknowledged that the Physiocrats had been accused of being "gens à systèmes" who proposed "abstract theories which have been established, it is alleged, without foreseeing obstacles or calculating possibilities, and which are therefore impossible to apply." But he brushed aside such "obstacles," physical or psychological, as irrelevant. We must, he said, let "theory establish the principles and suppose that all the obstacles will be eliminated. . . . Every true theory is based on facts, but they are general facts, and theories are to be combatted only by facts of a certain dimension; otherwise hundreds of years could be spent in gathering little facts, verifying them, and arguing about them. There would be no truth that could not be undermined by some obscure fact." [21]

The Physiocrats were also Cartesians, like the eighteenth-century naturalists, in that their point of departure was a mechanistic physics. "Natural law is physical," Mirabeau posited. The laws of psychology, morality, economics, and politics were all deducible from the operations of the physical universe. "Morality itself, celestial and divine though it be, does not exist for man except as an interest arising out of the physical world. It is in the physical that we must search for the source of our rights." [22]

21. [André Morellet], *Réflexions sur les avantages de la liberté d'écrire et d'imprimer sur les matières de l'administration, écrites en 1764. . . . .Par M. L'A. M.* (London [Paris], 1775), 45–49.

22. Mirabeau, "Discours pour l'ouverture des assemblées économiques," in Knies (ed.), *Carls Friedrichs von Badens brieflicher Verkehr,* II, 319.

The Physiocrats saw clearly a concrete chain of causes and effects by which natural physical laws determined economic laws, which in turn determined political laws, which thus were logically and actually implicit and ineluctable. "All laws," Baudeau said, "exist eternally and implicitly in a natural general and absolute code which allows no exceptions or modifications."[23] Du Pont put the concept most succinctly: "The physical order determines the moral order."[24] Consequently "it is the [positive] political laws," Boesnier de L'Orme wrote, "that must be adapted to economic relationships, not economic relationships to political laws. The first are established by nature; the second are the work of men."[25]

Among the physical laws, it had to be remembered, were those governing man's nature. Therefore "conformity to the laws which result from the nature of man considered comprehensively in all his different relationships [as a social, rational, and physical being] is the purpose of every political society, for man can be happy only if he observes these laws." Furthermore, the social behavior of individuals depended on how well the political laws of their societies conformed to the physical and economic laws. Boesnier de L'Orme continued:

> The particular behavior of individuals is necessarily a consequence of the model traced for them by [the government]. If this model contradicts Nature, then man, who is always forced to listen to her voice, will inevitably be torn between the necessity to obey natural laws and the obligations imposed on him by political laws. His conduct will therefore necessarily be irregular and inconsistent.
>
> The contradictions that are so often found between political and natural laws are incontestably the real causes of the evils that men have suffered in all ages and under all kinds of government.[26]

This sounds very much like the distinction made by Diderot (a friend of Boesnier de L'Orme) between the "code de la nature" and the "code civile," and also like D'Holbach's materialistic utilitarianism. Mercier de La Rivière in fact expounded a psychology that described man as moti-

23. [Nicolas Baudeau], *Première introduction à la philosophie économique, ou Analyse des états policés. Par un disciple de l'Ami des Hommes* (Paris, 1771), 402.
24. *Ephémérides du citoyen*, 1771, XII, 10.
25. Boesnier de L'Orme, *De l'Esprit du gouvernement économique*, 319.
26. *Ibid.*, 13, 14–15.

vated solely by pleasure and pain, by his natural desires to satisfy his senses, and by his self-interest or *amour-propre*. From these assumptions he argued that the only purpose of government was "to make man happy." Not all the Physiocrats were so frankly hedonistic, but Mirabeau himself wrote, "Nature has willed that man aspire only to his own advantages and always obey only his own needs."[27]

By asserting the primacy of physical causes the Physiocrats tended to empty natural law of ethical content and to fall sometimes into a sort of empirical moral utilitarianism. Boesnier de L'Orme, who held that happiness is the ultimate ethical good, wrote:

> It is not given to man to know the essence of things; he can have ideas about them only by their effects as he experiences them and by the relationships things have to him. What then is "justice"? What is "honor"? . . . They are the necessary laws which derive from the nature of man in his necessary relationships with his fellows, as he is capable of understanding these relationships through the operation of natural sanctions. . . . The "just" and the "honorable" are exactly the same as the "useful." What is truly useful to man and to society being necessarily just and honorable, and what is just and honorable being necessarily useful to man and society, morality and politics are the same science.[28]

This thesis was echoed and reechoed. "Let us show, let us prove that [self-interest] is in this world always in accord with the most severe justice and almost always in accord with beneficence, and we shall cut the roots of oppression and evil, which spring always from unenlightened self-interest. . . . Injustice is a foolish husbandman. It always buys too dear. It is justice that always buys at a fair price. It is beneficence that gets everything cheap." And the Abbé Roubaud: "There is no station in life in which the most honest and most just decision is not the shrewdest and the most profitable." The formula even worked in reverse. "To make men just and beneficent, the surest way is to make them rich."[29] Small wonder

27. Victor Riqueti, Marquis de Mirabeau, "Eloge de Fénelon," quoted by Weulersse, *La Physiocratie à la fin du règne de Louis XV*, 105.

28. Boesnier de L'Orme, *De l'Esprit du gouvernement économique*, 11–12.

29. *Ephémérides du citoyen*, 1771, VI, 222, 218; *Journal de l'agriculture, du commerce et des finances*, 1771, No. 12, p. 116; Victor Riqueti, Marquis de Mirabeau, "Eloge de l'abbé de Saint Pierre," quoted by Weulersse, *La Physiocratie à la fin du règne de Louis XV*, 107.

that the Physiocrats claimed as one of their own the American Philosophe who had preached that "honesty is the best policy."

This identification of justice and utility, this reassuring equation of the ethical precepts of the new utilitarianism with the dictates of the old natural-law morality and of Christian dogma, was made possible by the a priori assumption of the identity of the welfare of the individual with the welfare of the group. As Mirabeau posited, "Individual interest is at the same time the general interest of society."[30] "Enlightened self-interest" was merely the perception by educated reason of this natural identity. The principle applied not only among fellow citizens but also within the community of nations. The Physiocrats' pacificism followed from their reasoning that a nation by ravaging a neighboring state lost profitable markets for exports and destroyed needed sources of imports, and that the prosperity of one country increased the prosperity of all the rest. The ideal Physiocrat, said the Abbé Baudeau, was "a citizen of the world [who] embraces in his view all civilized nations; he considers them as constituting one single family; he sees them all naturally united by bonds of mutual advantage; and he concludes that only the state of peace is in their common interest."[31]

To posit that each individual was motivated only by the pursuit of his own happiness and that the achievement of his true, enlightened self-interest was the highest good, and therefore to argue for the welfare of society because it served the welfare of the individual, was a line of reasoning that obviously made the individual primary—ethically, economically, politically, and psychologically—and the state secondary. Thus Physiocracy was above everything else individualistic. The only purpose of government was to promote the welfare of the individual, and the best government, Mercier de La Rivière said, is the one "which men perceive to be most advantageous to them," the one "which assures them the greatest sum of enjoyment that they can reasonably desire" under the limitations of "the essential duties that our union in society imposes on us." Government achieves this end by assuring "the greatest possible abundance of

30. Victor Riqueti, Marquis de Mirabeau, *Supplément à la théorie de l'impôt* (The Hague, 1776), 298. (Written in 1774).

31. *Nouvelles éphémérides économiques*, 1775, No. 1, p. 183; Weulersse, *La Physiocratie à la fin du régne de Louis XV*, 108; *Nouvelles éphémérides économiques*, 1775, No. 3, p. 57.

things contributory to this enjoyment and the greatest possible liberty to take advanrage of them."[32]

To the modern mind such principles might suggest the welfare state, but to the eighteenth-century Physiocrat they indicated an opposite strategy. If one assumed that the enlightened pursuit of happiness would always be just, then all the government needed to do was to act as an educator to ensure enlightenment and as a policeman "to check our greed, which," as Mirabeau said, "is simply our self-interest blinded by its own ardor." Its sole useful function was to ensure the enjoyment of property, in the broadest eighteenth-century sense of the word, and do as little else as possible, letting the laws of nature operate. "Good government," Mirabeau wrote, "consists in doing the least possible amount of public business so that private business may prosper." He did not like Montesquieu's principle of *vertu* (active devotion to the republic) because it seemed "an unnatural prejudice that consecrates the individual to the maintenance of public interests at the expense of the extension of private property."[33] It was said that when the dauphin, the father of Louis XVI, once asked Quesnay what he would do if he were king, Quesnay replied, "Sire, I should do nothing." "And who would govern then?" asked the dauphin. Quesnay's answer was two words: "The laws."[34]

Consequently the Physiocrats opposed the proliferation of the government's bureaucracy, not for Malesherbes' reason that it was tyrannical but because it intruded on private enterprise. "If the government," Mirabeau complained, "is going to make everything run perfectly right down to the minute throughout the whole kingdom, it will have to be able to cause the rain to fall and the sun to shine whenever anyone wishes, grind every man's flour for him, and make the dough rise for every housewife." The individual neither needed nor wished to have his life managed by the government. "All a man wants to do is provide for his needs and enjoy the fruits of his labors. . . . He wants only to be protected, and all a government has to do is to inspire by instruction and example, to enforce by its authority absolute respect for property and liberty, and to create a sense

32. *Ibid.*, 1775, No. 9, p. 156.
33. Mirabeau, *Supplément à la théorie de l'impôt*, 269, 263–64; *Ephémérides du citoyen*, 1770, No. 4, p. 37.
34. Weulersse, *Le Mouvement physiocratique*, II, 41.

of complete and unalterable security."[35]

This doctrine of minimun government had two important corollaries. One was that the individual's attention to his private concerns should not be diverted to public responsibilities. The Physiocratic man wished neither to be governed nor to govern. Hence Mirabeau's dislike of Montesquieu's *vertu*. Second, there was to be no welfare state like that proposed by Lebrun. Physiocratic government left you alone—period. It neither interfered nor helped. There would be no sort of public assistance such as hospitals for the care of paupers.

The doctrine of the supremacy of individual self-interest also required a reexamination of the question of political sovereignty. If government was only an expedient device for the implementation of natural laws, its authority could not derive from anything as irrational as tradition or from a whimsical favoritism of the Almighty for the Bourbon family. It must somehow proceed from natural law operating through the collectivity of individual interests. Thus the Physiocrats were led to the theory of the general will. Mirabeau reasoned that the mere existence of a society of individuals automatically created what he called a "common will [*volonté commune*]," which should express itself through some constituted authority:

> The common will, or in other words the general will [*volonté général*], by its nature comprises the desire for the maintenance and preservation of the rights of all since it comprises the desire for the preservation of the rights of each, which is the natural will of every person, a will born of the sense of property and anterior to any desire to usurp the property of others. This union of individual wills forms the common will, whose expression, translation into action, and preponderance become a necessity. . . . Unity of interests is the natural bond holding societies together; unity of wills must be the result [of this bond] and is the necessary means for the satisfaction of these interests. All politics can be reduced to this truth; all government is instituted to indicate to those associated in society this locus of voluntary union.[36]

35. Victor Riqueti, Marquis de Mirabeau, "Eloge de Vauban," quoted by Weulersse, *La Physiocratie à la fin du régne de Louis XV*, 84; Mirabeau, "Eloge de Fénelon,," quoted *ibid.*, 85.

36. Mirabeau, *Supplément à la théorie de l'impôt*, 65–66, 262.

In his *De l'Instruction publique*, written for Gustavus III of Sweden, Mercier de La Rivière amplified and elaborated Mirabeau's reasoning. "A true political state," he posited, "is a body composed of a multitude of men so closely united that, having one single and identical will and one single and identical purpose, they form one single and identical individual. . . . This unity can have no other principle except a perfectly understood common interest. . . . This unity of will, purpose, and power supposes necessarily unity of opinion on what concerns and constitutes this interest."

Therefore a "true" government was necessarily the expression and embodiment of this common will of the "true state." "A common recognized interest being the sole and unique bond of a true body politic, it follows that such a body can truly exist only if it is governed by the common will of its members, and thus its government, considered as a power, is not and cannot be anything else but this common will itself translated into action for the common interest and by the common interest." This reasoning rested, of course, on the Physiocratic assumption that "it is impossible that a sensible and intelligent being not wish his own true best interest when he knows it," and that therefore a group of enlightened beings will likewise necessarily know and will their common interest, and having the same idea of this common interest will "all have the same will."

By Physiocratic definition "this common will is always just and always proposes the common good." Therefore if "laws are derived, as they should be, from the common interest and consequently are consonant with each reasonable individual's interest," then it follows that "such laws are consonant also with each individual's will, and so each member of the political body is a legislator who obeys only his own will because he obeys only his own laws. Thus the citizens are as free as they can aspire to be, once the government has done all that is necessary so that the laws may always govern, that is, so that no private will may ever . . . raise itself above the common will, of which the laws are the expression." Therefore the "legislative power" is "the body politic itself," and to suppose a legislating body politic is to assume one which has "the ability to assemble as a body and act as a body."[37]

37. Mercier de La Rivière, "De l'Instruction publique," in *Nouvelles éphémérides économiques*, 1775, No. 9, pp. 113–16, 120–21, 144–48.

On first reading, these conclusions seem to parallel those of Rousseau's *Contrat social*, published about ten years earlier, but there were fundamental differences in the premises. Chiefly, the Physiocrats denied the concept of the state of nature, as either a historical or a heuristic hypothesis. Man, Mirabeau taught, has always been a social animal and, however primitive, always has lived in some sort of society, even if it were no more than the family. Equally illusory was the concept of natural liberty. A savage alone in a forest would be the "least free of men, for he would be forced to flee at the slightest noise. . . . Where would be his liberty?" The theory that men had once lived in isolation and in perfect liberty and had agreed to sacrifice part of their natural freedom to join together in a society for mutual advantage was an "illusion." Even as a heuristic supposition (which Rousseau said he was making), it was misleading, for "society . . . is not the artifice of man. It is created by nature and is the natural result of the needs to which nature subjects us."[38] There was thus in the Physiocratic universe no dualism of nature and society, for society was natural.

Denying the hypothesis of a presocial and prepolitical state of nature, the Physiocrats perforce denied the first contract, by which Rousseau had supposed that men in the state of nature had joined to form a body politic and had *then* determined their general will. For the Physiocrats, the general will was naturally inherent in a society and manifested itself whenever the members became sufficiently enlightened. Second, property was not a right conferred on the invididual by society *after* its political institution (as Rousseau had said) but rather was a natural right because it was inherent in the nature of society. In fact there were no natural presocial or prepolitical rights, but only those which could be deduced logically from the "nature" of society. Third, the Physiocrats did not, contrary to Rousseau and most of the Patriotes, see any reason why a hereditary absolute monarch could not infallibly embody and implement the general will. Though Mercier de La Rivière said the legislative body politic had to have the ability to assemble as an actual body, this ability could remain "potential" and the people could tacitly delegate both their legislative and executive powers to a group of men or to a single man, preferably to a

---

38. Mirabeau, "Discours pour l'ouverture des assemblées économiques," in Knies (ed.), *Carl Friedrichs von Badens brieflicher Verkehr*, II, 321–22.

hereditary monarch.[39] This unconditional transfer of the authority of the general will to a prince was what Mercier, like Hobbes, called the social contract, whereas Rousseau had insisted that the transfer could only be a temporary and revocable "commission," the hiring of a public servant, and could not confer legislative authority but only a charge to execute the general will. Mirabeau was emphatic on the need for a single "imposing will to serve as a rallying point for the common will, expressed or tacit, . . . to evoke it, express it, and translate it into action." Finally, we must remember that while certain passages in the *Contrat social* seem rationalistic and mechanical, Rousseau never forgot that he was defining government "for men as they are." His political man was motivated as much by instinct and sentiment as by reason, and he had learned from Montesquieu the lesson that just government, like liberty, "is not the fruit of all climates."[40]

The Physiocratic definitions of political rights and duties and of the law also can be best understood in comparison with the corresponding ideas in Rousseau. According to the *Contrat social*, in a just state the laws, and consequently the citizens' rights and duties, are all "artificial," the creatures of a "convention," an agreement; they are not natural, and they are just only because the people to whom they apply have entered into a social contract and have each promised to abide by the decisions of the general will. These decisions may be wrong in the sense of impractical or inexpedient, and they are not necessarily in accord with a priori natural justice, but they are always "right" in that they are the expressions of the general will, the will of each and all. In the Physiocratic just state, on the other hand, the citizens' rights and obligations, and therefore the laws, derived *necessarily* from the nature of society. "The necessity of obedience is a consequence of the necessity of society," Mirabeau wrote. "The right of society is founded on the necessity for men to join forces and render one another mutual aid. . . . Every right has its principle in necessity."[41] Thus the enlightened general will, whose logical organ was a "tutelary authority," a hereditary monarch, did not really invent or choose laws, but sim-

39. Mercier de La Rivière, "De l'Instruction publique," in *Nouvelles éphémérides économiques*, 1775, No. 10, pp. 116, 122–25.

40. Mirabeau, *Supplément à la théorie de l'impôt*, 65–66; Jean Jacques Rousseau, *Du Contrat social*, Book III, Chap. 8.

41. Mirabeau, *Supplément à la théorie de l'impôt*, 64–65.

ply perceived them. "The sovereign authority," Du Pont de Nemours explained, "is not instituted to 'make laws,' for *the laws are already made* by the hand of Him who created our Rights and Duties."[42]

In order to understand the Physiocrats' disposition to implement their political system by the institution of an absolute monarch, by "legal despotism," we must go back to their economic theory, their point of departure. They were concerned only with the proper government for what they called a "nation agricole." There did exist, of course, "états trafiquants" and "états mixtes," whose economies were mainly commercial and industrial and which accumulated wealth "precariously and servilely" and fell outside the "natural order." The laws of such nations were "purely human, relative to time, manners, customs, circumstances, climate, and political institutions and hence fluid, variable, and, in a manner, arbitrary."[43] Such states were not describable by Physiocratic political theory and therefore should be ignored.

The problem they wished to resolve was the logically necessary government for a *nation agricole*, which France was. In such a state the only true citizens were the agricultural landowners, for they alone produced true wealth, they alone provided support for the government through taxes on the produce of their lands, and thus they alone had a true interest in the national welfare. Merchants, artisans, manufacturers, persons with merely pecuniary fortunes, and landless laborers were useful and to be tolerated, but their economic interests were not identical with those of the nation. They were not true citizens and so could not have an integral relationship to the nation's government. The "master class" or "national class," the true citizens, were the *propriétaires fonciers* (landowners), a term which was broadly used to cover various subgroups, from the *grands entrepreneurs de culture* (agricultural contractors) to the humblest landowning peasant. This was a kind of aristocracy, but one in which aristocratic status was conferred by ownership of land and in which "all the nobles are equal and wealth makes the only difference."[44]

The Physiocrats liked to speak of this class as a new *noblesse*, but it could

42. Du Pont de Nemours, "De l'Origine et des progrès d'une science nouvelle," in Albert and Bayet, *Les Écrivains politiques du 18ᵉ siècle*, 334. Italics *sic*.

43. [Baudeau], *Première introduction à la philosophie économique*, 397. See Weulersse, *La Physiocratie à la fin du régne de Louis XV*, 101.

44. [Baudeau], *Première introduction à la philosophie économique*, 108.

be described in modern terms as a capitalist agricultural plutocracy in which the richer plutocrats "naturally" enjoyed the greater power and prestige. Nevertheless this new nobility, like the old, had social obligations. "A landholder is really the owner only of that portion of his property which is necessary for his own subsistence, and he is the administrator of all the rest. That is, having more wealth than he can consume, he must, after having deducted his own portion, expend judiciously the remainder in such a way that it produces for him and for society the greatest possible good."[45] In working for himself he worked for all, and in working for all he worked for himself. His obligation was not mere almsgiving (though alms might be given in cases of dire need), for this sort of charity solved no economic problems, gave only momentary relief, and in the long run was pure loss. Instead, the landowner's duty was to live on his land, to increase its productivity, to provide workers and soldiers as needed for the maintenance and defense of the state, to assist in the education of the people, and to cooperate (though not too much) in the government.[46] In short, this was the classic apology for benevolent capitalism, stated for an agricultural economy.

At the head of this aristocracy stood the king, and here again was an analogy with the old nobility. Not only was he the greatest of all landowners, but also, just as the feudal king had ruled over his lords' domains, so he was the "co-owner" of all the lands of the nation. The kingdom was in a literal sense the king's property, for he derived income from it, a certain just percentage of the net income from all the land, which could be computed by dividing the expenses of government by the total national agricultural net product. Like any proprietor the monarch necessarily exercised all the rights of ownership; he could transmit his title to his heir, and he had the absolute right to manage his property according to his own best interests—which meant total legislative, executive, and judicial power, police power, the assessment and collection of taxes, and the responsibility for education and public works. The king's co-ownership created no injustice or conflicts of economic interest with private owners, for there was a natural identity of the enlightened best interests of the king-

45. Anonymous manuscript in Bibliothèque Nationale, quoted by Weulersse, *La Physiocratie à la fin du règne de Louis XV*, 212.
46. *Ibid.*, 213–14.

individual and of society. The king's share of the net income—the land tax—was a necessary expense to the private landowner for the security of his property. Moreovoer, since the king's income and the income of the private owner varied directly, whatever was in the best economic interest of one was in the interest of the other—provided, of course, that the only tax was on income from land.

Though the king had absolute authority to enunciate laws, his power was not arbitrary. As in the self-regulating absolutism of the royalists and conservative Patriotes, he was bound by inherent limitations. These were not, however, the traditional "fundamental laws" or Christian natural moral law, but the laws of the natural order. "Authority," Baudeau said, "is only the daughter of the law and never its rival. . . . The tutelary authority of sovereigns has essential limits, limits marked out by the nature of things, which are no less to the personal interest of the monarch than they are to the interests of his subjects."[47] Du Pont de Nemours went so far as to say that the authority of the law took precedence over the authority of the monarch, for "men were obliged by their consciences to submit" to the fundamental laws dictated by nature "even if [these laws] were not promulgated by the sovereign," and, conversely, if any positive law or arbitrary act of government were contrary to natural law the citizen could appeal from the king's authority to God and reason.[48] This position approached the Patriotes' appeal from tyranny to natural moral law.

This "monarchie économique" seemed to the Physiocrats the only logical—and therefore the "necessary"—form of government for a *nation agricole*. In the first place, it assured identity of interests between the producers of true wealth and the government. Second, by handing over the time-consuming tasks of government to one pair of hands it allowed the individual owner to concentrate on his proper business of producing wealth. Most importantly of all, it assured law and order. Like all utopias the Physiocratic state required a mechanism to enable enlightened reason to keep society at the point of perfection. It needed an absolute authority to "hold in line those unwilling to respect the rights of each and all."[49]

47. *Nouvelles éphémérides économiques*, 1775, No. 3, p. 49.
48. Du Pont de Nemours, "De l'Origine et des progrès d'une science nouvelle," in Albert and Bayet, *Les Ecrivains politiques du 18ᵉ siècle,* 335.
49. Mirabeau, "Discours pour l'ouverture des assemblées économiques," in Knies (ed.), *Carls Friedrichs von Badens brieflicher Verkehr*, II, 326–27.

Obedience to reason could not be enforced if the powers of government were separated as in England. "The idea of several authorities in a single state is a complete absurdity," Du Pont de Nemours had written in 1768, in agreement with the royalists' argument. "If they are equal there is no authority but only more or less anarchy; if one is superior, then it is the only authority, and the others are nothing."[50] Turgot spoke like a Physiocrat when he said, "Do not imagine that I approve of republican institutions. I do not believe there ever existed a good republic, and I agree with the Economistes that republicanism is a form of civil war and that what is called a balance of powers is worthless."[51] An obvious fear was that a republican legislature would represent interests opposed to those of the landowners. In a republic, Mirabeau warned, in which "the voice of the people [was] entrusted to representatives" the senators would be ruled by motives of private gain and ambition and would feel far less identity with the true interests of the nation than would a prince. The result would be corruption, disorder, and a reign of special interests.[52] In 1770, apparently already fearing demands for the recall of the States General, he spoke at length in his "Eloge de Sully" on the dangers of government by corporations:

> National assemblies participating in the sovereign authority can only impair an agricultural nation and fragment it. . . . If these men do not understand the laws [of the social order] they will be assemblies of blind men, suspicious of one another, malicious, and in the end dangerous. If they do understand these laws, then what is the good of taking them away from their own affairs? What is the good of having them assemble just to watch the sun rise and set? . . . In troubled times . . . if they are expected to remedy the problems and are consulted as spokesmen for the needs of the state, they can only give expression to the disruptive forces that are causing the difficulties. They will produce only

50. Du Pont de Nemours, "De l'Origine et des progrès d'une science nouvelle," in Albert and Bayet, *Les Ecrivains politiques du 18ᵉ siècle*, 334. Cf. *Nouvelles éphémérides économiques*, 1775, No. 3, p. 47.
51. Anne Robert Jacques Turgot to Pierre Samuel Du Pont de Nemours, June 21, 1771, in Turgot, *Oeuvres de Turgot et documents le concernant*, ed. Gustave Schelle (Paris, 1913–1923), III, 488.
52. Mirabeau, "Discours pour l'ouverture des assemblées économiques," in Knies (ed.), *Carls Friedrichs von Badens brieflicher Verkehr*, II, 317–18.

a confusion of tongues, conflicts of wills, mutual contempt and derision, plots, sound and fury, and even more disrespect for authority.[53]

This then was what was meant by "despotisme légal"—"despotisme" because the king would be absolute, but "légal" because he would rule according to the dictates of the natural laws of the social order. It was not a happy phrase, for *despotisme* had become a strongly pejorative word, even with extreme royalists, and the qualifier seemed paradoxical, for despotism was rule without law. To meet Turgot's objections Physiocratic writers began substituting in the 1770s the phrase "autorité tutelaire," which Turgot still found unsatisfactory.[54]

This was to be a secular bourgeois capitalist absolutism, and in this respect the Physiocrats were close to Voltaire's position. Although they were careful to avoid any appearance of anticlericalism and tried to reconcile their system with Christianity, they wished to eliminate the *dîme* (tithe) as contrary to their principles, and they opposed allowing the church any sort of fiscal immunity or special privilege. There was no place for ecclesiastical political or social power in a *despotisme légal*. By the same token the new agricultural aristocracy would displace from political and economic advantage the old hereditary nobility, whether its titles were *d'ancienne souche* or had been acquired by the purchase of *charges*. "They preempt authority for their own special advantage, . . . inevitably alienate the people," and create disunion, Mirabeau said. In the Physiocratic state, he predicted, "all claims for territorial franchises will be eliminated automatically. . . . Since all land in the state will owe taxes to the sovereign there will no longer be any such things as church lands or noble lands. . . . Every privilege is a dismemberment of the state."[55] The Abbé Baudeau perceptively remarked in 1774 that Turgot's Physiocratic economic policy was "not understood by the two extremities of the population, that is, the people at the Court and the upper class in Paris, on the one hand, and on the other the lower levels of the populace. . . . Enlightenment and virtue are to be found only in the middle class. A good gov-

53. Victor Riqueti, Marquis de Mirabeau, "Eloge de Sully," in *Ephémérides du citoyen*, 1770, VIII, 29–34.

54. See Anne Robert Jacques Turgot to Pierre Samuel Du Pont de Nemours, May 10, 1771, and March 25, 1774, in Turgot, *Oeuvres*, ed. Schelle, III, 486, 665.

55. Mirabeau, *Supplément à la théorie de l'impôt*, 264–65, 205, 247.

ernment, and the good education that good government provides, tend
to cut back more and more these two extremities and to increase the middle class. Which I think is a very good thing."[56]

Nevertheless the bourgeois capitalist individualism at the heart of *despotisme légal* began eroding the absolutism in the concept as soon as the
structure of the system was elaborated. Having granted the king absolute
power with one hand, the Physiocrats immediately began to take it away
with the other. The plan for a mathematically determined tax rate would
have deprived the crown of the essence of political power, control of the
public purse. But more important was the fundamental principle that the
king's will must be identical with the general will. This could be assured
only by some constitutional mechanism, and the Physiocrats' scientism
demanded that it be explicitly defined in an official document. "One of
the first and most necessary responsibilities of a reforming or founding
prince," Mirabeau advised, "must be to establish a national constitution
so written and so in conformity with nature that it will be consecrated by
the general will and will be respected by future ages."[57]

Obviously the English model would not be appropriate, for it entailed
separation of powers. Even worse would be a democratic constitution. "All
arbitrary government is bad," Du Pont wrote, "and no government is more
arbitrary than that by the populace."[58] Mirabeau strongly criticized the
recently published Virginia Bill of Rights because it included a guaranty
of the effective and active sovereignty of the people. He saw as highly dangerous precisely what Tocqueville was to consider the great strength of
democracy, the political involvement of the common citizen. Democracy
reversed the Physiocratic dictum that there should be the greatest possible private business and the least possible public business. It "makes a
public business of everything. Political passions replace and take on the
shape of domestic cares. Everyone is ambitious, everyone is discontented,
and such a government, if it existed, would be a prelude to anarchy, and
anarchy the signal for a dispersion of wills."[59]

56. Baudeau, "Chronique secrète," III, 414.
57. Mirabeau, *Supplément à la théorie de l'impôt*, 244.
58. Pierre Samuel Du Pont de Nemours to Carl Ludwig von Baden, in Knies (ed.),
Carls Friedrichs von Badens brieflicher Verkehr, II, 131.
59. Mirabeau, *Supplément à la théorie de l'impôt*, 263–64. Mirabeau by 1776 no longer
shared his disciples' enthusiasm for the American Revolution. To follow the example of
Virginia and institute popular sovereignty, he said, would "justify for all time the spirit

The task, then, was to conceive of a body which would represent the true citizens and provide the king the guidance of the enlightened general will without abridging his absolute authority. Quesnay and Mirabeau began to consider the problem as early as 1758, and the latter continued to work on it into the 1770s.[60] In a number of works but principally in his *Supplément à la théorie de l'impôt*, written in 1774, he elaborated in considerable detail a plan for annual provincial assemblies composed of elected landowning representatives from the various cantons. The clergy, the titled nobility (unless they owned land) and the urban bourgeois would be excluded. These bodies in cooperation with agents of the crown would assess properties, fix the tax rate, collect taxes, propose needed public works, and send the king reports of "notable examples of virtue, talent, devotion, or service"—but no grievances. Mirabeau stressed that his proposal was untainted by republicanism and did not infringe on the powers of the sovereign.[61]

Meanwhile Du Pont de Nemours became interested in Anglo-Saxon politics, and while remaining opposed to the introduction of separation of powers into the French monarchy, he apparently came to believe that it was a practical system for the British. He criticized the British government not so much for its constitutional principles but because he believed Parliament did not truly represent the nation. He ascribed this failure to a number of reasons but principally the underrepresentation of landowners and the contention of the members that they should speak not for their constituencies but for "the interests of Great Britain," which meant (Du Pont said) that they voted as they pleased. However, if these vices were corrected and the British adopted free trade and a single tax on the net agricultural product, they would have an acceptable government.[62]

Du Pont de Nemours' most interesting contribution was a plan for the constitution of an independent nation formed from the British North

of sedition." Victor Riqueti, Marquis de Mirabeau, "Observations sur la Déclaration des Droits du bon peuple de Virginie" (1776), quoted by Weulersse, *La Physiocratie sous les ministères de Turgot et de Necker*, 110.

60. Georges Weulersse, *Les Manuscrits économiques de F. Quesnay et du marquis de Mirabeau aux Archives Nationales* (Paris, 1910), 27; Weulersse, *Le Mouvement physiocratique*, II, 70–71, 79; Mathiez, "Les Doctrines politiques des Physiocrates," 200–201.

61. Mirabeau, *Supplément à la théorie de l'impôt*, 207–74.

62. Pierre Samuel Du Pont de Nemours to Carl Ludwig von Baden, in Knies (ed.), *Carls Friedrichs von Badens brieflicher Verkehr*, II, 228–30.

American colonies, which he published under the title "Lettres de Abraham Mansword" in the *Ephémérides du citoyen* three years before the American Declaration of Independence. The preamble contained a restatement of Physiocratic theories, a discussion of the nature of liberty, and a list of civil rights and constitutional principles: division of the government into legislative, judicial, and executive branches; limitations on the military; the guaranty of the possession and free use of property; and prohibitions against arbitrary taxation and interference with any civil rights except by due process of law. The government was to consist of a national states general, whose members would receive their instructions from the provincial legislatures; a senate of superior magistrates; and a *chef* who would preside over the states general and be the chief executive officer, assisted by a council. This surprising document deviated from some of the fundamental political dicta of Physiocracy; not only did it introduce separation of powers and abandon monarchism, placing instead sovereignty in "the proprietary corporation of the commonwealth [*le corps propriétaire de la chose publique*]," but it also took a first step toward democracy by incorporating decisions by majority vote, on the reasoning that "aside from the presumption of greater wisdom in the opinion of the greater number, . . . the majority, being by the nature of things endowed with the superior physical force, must possess the dominant moral force." Du Pont also eased slightly the Physiocratic restrictions on the franchise by admitting as voters besides landowners persons holding land in usufruct and those pensioned for past services, but he still relegated all the other inhabitants to the status of *Plebs*, "absolute aliens to the state."[63] These modifications seemed to show that, despite Mirabeau and Turgot, Physiocracy was susceptible to adaptation to republicanism.

This apparent anomaly is perhaps to be explained by the early and strong Americanism of the Physiocrats, who had been much impressed by Franklin during his trips to Paris in 1767 and 1769, by Dr. Benjamin Rush, who also visited them in 1769, and by John Dickinson's *Letters from a Farmer in Pennsylvania*, translated by Barbeu-Dubourg. The phenomenal demographic growth of the colonies and the prosperity of their agricultural economies seemed to confirm dramatically Physiocratic theory, and American opposition to British mercantilism, the high level of public

63. *Ephémérides du citoyen*, 1771, XI, 75–112; XII, 6–45.

education reported by Franklin, and the American Quaker antislavery movement first reported in Paris by Rush, all won the Physiocrats' enthusiastic approval. Du Pont proudly announced that Franklin had "adopted the principles and doctrines of the French Economistes."[64] This predilection was extended to all things American. Du Pont and Roubaud attacked Buffon and De Pauw for their theory of American degeneration.[65] Other Physiocrats joined the Rousseauists in propagating the mirage of the colonies as an Arcadia of simple virtuous yeomen.[66] Indeed many were vociferously cheering for American independence as early as 1771.[67] It is small wonder that Du Pont, the most vocal and persistent Americanist of the school, was receptive to American republicanism.

In 1775 Turgot was preparing for Louis XVI a plan for constitutional reform to be entitled *Mémoire sur les municipalités*, and he asked Du Pont to write it. Turgot endorsed the final document and the ideas it contained were certainly his. It was, however, basically an elaboration of Mirabeau's earlier plan, and Du Pont was unquestionably in sympathy with the scheme and may well have contributed suggestions. Moreover Turgot subscribed to most of the principles of the Physiocrats if not to their tactics, even though he refused to be formally enrolled in their ranks. Thus his *Mémoire* may properly be considered an extension of Physiocratic constitutional thought.

The proposal was essentially a multiplication of Mirabeau's consultive assemblies into a pyramid of *municipalités* representing parishes, towns, *arrondissements*, and provinces, capped by a national *municipalité* for the nation as a whole. Membership in these assemblies and the franchise were to be limited to landowners, including owners of urban properties, and no distinctions were to be made among nobles, clerics, and commoners. Voters would have fractional, single, or multiple votes proportionate to their incomes from real property. Turgot stressed that his plan did not

64. *Ibid.*, 1769, IX, 68.
65. *Ibid.*, 1769, X, 46; Pierre Joseph André Roubaud, *Histoire générale de l'Asie, de l'Afrique et de l'Amérique* (Paris, 1770–1775). See Durand Echeverria, "Roubaud and the Theory of American Degeneration," *French American Review*, III (1950), 24–33.
66. *Ephémérides du citoyen*, 1769, III, 68–78; VIII, 39–52; Gaspard Guillard de Beaurieu, *L'Elève de la nature* (new ed.; Amsterdam, 1771), II, 241–59; III, i–iii.
67. *Ephémérides du citoyen*, 1771, XI, 85–91; *Journal de l'agriculture*, June 1774, pp. 56–57; *Gazette d'agriculture, commerce, arts et finances*, July 23, August 2 and 20, 1774.

restrict the absolute authority of the king, for the role of the various bodies would be consultive. They would have, however, the important duty of assessing and collecting taxes; the king would present to the national *municipalité* the total sum needed for the fiscal year; this body would then allocate to the provincial *municipalités* their proper assessments, which would be progressively divided and passed down to the parish and town *municipalités*, which would distribute the burden proportionately among the landowners according to the income or value of their lands. Turgot expected that his scheme would provide an efficient and equitable system of taxation according to Physiocratic principles, counter the increasing social fragmentation and civic alienation he saw in France, and at the same time introduce considerable administrative decentralization, for the *municipalités* were to take an active though advisory role in local government.[68]

All these various constitutional proposals had the purpose of fostering unanimity and cooperation between the sovereign and the landowners. But there was also the additional need to educate the general will of the entire people so that the enlightened self-interest of every Frenchman would contribute to the integrity of the state. No group in France at this time was more keenly aware than the Physiocrats of the social and political power of public opinion or felt more strongly the need that this opinion be rational and informed. Indeed they believed that the first task of government was to instruct its citizens. "From all [their] knowledge is created a common reason, which then invariably creates the common will, and this in turn creates a society which will give unshakable support to its leader."[69] There was a beautifully simple logic in Physiocracy that made universal education essential: The Natural Order produced individual self-interests. The true knowledge of these interests through education resulted in an understanding of rights and duties. This collective knowledge constituted "common reason." The willing of this common reason was the common will, which created and supported the laws and society, which in turn supported the leader, the "tutelary authority." Conse-

68. Anne Robert Jacques Turgot, "Mémoire au Roi sur les municipalités," in Turgot, *Oeuvres*, ed. Daire, II, 502–50. On the "Mémoire" see Baker, "French Political Thought," 284, 295–98, 302–303.
69. Mirabeau, *Supplément à la théorie de l'impôt*, 271.

quently the government must provide all citizens with an adequate education. It has been supposed that the Physiocrats advocated general public education only in order to produce competent agriculturalists, but the political purpose was primary. Mirabeau called education the "indispensable bond of society," for its function was "to let men know and perceive their advantages in society" and to create between governors and the governed not merely "general mutual confidence" but "a meeting of minds and views."[70]

The Physiocrats intended a general education literally for all, male and female and of every social class. "To grant knowledge to some and abandon others in the same society to ignorance would create disunion or civil war." Rejecting doubts of the teachability of the masses, Mirabeau affirmed that individuals' natural faculties varied less than was generally believed, that everyone was capable of knowing and achieving more, and that among the lowest classes might be found geniuses capable of becoming valued citizens and fulfilling the highest positions in society. This universal education was to include reading, writing, arithmetic, and training in special skills, but the important purpose was the inculcation of what Mirabeau called "la morale économique": the citizen's rights and duties, the sanctity of property, respect for liberty, the identity of self- and group-interest, and the nature of law, sovereignty, and the tutelary authority. Although the curriculum was to be entirely secular in content and objectives, Mirabeau assured that it would not contradict religious training but supplement it. Above the primary schools there were to be colleges and academies to train leaders for the monarchy.[71] Mercier de La Rivière, who was influenced by Rousseau and cited by *Emile*, amplified Mirabeau's ideas and added the suggestion that even free primary schools for all would not suffice and that the government should use all its various branches to "spread enlightenment" and should take measures to see that citizens profited from their opportunities, "though without using violence or abridging their liberty."[72] The anonymous *Ferme de Pensilvanie*

---

70. *Ibid.*, 19, 29, 54, 156–57.

71. Victor Riqueti, Marquis de Mirabeau to Carl Friedrich von Baden, March 31, 1770, in Knies (ed.), *Carls Friedrichs von Badens brieflicher Verkehr*, I, 23–26; Weulersse, *La Physiocratie à la fin du règne de Louis XV*, 95.

72. Mercier de La Rivière, "De l'Instruction publique," in *Nouvelles éphémérides économiques*, 1775, No. 9, pp. 131–33; No. 10, pp. 133–36.

refuted those who claimed that "nothing would be more difficult to govern than a nation of people who could reason" by pointing to the example of Pennsylvania, where enlightenment had produced men like Dickinson and Franklin and brought forth a people who governed themselves by the eternal laws of the social order. "What we learn every day of their wisdom and virtue is unbelievable."[73]

By the same token the Physiocrats championed freedom of the press, which Mirabeau said would at last make public opinion truly "the queen of the world."[74] Their appreciation of the value of this freedom was certainly enhanced by the strict censoring they themselves suffered under Maupeou, and it was also encouraged by the example of the British colonies, particularly by Franklin, whose "noble reply" at the bar of Parliament, "No power, how great so ever, can force men to change their opinions," Du Pont proudly printed in the *Ephémérides* in 1768.[75] Yet their basic reason for advocating this liberty was that it was an essential means to enlighten the people and to bring to light economic and political truths. When Sartine suppressed the Abbé Baudeau's pamphlet *La Pierre de touche*, which proposed free publication of all political writings bearing the author's and publisher's names, for the reason that "there would be too many disadvantages to such freedom," Baudeau's comment was: "He is right. There would be a lot of disadvantages to ignorant and hypocritical ministers . . . and especially to the mob of presumptuous, absurd, and corrupt clerks [of the bureaucracy], but it is obvious that there would be no disadvantages to the prince and the nation."[76]

In 1771 Jacob Nicolas Moreau in his capacity as censor surprisingly responded to a request for views on the issue from Du Pont by writing that though he maintained that writings should be censored prior to publication he saw no reason to forbid discussion of the question of censorship itself. "In this way," he said, "we shall both give good examples of this liberty which always operates to the benefit of the instruction of the public and in the long run always assures the triumph of truth." So he au-

73. *La Ferme de Pensilvanie. Les Avantages de la vertu. Plan d'instruction pour le peuple; avec quelques observations sur la liberté de commerce des grains* (Philadelphia and Paris, 1775).
74. Mirabeau, "Eloge de Vauban," quoted by Weulersse, *La Physiocratie à la fin du règne de Louis XV*, 220–21.
75. *Ephémérides du citoyen*, 1768, VIII, 192.
76. Baudeau, "Chronique secrète," III, 62.

thorized publication in the *Ephémérides* of both his statement and Du Pont's reply. It is apparent that Moreau, who was the most libertarian perhaps of the royalists and who had marked sympathy for the Physiocrats, did not disagree with Du Pont on the essential point, that (in Du Pont's words) "with no other help than freedom to pursue the truth, reason always destroys error and falsehood." The only issue in debate was prior censorship. On this Du Pont argued that if authors signed their works and were subject to the penalties of libel, "errors could do no harm provided that more enlightened men were permitted to refute them. Errors are dangerous only when they are persecuted, and they are always spread by being prohibited." A free press was necessary to facilitate "the spread of the enlightenment, by which all men will learn to govern themselves in accordance with justice and their enlightened self-interest."[77]

This basic argument was voiced by Gustavus of Sweden in a speech printed by the Abbé Baudeau and by Mercier de La Rivière in applauding Gustavus' enlightenment.[78] The Abbé Roubaud engaged in a prolonged controversy with Linguet, who had contended that freedom of the press would instill disrespect for authority and "stir up the people to revolt." This, Roubaud answered, was a lie. "Ah, sir, between slavery and license stands liberty. Because you fear lest liberty degenerate into license you would choose slavery. . . . In darkness there is only anarchy."[79]

Thus working from their original economic premises the Physiocrats were led by their logic "necessarily" to a broad libertarianism that made *despotisme légal* much more legal than despotic. Their opposition to economic privileges for the titled nobility led them to oppose feudal dues and seignorial rights.[80] Similarly their denial of fiscal privileges to the church led them to religious toleration. Du Pont lauded the religious freedom in Catholic Maryland and Quaker Pennsylvania, and he urged Prince Frederick of Baden to "accomplish in Europe what has been begun in Penn-

77. *Ephémérides du citoyen*, 1771, I, vii–xviii. Du Pont de Nemours repeated the same arguments to Prince Carl Ludwig von Baden. See Knies (ed.), *Carls Friedrichs von Badens brieflicher Verkehr*, II, 221.

78. *Nouvelles éphémérides économiques*, 1774, pp. 98–100; Mercier de La Rivière, "De l'Instruction publique," *ibid.*, 1775, No. 10, pp. 139–40.

79. *Gazette d'agriculture, commerce, arts et finances*, December 27, 1774, p. 828. See also *ibid.*, November 5 and 22, 1774, pp. 709, 750.

80. *Journal de l'agriculture*, March 1771, pp. 139–63; August 1771, pp. 28–29. See Mackrell, *The Attack on 'Feudalism,'* 139–45.

sylvania, where, as Benjamin Franklin has told me, all the sects are gradually blending together of their own accord into one pure, simple, natural, and moral civil religion."[81]

Liberty did not, however, for the Physiocrats require equality. Their political philosophy is in this respect the most striking example of the fact that for an eighteenth-century mind (and as was still to be the case for Tocquevillian liberals of the nineteenth century) liberty and equality could be not merely distinct but even essentially incompatible. Boesnier de L'Orme seems to have been the only important Physiocrat who accepted the theory of the presocial state of nature, but even he said that, though man was naturally free, the idea of "natural equality" was a chimerical notion and an impossibility, for men were naturally unequal in abilities and faculties, and this natural inequality inevitably implied inequality of possessions.[82] For the others, who held that the social state was the only natural condition of man, the rejection of both the theory of "natural equality" and the ideal of economic equality was axiomatic. "Inequality of wealth," Mirabeau said, "exists in nature just as does inequality of size, strength, and health. As society expands, accidents, favorable or unfavorable, multiply. . . . The inequality becomes immense. . . . This is far from 'an evil destructive of society'; society is instituted for no other purpose but to protect and preserve this elemental disproportion."[83] Boesnier de L'Orme likewise stressed both the justice and desirability of inequality: "To constrain man to this so-called and chimerical equality [advocated by philosophers such as the Abbé Mably] is to take away the very principle of his life." A man forbidden to increase his property would have no incentive. Furthermore the whole fabric of social relationships was derived from the dependence of the weak and the obligations of the strong. Without inequality "there would no longer be fathers and sons, husbands and wives, friends or enemies, relatives or strangers."[84]

On the other hand, confronted with recurrent famines, the abject destitution of a large portion of the population, and conspicuous consump-

81. Pierre Samuel Du Pont de Nemours to Carl Friedrich von Baden, November 5, 1771, in Knies (ed.), *Carls Friedrichs von Badens brieflicher Verkehr*, I, 133.

82. Boesnier de L'Orme, *De l'Esprit du gouvernement économique*, 3, 17, 18.

83. Victor Riqueti, Marquis de Mirabeau, "Critique" of Morellet's *Réflexions*, quoted by Weulersse, *La Physiocratie à la fin du règne de Louis XV*, 83.

84. Boesnier de L'Orme, *De l'Esprit du gouvernement économique*, 9–10.

tion by the rich, the Physiocrats were open to charges from many besides Linguet that they were inhumanly callous. This accusation they could not ignore, especially since they believed that harmony and solidarity between classes was necessary in a Physiocratic society. "By the law of nature," a contributor to the *Ephémérides* wrote, "there cannot be two different interests, that of the poor and that of the rich. They are inseparable." Mirabeau himself admitted that "the prosperity of society . . . makes more shocking every day the inequality of wealth. . . . This increasing inequality brutalizes and antagonizes one group and enervates and hardens the other, and so tends to separate what the social law seeks to unite." Moreover, as Boesnier de L'Orme pointed out, a grave political danger lay in "the extreme inequality of the division of land." The Physiocratic ideal was an agricultural plutocracy, but a plutocracy that embraced the largest possible fraction of the population. "Can there be true laws," he asked, "in a nation in which a small number of citizens can make themselves the legislators merely by virtue of their wealth? . . . The rich then would be the entire state, and the people nothing."[85] To this dilemma the Physiocrats found no persuasive solution. They could only stress the obligation of the rich to contribute to society and predict that economic growth in a Physiocratic state while increasing inequality would benefit the poor on an absolute scale, so that "the most impoverished, . . . no matter how low their pay, will be much better off . . . than were the poor, and perhaps even the rich, in a savage and primitive state."[86]

Moreover the Physiocrats emphasized that they were defending inequality of property, not inequality of rights. They drew a sharp and clear distinction between what they called "égalité de fait" and "égalité de droit." The social order, Mercier de La Rivière wrote, "makes all men as equal as they possibly can be. . . . What they cannot be *in fact* they must be *by right*; every man must be equally protected by the law of property, equally protected against all wills inimical to this law, equally free in the exercise of his property rights. This is true social equality." The stress obviously was on equal property rights, but the Abbé Baudeau broadened

85. "Lettre du marquis de ***," in *Ephémérides du citoyen*, 1771, XII, 206–207; Mirabeau, "Eloge de Vauban," quoted by Weulersse, *La Physiocratie à la fin du règne de Louis XV*, 225; Boesnier de L'Orme, *De l'Esprit du gouvernement économique*, 295–306.

86. Pierre Samuel Du Pont de Nemours, "Fragment des Eléments de philosophie économique," in *Ephémérides du citoyen*, 1771, VII, 69–70.

égalité de droit to embrace equality under "one law common to all, a law which protects equally all legitimate claims and assures equally to each citizen the liberty to do anything in his own personal interest that does not harm the common interest." Du Pont de Nemours went so far as to urge Americans to extend *égalité de droit* across geographical and racial boundaries and to "take care not to discriminate against or degrade anywhere or by any privilege whatsoever either Virginians, or Pennsylvanians, or New Yorkers, or Marylanders, or Louisianians, or Mexicans, or savages, or Europeans, or Africans, or whites, or blacks, or redmen, or the bearded or beardless."[87]

The principle of the equal right to hold property paradoxically both increased *inégalité de fait* and implied a broad range of other liberties. The right to property was natural because it was identical with the natural right to the pursuit of happiness, "le droit de jouir." Man, by exercising this natural right to the pursuit of happiness, added his labor to the forces of nature and produced property for his own enjoyment, to which he obviously had a natural right. "The necessity of maintaining this right was the primary purpose for the union of men in a fixed and regular society."[88] When we examine in detail the operation of this basic liberty we see that it meant for the Physiocrats not merely protection from illegal or arbitrary seizure, but full freedom in the use of property—freedom from restrictions on acquisition, possession, and use; unlimited freedom to engage in foreign or domestic trade; freedom to exploit one's property as one saw fit; freedom to buy and sell without hindrance from feudal prescriptions, sumptuary laws, or any other restriction; freedom from search; freedom to choose one's occupation; freedom from arbitrary, inequitable, or unsound taxation. It even extended to the property of one's own person and so merged with civil liberty. In these broad extensions of the right of property the Physiocrats came into approximate agreement with the Patriotes.[89]

87. Mercier de La Rivière, "De l'Instruction publique," in *Nouvelles éphémérides économiques*, 1775, No. 9, pp. 170–71; *Nouvelles éphémérides économiques*, 1775, No. 3, p. 24; *Ephémérides du citoyen*, 1769, IX, 172.

88. Boesnier de L'Orme, *De l'Esprit du gouvernement économique*, 29.

89. Du Pont de Nemours printed in the *Ephémérides du citoyen*, 1769,, VII, 121, the *Lettre* of the Parlement of Grenoble of April 26, 1769, which stated: "There is a law, Sire, anterior to civil laws and founded immediately on nature, whose preservation is the unique

Nonetheless the core of the Physiocrats' right of property was the extreme economic individualism that so infuriated Linguet. Morellet, both a Philosophe and a Physiocrat, insisted that property rights should be limited only if they affected *directly* the property rights of others, but not because of any *indirect* result of their exercise:

> The only interest of another party that I am bound to respect and that is at issue here is his property, not the profit or loss to him resulting from my free use of my own property. Of course it is against the interest of a man freezing to death that I refuse to shelter him in my house, and it is against the interest of an established manufacturer that I cause his enterprise to fail; but if these two events detrimental to others occur only because I close my door or construct a factory of the same kind as my neighbor's, I may sin against humanity, or rather against charity, but I do not sin against the right of property or against justice. . . . If I have the right to prevent an *usage simple* [use affecting *directly* only the owner] that a citizen makes of his property (or that a large group of citizens such as landowners or farmers make of theirs) on the pretext of protecting the general welfare or the interests of another party, who then is to limit the applications I may make of this dangerous principle? Who can prevent me from impairing all rights, all properties, all kinds of liberty?[90]

This argument was what Linguet called "precepts for tigers" and Diderot called "the principle of cannibals." If the right of property was the preeminent ethical rule, then society and its members had no moral *obligation* to the destitute. "What do you ask of society? What do you expect?" Mercier de La Rivière asked the pauper. "If you were born of poor parents and possess no kind of property, do you think that society is obligated to provide gratuitously for all your needs? By what title do you impose this obligation on society? . . . Society recognizes no such right. . . . Nature has willed that we can procure things necessary for our needs only by our own efforts. You are probably going to tell me that we all

---

purpose of all human institutions, a law by which and for which you reign—the sacred law of property."

90. [André Morellet], *Réfutation de l'ouvrage qui a pour titre "Dialogue sur le commerce des blés"* (London [Paris], 1770), 108–10.

have from nature an equal right to the means of existence and the pursuit of happiness. Well, what do you conclude from that? That you have the liberty to enjoy free and for nothing all the good things you see us producing at our expense and by our labor?"[91]

By the same ethic there was no moral obligation to raise wages above the barest minimum. Since by Physiocratic theory the entire increase in a nation's wealth came from the agricultural net product, this net obviously should be diminished as little as possible by labor costs. Logically wages could never fall below what the Physiocrats called the "vital minimum," the least amount necessary to keep a laborer alive and working. This figure could be calculated as a multiple of the cost of living, and therefore there should be a constant correlation between wages and the price of food. But while this figure was theoretically a minimum only, in a surplus labor market it tended to become a maximum as well, as the Physiocrats readily admitted. Furthermore, in practice, when prices were rising wages rose more slowly, as the Abbé Roubaud conceded. Yet despite these discrepancies between theory and experience, there was no disposition to abandon the principle. In fact the Physiocrats suggested that if the worker's cost of living could be reduced by abolishing the taxes on him and by more efficient milling of the grain he ate, then it would be quite proper to reduce his wages to keep them down to the new lower "vital minimum." Thus the net product would be increased and the workers would still be "better dressed, better housed . . . and better fed than savages."[92]

Yet from the same premises and by the same sort of logic the Physiocrats opposed any form of colonial exploitation, since commercial colonial monopolies discriminated against the interests of the landowners of both the mother country and the colony and were infringements on the equality of property rights. If this meant the political independence of the colonies, so much the better. "It would be infinitely more advantageous," Boesnier de L'Orme predicted, "for Canada to become a very wealthy and

91. Denis Diderot, "Apologie de l'abbé Galiani," in Diderot, *Oeuvres politiques*, 118; Mercier de La Rivière, "De l'Instruction publique," in *Nouvelles éphémérides économiques*, 1775, No. 9, pp. 158–59.

92. Du Pont de Nemours, "Fragment des Eléments de philosophie économique," in *Ephémérides du citoyen*, 1771, VII, 65. See Weulersse, *La Physiocratie à la fin du régne de Louis XV*, 192–96.

well-populated independent kingdom than for it to remain forever dependent and undeveloped as it is today."[93] Therefore also, of course, the justice of American independence. By the same logic the Physiocrats took an early lead in the French antislavery movement, for slavery was not only supportive of colonialism but manifestly a violation of *égalité de droit*.

The conjunction of these various positions appears anomalous from the viewpoint of modern liberalism. Yet within the context of Physiocratic logic they were all consistent. Perhaps the best key to the understanding of the Physiocrats is their concept of liberty. Boesnier de L'Orme, reasoning from the hypothesis of a presocial state of nature, said "Man is naturally free." But, as we have seen, Mirabeau, like most of his colleagues, rejected this assumption. Liberty, he said, was derived from the natural right of property but was not itself a natural right. "Security and liberty," he wrote, "are inseparable annexes to property, but we do not hold them from nature as we hold property. It is up to man to win them. Security is nothing but the assurance of our properties and our happiness. Liberty is a faculty absolutely foreign to physical man; [it is] a faculty which he can acquire only through society and by the power of society, that is, through association with his fellows."[94] This was to say that liberty was a natural norm, an ideal toward which in the natural order of things all men could and should strive. But it was not something inherent in the natural order, like property. It was not something to which we all have a natural title at birth.

The reason for this distinction was that the Physiocrats conceived liberty not as the absence of restrictions or as a passive state of security, but as a dynamic condition, as action. This is why Roubaud rejected Montesquieu's "negative" definition, which he paraphrased as, "True liberty consists in doing nothing except what is permitted by law." According to this principle, Roubaud argued, "a slave would be free, for he can do all that the law permits him to do. . . . True liberty consists in the absolute power to enjoy one's rights without infringing the rights of oth-

93. Boesnier de L'Orme, *De l'Esprit du gouvernement économique*, 271–72. See *ibid.*, 261–70, and Weulersse, *La Physiocratie à la fin du règne de Louis XV*, 105, and *La Physiocratie sous les ministères de Turgot et de Necker*, 120–22.

94. Boesnier de L'Orme, *De l'Esprit du gouvernement économique*, 17; Mirabeau, "Discours pour l'ouverture des assemblées économiques," in Knies (ed.), *Carls Friedrichs von Badens brieflicher Verkehr*, II, 320.

ers."[95] "Man is born to act," Boesnier de L'Orme insisted, "to enjoy all the advantages he can procure for himself by the exercise of his moral and physical faculties, not to enjoy liberty of action by remaining in a state of apathetic repose."[96]

This freedom to act was economic in origin, for it derived from the possession of property and the desire for material security. "Man," Mirabeau said, "asks only to be free, and the first step to liberty or independence [*disponibilité*] is to have an income; the second is that it be a fixed income." Yet as property extended beyond tangible goods to the possessor, so did liberty denote not only unrestricted active use of material things but also unrestricted action by the person. Thus Mirabeau wrote, "For the fulfillment of the social order nothing is required but that each man enjoy his person and his possessions."[97] "Society," said Mercier de La Rivière, "must leave . . . you completely free to make whatever exchanges of goods you wish and also completely free to employ all your faculties and talents in whatever way you find most agreeable and useful to you personally. It must preserve your right to the *property of your person* [italics *sic*], the right to be the master of your own life, to live according to your own will, provided always that in so doing you do not injure the property of others." At the highest level social liberty was moral liberty and the opposite of slavery. Mercier de La Rivière wrote:

> Slavery is the annihilation of all virtue, the source . . . of all vices. It is from the inner sense of their liberty and equality that men conceive a noble idea of themselves as citizens. To make men virtuous, the first and essential condition is to make them free and equal, to let them enjoy the fullest liberty and the most perfect equality they can reasonably desire. . . .
>
> The loss of liberty produces in [the soul] the effect that we feel when our limbs are tightly bound, a numbness that deprives us of sensitivity and action. In order that the souls of citizens be sensitive and active, the government must grant them full and entire liberty and be so con-

95. Pierre Joseph André Roubaud, *Représentations aux magistrats, concernant l'exposition des faits relatifs à la liberté des grains* (1769), quoted by Weulersse, *Le Mouvement physiocratique*, II, 39. Cf. Baudeau, *Première introduction à la philosophie économique*, 54, 386–87.

96. Boesnier de L'Orme, *De l'Esprit du gouvernement économique*, 4.

97. Mirabeau, *Supplément à la théorie de l'impôt*, 224, 297.

stituted that the laws are fixed and that they are applied impartially.[98]

Thus in direct contradiction to Linguet's limited and pessimistic objective of freedom to exist, the Physiocrats erected the expansive ideal of freedom to act, to experience life in its fullest, just plenitude.

This purpose seems far removed from despotism of any sort. But we must remember that the Physiocrats always added that "citizens . . . can preserve their common liberty only by maintaining the constitution of the state in all its purity, the authority of the law in all its completeness, and public order, established by this authority for the common good, in all its integrity."[99] Liberty could exist only under the law, as Locke and Montesquieu had said, and the government must "force men to be free," as Rousseau had said. The Physiocrats differed only in the mechanism they chose to express and enforce the enlightened general will. Fearing, as Voltaire did, the weakness and corruptness of separated powers and government by corporation and regarding as absurd and archaic (as Rousseau surely would have agreed) the government of a large *nation agricole* by the total populace assembled in a public square, they saw the only logical solution in government by a benevolent absolute *roi-propriétaire* whose enlightened will would be constitutionally bound to the free and educated self-interest of each and all.

98. Mercier de La Rivière, "De l'Instruction publique," in *Nouvelles éphémérides économiques*, 1775, No. 9, pp. 159–60; No. 10, pp. 110, 128.
99. *Ibid.*, 1775, No. 10, p. 132.

PART III

The Third Position

Qu'on ne dise pas que je n'ai rien dit de nouveau,
la disposition des matières est nouvelle.

PASCAL, *Pensées*

EIGHT

Independents and the Maupeou Revolution

A PART FROM the directly opposed partisans of the parlements and supporters of Maupeou and absolutism stood an unorganized crowd of thinkers who did not espouse either cause. These "independents," as we may conveniently refer to them, included most—though not all—of those known as Encyclopedists or Philosophes, but also figures such as Turgot, who refused any party label, individualists such as Mably, who disassociated himself from the atheistic Philosophes, and various others of lesser note. They were by definition idiosyncratic; even the accepted denomination of Philosophe allowed room for disagreements on important questions. Some of these independents, despite their apparent neutrality, were not unsympathetic to absolutism, others abhorred it; some detested Maupeou as much as any Patriote, others had an equal contempt for the parlements, and others damned both houses; some revealed an interest in certain issues of the Maupeou revolution, others focused their attention on unrelated questions; some had declared war against the Physiocrats, others had incorporated fundamental Physiocratic concepts into their philosophies. Yet whatever their political or ideological orientations, none—so far as the record shows—favored either Maupeou's or any other form of monarchical absolutism or the parle-

ments' aristocratic corporatism. Thus they occupied a third position on
the political scene, that of uninvolved spectators.

Their uninvolvement did not, however, imply indifference or emo-
tional detachment, for it was difficult for anyone to remain unmoved
amidst the storms of political passion. But at the same time one cannot
assume that adoption of this third position indicated any particular ideology or set of ideas. Yet a reasonable inquiry is whether these French men
and women who seem to have refused both the *thèse royale* and the *thèse
parlementaire* were searching for some way out of the dilemma with which
they saw the nation faced, and whether a significant number of them
achieved any sort of consensus on the prime issue of the proper form of
government for France or on related social and political problems.

As they approached the problem of finding some alternative to choos-
ing between the irreconcilable and (to them) equally unacceptable Patriote thesis and royalist antithesis, these independent thinkers were simultaneously involved in the many other dialectical problems that confronted
French intellectuals as they entered the last quarter of the century. Every
philosophy, theory, or idea seemed to be producing a contrary philosophy, theory, or idea; every intellectual force seemed to create an equal and
opposite force. The more clear-sighted, or perhaps the more simplistic,
took one side or the other in these dialectics; the more muddled failed to
see the issues and wavered from one side to the other; and the more intelligent, such as Diderot, strove for syntheses. Some of these dialectical
problems, such as those opposing *sensibilité* and reason, providentialism
and determinism, primitivism and the apology for civilization, the affir-
mation and the denial of the state of nature, cosmopolitanism and na-
tionalism, or uniformitarianism and relativistic diversitarianism, were
peripheral, though not unrelated to the political and social issues raised
by the Maupeou revolution. Others, such as the choice between the
aprioristic and rationalistic *esprit de système* of a Helvétius and the revolutionary rhetoric of a Mercier, on one hand, and the prudent, empirical,
pragmatic gradualism of a Turgot on the other, were matters of style and
approach. Other dialectics, such as the contradiction between Turgot's
and Condorcet's belief in the theory of progress and Diderot's historical
pessimism, strongly colored responses to events. Still others, such as the
conflict between Catholicism and deism or between religion and materi-

alistic atheism determined the kinds of social or political solutions these philosophers could consider. And finally, the fundamental opposition of the utilitarianism of D'Holbach and others and the natural law position, perhaps best represented by Turgot, divided the ethical and philosophical bases on which stood their various proposals.

These philosophical differences inevitably affected the independents' attempts to find a third position which would offer a constructive synthesis of the Patriote thesis and the royalist antithesis. The fact that their thinking during these years was largely dialectical, not only on the political and social problems raised by the Maupeou revolution but on many other philosophical and historical problems as well, perhaps explains why the originality of the third position lay in the new arrangement of parts rather than in the generation of novel concepts.

In view of such a climate of thought, it is not surprising that the reactions of these independent thinkers to the parlements and the Maupeou ministry were ambivalent. Whatever support they voiced for one side was a function of their aversion for the other, and the historical problem is to determine which of the two they detested more. This is not an easy task, for it is necessary to distinguish, on one hand, between the independents' positions on the parlements' constitutional thesis and their feelings about the behavior of the magistrates, and, on the other hand, between their views on absolutism and their opinions of Maupeou's character and actions.

It would be impossible to recall too frequently that the crucial issue in the early 1770s was liberty, not equality. The word *liberté* had of course many different meanings, but for virtually everyone except the paradoxical Linguet it denoted the antithesis of *despotisme*. One has the impression that *despotisme* and *liberté* were the two abstract nouns with the highest frequency in the political vocabulary of the time. But precisely what was a *despote*? The word was sometimes a neutral term designating without prejudice any ruler with absolute power, as in the Physiocrats' phrase "despote légal" and in the concept of a "despote juste et éclairé," which Diderot and others were willing to consider as at least a theoretical possibility. This anodynic meaning corresponded with the concept held by the royalists and some Patriotes of a self-regulating absolute monarch who voluntarily obeyed the dictates of natural and divine law. But far more often *despote* had a strongly pejorative connotation and clearly meant an absolute ruler who acted arbitrarily and unjustly for his own private interests. This second usage corresponded with the positions of those Patriotes who held that absolute power was by its very nature unjust in both principle and practice.

The thesis of benign absolutism received at least sympathetic consideration from a few independents. Joseph de Lanjuinais, who despite his egalitarianism, utilitarianism, and defense of natural rights was writing in support of the enlightened absolutism of his patron Joseph II, expressed well the essential argument. In any society, he said, two forces are in opposition: one, the centrifugal disintegrating pressure from individuals for independence and dominance over their fellows, and the other the centripetal force exerted by "the weight of social law pressing down on the natural rights of the individual and keeping him submissive." Lanjuinais' political ideal was a dynamic equilibrium between the two, and he therefore argued that the power of the monarch must always be great enough to balance the disruptive energy of individualism.[1] Necker, a statist, held that the king's duties to control the people, provide their sustenance, and regulate the use of property were necessary to the fulfillment of his supreme obligation to maintain the strength and security of the state.[2] The Abbé Galiani, though he conceded the evils of *despotisme*, pointed out like Linguet that absolute government in order to survive had to assure an adequate supply of food to the lower classes and therefore by its nature it had to follow a *dirigiste* economic policy; similarly political liberty and laissez-faire economics by their natures always went hand in hand. Therefore he predicted that adoption of the Physiocratic economic system would inevitably produce democracy, and conversely that to grant political freedom was to force everyone to be economically self-dependent and fend for himself—which for the poor would mean starvation. Galiani was less concerned, however, about the fate of the lower classes than he was about the libertarian political consequences of Physiocratic econom-

1. Joseph Lanjuinais, *Le Monarque accompli, ou Prodiges de bonté, de savoir et de sagesse qui font l'éloge de Sa Majesté Impériale Joseph II . . . Par Mr. de Lanjuinais. Principal du Collège de Moudon . . .* (Lausanne, 1774), I, 95–100.

2. Jacques Necker, *Eloge de Jean-Baptiste Colbert, discours qui a remporté le prix de l'Académie Françoise en 1773* (Paris, 1773), 20, 33, 44–45, 72; Necker, *Sur la législation et le commerce des grains* (Paris, 1775), I, 170, 182, 183; II, 170.

ics. "Constitutional change is a very fine thing," he warned, "when it is completely accomplished, but it is a very dirty business to live through. It upsets the lives of two or three generations, and benefits only posterity."[3] So his advice was to not disturb the absolutist status quo.

These apologists of unlimited monarchism were, however, relatively few. Those who denounced the theory of absolutism were far more numerous and vociferous. They cited both the evidence of history and the principles of natural law and utilitarianism. The historical argument was strongly buttressed by Delolme's popular *Constitution de l'Angleterre* (ten editions from 1771 to the Revolution), which demonstrated the social benefits the English had happily achieved by the alliance of the people and the nobles against the crown, which had created a constitution that effectively checked royal power. Mably's *Observations sur l'histoire de France* (written before 1771 but published with important additions composed during the Maupeou revolution) explained why the French had not been so fortunate. Rejecting both Du Bos' *thèse royale*, which ascribed to the early Frankish kings by right of conquest the absolute power of the Roman emperors, and likewise Boulainvilliers' *thèse nobiliaire*, which claimed that the French nobility were heirs to the rightful sovereignty of the Frankish lords, Mably advanced what may be called the *thèse démocratique*. According to this theory the primitive Frankish state had been governed by a popular general assembly which had merely delegated executive power to the king and a council of nobles. Charlemagne had overthrown the first usurpation by nobles and had returned legislative power to the people, creating a golden age of peace, security, and liberty. But during the Middle Ages the great lords had again seized power, and when the kings eventually subdued them it was only to substitute for feudal tyranny a vicious personal despotism that continued to modern times.[4]

The utilitarian argument against absolutism was most cogently given

3. Ferdinando Galiani to Jean Baptiste Suard, September 8, 1770, in Galiani, *Sa Correspondance* (Paris, 1881), I, 245. See also Galiani to Suard, December 15, 1770, and to Louise F. M. Tardieu d'Esclavelles, Marquise d'Epinay, November 2, 1771, *ibid.*, I, 318–20, 474; Ferdinando Galiani, *Dialogues sur le commerce des blés* (London, 1770), 242–47.

4. Gabriel Bonnot de Mably, *Observations sur l'historie de France* (Paris, An III [1795]), I, 133 ff.; II, 244 ff.; III, 319. Vols. I–III of Mably, *Collection complète des oeuvres*, 15 vols. See note 59. For a recent suggestive consideration of Mably's political thought, see Keith Michael Baker, "A Script for a French Revolution: The Political Consciousness of the Abbé Mably," *Eighteenth-Century Studies*, XIV (1981), 235–63.

by D'Holbach. Liberty he defined as "the right to use all the means one judges appropriate to produce one's own happiness without detracting from that of others." Despotism was the logical opposite, the misdirection of the forces of society to the satisfaction of the passions of one man and the sacrifice of the happinesses of all others. The effects were symmetrically contrary: "Everything languishes and deteriorates under absolute power; everything grows strong and vigorous under the reign of liberty." A just and enlightened despotism was psychologically impossible, D'Holbach said, anticipating Lord Acton, for "unlimited power corrupts the mind and heart and perverts even those with the best moral instincts." He cataloged all the evil products of despotism: it perverted the nobility, made impossible a legitimate class structure, and reduced everyone to a uniform condition of slavery. It kept men in a state of ignorance, subjected them to the constant threat of capricious violence, violated their rights to property and personal security, destroyed all patriotism, imposed excessive taxes and squandered the public wealth, corrupted justice, stifled the arts and sciences, encouraged luxury, and produced moral corruption, militarism, war, poverty, and economic stagnation. It was both the easiest and the most self-contradictory and unstable form of government. If it still infested the earth this was because despots were theocrats kept in power by the religious superstition, fear, and ignorance fomented by priests.[5]

On all this Helvétius concurred, writing, "Despotism, under which the purpose of everything is the happiness of one man, and superstition, whose purpose is the power and happiness of priests, are both equally contrary to good government."[6] Georg Jonathan von Holland, a German mathematician and philosopher, published in 1772 his *Réflexions philosophiques sur le Système de la nature*, which while criticizing D'Holbach's philosophy endorsed his politics. Any political authority, Von Holland said, is legitimate if it promotes the general welfare, and contrariwise absolutism must be always evil: "Knowing no law except the capricious momentary will of the sovereign, it is in contradiction to all the interests of

5. [Paul Henri Dietrich, Baron d'Holbach], *La Politique naturelle, ou Discours sur les vrais principes du gouvernement, par un ancien magistrat* (London, 1773), I, 38, 105, 145–46, 155, 165–66, 216; II, 12–20, 31, 39–57, 69, 71, 101–69, 260; [D'Holbach], *Système social. Ou Principes naturels de la morale et de la politique. Avec un examen de l'influence du gouvernement sur les moeurs* . . . (London [Amsterdam], 1773), II, 16–17.

6. Claude Adrien Helvétius, *Le Bonheur, poème en six chants. Avec des fragments de quelques épîtres. Ouvrages posthumes* (London, 1772), 69.

the body politic. A people who resolve to free themselves from despotic rule risk nothing, for slavery is certainly the lowest level of human misery." Similarly Chastellux condemned absolutism not only because of its historic record of injustice, immorality, and cruelty, but because it hampered the progress of reason and the achievement of human felicity, and negated the essential element of this felicity—freedom from arbitrary, oppressive power.[7]

The pervasive fear of uncontrolled centralized authority is exemplified by Rouillé d'Orfeuil's sharp objection to Montesquieu's statement that the necessary condition of political liberty is that "the government be such that one citizen cannot fear another citizen." It was not other citizens one had to fear, Rouillé d'Orfeuil objected, but the government. "The leaders no longer consider themselves citizens, and indeed they no longer are citizens—that is the great evil." Like D'Holbach he listed the manifold impacts of absolutism on the individual: "Abuses of authority, vexations, injustices, forced taxes, violence. . . ."[8] In similar language Mercier's citizen of 2440 described eighteenth-century France:

> We know how much absolutism was opposed to the true interests of the nation. The fine art of exacting taxes, the full force of that terrible leverage progressively multiplied, the confused and contradictory laws, chicanery that devoured private property, cities filled with privileged tyrants, venality of office, ministers and intendants treating parts of the kingdom like conquered territories, the subtle cruelty of rationalized inhumanity, royal officers who felt no responsibility to the people and who insulted them instead of listening to their petitions—such were the effects of sharp-eyed despotism. . . . One traveled the length and breadth of France. . . . What did one see? Cantons left desolate by tax collectors, cities reduced to towns, towns diminished to villages, and villages to hamlets, their inhabitants gaunt and bent—beggars in fact, not inhabitants.[9]

7. Georg Jonathan von Holland, *Réflexions philosophiques sur le "Système de la nature"* (London, 1773), 133; François Jean, Marquis de Chastellux, *De la Félicité publique; ou Considérations sur le sort des hommes dans les différentes époques de l'histoire* (Amsterdam, 1772), I, 106–107, 114; II, Chap. 4.

8. [Augustin Rouillé d'Orfeuil], *L'Alambic des loix, ou Observations de l'Ami des François sur l'homme et sur les loix* (Hispaan, 1773), 176–77.

9. [Louis Sébastien Mercier], *L'An deux mille quatre cent quarante. Rêve s'il en fût jamais* (London, 1771), 302–303.

Thus the two essential points in the utilitarian critique of absolutism were, first, the inherently contradictory interests of the omnipotent prince and the impotent generality, and, second, the catalog of social evils that in fact resulted. What may be called the natural-law critique (which of course was not exclusive to the natural-law philosophers) stressed questions of principle and conscience: the violation of natural rights, the absurdity of the Hobbesian contract, and the degradation of the human spirit under even the most benign absolutism.

Raynal's *Histoire des deux Indes* won for its author the name of "a great enemy of despotism" as soon as it appeared in Paris in March 1772, and this reputation was enhanced by the additions to the 1774 edition, on which Diderot collaborated. Opposition to despotism was indeed the central tenet of Raynal's politics. To place absolute power in the hands of one man, he said, was to degrade all others and to destroy their humanity. "Bound by the chains of servitude, their spirits grow too weak to assert the rights inherent in their nature. One may wonder whether these slaves are not as guilty as their tyrants, and whether liberty has greater reason to complain of the insolence of those who violate her or of the imbecility of those who will not defend her." India, for instance, exemplified how "political and civil slavery . . . destroys the energy of the soul and makes it incapable of the sacrifices that courage demands."[10]

D'Alembert as early as 1759 had written, "Both the mind and heart of man refuse to accept the idea that a multitude of men could have said without conditions to a single man, or to several, 'Command and we shall obey you.'"[11] Like so many others he was deeply worried by the accumulating victories of absolutism throughout Europe. In 1772 he wrote Turgot, "The Swedish adventure [the coup d'état by Gustavus III] seems to me a consequence of absolutism's general offensive now in progress over all of Europe against liberty. Liberty writes fine books, but tyranny chains her feet, while it is waiting for the chance to bind her hands. Liberty can only say like Pourceaugnac, 'He slapped my face, but I certainly told him what I thought of him.'"[12]

    10. Guillaume Thomas François Raynal, *Histoire philosophique et politique des établissemens et du commerce des Européens dans les deux Indes* (The Hague, 1774), VII, 216; II, 372.
    11. Jean Le Rond d'Alembert, "Eléments de philosophie" in D'Alembert, *Oeuvres* (Paris, 1821–22), I, 225.
    12. Jean Le Rond d'Alembert to Anne Robert Jacques Turgot, September 24, 1772,

The young Count de Mirabeau's first serious work, his *Essai sur le despotisme*, was an undigested mixture of hedonistic utilitarianism with rationalistic natural-law and natural-rights arguments, and he himself later "repented having mutilated so fine a subject." Nevertheless the sheer force of his passionate indignation made his central point clear—that absolutism violated natural law and man's natural right to the pursuit of happiness and therefore had no moral justification. [13] It was the outrageousness of the proposition of absolutism that shocked these philosophers. "When one sees a print of Gargantua," Mercier wrote, "whose mouth is as large as an oven, swallow in a single meal twelve hundred loaves of bread, twenty oxen, a hundred sheep, six hundred chickens, fifteen hundred hares, two thousand quail, twelve hogsheads of wine, six thousand peaches, etc., who does not say, 'That great mouth is a king's'?" [14]

One could prolong the list of those who opposed absolutism on natural-law grounds, such as the poet Thomas, Laharpe, and the Abbé Maury, but the most interesting ideas, as always, were those of Diderot. His stay in Saint Petersburg during the winter of 1773–1774 had allowed him a close look at absolutism in action, and he came back badly shaken. During his return journey he wrote Mme Necker, "Our Philosophes, who seem to be experts on despotism, have only looked at it through the neck of a bottle. There is a big difference between viewing a tiger painted by Oudry and facing the live beast in a jungle." Like D'Alembert he saw no hope of stemming the wave of absolutism that was inundating Europe: "Enlightenment [on the problems of political theory] has been carried as far in our day as it can go, and what has it produced? Nothing. Despite the protests by the magistrates and philosophers of all civilized peoples despotism is spreading in every direction." [15]

---

in D'Alembert, *Correspondence inédite . . . avec Cramer, Lesage, Clairaut, Turgot, Castillon, Béguelin, etc.* (Rome, 1886), 30. The reference is to Molière's *Monsieur de Pourceaugnac*, Act I, Scene 4.

13. [Honoré Gabriel Riqueti, Count de Mirabeau], *Essai sur le despotisme* (London [Neuchâtel], 1775). This work was written in 1774, largely before the death of Louis XV, and printed in 1775, but copies did not reach Paris until 1776. See "Avis de l'éditeur," *ibid.*, 4; *Mémoires secrets*, January 22, 1776 (IX, 157); Oliver J. G. Welch, *Mirabeau: A Study of a Democratic Monarchist* (London, 1951), 49.

14. Mercier, *L'An 2440*, 164.

15. Denis Diderot to Mme Necker, September 6, 1774, in Diderot, *Correspondance*, XIV, 72–73. Jean Baptiste Oudry (1686–1755) was a well-known painter of animals. Denis Diderot, "Observations sur le Nakaz," in Diderot, *Oeuvres politiques*, 405.

Diderot subscribed to the utilitarian arguments against despotism, listing all the practical consequences of absolutism: reliance on a large standing army, reduction of all citizens to a common level of servitude, denial of the right of property, moral corruption, and so on.[16] His *Principes de politique* (1774), a satire directed at Frederick of Prussia, was in effect a long catalog of the manifold evils and dangers of absolutism. He also made the practical argument that the chance that a hereditary monarch would be born endowed with all the qualities necessary for an acceptable ruler was mathematically so small that it was absurd to endure a long succession of bad kings in hopes of one good one.[17]

But these were not Diderot's essential arguments. Even if all the practical and utilitarian objections were without merit, absolutism, no matter how benign, would still be wholly evil, he insisted, for it destroys human dignity by denying men the freedom to will or not to will, by depriving them of the liberty to deliberate their own destinies and to resist—even to resist what is for their good if they so choose. "The right of opposition . . . in a society of men is a sacred and inalienable natural right. A despot, even if he is the best of men, by governing as he thinks best commits a heinous crime. He is a good shepherd who reduces his subjects to the condition of animals by seducing them from their love of liberty, which once lost is very difficult to regain." For what characterizes a despot? Whether he is good or evil? "No, these notions have nothing to do with despotism. It is the extent of the authority that he arrogates, not the use he makes of it. One of the worst misfortunes that could befall a nation would be two or three successive reigns by just, moderate, and enlightened but absolute rulers, for the people would be beguiled into forgetting completely their rights and led into a state of utter slavery."[18] Thus Diderot categorically

16. Denis Diderot, "Observations sur le Nakaz," in Diderot, *Oeuvres politiques*, 353; Diderot, "Principes de politique des souverains," *ibid.*, 179; Diderot, "Réfutation de l'ouvrage d'Helvétius intitulé L'Homme," in Diderot, *Oeuvres complètes*, ed. J. Assézat and M. Tourneux (Paris, 1875–77), II, 383, 414–16; Diderot, *Mémoires pour Catherine II*, ed. Paul Vernière (Paris, 1966), 123; Diderot, "Rêveries à l'occasion de la révolution de Suède," in Herbert Dieckman, "Diderot, Grimm et Raynal: Les Contributions de Diderot à la 'Correspondance litteraire' et à l'"Histoire des deux Indes,' " *Revue d'histoire littéraire de la France*, LI 1951), 434.
17. Diderot, *Mémoires pour Catherine II*, 118. Cf. Diderot, "Observations sur le Nakaz," in Diderot, *Oeuvres politiques*, 354.
18. Diderot, *Mémoires pour Catherine II*, 117–18; Diderot, "Réfutation de . . . L'Homme," in Diderot, *Oeuvres complètes*, II, 381.

rejected the proposition "that the best of all governments would be a just and enlightened despot. . . . It could easily happen that the will of this absolute ruler would be contrary to that of his subjects. In this case, despite all his justice and all his enlightenment, he would be wrong to deprive his people of their rights, even to their advantage. Power can be abused for good as well as for evil. . . . One may drive sheep to greener pastures, but it is tyranny to use the same violence against a society of human beings."[19]

Diderot's denial of absolutism proceeded from his humanism, a humanism that was sustained by strong passion. He generally kept his emotions off the printed page, but occasionally they burst forth in his private writings, as in the poem "Les Eleuthéromances," in which the "child of nature" cries,

"La nature n'a fait ni serviteur ni maître;
Je ne veux ni donner ni recevoir des lois."
Et ses mains ourdiraient les entrailles du prêtre,
Au défaut d'un cordon pour étrangler les rois.[20]

This linking of the two *infâmes*, despotism and religion, of which Helvétius and D'Holbach were so frequently guilty, worried D'Alembert, who feared it would "land us in a ditch."[21] It disturbed even more Condorcet and Turgot. The latter consequently has sometimes been accused of being a proponent of enlightened despotism. We probably should take him at his word, however, when he said he "hated despotism as much as any man," for he had had enough experience as an administrator to know how much enlightenment to expect from the absolutism of either Louis or from the bureaucracy at Versailles. As a pragmatic gradualist, he chose in combating despotism to shun the political error of attacking the church and the government simultaneously, to avoid broad frontal attacks on the the-

19. Denis Diderot, "Fragments échappés du portefeuille d'un philosophe," in Diderot, *Oeuvres complètes*, VI, 449–50. This passage reappeared, undoubtedly as a result of Diderot's collaboration, in Raynal's *Histoire des deux Indes* (The Hague, 1774), VII, 216.

20. Denis Diderot, "Les Eleuthéromanes," in Diderot, *Oeuvres complètes*, IX, 15–16. "'Nature created neither masters nor servants. I will neither give nor accept laws.' And his hands would twist the guts of a priest to make a rope to strangle kings."

21. Jean Le Rond d'Alembert to Frederick II of Prussia, June 8, 1770, in D'Alembert, *Oeuvres*, V, 294.

ory of French monarchism, and to concentrate his efforts on eliminating specific despotic practices. He believed that the way to lessen the evil was not by grand "déclamations," broad generalizations, and panaceas like those of Helvétius, who, he said, "gives the impression of being the enemy of all government though he pretends to be writing about France." Such talk gratuitously aroused the opposition of those in power with an interest in preserving the status quo. Instead of attacking the entire government on principle one should concentrate on righting specific evils and in this way "establish clearly the rights of man." "There are a host of despotic abuses," he pointed out, "in which princes have no interest at all, and there are others that they permit only because public opinion has not yet taken notice of their injustice and harmful effects. We shall do far more to deserve the gratitude of nations if we attack these abuses with clear reasoning and with courage, and especially if we appeal to respect for humanity, than we shall if we do nothing but mouth eloquent insults."[22] He therefore proposed changes in the system of military conscription, urged Louis XVI to grant religious freedom to the Protestants, and suggested a wide variety of other specific reforms. Turgot's essential moral and social intent seems not to have been far from that of Diderot, and the same might be said of his admirer Condorcet.[23]

This opposition to the theory of absolutism logically implied sympathy, in principle at least, with any political effort to limit monarchical authority. In fact there had long existed evidence of compatibility on the abstract level between the politics of the Philosophes and the parlements. If this were not true, the accusation that the latter had been infected by the Encyclopedic *esprit de système* would not have been credible. Indeed Pa-

22. Anne Robert Jacques Turgot to Marie Jean Antoine de Caritat, Marquis de Condorcet, December, 1773, in Turgot, *Correspondance inédite de Condorcet et de Turgot*, 145–46. For a good summary of the various interpretations of Turgot's position on absolutism, see Gerald J. Cavanaugh, "Turgot: The Rejection of Enlightened Absolutism," *French Historical Studies*, VI (1969), 30–58. Also see Keith Michael Baker, *Condorcet: From Natural Philosophy to Social Mathematics* (Chicago, 1975), 212, 443.

23. See Marie Jean Antoine de Caritat, Marquis de Condorcet to Anne Robert Jacques Turgot, December 4, 13, and 20, 1773, in Condorcet, *Correspondance inédite de Condorcet et de Turgot*, 141, 148, 152. For examples of Condorcet's attacks on specific "despotic abuses," see [Marie Jean Antoine de Caritat, Marquis de Condorcet], *Lettres sur le commerce des grains* (Paris, 1774), 26; Condorcet, "Lettre d'un laboureur de Picardie," "Réflexions sur les corvées," and "Sur l'abolition des corvées," in Condorcet, *Oeuvres*, ed. A. Condorcet O'Connor and F. Arago (Paris, 1847–49), XI, 1–34, 59–86, 87–97.

triote writers did not hesitate to quote from the *Encyclopédie*.[24] On the other hand, the *Encyclopédie* articles on topics related to the French constitution were in essential agreement with the parliamentary position. These contributions were in large part the work of De Jaucourt, Diderot's indefatigable collaborator, of Boucher d'Argis, a lawyer of the Paris Parlement whose family had worn the robe for three generations, and of Diderot himself. Diderot's first and most daring political article, "Autorité politique," which with the Prades affair led to the first suspension of the publication of the *Encyclopédie* in 1752, presented a contractual theory of government based on natural law and French constitutional tradition that was quite consonant with the *thèse parlementaire*. The initial attacks on it came, significantly, from the church, particularly the Jesuits, and the Court, not from the Parlement. Volume III (1753) of the *Encyclopédie* contained a note inserted in defense of this controversial article, in which the editors, Diderot and D'Alembert, claimed that its essential thesis was admirably defined by a quotation they copied from the remonstrances of the Parlement of Paris of April 9, 1753. Moreover in his *Suite de l'Apologie de M. l'abbé de Prades* Diderot boldly asserted that the principles enunciated in "Autorité politique" were the basic principles of the Parlement.[25] Diderot's other political articles in the *Encyclopédie*, though they may have contained philosophic implications and democratic tendencies disturbing to some magistrates, could scarcely have offended by maintaining such principles as natural rights, the delegated conditional authority of the king, his obligation to rule according to law, the right of the nation to political power through a representative corporation, and the supremacy of the fundamental laws.[26] D'Holbach's article "Représentants" held that in a mod-

24. E.g., *Les Efforts de la liberté*, IV, 76.

25. Denis Diderot, "Suite de l'Apologie de l'abbé de Prades," in Diderot, *Oeuvres complètes*, I, 469. See John Lough, "The Article *Autorité politique*," in Lough, *Essays on the Encyclopédie of Diderot and D'Alembert* (London, 1968), 424–62.

26. E.g., "Droit naturel," "Indépendance," "Magistrat," "Obvier," "Parlementaire," "Pouvoir," "Souverains," "Vouloir." On the attribution of these and other articles, see John Lough, "The Problem of the Unsigned Articles in the *Encyclopédie*," *Studies on Voltaire and the Eighteenth Century* (Geneva, 1965), XXXII, 327–90; Lough, *The Encyclopédie in Eighteenth-Century England and Other Studies* (Newcastle-upon-Tyne, 1970); Lough, *The Contributors to the "Encyclopédie"* (London, 1973); Jacques Proust, *Diderot et l'Encyclopédie* (Paris, 1962); Proust, *L'Encyclopédie* (Paris, 1965); Richard N. Schwab, Walter E. Rex, and John Lough, *Inventory of Diderot's Encyclopédie* (Geneva, 1971). Vol. LXXX of *Studies on Voltaire and the Eighteenth Century*.

erate (nondespotic) monarchy the king must share power with representatives of the nation, who should be delegates from the church, the nobility, the magistrates, the merchants, the manufacturers, and the agricultural landowners. De Jaucourt's concept of personal liberty seemed to come mainly from Locke (as in "Liberté naturelle [Droit naturel]"), but his definitions of civil and political liberty and his concepts of natural and positive law derived from the great authority of the parlements, Montesquieu (as in "Liberté civile," "Liberté politique," "Loi," "Loi naturelle," "Monarchie absolue," "Monarchie limitée"). His article "Loi fondamentale" developed the concepts of constitutionalism, the contract, and limited monarchy; his "Puissance" dwelt on the corrupting effects of absolute power; and his "Souveraineté" followed the lines of Diderot's "Autorité politique." Boucher d'Argis' article "Etats" expounded the theories that the *noblesse de robe* was coequal with the *noblesse d'épée* and that the Parlement, descended from the early Champs de Mars, was a more ancient institution than the States General.

This ideological linkage does not of course mean that the Philosophes and the other independent thinkers we are studying believed that the parlements were by any means the ideal institutions to represent the will of the nation, or that they approved of the hereditary and aristocratic prerequisites for membership or condoned the abuses within the system such as venality. Nevertheless these thinkers apparently did generally believe that the powers the courts claimed should somehow be guaranteed within the French constitution. Diderot called the right of free registration "that great, beautiful, sacred law . . . [which] if entrusted to truly patriotic hands would have been enough to halt all the machinations of a perverse minister" or check "the mistaken will of the sovereign," and he said that verification should be no empty formula but "the confrontation of [the written will of the sovereign] with the law of the state and the law of common reason." Moreover it was generally conceded that in the absence of a true national legislature the parlements could and should perform a useful function. D'Holbach wrote, "When the fundamental laws of a state have neglected to establish corporations with the duty of affirming the interests of the people, or when tyranny has succeeded in closing the mouths of those originally designated to speak in the name of the people, then by the very necessity of things bodies are created to represent to the sovereign the truths of which his courtiers and ministers leave him ignorant."[27]

What turned the independents against the magistrates was not, then, so much the latter's constitutional thesis as their failures to meet their moral and patriotic responsibilities—their irresponsible neglect of the welfare of the nation in favor of their own private and class interests, their abuses of judicial power, their religious fanaticism, and so forth. Accusations of collective malfeasance were often, as we shall see, bitter, sweeping, and unqualified.

Yet these same independents detested with even greater passion, if we may judge by what they wrote, "that scoundrel Maupeou" (Diderot's epithet), and they held the new courts he had concocted in even greater contempt than the old ones he had abolished.[28] Furthermore, as the months passed by after the coup, immediate and present dangers tended to override in the independents' minds the memories of past evils. In addition, the Patriotes seem to have won a clear propaganda victory by deemphasizing the parlements' claims to aristocratic and caste privileges and identifying, at least in the minds of many, the *thèse patriotique* with popular libertarianism. When to all these elements in the situation was added the independents' adamant opposition to the principle of absolutism, which Louis XV had so boldly and unequivocally proclaimed in the edict of December 1770, it was predictable that while these uninvolved spectators in the Maupeou revolution would damn both houses, they would damn more vehemently the triumphant chancellor than the exiled magistrates. Particular reactions could, of course, be expected to vary according to special convictions on the abstract issues and in proportion to the relative strength of a person's prejudices against one side or the other. It is impossible here to examine in detail the reactions of all those on whom we have some documentation, but a representative sample may be enlightening.

Turgot is perhaps the best example of those who approximated a balanced neutrality. He was initially predisposed against the parlements, first, because he had been a member of the Chambre Royale that had replaced

27. Denis Diderot, "Essai historique sur la police," in Diderot, *Mémoires pour Catherine II*, 14–15, 25; [D'Holbach], *La Politique naturelle*, II, 59. Cf. *ibid.*, I, 135, 223. See Carcasonne, *Montesquieu et le problème de la constitution française*, 334.

28. "Ce scélérat Maupeou." Diderot, "Réfutation de . . . L'Homme," in Diderot, *Oeuvres complètes*, II, 380.

the exiled Paris Parlement in 1753–1754 and consequently still had many enemies among the magistrates, and, second, because this prejudice was reinforced by his opposition on principle to aristocratic republicanism. After the edict of December 1770 he wrote Du Pont de Nemours, "Though I detest the [ministry's] reasons, their motives, and what is going on under the table, I do not on the whole disapprove of the job, and it seems to me that if it can be made to stick, in the long run the public will gain more than it will lose." Yet a few weeks later he was more pessimistic: "From all I hear, it looks to me as though the new ministry has failed. We shall be delivered from ravenous wolves [Maupeou's ministry] and the *boeufs-tigres* [the magistrates] will come back as stupid or even stupider than before. From neither side can we expect any good. These men [Maupeou, Terray, and D'Aiguillon] have undertaken with the very worst intentions a task that with the best motives would have been very difficult; the obstacles they have encountered will for a long time be hindrances to progress and to any change for the better."[29] Nevertheless when he became minister himself in 1774 he approved and helped implement the decision to recall to office the "boeufs-tigres." There is no need here to reexamine this complicated and fully studied episode.[30] Suffice it to say that it seems evident that Turgot knew that if he were to succeed in reuniting the nation behind the new king and achieve the reforms he had in mind he had to get rid of the discredited Maupeou Parlement and explicitly disassociate himself from Maupeou's provocative absolutist coup. He no doubt hoped that Maurepas' compromise settlement would avoid both extremes of undisciplined aristocratic republicanism and irresponsible absolutism.

Condorcet's inveterate prejudice against the parlements was even stronger than Turgot's. In one of his earliest writings he called them tyrannical and blamed them for having consistently opposed any sort of legal, judicial, or financial reform and for having destroyed all mutual trust between the throne and the people.[31] In 1770 he said the magistrates and

29. Anne Robert Jacques Turgot to Pierre Samuel Du Pont de Nemours, February 28 and March 13, 1771, in Turgot, *Oeuvres*, ed. Schelle, III, 475, 477–78.
30. See Henri Carré, "Turgot et le rappel des Parlements"; Dakin, *Turgot and the Ancien Régime*, 136–45.
31. Marie Jean Antoine de Caritat, Marquis de Condorcet, "Un Fragment inédit de Condorcet," ed. Léon Cahen, *La Révolution française*, XLII (1902), 115–31.

the laws under which they operated constituted "the principal cause of France's troubles, . . . the main source of fanaticism, and the greatest obstacle to progress that could ever be erected."[32] Like Voltaire, he hated the magistrates for their record of religious persecution (as in the La Barre case), for the rigorous way they had exercised their powers of censorship, and for their opposition to a more liberal economic policy.[33] The roots of Condorcet's antagonism were undoubtedly his passionate anti-religious convictions.[34] Nevertheless Condorcet was jarred by Maupeou's absolutism. He had two friends among the Paris magistrates, and their exile seemed to him vindictive and unjust. He thought Voltaire might have forgone his jokes about their hardships, and he could not forget Maupeou's share of responsibility for the La Barre case. Moreover he joined in the general admiration for the energy and nobility of Malesherbes' defense of the rights of the judiciary. Though he hoped that Maupeou's new parlements would be less intolerant, he feared they might be even more corrupt than the old ones.[35] But despite this disillusion with the chancellor's reforms, Condorcet remained to the end opposed to the recall of the dismissed magistrates. "The colossus [of religious fanaticism] is half demolished," he wrote Turgot, "and we must complete its destruction, for it is essential that we erect something else in its place." By this "something else" he meant an entirely new "third Parlement."[36] Consequently he accepted Turgot's reassurances about the ministry's settlement of the problem reluctantly and pessimistically.[37] His opposition implied, how-

32. Marie Jean Antoine de Caritat, Marquis de Condorcet to Anne Robert Jacques Turgot, June 29, 1770, in Condorcet, *Correspondance inédite de Condorcet et de Turgot*, 16.

33. Marie Jean Antoine de Caritat, Marquis de Condorcet to Anne Robert Jacques Turgot, April 15, June 29, August [?], August 22, 1770, January 20, spring, 1771, July 20, fall, 1774, etc., *ibid.*, 11, 16, 17, 18, 38, 48, 184, 202.

34. E.g., [Marie Jean Antoine de Caritat, Marquis de Condorcet], *Lettre d'un théologien à l'auteur du "Dictionnaire des trois siècles"* (Berlin, 1774), 86–88.

35. Marie Jean Antoine de Caritat, Marquis de Condorcet to Anne Robert Jacques Turgot, January 22, February [?], February 17, March [?], spring, 1771, in Condorcet, *Correspondance inédite de Condorcet et de Turgot*, 39, 42, 44, 47, 48, 79.

36. Marie Jean Antoine de Caritat, Marquis de Condorcet to Anne Robert Jacques Turgot, October or November, 1774, *ibid.*, 201–203, 204–206; Marie Jean Antoine de Caritat, Marquis de Condorcet to François Marie Arouet de Voltaire, July 22, 1774, in Voltaire *Correspondence*, LXXXVIII, 118.

37. Marie Jean Antoine de Caritat, Marquis de Condorcet, "Une Lettre de Condorcet à Diderot sur le Parlement," *Révolution française. Revue d'histoire moderne et contemporaine*,

ever, no endorsement of Maupeou's or anyone else's absolutism. "I fear greatly," he wrote Turgot in 1774, "that the King of Prussia may have the honor of having set the style, not of conquerors like Caesar or Alexander who ravaged the world in their progress, but of tyrants who oppress gradually, coldly, and deliberately."[38]

D'Alembert's initial reaction to the coup was like Turgot's, to whom he wrote in February 1771, "The king is without doctors, and none the worse. Maybe the same would be true of the state if it could be without a parlement and without a ministry." Though he was grateful for the magistrates' expulsion of the Jesuits, he remained convinced they had formed with the clergy "a defensive and offensive league against philosophy and the progress of the enlightenment."[39] Yet he became disheartened by the deplorable state of the nation's finances under Terray, by "the atrocities and absurdities of every sort that dishonor my dear country," the intensification of the censorship of the Philosophes, and the threatened restoration of the Jesuits.[40] So when Maupeou fell he approvingly reported to Frederick, "The ministers whom [the king] has dismissed were the horror of the nation and their expulsion has been the cause of universal joy." He accepted with equal satisfaction the abolition of the Maupeou Parlement, for he had come to the conclusion that it "was too badly organized to be able to hold the confidence and public respect that magis-

LXV (1913), 365–66. Other factors alienating Condorcet from the Maupeou Parlement were the court's favoritism to the Farmers General, the Beaumarchais affair, and the Parlement's censorship of philosophic writings. On these issues, see respectively *ibid.*, 365; Marie Jean Antoine de Caritat, Marquis de Condorcet to Anne Robert Jacques Turgot, December 20 and 27, 1773, and January 16, 1774, in Condorcet, *Correspondance inédite de Condorcet et de Turgot*, 152–53, 162. See also François Marie Arouet de Voltaire to Marie Jean Antoine de Caritat, Marquis de Condorcet, September 28, 1774, in Voltaire, *Correspondence*, LXXXIX, 29.

38. Marie Jean Antoine de Caritat, Marquis de Condorcet to Anne Robert Jacques Turgot, April 18, 1774, in Condorcet, *Correspondance inédite de Condorcet et de Turgot*, 166. On Condorcet and the parlements, see also Baker, *Condorcet*, 32–33, 59.

39. Jean Le Rond d'Alembert to Anne Robert Jacques Turgot, February 3, 1771, in D'Alembert, *Correspondance inédite*, 29; Jean Le Rond d'Alembert to Frederick II of Prussia, October 15, 1775, in D'Alembert, *Oeuvres*, V, 367.

40. Jean Le Rond d'Alembert to Frederick II of Prussia, August 17 and November 8, 1771, April 9, May 14, and December 10, 1773, July 1 and September 12, 1774, *ibid.*, V, 313, 315, 335, 337, 343, 351, 353; Jean Le Rond d'Alembert to François Marie Arouet de Voltaire, December 26, 1772, and March 22, 1774, in Voltaire, *Correspondence*, LXXXIII, 221–22, and LXXXVII, 139–40.

trates must enjoy," and though "the old [parlement] had very serious faults too," he hoped that "its four years of disgrace [had] made it reasonable and well behaved." He was reassured by the fact that "the religious fanatics [were] screaming against its reestablishment."[41]

Despite the parliamentary tenor of the politics of the *Encyclopédie*, by 1770 Diderot was (privately) lambasting the magistrates in language that was unadulterated vitriol. He gave unqualified endorsement to Voltaire's *Histoire du parlement de Paris*, but went far beyond that author's polished irony. He forthrightly condemned the magistrates for their corruption, for their refusal of justice to the people, for their indifference to the public welfare, for their stupidity, for their uninformed meddling in all branches of the government, for their reactionaryism, for their defense of feudal privileges, for being "the most violent enemies of all liberties civil and religious," and for serving as "the slaves of the powerful and the oppressors of the weak." In sum, the Parlement of Paris was "the shabbiest, the most ignorant, most petty, most pretentious, most stubborn, most evil, most vile, most vindictive body of men that it is possible to imagine. They always oppose what is good, or support the good with bad motives; they have no sound ideas on public administration or the general welfare, no feeling for the importance and dignity of the nation; and they are the irreconcilable enemies of philosophy and reason."[42] After the coup Diderot conceded, as we have seen, the potential value of the court's claimed powers, even though they had no substantial historical justification, but he blamed the magistrates all the more for failing to exercise their authority courageously and in the nation's interest, which might have won them the support and trust of the people. In 1773 he was still attacking the former magistrates of the Paris Parlement in the same unqualified terms as "gothic . . . intolerant, bigoted, superstitious . . . petty busybodies . . . vindictive, proud, and ungrateful."[43]

"But," Diderot said to Catherine, "did all this mean that the destruc-

41. Jean Le Rond d'Alembert to Frederick II of Prussia, September 12, October 31, 1774, in D'Alembert, *Oeuvres*, V, 352, 354.

42. Denis Diderot, "Sur l'Histoire du parlement de Paris de Voltaire," in Diderot, *Oeuvres complètes*, VI, 402–404. Cf. Denis Diderot, "Salon de 1767," *ibid.*, XI, 93, on venality of office.

43. Diderot, "Essai historique sur la police," in Diderot, *Mémoires pour Catherine II*, 8, 16, 18.

tion of the parlements was a good thing? . . . Did the nation rejoice over the devastation of its courts?" By no means. The Maupeou revolution had caused "the ruin of twenty thousand families," and the former magistrates, who for all their faults had had some measure of dignity, experience, and competence, had been replaced by "a pack of wretches, malefactors, sycophants, tramps, ignoramuses—a miserable rabble that now hold the fatal urn containing our liberty, our fortunes, and our honor."[44] But Maupeou's worst crime was that he had destroyed Frenchmen's self-respect and dignity as human beings. Before December 1770 they had not in fact been free, yet they had still enjoyed a precious belief in their freedom. "There was between the face of the despot and our eyes a huge spider web on which the multitude worshipped a great image of liberty. The perspicacious had for a long time been looking through the little holes in the web and they had a good idea of what was behind it. But now the web has been torn to shreds, and tyranny has shown its face. . . . Now the people are slaves, they feel they are, they see they are." Moreover the unabashed *despotisme* of Louis XV did not even make pretension to being "juste et éclairé." It was weak and morally corrupt misgovernment by a "breed of vipers that tear each other to pieces at the foot of the throne," and by royal mistresses who "twist as they please the will of their lover, depose ministers, assign generals to armies, and use beauty spots to lay out on a map the line of march for the troops—and twenty thousand men are murdered."[45] Maupeou himself was "a vicious man," "a nobody, without wealth, without birth, without great ability, but a man who has made up for his lack of such qualities with baseness, duplicity, vindictiveness, ambition, and audacity." His "reforms," which so impressed Voltaire, Diderot called a pack of frauds. "To deceive the people (who cannot be deceived) they said they were going to make justice free, and it became more costly than before. They said that in order to spare litigants long journeys, extended absences from home, and immense expenses they would replace the abolished courts with a large number of Cours Souverains . . . ; which they did, but only by accepting [as magistrates] every wretch that

44. *Ibid.*, 18–20. The "twenty thousand families" refers of course, not to the exiled magistrates but to those like Mme D'Epinay who were (relatively) "ruined" by Terray's financial operations.

45. *Ibid.*, 20–21, 79; Denis Diderot, "Essai sur les règnes de Claude et de Néron," in Diderot, *Oeuvres complètes*, III, 71.

had the impudence to offer himself for the paltry salary they paid. I have seen these respectable appointments to the magistracy peddled from house to house, and not a single honest citizen could be found to take one. . . . We have in an instant leaped from monarchical government to the most perfect form of despotism."[46]

Diderot's despair over the Maupeou revolution was woven into the fabric of his historical pessimism. As early as April 1771 he told the Princess Dashkoff, "We have reached a crisis that will lead either to slavery or to liberty. If it is to slavery, it will be a slavery like that in Morocco and Constantinople." The Count de Broglie once twitted him about a black coat he was wearing, asking if he were in mourning for the Russians. Diderot replied, "If I had to wear mourning for a nation, my lord, I should not have so far to seek."[47]

Mme d'Epinay shared Grimm's acid opinion of the regime, and like her lover she expressed contempt for Voltaire for "having written twenty of so [!] detestable little pamphlets against the parlements, which no one reads and against which everyone is indignant."[48] She held no brief for the parlements and feared lest their victory might mean that "the king would have little more authority than the king of England," but she abhorred turmoil. She predicted that the current revolution would cause a lot of trouble and no benefits, and that if it continued it would change the character of the nation. If this did have to happen, she would prefer "the despotism of the Parlement, for [at least] it keeps to formal procedures, which a despotic sovereign spurns."[49] Indeed she spoke with reason, for Terray's extralegal financial maneuvers had seriously reduced her income.[50] Like all the Philosophes she was shocked by the suppression of

46. Diderot, *Mémoires pour Catherine II*, 29, 28; Diderot, "Observations sur le Nakaz," in Diderot, *Oeurves politiques*, 31–32.

47. Denis Diderot to Princess Dashkoff, April 3, 1771, in Diderot, *Correspondance*, XI, 20; *Mémoires secrets*, January 5, 1772 (VI, 70).

48. *Correspondance littéraire*, October 15, 1772, and January 1, 1773 (X, 80–81, 138); Louise F. P. Tardieu d'Esclavelles, Marquise d'Epinay to Ferdinando Galiani, May 20, 1771, in Epinay, *La Signora d'Epinay et l'abate Galiani. Lettere inedite*, 177.

49. Louise F. P. Tardieu d'Esclavelles, Marquise d'Epinay to Ferdinando Galiani, April 11, 1771, in Galiani, *Sa Correspondance* (Paris, 1881), I, 374–76.

50. Louise F. P. Tardieu d'Esclavelles, Marquise d'Epinay to Ferdinando Galiani, May 11 and March 8, 1771, *ibid.*, I, 371–72, and in Epinay, *La Signora d'Epinay et l'abate Galiani. Lettere inedite*, 154.

the Cour des Aides, over which her friend Malesherbes presided. "We expected [it]," she wrote Galiani, "and guessed the reason for the precipitation with which it was carried out, and no one doubts that it will achieve its purpose. We are heartbroken to be deprived of all justice. . . . The consternation is tremendous. . . . A number of people are thinking seriously of leaving the country. . . . We don't know what to expect and we are frightened. Yet our ideas remain unchanged, for no one can order people what to think. As for what is being written, there is such general contempt for the way the chancellor operates that we scarcely bother to read what appears. We know before we look at it that it is full of lies and tricks."[51]

Mme d'Epinay and Grimm were collaborating with Diderot, Pitra, and Meister during the years 1771–1775 in writing the *Correspondance littéraire*. This clandestine manuscript newsletter, though not oriented to politics, mirrored the development of Philosophic opinion on the crisis. Through December 1770 it was clearly hostile to the Paris Parlement, which the editors described as the ally of the church and the enemy of the Philosophes.[52] But after the exile of the magistrates and the suppression of Malesherbes' Cour des Aides there was an abrupt shift in editorial policy, first clearly manifested in the May 1771 issue. The *Correspondance* reported in some detail the struggles between the Parti Dévot and the Parti Encyclopédique for domination of the French Academy, in which occurred the demonstration in support of Malesherbes, and the furor over the censorship imposed on that august body after Laharpe's and Maury's mildly libertarian eulogies of Fénelon.[53] In all these skirmishes the Patriotes and the Philosophes of course stood side by side.

Helvétius, writing before his death in 1771 for posthumous publication, could dare to speak his mind. He was critical of the parlements, but like Diderot not so much because of their constitutional position as for their abuse of their powers.[54] He was grateful to them for their expulsion of the Jesuits and wished they had acted with equal vigor against the pa-

51. Louise F. P. Tardieu d'Esclavelles, Marquise d'Epinay to Ferdinando Galiani, May 11, 1771, in Galiani, *Sa Correspondance* (Paris, 1881), I, 373.

52. E.g., *Correspondance littéraire*, September 1, 1770, and January 1, 1771 (IX, 111–12, 203–14).

53. On the demonstration in support of Malesherbes, see *ibid.*, May, 1771 (IX, 313).

54. Helvétius, *Le Bonheur*, 79.

pacy. On the other hand, Maupeou filled him with despair. In the preface to *De l'Homme* he wrote, "In the time I have spent composing this work the evils with which my fellow citizens are faced have changed in nature, and so has their government. The ills for which I thought I could offer some remedy have now become incurable; I have lost hope of being useful, and so I am postponing the publication of this work until after my death. My country has finally been forced to bow to the yoke of despotism. It will therefore no longer produce famous writers, for despotism always stifles thought in men's minds and virtue in their hearts. This degraded nation is today the scorn of all Europe."[55] Saint Lambert in the preface to Helvétius' poem *Le Bonheur* (also published posthumously) testified to the mental depression his friend suffered after January 1771 because of the "public misfortunes," the "financial chaos of the government, and the change in the constitution of the state."[56]

In the works D'Holbach published during the years 1771–1774, even though they were printed abroad or clandestinely, he prudently limited himself to oblique references to the political struggle. As a utilitarian he rejected the parliamentary (and royalist) tenet that a fundamental law could be justified merely by tradition or historical precedent; he denounced venality of judgeships; he blamed magistrates who sacrificed the public good to their private interests; and he even wrote, "A despot is preferable to a despotic corporation." At the same time he repeatedly conceded that bodies such as the parlements could serve as valuable "barriers against authority."[57] None of these general comments was specifically applied to the politics of the moment. In his *Morale universelle*, however, which though in part written in 1774 or earlier was not published until 1776, he felt he could safely call a spade a spade. On one hand, he sharply attacked the magistrates. They had asserted that as representatives of the nation they were defending the law and the people's rights, and indeed if they had acted equitably, honestly, and moderately this claim might have gained acceptance. But instead, "puffed up with their prerogatives," they had

55. Claude Adrien Helvétius, *De l'Homme, de ses facultés intellectuelles, et de son éducation, ouvrage posthume de M. Helvétius* . . . (London, 1773), II, Chap. 22, I, viii.

56. Helvétius, *Le Bonheur*, cxvi.

57. [D'Holbach], *Système social*, I, 190; II, 11, 31; III, 29–30; [D'Holbach], *La Politique naturelle*, I, 135. Cf., *ibid.*, I, 223; II, 59.

arrogantly "abused their power and cruelly imposed the weight of their authority on their fellow citizens." On the other hand, the pride of the magistrates gave no license to despotism. "At this very moment," D'Holbach wrote in the summer of 1774, "a nation long oppressed is transported with joy by the deserved disgrace of two tyrannical ministers, the Chancellor Maupeou and the Abbé Terray. One, after having insolently destroyed the laws and tribunals of his country and cruelly dispersed its magistrates, now finds himself in his turn exiled to an isolated retreat where he hears the shouts of joy of an entire people rejoicing over his downfall. The other, after having heartlesssly squeezed the last drops of blood from his fellow citizens, is now forced, despite his hard, insensible heart, to blush for the vile way he made himself the executioner of his nation."[58]

One of the strongest indictments of both the parlements and the Maupeou regime was that written by Abbé Mably between 1771 and 1774 but not published until 1788. In accord with his *thèse démocratique* he refused to allow the Parlement of Paris any of the constitutional or historic rights and powers it claimed; he denounced *épices* and venality of office as "vile and unjust practices"; and he blamed the magistrates for failing to perform what proper functions they did possess with integrity and devotion to the public interest. Instead of truly defending the people against arbitrary authority, the Parlement had only proved that it "loves despotism provided it can share it."[59] On the other hand, "the depredations of the Abbé Terray and the tyranny of the Chancellor Maupeou" heralded a new insidious kind of despotism that was already demoralizing the French people and spreading throughout the nation poverty, corruption, and decadence. This degeneration Mably saw already manifested in the character of the magistrates Maupeou had appointed: "Rascals, fanatics, or fools, they are a pack of dishonored men who have brazenly lent them-

58. [Paul Henri Dietrich, Baron d'Holbach], *La Morale universelle, ou le Devoirs de l'homme fondés sur la nature* (Amsterdam, 1776), II, 170–71, 95.

59. Mably, *Observations sur l'histoire de France*, III, 547, 25–55, 126, 141–46, 313–14. This final version of the *Observations*, a considerable expansion of the 1765 edition, was first published after the author's death as *Observations sur l'histoire de France. . . . Nouvelle édition continuée jusqu'au règne de Louis XV* (Kehl, 1788). It contained the continuation indicated and a "Conclusion." According to Lanson, the additions were by Rulhière, but the references to the Maupeou revolution as a contemporary event and the style indicate that these passages at least were written by Mably himself, certainly before 1775 and according to Baker in 1772. See Baker, "A Script for a French Revolution," 245, 247, 261.

selves to all the inequities perpetrated by the ministry. Their morals will constitute our new jurisprudence, and their successors, brought to office by the intrigues of valets, clerks, and *femmes galantes* of Versailles, will squander our money and keep swords hanging over the heads of those of us they have marked for execution."[60]

Mably saw no hope for his poor country caught in this dilemma between the alternatives of government by self-serving magistrates or obscene despotism. "The small prestige that the Parlement still possesses cannot be the means to a successful reform of the government," nor could saving leadership be expected either from the nobility or the clergy, both of whom were intent on protecting their own privileges, or from the sophistic and irreligious Philosophes, or even from a "new Charlemagne," who would find himself balked by all those "interested in keeping the government the way it is."[61] The real culprit was neither the Parlement nor Maupeou, but the people who tolerated both. "The vices that indolence, luxury, avarice, and servile ambition have been implanting in the French character since the reign of Louis XIII have so corrupted the soul of the nation that no matter how much reason the French have to fear despotism they lack sufficient courage to love liberty. . . . Our character befits our government, and . . . we have within us no spirit of revolution." Instead of rebelling against Maupeou's tyranny the French people had been so cowed they had been frightened by their own complaints and had had only enough courage to long for the Duke de Choiseul and hope for the fall of the cabal that had ousted him. The insidious quality of absolutism was its ability to feed on itself and continually wax stronger. "Our government . . . is capable of producing nothing but more Maupeous."[62]

One might continue citing other examples. There was Julie de Lespinasse, who was "intoxicated with joy" at the fall of Maupeou. There was Mme Du Deffand, who wrote Walpole that the chancellor "is not a man; he is a devil."[63] And there were the Count de Guibert, Galiani, Mercier,

---

60. *Ibid.*, III, 542, 544.

61. *Ibid.*, III, 301, 303, 308–313, 317, 549–53.

62. *Ibid.*, III, 305–306, 542, 546.

63. Julie Jeanne Eléonore de Lespinasse to Jacques Antoine Hippolyte, Count de Guibert, August 27, 1774, in Lespinasse, *Correspondance entre Mlle. de Lespinasse et le comte de Guibert* (Paris, 1906), 132. Marie Anne de Vichy-Chamrond, Marquise Du Deffand to Horace Walpole, May 1, 1771, in Horace Walpole, *Correspondence with Madame Du Deffand and Wiart*, ed. Wilmarth S. Lewis and W. H. Smith (New Haven, 1939), III, 67.

Morellet, the younger Mirabeau, Raynal, and more. The pattern that emerges in these years is that of a pervasive historical pessimism intensified if not produced by the apparent futility of the struggle between Maupeou and the Patriotes and by the spread of absolutism across continental Europe. The eighteenth century has sometimes been described as the age of optimism, and indeed it so appears if one considers only the Philosophes' alleged faith in the power of human reason to build the new "Heavenly City" of the Enlightenment, or reads only the confident formulations of the theory of progress sketched by Turgot in his *Discours* of 1750 and 1751, echoed by the Physiocrats, Morellet, and Chastellux, and later fully developed by Condorcet in his *Esquisse d'un tableau du progrès de l'esprit humain*. But in the early 1770s among the independent philosophers we are examining, pessimism was certainly dominant, both in short-term predictions for French society and long-term philosophies of history.[64]

The Count de Guibert painted a gloomy picture of a Europe bowed down under "tyrannical, ignorant, and weak governments; the vigor of nations sapped by vice; private interests prevailing over the public good; public morals . . . corrupt and the corruption viewed with indifference; systematic oppression of the people; public expenditures exceeding receipts; taxes higher than the people can pay; the population in decline; the essential arts neglected for frivolous pursuits; all classes corrupted by luxury; governments indifferent to their people, and the people reciprocating by an equal indifference to the fate of their governments. . . . The people . . . live in a state of apprehension and anguish, sick of life, existing mechanically . . . enchained by habit and vice."[65] In spite of all this, Guibert still had hopes for the regeneration of France. But to most of his contemporaries the expectation of renewal seemed an idle dream. "He [Guibert] depicts," Grimm said, "a beautiful era which will dawn on some utopia, but it is still a long way from this unhappy globe." Chastellux's progressionism met with the same bitter skepticism. D'Alembert commented, "He proposes to prove that the human race is less unhappy

64. See the excellent but not exhaustive study, Henry Vyverberg, *Historical Pessimism in the French Enlightenment* (Cambridge, Mass., 1958).

65. [Jacques Antoine Hippolyte, Count de Guibert], *Essai général de tactique, précédé d'un discours sur l'état actuel de la politique et de la science militaire en Europe, avec le plan d'un ouvrage intitulé: La France politique et militaire* (London, 1772), v–vi.

than it was before and that its unhappiness will keep decreasing by virtue of the progress of the enlightenment. I wish this more than I expect it." Mme d'Epinay was even more derisive: "No doubt it is good to preach to men the necessity of ridding themselves of prejudices and errors and of perfecting education, but to believe that the enlightenment of men will make them better or perfect, and that everyone's passions will yield to the speculations of philosophy and the sheer power of enlightenment and reason is a lovely fantasy."[66]

Thus the few sparks of optimism were being lost in the pervading gloom. Helvétius predicted that France, infected by the consumption of absolutism, would waste away, and the only imaginable "cure of the malady she suffers" would be "conquest by another power." His friend Saint Lambert wrote, "These recent years have been a period of public disaster. . . . The financial chaos and the change in the constitution have produced a general mood of despair which has been sadly evidenced by the large number of suicides."[67] Meanwhile Voltaire was writing his friends, "All is lost. We are in the hands of barbarians," and reaffirming his resolve to cultivate his own garden.

Materialistic naturalism logically implied historical pessimism, for it conceived of a universe in an eternal cyclical process. "Everything changes, everything passes, and only the whole remains," Diderot wrote. "All is in perpetual flux. . . . What will the passage and vicissitudes of some millions of centuries not produce here and elsewhere? . . . The imperceptible worm wiggling in the slime is perhaps on its way to become a great animal; the enormous beast that terrifies us by its size is perhaps in the process of being transformed into a worm."[68] What was true across the millenia for life forms was equally true across the centuries for human societies, as D'Holbach showed in his passages "On the Dissolution of

66. *Correspondance littéraire*, September, 1772 (X, 56); Jean Le Rond d'Alembert to Frederick II of Prussia, August 22, 1772, in D'Alembert, *Oeuvres*, V, 327; Louise F. P. Tardieu d'Esclavelles, Marquise d'Epinay to Ferdinando Galiani, January 12, 1773, in Galiani, *Sa Correspondance*, ed. Lucien Perey and Gaston Maugras (Paris, 1881), II, 167.

67. Helvétius, *De l'Homme*, I, viii; Jean François de Saint Lambert, "Préface" in Helvétius, *Le Bonheur*, cxvi.

68. Denis Diderot, "Le Rêve de d'Alembert, Entretien entre d'Alembert et Diderot," in Diderot, *Oeuvres philosophiques*, ed. Paul Vernière (Paris, 1956), 299–300, 311, 308, 268. On eighteenth-century naturalism, see Aram Vartanian, *Diderot and Descartes: A Study of Scientific Naturalism in the Enlightenemnt* (Princeton, 1953).

Nations." Every form of government, he believed—absolutism, limited
monarchy, aristocracy, or democracy—each had its own peculiar malignancy. The best he could offer his readers was a sort of meliorism, the
argument that reason, virtue, and liberty were worth working for, even
though their attainment would at best be relative and temporary. "Are
we to scorn good health because sooner or later it is followed by pain and
sickness?"[69]

Diderot's philosophy of history was even more pessimistic. He called
the American Revolution "one of the most extraordinary phenomena in
the history of the world," yet he felt compelled to warn the new repub-
licans of the seeds of degeneration within their triumph and of "the sad
and almost necessary influence of time, which brings more or less rapidly
the ruin of the most wisely ordered things."[70] As for France, the catastrophe was now, he told Catherine: "O unhappy nation, I weep for you! There
is a high mountain, of which one side is a steep slope and the other a precipice; between the two is a more or less extensive plain. A young nation
is one climbing the steep slope. A mature nation is one crossing the plain.
A nation in decline drops swiftly down the precipice. This is where we
French are now." And on another occasion (before the death of Louis XV):
"Our monarch is a superannuated old man. The last years of the long reign
of a great king have often spoiled the record of the first years, but never
have the last years of the long reign of a mediocre king compensated (to
speak charitably) for the preceding disasters. So we still have perhaps a
way to go on the road of decadence. Who knows our fate under the next
king? Speaking for myself, I am pessimistic. Would that I may be
wrong."[71] "One might be consoled," he bitterly wrote after returning from
Russia, "for past and present evils if the future were to bring a change in
our destiny. But this is an impossible hope. If a philosopher were asked
what good was the advice he kept giving to nations and their rulers and
if he answered honestly, he would say he was satisfying an invincible de-

69. [D'Holbach], *La Politique naturelle*, II, 226–27.
70. Diderot, "Essai sur les règnes de Claude et de Néron," in Diderot, *Oeuvres complètes*, III, 393.
71. Diderot, *Mémoires pour Catherine II*, 21, 40–41. See also *ibid.*, 13, 22, 34–35, 62,
66, 145–48, and Denis Diderot to John Wilkes, October 19 and November 14, 1771,
and to Catherine II of Russia, September 13, 1774, in Diderot, *Correspondance*, XI, 210–
11, 223; XIV, 80–81.

sire to tell the truth at the risk of arousing indignation and even of having to drink the cup of Socrates." But Diderot had long since decided to avoid the hemlock, and he had written Sophie Volland, "Don't worry, my dear, the time when I committed that sort of folly is passed."[72]

In analyzing the independent thinkers' constructive reactions to the Maupeou revolution it is obviously important to bear in mind this mood of pessimism. It is equally important, however, to appreciate the power of the countervailing forces, for the pessimism did not, after all, produce apathy in the face of the crisis. There were the progressionists such as Turgot and Condorcet, who denied historical pessimism; there were the limited meliorists, those who believed like D'Holbach that there was no reason to "scorn good health because sooner or later it is followed by pain and sickness"; and there were those like Diderot, who despite his conviction that France was a "nation in decline," could not abandon humanity by stifling his "invincible desire to tell the truth." Furthermore the pessimism, despite its scientific justification for the naturalists, was indeed in large part a mood, and one which was at least partially dispelled by the events of 1774. Rejecting the despair of Helvétius' *De l'homme* (which he himself had earlier shared), Diderot now wrote, "If the honorable men now in power remain in office for only ten years, all our troubles are over."[73]

Thus these independents emerged from the Maupeou revolution deeply troubled but committed to chart a better course for at least the immediate future. The pattern of their reactions, despite variations between different writers with different philosophic perspectives, is clear: a refusal to accept the parlements as the key institutions of the French constitution; a qualified acknowledgment of the courts' potential limited value in the existing circumstances; a general condemnation of the magistrates' failure before 1770 to fulfill their responsibilities; and, finally, the rejection of the principle of absolutism and profound contempt and even hatred for Maupeou and his ministry. The independents thus found themselves faced with two contradictory but equally unacceptable alternatives, the *thèse royale* of absolutism, totally reprehensible in both theory and practice, and the *thèse parlementaire*, inadequate and unjustifiable in theory and perverse in practice. Their only decision could be to reject both and seek a third option.

72. Diderot, "Observations sur le Nakaz," in Diderot, *Oeuvres politiques*, 367; Denis Diderot, *Lettres à Sophie Volland*, ed. André Babelon (Paris, 1930), III, 267.

73. Diderot, "Réfutation de . . . L'Homme," in Diderot, *Oeuvres complètes*, II, 275.

NINE

The Political Design

LIBERTY AND LIMITED MONARCHY

THE POLITICAL problem for the independent thinkers in the 1770s was to conceive a constitution which would deny the unacceptable alternatives of aristocracy and absolutism presented by the parlements and the crown, yet which would reconcile the royalists' argument for rational reorganization with the libertarianism of the Patriotes, and would do so without threatening property owners with anarchic populism. Unlike their opponents, the independents were not bound by commitments to existing institutions, traditions, or precedents and they could freely seek inspiration in foreign constitutions and in their own fertile imaginations. Their two essential problems were, first, to define the liberty which the new state was to guarantee, and then to invent a political structure which would make this guaranty effective. What negative liberties needed to be assured? That is, what kinds of individual behavior had to be protected against restrictions or interference by either the government or powerful individuals? And what positive liberties was it safe to grant? In whose hands should political power be entrusted?

It is possible to distinguish three current concepts of negative liberty. For the utilitarians, liberty was the power to pursue happiness. D'Holbach, our most typical example, gave a definition which he frequently repeated without significant variations: "Liberty is the faculty to use all the means that one judges appropriate to produce one's own happiness without detracting from that of others."[1] "Love of liberty," he said, "is the strongest of human emotions"; it was an instinctive "sentiment" engraved in our hearts by nature. Yet like all emotions it could be destructive if not controlled by enlightened reason and directed to activities productive of the good of society and the individual's true best interests—which by hypothesis were always compatible. "To be free is . . . to do what can contribute to one's permanent happiness."[2] It is important to note that in his *Politique naturelle* (1773) and his *Système social* (1773) D'Holbach called liberty a "faculté" or a "pouvoir," not a right, and when he used the term "droit" in his *Ethocratie* (1776) he meant only a power that all men rightly possess. He never conceived of liberty as an end, as an absolute good; it was a *means* for achieving the purpose of society, the greatest good of the greatest number. He listed the specific benefits of liberty: It made workers industrious, stimulated trade, manufacturing, and agriculture, increased population, instilled patriotism, etc. "There are no true virtues without liberty." For Helvétius likewise liberty was a right only in the sense that it was a rightful power which served human happiness.[3]

For certain natural-law philosophers, notably Turgot and Condorcet, liberty was also a means, but a means to a quite different absolute good—justice. To be free was to be protected from injustice. Restrictions on the civil rights of Protestants, for example, or the *corvée*, were unjust by natural law, and liberty consisted in the elimination of these wrongs. This is why Turgot refused to indulge in "déclamations" about "liberté" as an abstraction and instead worked to eradicate despotism "by clearly establishing the rights of man"; he strove to make men free by eliminating injustices.

Thirdly there was the position, also based on natural-law assumptions, that liberty was not a means to anything but an absolute good and end in itself, a natural right coequal with justice. Here Diderot seems our best

1. [D'Holbach], *La Politique naturelle*, I, 38. Cf. *ibid.*, II, 61; [D'Holbach], *Système social*, I, 145; II, 40; [Paul Henri Dietrich, Baron d'Holbach], *Ethocratie, ou le Gouvernement fondé sur la morale* (Amsterdam, 1776), 20.

2. [D'Holbach], *La Politique naturelle*, II, 59–60; [D'Holbach], *Système social*, I, 146.

3. [D'Holbach], *La Politique naturelle*, II, 100. Cf. *ibid.*, II, 75–77, 94, 99, etc.; Helvétius, *De l'Homme*, II, 325.

example. Though he sometimes sounded like a hedonist or a utilitarian, or even a moral anarchist, he always held firm to his basic conviction that man's good included but transcended material well-being and pleasure— that its essence was the enjoyment of the natural right of liberty to pursue the true, the good, and the beautiful. "Liberty," he wrote, "is a gift of heaven, and every individual of the same species has the right to enjoy it as soon as he has the use of reason."

> L'enfant de la nature abhorre l'esclavage;
> Implacable ennemi de toute autorité,
> Il s'indigne du joug; la contrainte l'outrage;
> Liberté, c'est son voeu; son cri, c'est Liberté.[4]

Diderot's hatred of despotism was, of course, simply the obverse of this love of liberty as the summum bonum of the species. His conception of human freedom was most clearly illustrated by his repeated assertions that any act of absolute authority, no matter how wise or beneficial to the individual or society, demeaned humanity by denying freedom of choice, the freedom to make, if a man so wished, stupid decisions against his own interests. Human beings could not be treated like a flock of sheep.

These three definitions of liberty—as a means to happiness, as a means to justice, and as an absolute natural good and right—were philosophically distinguishable, but the distinctions were not being argued in the 1770s, and in some cases they apparently were not clearly seen. Rather the practice was to synthesize—or confuse—the three concepts. Often this confusion made little practical difference, as in the case of property rights. Sometimes, however, differences in premises led to conflicting conclusions, as on the issue of enlightened despotism, or produced contradictions within the writings of the same man, for instance Rousseau's subordination of the Polish serfs' right to liberty (which was certainly primary according to the *Contrat social*) to the welfare of the state.[5]

4. Denis Diderot, "Autorité politique," in Diderot, *Oeuvres politiques*, 9; Diderot, "Les Eleuthéromanes," in Diderot, *Oeuvres complètes*, IX, 14. "The child of nature abhors slavery. He is the implacable enemy of all authority. Every yoke fills him with indignation; every constraint outrages him. Liberty is his great desire. His single cry is for Liberty."
5. Jean Jacques Rousseau, "Considérations sur le gouvernement de Pologne," in Rousseau, *Oeuvres complètes*, ed. Bernard Gagnebin and Marcel Raymond (Pléiade edition; Paris, 1959–1969), III, 974.

The weight given to the three concepts varied from writer to writer. For example Rouillé d'Orfeuil, who called liberty "the ability to do peacefully and safely whatever is necessary, useful, and agreeable to us," remained consistently in D'Holbach's camp.[6] Mercier like Turgot saw liberty as existence under the law of justice. D'Alembert, however, was more ambiguous. Initially he seems to have been close to Diderot, defining liberty as a natural right derived from natural moral law, but by the 1770s he was less interested in repeating Diderot's "déclamations" than in imitating Turgot (whose appointment he enthusiastically applauded) by campaigning against specific injustices, particularly the "literary inquisition" to which the Philosophes were being subjected.[7] The younger Mirabeau usually seemed to follow D'Holbach in conceiving liberty as the power of enlightened pursuit of self-interest and pleasure, but he also sometimes appeared to think of it as an absolute good, as when he wrote, "Men, equal in their rights, . . . all demand liberty by the same title and all have the same right to defend it when it is attacked." The Abbé Morellet, on the other hand, started with the natural-law premise that liberty is an "inalienable and indefeasible right," but then gave a definition certainly colored by utilitarianism: "Human liberty consists both in acting in a way useful and agreeable to oneself and in being protected from actions of others which would be harmful and disagreeable." Chastellux leaves us in doubt as to whether he paralleled D'Holbach in thinking of liberty as simply a means to achieving "the greatest happiness of the greatest number" or whether he believed like Diderot that it was an essential ingredient of this happiness, as when he wrote, "A happy people is one who enjoys prosperity [*aisance*] and liberty, which is linked to property."[8] Mably fits no pattern, for he held that liberty (which he believed

6. [Augustin Rouillé d'Orfeuil], *L'Alambic moral, ou Analyse raisonnée de tout ce qui a rapport à l'homme. Par l'Ami des François* (Maroc, 1773), 378.

7. D'Alembert, "Eléments de philosophie" (1759), in D'Alembert, *Oeuvres*, I; Jean Le Rond d'Alembert to Frederick II of Prussia, April 9 and May 14, 1773, September 12, 1774, February 7 and May 27, 1775, in D'Alembert, *Oeuvres*, V, 335, 337, 352, 354, 358, 361–62, 363; and Jean Le Rond d'Alembert to François Marie Arouet de Voltaire, October 7, 1771, and December 26, 1772, in Voltaire, *Correspondence*, LXXX, 72–73; LXXXIII, 221–23.

8. Mirabeau, *Essai sur le despotisme*, 71; [Morellet], *Réflexions sur les avantages de la liberté d'écrire*, 52; [André Morellet], *Théorie du paradoxe* (Amsterdam, 1775), 18; Chastellux, *De la Félicité*, I, 106–107.

possible only if men freed themselves from materialistic ambitions by abolishing property and economic inequality) was a means neither to happiness nor to justice, but to virtue.

The one point of agreement, regardless of philosophical premises, was that liberty was a universal, a right or power that should be enjoyed by all men. Beyond this, however, the philosophers obviously were far from a clear and unanimous definition of this word *liberté* which they and everyone else were beginning to use with such abandon. If Montesquieu had been alive he would no doubt have still said that no word had so many different meanings. The semantic problem was not limited to the question whether the word denoted a power or condition for the achievement of some higher absolute good—happiness, justice, or virtue—or whether it was an ultimate, absolute good in itself. There were also other uncertainties: liberty from what? Liberty to do what? It was in specific applications of the right or power of liberty that the means/end dichotomy often became most visible. Such applications were the rights of life and property, economic liberty, and freedom of person, of religion, of speech, and of the press.

The right to property was asserted mainly on utilitarian grounds and tended to be identified with economic liberty. For D'Holbach the free use of private property was obviously the primary means of promoting individual happiness and the public welfare. As a Physiocrat on economic questions, he interpreted this freedom to mean equality before the law, fairly proportioned taxation, prohibition of tax exemptions, the removal of all other restrictions on economic activity, and of course protection from confiscation, either outright or by inequitable taxation. Yet he went beyond the Physiocrats in emphasizing that economic liberty should be granted to salaried workers as well as to property owners. "The government," he wrote, "shall not fail to open up the freest possible field for the activity of all citizens disposed to work. Exclusive privileges, the powers and rights of trade guilds, etc., are all obstacles to industry and prevent the indigent from improving their lot."[9] This basically utilitarian position on property was shared with modifications by Chastellux, Rouillé d'Orfeuil, the younger Mirabeau, and Raynal.

Morellet, as we have seen, carried the economic individualism of the

9. [D'Holbach], *Ethocratie*, 151.

Physiocrats to its ultimate limits, insisting that the free use of property was an absolute right, limited only by the like right of others, but otherwise unrestricted regardless of the indirect harmful effects it might have on individuals. One acted within one's absolute rights (though perhaps without charity) in shutting one's door on a man freezing to death. This sounds like an extreme natural-right position, but Morellet's justification was utilitarian, for he argued that despite the incidental injuries suffered by others from such total economic liberty, society as a whole benefited: "The general interest . . . is that each citizen make the most varied, extensive, and unlimited use possible of his property, provided that he is limited to his own possessions and his own person. It is from this activity and this liberty exercised by each individual that the general good results. . . . From the very opposition of private interests springs the public welfare."[10]

Predictably it was Diderot who most clearly took an authentic natural-rights position on property. True, he sometimes gave utilitarian justifications for the right, arguing that it was essential for demographic growth, the happiness of the people, the prosperity and viability of the state, etc.[11] Informed by his observations of the Dutch economy, he was a strong advocate of free enterprise and the profit motive as the keys to national prosperity. "Protect business," he wrote, "but be careful not to control it. Inspections, restrictions, prohibitions, and regulations are never without disadvantages in something as variable as trade." The natural operations of economic laws provided all the regulations needed: "There must be no legislation where nature has installed an attentive, just, firm, and enlightened despot who always rewards and punishes with an even hand. Self-interest, always favorable to those who consult it wisely, is cruel only to those who fail to understand its true nature."[12] Thus economic freedom and the right of property required not only legal safeguards but also the principle of minimum government.

10. [Morellet], *Réfutation {du}* . . . *"Dialogue sur le commerce des blés,"* 109–10.

11. E.g., Diderot, "Observations sur le Nakaz," in Diderot, *Oeuvres politiques*, 380, 394, 403, 407, 440, 457; Diderot, "Fragments échappés du portefeuille d'un philosophe," in Diderot, *Oeuvres complètes*, VI, 450; Diderot, "Rêveries à l'occasion de la révolution de Suède," in Dieckman, "Diderot, Grimm et Raynal," 434.

12. Denis Diderot, "Voyage de Hollande," in Diderot, *Oeuvres complètes*, XVII, 391. Cf. Diderot, "Lettre sur le commerce de la librairie," *ibid.*, XVIII, 29.

Yet Diderot's definition of property, "the taking of possession by labor," was Lockean. He saw economic freedom as an extension of the general right to liberty as an absolute good:

> The individual must be able to leave his land fallow, if he so wishes, without the government or the police intervening. If the ruler makes himself the judge of the abuse he will soon make himself judge of the use, and then all true notions of property and liberty will be lost. If he can demand that I use my possessions as he happens to will, if he inflicts penalties for violations of his regulations, for negligence, or for stupidity, and does so under the pretext of acting in the public interest, then I am no longer absolute master of my property; I am only an administrator acting at the pleasure of another. Man in society must in these matters be allowed the freedom to be a bad citizen, for he will soon enough be severely punished by poverty, and by the contempt of others, which is even more painful than poverty. [13]

Economic men, like political men, should not be treated like a flock of sheep. It is important to note that this absolute right of property was quite different from that maintained by Morellet and the Physiocrats, for while Diderot defended economic man's right to be stupid or negligent he did not defend his right to exploit his fellows. On this point he was in accord with Turgot and Condorcet.

Around the proponents of these two basic positions on property were those whom we may call the eccentrics, notably Linguet, who opposed of course both Morellet's and Diderot's kinds of economic liberty, and Mably, who believed that all property was an unnatural institution which fostered materialistic ambitions and corrupted man's natural virtues.

Life, though first in the triumvirate of rights proclaimed by Locke and the Patriotes, received no more than formal mention by these independents—except, as we shall see in the following chapter, Jacques Henri Meister, who like Linguet turned the right into something far removed from the Lockean concept. No doubt the right to life was included under freedom of person, but even this latter right received far less attention than the Patriotes gave to it. We may assume that despite incidents such as

13. Denis Diderot, "Entretien d'un père avec ses enfants," *ibid.*, V, 297; Diderot, "Fragments échappés du portefeuille d'un philosophe," *ibid.*, VI, 449.

Diderot's incarceration at Vincennes, Voltaire's exile from Paris, and the miscarriages of criminal justice that Voltaire made causes célèbres, neither the right to live nor the right to freedom of person appeared as pressing social problems. This is not to say, of course, that they were ignored. D'Holbach said that security of person—that is, protection against arbitrary imprisonment, exile, or execution—was as important as security of property. The abuse that drew the most attention was that of *lettres de cachet*, against which the younger Mirabeau and Mercier spoke out with special vigor. Morellet praised the protection afforded by the British writ of habeas corpus.[14] Serfdom, which was still in force in eastern Europe and of which vestiges still existed in France, was condemned, and slavery and the slave trade were denounced not only by the Physiocrats but by Diderot, Condorcet, Lanjuinais, Mercier, Turgot, and most especially Raynal. One has the impression, however, that on these matters the independents were not defending a basic principle as they were in their defense of property but were rather following Turgot's lead in promoting justice by attacks on specific inequities.

Positions on religious freedom were complicated by the wide range of opinions on religion itself (Was God a vicious *chimère*, a necessary invention, or the architect of the universe?) and by the various views on the social utility of religion and the political danger of the Catholic Church. Freedom of conscience as a distinct natural right, inferred either from Bayle's "droit de la conscience errante" or from Locke's principle of fallibility, found few apologists other than Rousseau and Turgot. Moreover one finds no consideration of the American concept of total separation of church and state, as is made abundantly clear by all the talk about salaried priests. Of course the continued official policy of intolerance against the Huguenots was deplored by all and religious freedom was vaguely included in the general concept of personal liberty, but as we shall see in Chapter 10, religious liberty was more a political tactic than a moral principle, for the central interest was in destroying the Catholic Church's privileged position and its political support of absolutism.

14. [Paul Henri Dietrich, Baron d'Holbach], *Système de la nature, ou Des lois du monde physique et du monde moral.* . . . (London, 1770), Chap. 9; [D'Holbach], *La Politique naturelle*, II, Discours VI; [D'Holbach], *Ethocratie*, 20; [Mirabeau], *Essai sur le despotisme*, 33–35, 65–66; [Mercier], *L'An 2440*, 98; [Morellet], *Théorie du paradoxe*, 31.

Freedom of speech and press were likewise seldom championed as specific, distinct natural rights or even as extensions of the general right of liberty. Notable exceptions were Turgot and Mercier. "Freedom of the press," the latter wrote, "is the true measure of civil liberty. If one is infringed the other is destroyed. Thought must have full expression. To restrict it, to stifle it in its sanctuary, is a crime of *lèse-humanité*. What shall I possess if I do not possess my own thoughts?" [15]

Far more frequent, however, was the argument that freedom of speech and press was good policy, that it was an efficacious means of advancing the general welfare, spreading enlightenment, and achieving the sovereignty of the nation. It was justified not absolutely as an ultimate good but relatively by its special benefits. D'Alembert could be infuriated by Maupeou's "literary inquisition" against the Philosophes but he was no less indignant when anti-Philosophes like Clément were afforded freedom of the press to vilify his friends. [16] Diderot's *Lettre sur le commerce de la librairie*, which in 1769 he planned to entitle *Sur la liberté de la presse*, was merely a plea for the protection of the property rights of authors and publishers. He dismissed as irrelevant to his purpose the "usual arguments" for freedom of the press—that books were not as dangerous as was believed, that truth always drives out error, and that there is no danger in truth. [17]

These were indeed the usual utilitarian arguments. D'Holbach saw freedom of the press as an efficient means of implementing the general will and of disseminating truth. Nothing was more unreasonable, he wrote, than to prevent freedom to speak and write on "subjects important to the happiness" of citizens. "The public has the right to regulate the conduct of its leaders and legislators. . . . It is only through enlightenment that a nation can improve its lot." A man who thinks "is a useful man, and freedom of thought is a strong and necessary barrier against . . .

15. See Anne Robert Jacques Turgot to Josiah Tucker, September 12, 1770, and to Pierre Samuel Du Pont de Nemours, January 4, 1771, in Turgot, *Oeuvres*, ed. Schelle, III, 11, 468; [Mercier], *L'An 2440*, 52.

16. *E.g.*, Jean Le Rond d'Alembert to François Marie Arouet de Voltaire, March 6, 1772, in Voltaire, *Correspondence*, LXXXI, 103–104, on D'Alembert's reaction to Clément's *Boileau à M. de Voltaire* (1772). See also D'Alembert, "Eléments de philosophie," in D'Alembert, *Oeuvres*, I, 223, and page 114 herein.

17. Denis Diderot, "Lettre . . . sur le commerce de la librairie," in Diderot, *Oeuvres complètes*, XVIII, 7–75. See Jacques Proust, "Pour servir à une édition critique de *La Lettre sur le commerce de la librairie*," *Diderot Studies* (Geneva, 1961), III, 321–45.

tyranny." "Truth is dangerous only to the evil, and public calumny cannot harm men whose good works the public knows. . . . Truth always gains by discussion; only lies and crime profit from the concealment of darkness."[18] This basic argument of the social utility of truth was repeated in almost identical language by Helvétius, and even by Condorcet and the Abbé Morellet, who might have been expected to use natural-law arguments.[19] In fact freedom of the press was more closely associated with education as a key strategy in the program for the Enlightenment of Mankind than it was with property as an inalienable natural right.

Since by Lockean psychology all ideas, including moral concepts, are acquired by experience, and since as a consequence "education makes us what we are," as Helvétius said, it followed that "education" of the young by formal instruction and of adults by the diffusion of information and ideas was the primary means of achieving moral, social, and political reform.[20] On this reasoning everyone agreed; the differences arose over the questions of what should be taught, either in schools or through the press, and to whom. Rousseau in his *Emile* had said he saw no hope of giving the youth of modern France a true "éducation publique" in civic virtue and therefore proposed his alternative of an "éducation domestique" to develop the moral and intellectual faculties of the apolitical individual. Maupeou was happy to extend freedom of the press to Voltaire as long as he wrote in support of the ministry, and Lebrun made elaborate plans for schooling which would have inculcated the youth of France with what he considered the proper virtues. The independent philosophers were demanding freedom of the press to propagandize their own ideas (not defending to the death—despite the legend—the right of their enemies to publish theirs) and their proposals for the instruction of the young had the same purpose.

D'Holbach hoped for a national system of education which, no longer

18. [D'Holbach], *La Politique naturelle*, II, 84; [D'Holbach], *Système social*, II, 53; [D'Holbach], *La Politique naturelle*, II, 83–84.

19. Helvétius, *De l'Homme*, II, 233, 314, 321, 325, 333. See Marie Jean Antoine de Caritat, Marquis de Condorcet to Anne Robert Jacques Turgot, August, 1770, January 20 and February or March, 1771, January 16, 1774, 1776, in Condorcet, *Correspondance inédite de Condorcet et de Turgot*, 18–19, 38, 46, 162, 272. Condorcet did not recommend the total abolition of censorship but rather urged that the authority to censor be transferred from the Parlement to the conseil and the courts act only on suits for libel brought by private citizens. [Morellet], *Réflexions sur les avantages de la liberté d'écrire*, 19.

20. Helvétius, *De l'Homme*, II, 401.

perverted by priests, would "make men reasonable and teach them their true interests." Diderot was primarily interested in education as a means of creating equality of opportunity in a fluid society. Mably, disdaining the aims of these atheistic "sophists," would have directed national education toward the moral regeneration of the French people. He proposed a plan of instruction for both sexes which would have included physical as well as mental instruction and would have inculcated civic virtue, patriotism, and the spirit of egalitarianism. Turgot likewise posited that the primary purpose of education was moral and that a high level of public morality (*moeurs*) could be achieved by "instruction from childhood in all the duties of man in society." His aim, however, was not to instill the spirit of equality but a sense of social responsibility and an openness to reform that would accelerate "the progress of the enlightenment." He proposed to Louis XVI the establishment of a *conseil d'instruction nationale* to supervise all the primary schools, academies, colleges, and universities in France and to promulgate a curriculum in which the various subjects "would be arranged in the order of their utility to the nation" and whose central goal would be teach each Frenchman the "duties of the citizen as a member of a family and as a member of the state."[21] Whether the rationale for general education was moral as with Mably, progressionistic as with Turgot and Condorcet, or utilitarian as with D'Holbach or Helvétius, the general proposal received wide support not only from libertarians like Chastellux, Morellet, and Raynal but also, as we know, from the Physiocrats and Lebrun among the absolutists. This support was not, however, unanimous, for Necker, like the Abbé Galiani, shared Voltaire's doubts and fears.

From all the foregoing it should be obvious that the concept of liberty in the 1770s still focused on security of life, person, and property and that it was only just beginning the two-century process of progressive proliferation into increasing numbers of special and specific rights, starting with the rights of religious liberty and freedom of the press and ending with the right to practice sodomy. This process was to be triggered by the

21. [D'Holbach], *La Politique naturelle*, I, 188; Gabriel Bonnot de Mably, *De la Législation, ou Principes des lois* (Amsterdam, 1776), II, 133–64; Book IV, Chap. 1; Turgot, "Mémoire sur les municipalités," in Turgot, *Oeuvres*, ed. Schelle, IV, 578–80; Anne Robert Jacques Turgot to Marie Jean Antoine de Caritat, Marquis de Condorcet, July 16, 1771, *ibid.*, III, 523.

American and French bills of rights and was to constitute the rationale of nineteenth- and twentieth-century liberalism. Only Meister's and Linguet's new principle of the right to minimal economic security foreshadowed what was to come.

Security of person and property could, of course, exist only under the rule of law. This principle of Locke, of Montesquieu, and of the Patriotes was accepted without question. Liberty, the poet Thomas said, was simply "the right to obey the law and fear only the law."[22] The only alternatives to existence under the rule of law were the servitude of anarchy or servitude to the whims of arbitrary authority. This simple formula was becoming, however, more and more inadequate in the face of the objection: Yes, but what law?

The first and most important qualification was that the law had to be a law that applied equally to all, that allowed no exceptions by reason of profession, birth, or ecclesiastical privilege. D'Alembert had laid down in his *Eléments de philosophie* (1759) the principle that "the only good government is one under which citizens are equally protected and bound by the laws. . . . In this sense they are equal, not by virtue of that metaphysical equality which makes no distinctions between differences in fortune, honor, or condition, but by virtue of an equality one may call moral, which is more important to man's happiness. Metaphysical equality is an illusion which cannot be the purpose of law and which would be more harmful than advantageous. . . . But establish moral inequality and you will see one part of the members of the state oppress the others, despotism will take over, and society will be destroyed." He was still of the same mind in 1770 when he wrote Frederick, "True equality between citizens consists in their being equally subject to the law and equally subject to its penalties when they break it."[23] Rousseau did not subscribe to D'Alembert's distinctions between kinds of equality, but an essential principle of the *Contrat social* was that all laws must apply to all equally. On this D'Holbach, despite his differences with Rousseau, fully concurred. So did Diderot, who said that laws must be "so general that they except no one. The generality of the law is one of the great principles of

22. Antoine Léonard Thomas, *Eloge de Marc-Aurèle* (Amsterdam, 1775), 39.
23. D'Alembert, "Eléments de philosophie," in D'Alembert, *Oeuvres*, I, 218; Jean Le Rond d'Alembert to Frederick II of Prussia, June 8, 1770, *ibid.*, V, 294.

the equality of subjects." Catherine had written in her *Instructions*, "The equality of citizens consists in all being subject to the same laws," and Diderot commented, "The word *equally* must be added." [24]

The second qualification, which Montesquieu had anticipated, was that the applications and penalties of the law had to be reasonable, appropriate, just, and humane. Miscarriages of justice, badly written laws, and inappropriate or excessive punishments such as torture, however legal in a strict sense, were nonetheless violations of personal liberty. Beccaria and Voltaire were the leading advocates of such reforms, but they were seconded by D'Holbach, Diderot, Mably, Mercier, Lanjuinais, Turgot, Condorcet, D'Alembert, and others.

The utilitarian theory that the nature of the government determined the nature of society meant that the solution of the political problem was of paramount importance. The objective was easy to define: a constitution which would ensure liberty by the equal application of equal, just, and humane laws. Since, it was held, the principle of law itself precluded an absolutistic solution, for a law could not be the arbitrary will of one man, and since the principle of equal laws equally applied precluded an aristocratic solution, the only answer could be some sort of non-aristocratic "republic" (in the eighteenth-century sense). Moreover the majority view was rapidly swinging to the opinion that Rousseau, in contradiction to Montesquieu, had been right in asserting that negative liberty is assured only to those who possess the effective power of positive liberty—that if the French people were to be truly free they had to be truly sovereign.

The concept of the sovereignty of the people or of the nation was, as we have seen, an idea whose sources can be found in classical philosophy; it was fundamental to the Patriote thesis; it could be reconciled with monarchical absolutism; or it could become, as it did in Rousseau's *Contrat social*, the rationale of what we should today call direct democracy. What is significant, therefore, is not the idea itself but the applications these independent thinkers were now giving it—the extent to which they proposed to translate the abstract principle into positive liberty, that is, effective political power, for persons who hitherto had been politically powerless.

24. [D'Holbach], *La Politique naturelle*, Discours I–III; [D'Holbach], *Système de la nature*, Chaps. 9 and 12; [D'Holbach], *Système social*, II, Chap. 1; Diderot, *Mémoires pour Catherine II*, 63; Diderot, "Observations sur le Nakaz," in Diderot, *Oeuvres politiques*, 366. Cf. *ibid.*, 378, 403, 407, 430, 447; Diderot, *Mémoires pour Catherine II*, 5, 64, 152–53.

Diderot as early as 1751 in his *Encyclopédie* article "Autorité politique" had followed Locke in asserting that men possess not only the natural right to negative liberty but also the natural right of positive liberty, that is of "authority" (or "executive power" as Locke called it) over themselves— and *only* over themselves. Therefore "no man has received from nature the right to command others," save a father until his children have reached the age of reason. The only possible legitimate authority of a government was that exercised by the free consent of a people who had delegated their natural separate authorities by a conditional contract, restricted to the needs of the public welfare and limited by natural law and the fundamental laws of the state.[25] Diderot held to this theory all his life, and as he grew older he reiterated it in increasingly radical terms. "There is no true sovereign except the nation," he wrote in the *Observations sur le Nakaz.* "There can be no legislator except the people. . . . The consent of the nation, represented by deputies or assembled as a body, is the source of all political and civil power."[26] This Lockean, natural-law theory was echoed by Raynal (in passages probably supplied by Diderot himself), by the Abbé Morellet, and by Condorcet. D'Alembert, who subscribed to the theory of the double contract, emphasized that any transfer of sovereignty to a governmental authority must be contractual and by consent of the people.[27]

Mercier, however, like Rousseau, vehemently denied that there could

25. Diderot, "Autorité politique," in Diderot, *Oeuvres politiques*, 9 ff. Cf. Diderot, "Fragments échappés du portefeuille d'un philosophe," in Diderot, *Oeuvres complètes*, II, 450; "No man can be the property of a sovereign, no child the property of a father, no wife the property of a husband, no servant the property of a master, and no Negro the property of a colonial."

26. Diderot, "Observations sur le Nakaz," in Diderot, *Oeuvres politiques*, 343, 357. Cf. Diderot, "Réfutation de . . . L'Homme," in Diderot, *Oeuvres complètes*, II, 381.

27. The parallel passages published by Raynal first appeared in the new Book XIX added in the revised 1774 edition and were elaborated in the 1780 revision; Raynal, *Histoire des deux Indes* (The Hague, 1774), VII, 216, 230–31, 252–54 (Book XIX, Chap. 35); Raynal, *Histoire des deux Indes* (Geneva: Pellet, 1781), X, 25–26, 45, 86–90 (Book XIX, Chap. 2). See Anatole Feugère, *Un Précurseur de la Révolution, l'abbé Raynal (1713– 1796): documents inédits* (Angoulême, 1922), 234–35, 258. [Morellet], *Réflexions sur les avantages de la liberté d'écrire*, 2: "When men united in societies they surely could not have renounced any portion of their liberty except that part which would be contrary to the welfare of the very societies they were forming." [Condorcet], *Lettre d'un théologien*, 82: "Princes have received their authority from the people and must use it for the advantage of the people." D'Alembert, "Eléments de philosophie," in D'Alembert, *Oeuvres*, I, 225; D'Alembert, "Mémoires pour Christine," *ibid.*, II, 134.

be any transfer at all of the people's sovereignty under any conditions whatsoever. "Is there anything more ridiculous," he demanded, "than the idea that intelligent beings should say to one or to several persons, 'Exercise our wills for us'? People have always said to monarchs, 'Act for us, according to our clearly expressed will.'" Similarly Mably subscribed to Rousseau's theory that the citizen was simultaneously subject and part of the legislating sovereign, writing: "If I consent to obey the laws, if I recognize a sovereign of which I am part, as are all the other citizens, am I not the equal of all those who enjoy no more than the same rights that I enjoy?" Under such a compact, all citizens were equally and collectively sovereign, and the "government," the executor of the law, did not exercise even delegated sovereign authority but was merely the agent and servant of the sovereign. It is interesting that Turgot, who publicly kept reassuring Louis XVI of his personal sovereignty, nevertheless privately wrote Hume that Rousseau's *Contrat social* "is essentially a precise distinction between the sovereign and the government, but that distinction is a brilliant truth, and it seems to me to make imperishable the idea of the inalienable sovereignty of the people, whatever may be the form of government."[28]

Similar conclusions could be reached from utilitarian premises. D'Holbach, who rejected the theory of the state of nature, could not accept Rousseau's hypothesis of a primitive contract to explain the origin of the authority of the political collectivity. He merely substituted, however, the concept of "a tacit pact, which though not written or explicitly stated is nonetheless real," between each individual and the community into which he is born. By this pact or agreement "society" guaranteed to its members justice and the protection of their liberty and property, and the citizens in return promised to be just, observe the law, and defend and serve society, subordinating their wills to its will. Thus society had a "general will," and this "will of society" was the only legitimate source of law. Government was merely "the totality of the power of society placed in the hands of those whom [society] judges best fitted to bring about its happiness," and "a nation has . . . the right to revoke, annul, extend,

28. [Mercier], *L'An 2440*, 307, Cf. [Mercier], *Jean Hennuyer*, 88–89; Mably, *De la Législation*, I, 70; Anne Robert Jacques Turgot to David Hume, March 27, 1767, in Turgot, *Oeuvres*, ed. Schelle, II, 660.

restrict, explicate, or alter all the powers it has granted."[29] Another who subscribed to this utilitarian version of the social contract was Helvétius. Likewise the younger Mirabeau had the temerity to tell Louis XVI he was nothing more than the people's "premier salarié."[30]

Such words may sound like pure democracy to the modern reader, but they must be read in the eighteenth-century context. In the first place, everyone assumed that the nation would still need a hereditary king, even though he might be only the "number-one employee." In spite of Diderot's gloomy calculations of the minimal chance of the accident of birth producing a properly qualified monarch, Poland's disastrous experience with elective monarchy seemed to preclude the alternative of an elected executive.[31]

Second, while there was general acceptance of the principle that equality before the law—D'Alembert's "moral equality"—was the necessary condition of negative liberty, there was also, as we have noted, an equally general agreement on the necessity and justice of "metaphysical inequality" of wealth and social status. Such "inégalité de conditions" inevitably connoted to even the most "liberal" eighteenth-century mind inequality of political status and power. The philosophers, despite the compassion some felt for the destitute, had an inveterate distrust of the political capacities of the laboring class. D'Holbach was careful to explain that by "people" he did not mean "the imbecilic populace, unenlightened and devoid of common sense, who can at any moment be turned into the instrument or accomplice of demagogues." In democracies, he said, "the least reasonable and the least enlightened part of the nation dictates to those to whom experience and enlightenment should give the right to rule. . . . Whenever the populace are in possession of power, the state carries within itself the principle of its own destruction. Liberty degenerates into license and is followed by anarchy."[32] Raynal too agreed that democracy "tends to anarchy," and Chastellux called "the despotism of the popu-

29. [D'Holbach], *Système social*, II, 4–5; [D'Holbach], *La Politique naturelle*, I, 163; [D'Holbach], *Système social*, II, 6, 57.

30. Helvétius, *De l'Homme*, II, 314, 384; [Mirabeau], *Essai sur le despotisme*, 67.

31. Diderot, "Observations sur le Nakaz," in Diderot, *Oeuvres politiques*, 353; Diderot, *Mémoires pour Catherine II*, 118.

32. [D'Holbach], *Système social*, II, 52. Cf. [D'Holbach], *La Politique naturelle*, I, 66; [D'Holbach], *La Politique naturelle*, II, 238–40.

lace" in ancient Rome "the most disastrous tyranny of all."[33]

Diderot was probably, after Rousseau and Mably, the philosopher most sympathetic to democracy in the sense of universal franchise. He believed that the "social order" should "result from a general concord of wills," and that "the concourse and opposition of the general will with private wills" was "the special advantage of democracy over all other forms of government." He even wrote, "Liberty is in democracies. The spirit of liberty may be in a monarchy, but its sources are very different." Nevertheless he reluctantly accepted Montesquieu's dictum that democracy was possible only in small states; in his *Réfutation de l'Homme* he wrote, "Since a democratic government supposes a concert of wills, and since a concert of wills supposes men assembled in a rather restricted space, I believe that only small republics can exist and that the stability of this kind of society, the only one that can bring happiness to men, will always be precarious."[34]

There was a second and equally compelling argument for a limited franchise. Whether one held with the Physiocrats that the only citizens whose interests were truly identified with the nation were landowners, or whether one took the utilitarian position that a citizen's political status should be relative to his contribution to society, in either case it followed that there would be many inhabitants who had no title to an effective share in the sovereignty. The disenfranchised would be mainly the ignorant and unpropertied masses but might also include unproductive rich such as bankers. Turgot's *municipalités* plan extended the franchise only to owners of real property (agricultural or urban) on the grounds that such property, "inextricably binding the owner to the state, constitutes the true right of citizenship." Day laborers (*journaliers*) were itinerant by profession, belonged to no village or region, had no "necessary" motives for patriotism, and usually tried to evade taxes and the constraints of authority. On the other hand, it seemed to Turgot reasonable to grant to large landowners multiple votes, for this arrangement "by giving the plurality to the best

33. Raynal, *Histoire des deux Indes* (The Hague, 1774), VII, 231; Chastellux, *De la Félicité*, I, 114.

34. Diderot, *Mémoires pour Catherine II*, 10, 121; Diderot, "Observations sur le Nakaz," in Diderot, *Oeuvres politiques*, 357; Diderot, "Réfutation de . . . L'Homme," in Diderot, *Oeuvres complètes*, II, 390. Cf. Diderot, "Fragments échappés du portefeuille d'un philosophe," *ibid.*, VI, 447.

educated would make the deliberations of the assemblies more rational than they would be if the uneducated formed the majority."[35]

Though we lack adequate documentation on Condorcet's views on this question during the early 1770s, there is little doubt that they were similar. As late as 1786 he wrote, "The right to contribute equally to the creation of the laws is no doubt an essential right, inalienable and imprescriptible, *which belongs to all owners of property*. But in the present state of society the exercise of this right would be almost illusory for the majority." The other basic rights—security of person and property and equality before the law—were, he said, much more important to the general happiness, and as long as laws were in accord with reason and natural law it mattered little whether or not they were enacted by a majority. In fact history showed that democracies such as Athens had often abridged their own liberty by popular votes for unjust laws. In short, to attempt to create a popular representative legislature in France would be an act of "hypocritical cruelty."[36]

D'Holbach took the same position as the Physiocrats: "Every man who can subsist honorably on the profits from his property, every father of a family who owns land in some section of the country, must be considered a citizen. The artisan, the merchant, and the mercenary soldier, though they should be protected by the state they usefully serve, nevertheless are not true members of a nation until by their labor and enterprise they have acquired real property. It is land that makes the citizen." Raynal agreed that only landowners should have the right to serve as "representatives of the nation."[37] And the Abbé Morellet, a self-proclaimed republican and devotee of liberty, was careful to assure his friend Lord Shelburne that in

35. Turgot, "Mémoire sur les municipalités," in Turgot, *Oeuvres*, ed. Schelle, IV, 583–85, 588.

36. Marie Jean Antoine de Caritat, Marquis de Condorcet, *Vie de Turgot* (London, 1786), 154–64, 250, 289–92. Italics added. Cf. Condorcet, "L'Influence de la révolution de l'Amérique sur les opinions et la législation de l'Europe," in Filippo Mazzei, *Recherches historiques et politiques sur les Etats-Unis de l'Amérique septentrionale* (Colle [Paris], 1788), IV, 241–42, which repeats the same ideas. This latter work was first published separately with the imprint "Amsterdam, 1786." For an excellent analysis of the subsequent development of Condorcet's ideas on the franchise and "societal choice," see Baker, *Condorcet*, 56–57, 193–94, 253–54, 321, and *passim*.

37. [D'Holbach], *Système social*, II, 52; Raynal, *Histoire des deux Indes* (The Hague, 1774), VII, 376.

espousing the American slogan "No taxation without representation" he meant of course representation of tax-paying property owners—"as though one could mean by a nation anything other than the landholding heads of families."[38] Even Diderot observed with approval that in Holland "a voter is always a large property owner. This seems to me just, for personal interest is always the measure of patriotism. There is no fatherland for a man who possesses nothing, or who can carry away everything he owns." Consequently he advised Catherine that the deputies to the Russian legislature that he proposed should all be "grands propriétaires."[39]

From all these assumptions it followed that for most of the independent thinkers of the early 1770s the best French constitution seemed to be a limited monarchy with a legislature elected by limited franchise. The only open questions were how much to limit the powers of the king and how far to extend the powers of the legislature. During the years we are examining, reasonably precise models were suggested by D'Holbach, Diderot, Turgot, and Rouillé d'Orfeuil; Mably and Mercier indicated the principal features of their proposals; and other writers gave definite but undetailed support of the general concept. The tendency of the various proposals during this brief period was to gravitate progressively toward greater limitations on the crown and greater powers for the legislature.

These independents, far more than the Patriotes and the royalists, examined problems from a cosmopolitan point of view and were inclined to seek in the experiences and institutions of alien cultures and societies solutions for French problems. Consequently in their speculative political constructions they inevitably kept in mind the British constitution, which Voltaire's *Lettres philosophiques* and Montesquieu's *Esprit des lois* had established as the prime model to be studied, if not imitated, and on which Delolme had just provided up-to-date information in his *Constitution de l'Angleterre* (1771). They did not, of course, unanimously approve of all they saw across the Channel. D'Holbach believed that the British system of government fostered bribery and inordinate party spirit and gave excessive influence to commercial interests.[40] Turgot strongly disapproved

38. André Morellet to Lord Shelburne, December 13, 1774, in Morellet, *Lettres à Lord Shelburne . . . 1772–1803*, (Paris, 1898), 58–59.

39. Diderot, "Voyage de Hollande," in Diderot, *Oeuvres complètes*, XVII, 385; Diderot, "Observations sur le Nakaz," in Diderot, *Oeuvres politiques*, 369.

40. [D'Holbach], *La Politique naturelle*, I, 73; II, 234–37.

of the separation of powers and representation by classes, and there was generally little disposition to imitate the bicameral system. Diderot, however, told Catherine, "If it were proposed to Her Imperial Majesty to see suddenly the constitution of the Russian Empire transformed into the English constitution, I doubt that she would refuse," and he advised her to send her son, the Grand Duke Paul, to England for his political education. Raynal called the British constitution "a creation . . . of reason and experience" which should serve as a model for posterity. The Abbé Morellet wrote that the British "system of government and legislation is considered to be, if not free from defects, at least one of those which has best reconciled the liberty of the individual with the state of society." Sébastien Mercier wondered why the French had not yet been able to achieve a republican government like the English.[41] Mably hoped that a revolution in France like the English revolution of 1688 might permit the French to create a similar constitution. Chastellux particularly admired the House of Commons as that part of the British government "most firmly founded on reason and most supportive of the right of property."[42] Thus it may be said that these independent thinkers were, for the most part, working toward some sort of French equivalent of the British constitution, adapted to French conditions, problems, and traditions, and in conformity with their particular philosophies.

Only Turgot deliberately eschewed the Anglo-Saxon political tradition. His plan for a pyramidal structure of advisory *municipalités* whose powers would have been limited largely to the assessment and collection of taxes was, on paper, the most moderate, and indeed his proposal seemed to strengthen the crown by leaving the royal legislative, executive, and judicial powers intact, freeing the government from dependence on the tax farmers, and eliminating the parlements' power to obstruct additional taxation. It might well have proved, however, to be revolutionary, for it is difficult to believe that the various *municipalités*, holding control as they would have over the government's income, would have confined their discussions to the repair of roads.

41. Diderot, *Mémoires pour Catherine II*, 123, 71; Raynal, *Histoire des deux Indes* (The Hague, 1774), VII, 231; [Morellet], *Théorie du paradoxe*, 31; [Mercier], *L'An 2440*, 312. Cf. *ibid.*, 405.
42. Mably, *De la Législation*, II, 48–51; Chastellux, *De la Félicité*, II, 32.

D'Holbach in his *Politique naturelle* and his *Système social* (both 1773) outlined a constitution which was also relatively moderate but which would have given to a national legislature of "representatives" more power than would have been granted to Turgot's *municipalités*. These representatives were to be elected only by "true citizens," that is, landowners from any of the three estates.[43] In principle, D'Holbach said, "the power of the monarch should always be subordinate to that of the representatives of the people, and these representatives should constantly depend on the will of their constituents, from whom they derive all their rights and of whom they are the interpreters, not the masters." The nation, represented by the constituents and their representatives, would therefore have been sovereign and would have possessed the essential powers of sovereignty, notably the power to tax. Nevertheless D'Holbach left governmental initiative and broad authority in the hands of the king, and he seems to have envisaged his unicameral legislature as a "proportional mean" between the monarch and the people rather than a true governing body.[44] In his *Ethocratie*, published three years later, however, D'Holbach gave to his "Corps de Représentants" the power to make all laws, vote all taxes, authorize all governmental loans, declare war and peace, and assemble on its own initiative.[45] In his earlier works D'Holbach had wavered between the disadvantages of both elective and hereditary monarchism, but now in the *Ethocratie* he resolved the dilemma by reducing the king to the role of a hereditary symbolic figurehead and giving all effective political authority to the legislature.[46]

Diderot's ideas on limited monarchy during the years 1770–1774 are found mainly in the memoirs he wrote for his conversations with Catherine at Saint Petersburg during the winter of 1773–1774 and in his *Observations sur le Nakaz*, written in The Hague in 1774 after his return and

43. [D'Holbach], *Système social*, II, 51; [D'Holbach], *La Politique naturelle*, I, 73.

44. [D'Holbach], *La Politique naturelle*, I, 73, 183; II, 74; I, 124, 127, 136, 176–77. A similar constitution, under which the corps of representatives would have been elected by five classes of landowners (the clergy, nobles, magistrates, businessmen, and agriculturalists) had been suggested by D'Holbach's *Encyclopédie* article "Représentants." On the attribution, see Herbert Dieckman, "L'*Encyclopédie* et le Fonds Vandeul," *Revue d'histoire littéraire de la France*, LI (1951), 332.

45. [D'Holbach], *Ethocratie*, 16–19 and *passim*.

46. [D'Holbach], *La Politique naturelle*, II, 232–33; [D'Holbach], *Système social*, II, 29; [D'Holbach], *Ethocratie*, 33.

addressed but not sent to Catherine. These two writings reveal the same evolution to more radical republicanism, a shift explainable in part by Diderot's initial effort to be prudent and diplomatic in his discussions with the empress and by his subsequent disillusion with the results of his moderation.

The essential problem, Diderot saw clearly, was to minimize restrictions on liberty by making the monarch "the slave of the law." "We always keep coming back to this great difficulty, that of limiting the sovereign power."[47] Faced with the reality of firmly entrenched absolutisms all over continental Europe, he initially thought that the most reasonable hope would be to enlighten the heads of state and persuade them to bind themselves and their successors to the rule of law. He tried this unsuccessfully with Catherine, but he was encouraged by the possibility that Turgot might do better with Louis XVI. Thus he started as a proponent of enlightened monarchism, though not of enlightened despotism.[48]

In the memoirs Diderot concentrated on urging Catherine to profit from the horrendous example of the irrational and chaotic French constitution, a welter of "mad, absurd, contradictory institutions," and to construct for Russia a rational, precisely defined, and coherent constitutional edifice. As a start he proposed that she convert the advisory commission to which she had addressed her *Instructions* into a permanent legislative body responsible (subject to royal veto) for writing and preserving the laws, but without executive functions and without authority over foreign policy or even taxation. Diderot had no illusions about what this modest proposal—radical enough, however, for eighteenth-century Russia—might accomplish, but he hoped that it would obtain for the nation "the right to deliberate, to wish or to not wish, to oppose, even to oppose the good," and that this would give the Russian people at least a feeling of liberty, if not liberty itself.[49]

The *Observations* were far more extreme, for in writing them Diderot threw pragmatism and prudence out the window and resolved to set down what he really thought the constitution of a free nation should be. He

47. Diderot, "Observations sur le Nakaz," in Diderot, *Oeuvres politiques*, 353, 447. Cf. *ibid.*, 355, 368, 440.
48. Denis Diderot, "Pages contre un tyran," in Diderot, *Oeuvres politiques*, 141–42.
49. Diderot, *Mémoires pour Catherine II*, 22, 34, 59–60, 78–83, 117–18, 127.

spelled out the principles of popular sovereignty, government by consent, and the accountability of the monarch. The contract between the Russian people and Catherine was to read: "We the people, and we the sovereign of the people, jointly swear to obey these laws, by which we shall both be equally judged; and if we the sovereign should change or violate these laws and thus become an enemy of the people, then it would be just that the people be our enemy, that they be absolved from their oath of fidelity, that they prosecute us, that they depose us, and even that they condemn us to death if the case warrants."[50] Diderot was still working out his constitutional principles and did not get to specifics, but there are interesting coincidences between these principles and those soon to be followed in the writing of the American constitutions. Diderot's constitution was to be subject to amendment and was to be periodically re-ratified; there was to be clear separation of powers; a "depository" of the fundamental laws of the nation independent of the executive, a sort of supreme court, would safeguard the interests of the people; the legislature would have total legislative power; and while the executive would enjoy broad prerogatives its conduct would be reexamined every five years. As was to be true in the American constitutions, the legislature as the representatives of the people would have the final authority, by virtue not only of power of impeachment but also by power "to revise, approve, or disapprove of the will of the sovereign and transmit it to the people." Finally, there was to be complete separation of church and state, or rather complete subordination of the church to the state.[51]

Rouillé d'Orfeuil's scheme, the most elaborate and detailed but of course the least important in the history of ideas, is of interest mainly as a further example of the prevalence of the philosophic vogue of constitution writing. His completely secularized state was to be ruled by a unicameral tribunal representative of the nobility, merchants, and "notables agriculteurs" which would possess full legislative powers, major executive functions, authority over the judiciary, supervision of the nation's finances, guardianship of the constitution, and the power to grant the crown by contract or to refuse the king's heir if he were judged unworthy of the responsibility.[52]

50. Diderot, "Observations sur le Nakaz," in Diderot, *Oeuvres politiques*, 343–44.
51. *Ibid.*, 343, 344, 346–49, 355, 357, 358, 360–64, 369, 436.
52. [Augustin Rouillé d'Orfeuil], *L'Ami des François* (Constantinople, 1771), 115 ff.,

The Abbé Mably sadly acknowledged that the present moral corruption of the French people created "insurmountable obstacles" to the realization of his ideal of a communistic state governed by "modest magistrates drawn from the plow." Yet after Turgot's accession to power he came to hope that France might be capable of liberty, if not of equality.[53] He left no detailed constitutional plan, but from his earlier description of the Carolingian monarchy and from certain passages in *De la Législation* (1776) we may infer the broad lines of what he had in mind. Though he denied that the States General were the true continuation of the Carolingian national assemblies, he apparently thought they should be convoked and established as a legislature representative of the sovereignty of the people. He would have gone further than the British constitution, which he admired, in enforcing complete separation of judicial, executive, and legislative powers, for he observed that the British king should have no share in legislation, not even the power of veto, and should be subject to the law and the courts. He would also have further democratized the government by abolishing all venal, hereditary, and appointive offices and electing magistrates by popular vote.[54]

Mercier advocated for France a "republican government" more or less on the British model. Legislative power should be vested, he said, in the "assembled estates of the kingdom," the representatives of the people, who would meet every two years. He would have kept the king as a symbol of the people's power and as "an image to check the ambitious," and he would have made him and his ministers responsible for the execution of the laws and answerable to the national legislature. An exceptional aspect of Mercier's thinking was that he saw a further safeguard of liberty in a decentralized federal system which would give to the several regions of France considerable self-government and the power to enact local laws.[55]

---

142 ff.; [Rouillé d'Orfeuil], *L'Alambic des loix*, 63, 99, 135, 175, 433 ff.; Book VI.

53. Mably, *De la Législation*, I, 43; II, 43–44.

54. *Ibid.*, I, 238–45, 261–62; Mably, *Observations sur l'histoire de France*, II, 115–16; III, 302, 306. See Baker, "A Script for a French Revolution."

55. [Mercier], *L'An 2440*, 301, 304–306, 312. In 1771 Mercier was using the word *république* in the sense of "limited monarchy." It is interesting to note, however, as a sidelight on the history of political terms, that he added a passage to the 1787 edition of *L'An 2440* in which he used the word in the sense of a representative government without a monarch, citing the United States as proof that the age of republics was not passed (*L'An 2440* [N.p., 1787], I, 176–77).

Most of the other independents and Philosophes—excepting of course Voltaire—seem to have been thinking along similar lines. Helvétius called the king the "premier commis" of the people. Morellet apparently would have been satisfied with a duplication of the British constitution, for he approved highly of the balance and separation of power between the two houses of Parliament and the crown. The Count de Guibert proposed an assembly of representatives, which he compared to the British Parliament, to serve as "a permanent body whose responsibility would be to gather information, systematize the interests of the state, and take counsel from the past to plan for the future." Raynal also favored a government on the British model under which taxes would be imposed by the "representatives of the nation." The younger Mirabeau likewise believed that legislative and taxing powers should be vested in a legislature representative of the people.[56] Chastellux was especially emphatic on the advantages of representative government. "Assemblies," he wrote, "are the source of all liberty. Every nation that enjoys representation, whatever may be its laws and customs . . . will in the end acquire great power. . . . M. Rousseau has said that in any country where the citizens are so numerous that it is necessary to make the government representative there can be no true liberty. For my part, I believe that there will be no solid and enduring liberty, and certainly no public felicity, except for peoples whose governments are wholly representative."[57]

Thus, despite variations in details, there emerged what might be called a majority report on the broad outlines of a political solution. This was the rejection of both absolute monarchism and rule by aristocratic corporations, and an abrupt break with French political tradition by the creation of some sort of limited monarchy, perhaps not unlike that of Great Britain, which would guarantee certain legal and civil rights and under which the power to legislate and tax would be vested in a national assembly elected by limited franchise. Such a constitution could not, however, be readily imposed on French society as it was then constituted. Since it was to be a secular government, French society had to be secularized

56. Helvétius, *De l'Homme*, II, 384; [Morellet], *Théorie du paradoxe*, 31; [Guibert], *Essai général de tactique*, xv; Raynal, *Histoire des deux Indes* (The Hague, 1774), VII, 231, 376; [Mirabeau], *Essai sur le despotisme*, 74–75, 81–83.

57. Chastellux, *De la Félicité*, II, 33; I, 43. The reference is to Rousseau's *Du Contrat social*, Book III, Chap. 15.

and the church had to be divested of its privileged functions and rights. And since it was to be a government of and by the nation as a whole, social and political status, and consequently economic status as well, had to be reformed according to some new rationale.

TEN

The Design for a New Society

T HE INDEPENDENTS' various plans for the political reorganization of France generally made two assumptions: that the state
of the future would be secular, not theocratic; and that French
society would be restructured on rational and humane principles.

SECULARISM: TOLERATION AND ANTICLERICALISM

The intense interest in political issues and problems fomented by the
Maupeou revolution had the unexpected effect of diminishing attention
to the religious question, which had preoccupied the Philosophes and their
readers since about 1758. Insofar as the religious debate continued, it did
so mainly in politicized form. The discussions centered on the relationship of the French Catholic Church to monarchical absolutism and to fiscal reform, rather than on the metaphysical or theological truth of religious beliefs or on the need to liberate men's minds from "superstition."
It was this ideological shift that Delolme was describing when he wrote
in 1771, "The philosophic spirit, which particularly distinguishes this
century, after having cured society of many fatal errors, now seems to be
turning its attention to the basic principles of society itself."[1]

The decline of interest in religion as religion was also due to the fact
that the tide of opinion among those who mattered had already turned

1. Jean Louis Delolme, *Constitution de l'Angleterre* . . . (Amsterdam, 1771), 1.

against the Catholic Church. In prolonging his mockeries of biblical absurdities and papal atrocities Voltaire seemed to be beating a dead horse. It would be difficult to document this conclusion with statistics, but it is the inescapable impression one receives, especially from reading the documents issued by the church itself. For instance the Assemblée Générale du Clergé of 1775 remonstrated thus against the government's inability to stem the flow of irreligious publications: "They are advertised in catalogs; they are publicly offered for sale; they are taken into private homes; the great display them in the vestibules of their mansions and perhaps, Sire, even within the walls of that august palace where Your Majesty receives our homage." The infection of unbelief was spreading in all directions. "History, philosophy, poetry, the sciences, the theater, even the arts, all have become enmeshed in its deadly plots. . . . Already its ravages have penetrated our provinces; it invades our cities and the countryside, the study of the man of letters and the everyday conversations of society; it affects those of high degree and those of humble condition, those of all ages, of all professions, and of all social classes."[2]

The inroads of agnosticism into the machinery of government were revealed by the de facto toleration of Protestantism in spite of Maupeou's policy of continued repression. Plans for an edict of toleration had in fact been under active consideration in the government as early as 1767.[3] The timid, inept, and confused efforts of the Duke de La Vrillière, secretary of state in charge of the Département des Affaires Générales de la Religion Prétendue Réformée, could not prevent municipal officials and intendants such as Turgot and the Prince de Beauvau from practicing willful leniency to the Huguenots or stop powerful figures like the Duke de Richelieu from intervening on their behalf. In Toulouse, the scene of the Calas trial, the parlement upheld in the famous case of Marie Roubel the legality of Protestant marriages, and in the same city the Académie des Jeux Floraux in 1770, 1771, and 1772 held competitions for the best eulogies of Protestant heroes.[4] The Assemblée du Clergé of 1772 charged

2. *Procès-Verbal de l'Assemblée-Générale extraordinaire du Clergé de France, tenue à Paris, au Couvent des Grands-Augustins . . .* (Paris, 1775), 260–61.

3. Joseph Dedieu, *Histoire politique des Protestants français, 1715–1794* (Paris, 1925), II, 60 ff.

4. *Ibid.*, II, 96–116, 118–19, 131–34, 139–51; Burdette C. Poland, *French Protestantism and the French Revolution: A Study in Church and State, Thought and Religion, 1685–1815* (Princeton, 1957), 62, 70–71.

that this official connivance at toleration was permitting "the Protestants to assemble in a number of dioceses with greater liberty than ever." In 1775 it complained that they were celebrating their sacraments "almost under the walls of our churches."[5] These accusations were not exaggerated, for in 1773 the pastor Desmont reported from western France that the area "enjoys a liberty unknown to French Protestants since the Revocation [of the Edict of Nantes]. Saintonge and Angoumois have temples in every town and city of any importance, [where] . . . our faithful freely . . . assemble regularly twice every Sunday."[6]

Moreover the pressure to erode the church's fiscal immunities, which had long existed, was increased by the state's financial difficulties and was meeting less resistance. The Assemblée of 1772 was summoned to approve a special *don gratuit* to the royal treasury of ten million livres, and that of 1775 was asked for sixteen million. In addition, the clergy complained that they were being subjected to hidden taxation, which "disguised and multiplied under a thousand different forms, was gradually eating up the church's revenues," and they requested formal exemption from a long list of levies and forced contributions which they said they were being obliged to pay.[7]

This creeping secularism had certainly been accelerated, though not solely caused, by the controversies within the French church instigated by the Jansenists and supported by the parlements. Archbishop Vintimille's attempts to discredit the Jansenistic miracles of Saint Médard had suggested skepticism about all miracles and indeed about all the supernatural in Catholic doctrine. The suppression of the Jesuits could be understood to imply a general condemnation of all monasticism. Both Gallicanism in attempting to limit the authority of the papacy and Jansenistic Richerism in attempting to limit the authority of the episcopacy had diminished respect for the ecclesiastical and spiritual authority of the church as a whole. In addition, the Jansenistic-parliamentary efforts to increase the authority

5. *Procès-Verbal de l'Assemblée Générale du Clergé* (Paris, 1772), 169; *Procès-Verbal de l'Assemblée-Générale extraordinaire du Clergé* (1775), 268.

6. Edmond Hugues, *Les Synodes du désert: Actes et règlements des synodes nationaux et provinciaux tenus au désert de France, de l'an 1715 à l'an 1793* (Paris, 1886), III, 77 note. See also Dedieu, *Histoire politique des Protestants*, II, 117 ff.

7. *Procès-Verbal de l'Assemblée Générale du Clergé* (1772), 202–205; *Procès-Verbal de l'Assemblée-Générale extraordinaire du Clergé* (1775), 1025–31.

of the civil government over the church, even in doctrinal matters over which the parlements clearly had no jurisdiction, pointed toward some sort of civil constitution of the clergy and subordination of the church to the state, a reform which the Philosophes were already demanding and which indeed some Jansenists were to support in 1790.

On the other hand, the throne was not without some responsibility for the decline of ecclesiastical prestige. Louis XV did, however unwillingly, acquiesce to the destruction of the Jesuits in France, and Maupeou's concept of the French monarchy was, as we have indicated, essentially statist and secular rather than theocratic, a fact which, incidentally, helps to explain the ministry's failure to respond to the clergy's demands for effectual action against unbelief and de facto toleration.

In spite of the effective progress toward toleration, some independents, as we have seen, especially those of the natural-law stamp, continued to press for explicit official guaranties of religious freedom. Turgot soon after his appointment as minister presented to the young king a memoir urging that "every one of his subjects be allowed the liberty of following and professing the religion his conscience persuades him is true." By the principles of natural justice, Turgot argued, every individual has a sacred obligation to follow the dictates of his own conscience, which is his only authoritative guide to his search for truth. His friend, Du Pont de Nemours, of course, seconded his efforts, as did the Abbé Morellet, who championed toleration for the Huguenots and asserted that religious freedom was an inseparable aspect of the general natural right of liberty.[8] Similarly Chastellux stood in support of "toleration and freedom of conscience." The Abbé Maury's and Laharpe's eulogies of Fénelon stressed that prelate's opposition to Louis XIV's policy of conversion by terror. D'Alembert had called religious persecution "unjust both in principle and in effect."[9] D'Holbach, though a militant atheist and a utilitarian, sur-

8. Anne Robert Jacques Turgot, "Mémoire sur la tolérance," in Turgot, *Oeuvres*, ed. Daire, II, 492–93; André Morellet to Lord Shelburne, November 26, 1774, in Morellet, *Lettres à Lord Shelburne*, 71; Morellet, *Mémoires*, I, 31–32.

9. Chastellux, *De la Félicité*, I, 222; Jean Siffrein Maury, *Eloge de François de Salignac de La Motte-Fénelon, Discours qui a obtenu l'accessit* (Paris, 1771), 8, 9, 18; Jean François de Laharpe, *Eloge de François de Salignac de La Motte-Fénelon, Discours qui a remporté le prix de l'Académie Françoise en 1771* (Paris, 1771), 8–9, 32; D'Alembert, "Eléments de philosophie," in D'Alembert, *Oeuvres*, I, 222.

prisingly made what was in effect the natural-law argument couched in utilitarian language. He recognized that because of differences in education and customs "men do not and cannot have identical ideas about the divine essence that all worship in equal ignorance." Therefore, he said, freedom of religion was an essential ingredient of human liberty and of the right to the pursuit of happiness. "The heart of man is an inviolable sanctuary. . . . The sovereign can never reasonably claim the barbaric right to intrude upon men's consciences."[10]

One of the most effective pieces of writing in support of religious freedom to appear during these years was Mercier's play *Jean Hennuyer*, which of course could not be publicly produced in France. Printed copies, however, reached Paris in 1772, the anniversary of the Saint Bartholomew's Day massacre. Grimm was moved to uncharacteristic enthusiasm by the work's attack on "the hydra of fanaticism" and by its simplicity and warmth, even if it was "not a work of genius."[11] Mercier, "more a Protestant than a Philosophe," as Grimm said, proclaimed through his characters the right of freedom of conscience ("What shall be left a man if he is deprived of even his freedom to think! . . . Can a man act against his conscience?") and at the same time denounced the instruments of Catholic fanaticism as a "mad herd of murderers . . . infernal monsters suckled on the poisons of Italy."[12]

Yet this sort of high moral indignation over the denial of natural rights to the Huguenots was not the dominant note. A sizeable portion of the independents, perhaps the majority, were more interested in the destruction of theocratic absolutism, and consequently—secretly or openly—they regarded religious toleration primarily as a political tactic. Diderot, who held that any religion was a vicious deception, had no great interest in helping the Protestants to practice theirs. "Toleration," he said, "is a virtue of character rather than a matter of reason." It seemed to him perfectly reasonable for Saint Louis to say " 'Take your sword and slit open the belly of any man you hear speak ill of God' (that is, the God of Saint Louis and of Joinville). For when you realize that Saint Louis based all morality, all

10. [D'Holbach], *La Politique naturelle*, II, 77–78. Cf. [D'Holbach], *Système social*, II, 54.
11. *Correspondance littéraire*, September 1, 1772 (X, 53–55).
12. [Mercier], *Jean Hennuyer*, 30, 53. Cf. [Mercier], *L'An 2440*, 98 ff., 143.

public and private security, all bonds between men, and all virtue, on the notion of divinity, then there appears nothing atrocious in his command." Similarly, "a priest is intolerant because he is a priest; he would wreck his own creed if he admitted that a man could please God just as well by following another religion."[13] Religious intolerance was not bad because it was intolerant but because it was religious, and it should be combatted for that reason. Any notion of divinity, even one conceived by an atheist, inevitably became in a man's head an overriding idea. It dehumanized. It led to sectarianism, controversies, fanaticism, disregard of law, subversion of good government, discrimination against merit, calumny, hatred, prejudice, ignorance; it perverted great minds, as it had Pascal's. In all societies there was a constant contradiction between religious law and the "code de la nature."[14] "Show me," he challenged, "in the history of all the different peoples of the world an innocent act that religion has not made into a crime, or a crime that it has not made into an innocent act." Diderot's objective was to secularize the state by stripping the church of political and social power and by making priests salaried employees of the government on a status "just above or just below that of actors."[15] By thus reducing them "to a state of bare competence, or rather indigence (which will make them as contemptible as they are useless)" he hoped to root out religion from men's minds. Diderot's respect for property and contractual obligations prevented him, however, from seriously proposing confiscation of church lands or unilateral abolition of legal rights; he suggested rather a policy of gradual impoverishment of the church by the denial of pensions, exactions of large *dons gratuits*, and the abolition of benefices as they became vacant.[16]

The Abbé Galiani was even more frankly cynical about toleration. He called Voltaire's *Sermon de N. Charitoski* "a lot of drivel": "His Catherine is a masterful woman because she is intolerant and conquers her enemies. All great men have been intolerant, for they have had to be. If a prince is

---

13. Diderot, *Mémoires pour Catherine II*, 108, 107, 185.

14. *Ibid.*, 99, 101, 110–11, 185; Denis Diderot, "Supplément au Voyage de Bougainville," in Diderot, *Oeuvres philosophiques*, 461, etc.

15. Diderot, *Mémoires pour Catherine II*, 106–107; Diderot, "Observations sur le Nakaz," in Diderot, *Oeuvres politiques*, 348.

16. Denis Diderot, "Discours d'un philosophe," in Diderot, *Oeuvres complètes*, IV, 33–34.

stupid, preach toleration to him and he will fall in the trap; toleration will give the outs time to recover and crush the ins. This sermon on toleration is a sermon for fools and dupes, or for the uninvolved. Sometimes a secular ruler should listen to talk about toleration, but only when it is a toleration of priests which does not affect kings." [17]

Even those who talked loftily of natural rights and freedom of conscience were aware that toleration was the trap for kings that Galiani said it was—that it was a tactic to abolish theocracy, secularize the state, and deprive monarchical absolutism in France of its one sturdy prop. D'Holbach was notably loud in his denunciations of "théocratie," the alleged age-old conspiracy between priests and the crown to use the weapons of ignorance, fear, and superstition to deprive "the inhabitants of this world of liberty and happiness." In his *Ethocratie* he proposed total expropriation of all church properties and the support of the clergy by salaries "proportionate to the real services they render the country." [18] Similarly Helvétius asserted that "the spiritual power is always the open or secret enemy of the temporal," and he urged religious toleration as a weapon against clerical influence. "Tolerance subjugates the priest to the prince; intolerance subjugates the prince to the priest." Condorcet likewise said that "the enemies of kings are not the philosophers; they are the priests." He suggested that Turgot present to the king "a clear, moderate, well-documented study recounting all the assassinations, massacres, rebellions, wars, tortures, poisonings, filth, and scandal that for 1774 years have formed the history of the Catholic clergy." [19] Raynal, who after all was an abbé and a former Jesuit, could grant that a purified form of Christianity might contribute to the progress and liberty of mankind, but in the successive revisions of his *Histoire des deux Indes* he stated in increasingly stronger terms his thesis that the church had a long record of support of absolutism and that the achievement of liberty required the supremacy of secular author-

17. Ferdinando Galiani to Louise F. P. Tardieu d'Esclavelles, Marquise d'Epinay, June 22, 1771, in Galiani, *Sa Correspondance* (Paris, 1881), I, 407–408.

18. [D'Holbach], *Système social*, III, 16–17; [D'Holbach], *La Politique naturelle*, I, 105; II, 12; [D'Holbach], *Ethocratie*, 111–12. Cf. [D'Holbach], *La Politique naturelle*, I, 226–28.

19. Helvétius, *De l'Homme*, II, 375, 376; [Condorcet], *Lettre d'un théologien*, 83; Marie Jean Antoine de Caritat, Marquis de Condorcet to Anne Robert Jacques Turgot, October or November, 1774, in Condorcet, *Correspondance inédite de Condorcet et de Turgot*, 206.

ity over the spiritual, the abolition of all state religions except for a code of civic ethics, the denial of any civil or fiscal privileges to the church, and the transfer to civil authorities of responsibility for social services such as care of the aged, sick, and destitute.[20]

Mably, another abbé and one who condemned "those philosophers so common today who deny the existence of a Supreme Being and of Providence and who believe that everything is material," nevertheless denounced in equally strong terms the French clergy for having "for a long time separated their own interests from the interests of the nation" and for having made themselves, in their greed for rich benefices, servile supporters of arbitrary absolutism, "because if [was] easier to circumvent and manipulate a prince than to deceive a free people enlightened by liberty." He proposed that a purified form of Catholicism be retained as the state religion but that the church be subordinated to the secular government, which would pay the priests' salaries, and that full toleration be extended to all the other sects.[21]

Behind all this talk of theocracy were the hard economic issues—which were growing crucial in the current financial crisis—of the exemption of the clergy and church property from taxation and of the burden of the *dîme* (tithe) on taxpayers. Richard Des Glanières published in 1774, with Turgot's permission but not his endorsement, a *Plan d'imposition économique et d'administration des finances* for the abolition of the *dîme* and the taxation of the clergy in proportion to their incomes.[22] A significant earlier proposal had been *Du Droit du souverain sur les biens fonds du clergé* (1770), attributed to the Chevalier de Cerfvol. The author drew a revealing contrast between the demeaning poverty of the lower clergy and the opulence of "idle monks and scandalous abbés," and he charged that the church by arrogating civil authority had denied Christ's word "that His realm is not of this world" and had "separated the interests of the clergy from those of other believers." Convinced that the state's financial crisis could never be solved merely

20. Raynal, *Histoire des deux Indes* (The Hague, 1774), Book IX, Vol. VII, 263, 205, 255. See Feugère, *Un Précurseur de la Révolution*, 234 ff.

21. Mably, *De la Législation*, Book IV, Chaps. 2–4; Mably, *Observations sur l'histoire de France*, III, 308.

22. [Richard Des Glanières], *Plan d'imposition économique et d'administration des finances, présenté à Monseigneur Turgot, ministre et contrôleur général des finances* (Paris, 1774). On Turgot's position on this work, see *Nouvelles éphémérides économiques*, 1774, pp. 75–76.

by increased taxes, further loans, or greater economy, he saw as the only recourse the confiscation and sale of all church property to provide funds to liquidate the towering national debt. Monasteries and nunneries, he suggested, could be administered by the state and the clergy could be supported on a reduced scale by the proceeds from the *dîme*.[23]

These suggestions, which so closely anticipated the actions of the Assemblée Nationale, were of course not the only ones. Rouillé d'Orfeuil likewise advocated exclusion of the clergy from all civil authority, the confiscation of church property, the abolition of monastic orders, and the salaried support of the clergy by the *dîme*. Chastellux opposed clerical privileges, the intervention of ecclesiastical authority in civil affairs, and monasticism.[24] And we must of course remember that Turgot's *Mémoire sur les municipalités* would have subjected ecclesiastical properties to the general rates of taxation, and that Voltaire was the most ardent advocate of all of the secularization of the state. In fact, though the ministry could not overtly offend the political support it received from the Dévots, Maupeou's and Lebrun's statism was essentially secularistic.

The ruling clergy had no illusions about the political and economic implications of the Philosophes' drive for "toleration," or about the threat of secularism, whether statist or libertarian. Without using the word *theocracy* they fully recognized the necessity of maintaining the conjunction of the interests of church and throne. The only plausible justification of royal authority was the doctrine of divine right, and on the level of practical politics the king, surrounded as he was by disaffected Patriotes and Philosophes and a sullen populace, had no firm allies but the clergy and

23. [Chevalier de Cerfvol (?)], *Du Droit du souverain sur les biens fonds du clergé et des moines, et de l'usage qu'il peut faire de ces biens pour le bonheur des citoyens* (Naples, n.d. [Rouen, July 1770]), 155–56, 39, 45, 121 ff. Barbier attributes this work to Cerfvol, but the *Mémoires secrets* (V, 172–73) ascribe it to the Marquis de Puységur. Hardy ("*Mes Loisirs,*" 212) says the ministry was inclined to look favorably on the publication but suppressed it under pressure from the Assemblée du Clergé meeting during the summer of 1770. Van Kley sees a relationship between the author and "indisputably Jansenist pamphleteers such as Le Paige" and considers the work as a delayed extension of the controversy occasioned by the Paris Parlement's declaration nullifying the *Actes* published by the General Assembly of the Clergy of France in 1765. See Van Kley, "Church, State, and the Ideological Origins of the French Revolution," 649–52.

24. [Rouillé d'Orfeuil], *L'Ami des François*, 188 ff., 389 ff., 409, 425; [Rouillé d'Orfeuil], *L'Alambic des loix*, 92–93, 305 ff., 436; [Rouillé d'Orfeuil], *L'Alambic moral*, 126 ff., 352 ff.; Chastellux, *De la Félicité*, I, 193 ff., 199 ff.; II, 35–36, 89, 203.

the Dévots. On the other hand, the church could expect no support against the insidious progress of unbelief and the increasing challenges to its economic and civil privileges except from the crown. The churchmen repeatedly warned the king that every attack on the authority of Catholicism was an attack on the authority of monarchical absolutism. Religious skepticism and political skepticism were twin manifestations of the same evil. The "prétendus philosophes" were worse than atheists; they were seditious. The clergy's *Remontrances* of 1775 explicitly spelled out the threat:

> There is another fatal danger in unbelief, namely the spirit of independence that it inspires. God grant that we should not wish to render suspect the attachment of the nation for its kings; this will be the last virtue to die in the hearts of Frenchmen. But what is the cause of this general ferment which works to dissolve the bonds of society? Whence comes this restless and curious examination, in which all indulge, of the operations of the government and of its rights and limits? Whence come these principles, so destructive of all authority, which are sown by a multitude of writings and which all classes delight in reading and repeating? All these disorders, Sire, are connected and follow inevitably one from another. The foundations of morals and of authority must crumble if the foundations of religion are undermined. Religion alone maintains the thrones of kings in the most secure and most inaccessible of all places, in the conscience [of the subject], where God has his throne. This is the one firm basis of public tranquillity.[25]

The Philosophes and other independent thinkers have generally been discounted by modern historians as an effective cause of the French Revolution. Their writings may, however, have been an important indirect cause of the sort the clergy predicted. By 1789 the church, long a solid buttress of the French throne, had been so weakened by the attacks of unbelief epitomized by Voltaire's slogan *écrasez l'infâme*, as well as by the Jansenists' campaigns against the Jesuits and ecclesiastical authority, that it offered scant support against the wave of revolution.

POVERTY AND STATUS

The independents' vision of the social structure of the new France was far

25. *Procès-Verbal de l'Assemblée-Générale extraordinaire du Clergé* (1775), 263.

less clear and considerably more conservative than their secularism. For the modern liberal it is difficult to understand men like the Physiocrats who could couple opposition to slavery, feudal and seignorial rights, and colonialism with a happy acceptance of minimum subsistence wages. The apparent anomalies in the social thought of the independent thinkers were no less striking. It is important to remember that none of the men we are studying here were capable of conceiving of a classless society, and only the utopian Mably dreamed of economic equality. Moreover, while there was general advocacy of legal equality and equality of rights, political democracy in the modern sense was a still unborn idea. Only two issues were under active debate: What and how much should be done to alleviate poverty? How could the social structure be made more rational and just?

Attitudes to the problems of poverty and the laboring class varied greatly. At one extreme was Jacques Necker, who thought that the vast distance between the luxury of the rich and the bare subsistence of the poor was not only inevitable but in fact necessary in the best possible social system. The suggestion that the wealthy share their superfluity with the destitute struck him as absurd:

> The poor man, fed in idleness and a prey to boredom, would miss the hard labor he is used to, and the rich man, restricted in the enjoyment of his property, would take his money and flee a country where he could not enjoy it. . . . In a monarchy . . . distinctions of wealth cannot give offense; on the contrary, they provide encouragement by showing to talent a path to advancement. As for those whom the institution of property condemns to labor for bare necessities, they look upon the rich as beings of another species and regard magnificence as an attribute of grandeur. The spectacle of wealth does not make the poor man unhappy. Displays of luxury, like the rays of a bright sun, dazzle his eyes and keep him from falling into the sin of envy.[26]

Since population was the basis of the power of the state, Necker argued, it was obviously preferable to have a large number of laborers existing at the subsistence level than a smaller number better nourished and clothed. Moreover "two thousand men reduced to bare necessities add up to [*ré-*

26. Necker, *Eloge de Colbert*, 43–44.

unissent] (if I may so express myself) a greater quantity of happiness than a thousand a little better dressed or a bit more delicately fed. Such no doubt is the benevolent purpose of Nature when she induces men to multiply."[27]

The Abbé Galiani regarded the bottom social stratum with a mixture of fear and contempt:

> As for that class of men, the lowest of all and so much the lowest that they are almost a transitional species between men and beasts of burden, . . . the dregs of city and country, who use their backs instead of their brains, . . . it is very important to keep them busy and contented. Make no mistake, they are the sole instigators of riots; they attack with their throats and defend themselves with their stupidity. . . . They are worse than frightening; they are pitiful. . . . What can we do with them? Conquer them? They are cowards. Kill them? They are innocent. Persuade them? They are stupid. Leave them alone? They are madmen. We have to give them work, let them earn money, keep them dispersed, and encourage their unquenchable throats to drink and shout "Long live the King!"[28]

To advocate the economic betterment of lower-class landowners, as the Physiocrats did, was madness, Galiani warned, for the rich peasant would be a litigious and even violent rebel against established authority.[29]

Necker and Galiani were merely expressing, in their particular styles, an image of the poor traditionally held by the elite classes, the possessors of wealth, power, and high culture, including the Philosophes. Those whom the eighteenth century designated, in economic and social contexts, as the *peuple*, the members of society dependent on the resources of others to find work, had long been seen by the higher classes as base, stupid, ignorant, unreasoning, capricious, superstitious, violent, cruel, and even ferocious. Yet this "vile multitude" was nevertheless the majority of the population and as *gens de bras* the producers of the nation's wealth, and thus not merely useful but indeed necessary. Furthermore by the 1770s

27. Necker, *Sur la Législation et le commerce des grains,* I, 32.
28. Galiani, *Dialogues sur le commerce des blés,* 223–24.
29. Ferdinando Galiani to Louise F. P. Tardieu d'Esclavelles, Marquise d'Epinay, January 2, 1773, and January 22, 1774, in Galiani, *Sa Correspondance* (3rd ed.; Paris, 1890), II, 154, 290.

the independent thinkers—with exceptions such as Galiani and Necker—were moved by the growing spirit of humanitarianism and libertarianism to see that the *peuple* might be the victims as well as the economic supports of society. Though certainly too irrational to be trusted with political power, they nevertheless did seem to deserve the equality before the law that was being claimed for all, equitable taxation, freedom from the harassment of feudal dues, perhaps some minimal education, and assurance of subsistence (or more) in a stable economy.[30]

It is true that the Physiocrats and their allies, though opponents of Galiani and Necker in the area of economic theory, did not appear to be effectively much different from either when they defended economic inequality as a necessary consequence of the operation of natural law or when they argued for minimal agricultural wages. Yet the humanistic individualism of the school and of their allies among the Philosophes did save them from Necker's arrogance and Galiani's ironic cynicism. Though the Abbé Morellet preached the natural justice of unlimited free enterprise, he nevertheless believed that the achievement of the essential purpose of government, the increase of the total sum of the nation's material well-being (*jouissances*), required not merely overall economic growth but also the elimination of "excessive and unnatural inequality" and the elevation of the lowest group of wage earners above the level of bare subsistence.[31] Chastellux, though certainly an aristocrat by instinct and later accused by Brissot with some justice of condoning Negro slavery, nevertheless believed that progress toward "the sole purpose of government, . . . the greatest good of the greatest number of citizens" would be possible only when the people had been "assimilated" through enlightenment.[32] Nor was Turgot an advocate of political, social, or economic equality; yet as a man of principle he did his best to right the obvious inequities in the system. "Artificial institutions like the nobility and the Indian caste system," he wrote, "give to vanity a legal basis; they set in conflict pride and lowly birth and often make us forget the rights of justice and humanity.

30. See Harry C. Payne, *The Philosophes and the People* (New Haven, 1976), to whom I am indebted for his definition of the word *peuple* in eighteenth-century economic and social usage and for his excellent general analysis of the subject.

31. [Morellet], *Rèfutation {du} . . . "Dialogue sur le commerce des blés,"* 59–62; [Morellet], *Réflexions sur les avantages de la liberté d'écrire*, 13.

32. Chastellux, *De la Félicité*, II, 212–13.

. . . In our present society the laws are far too favorable to the rich and often oppressive to the poor." As an intendant Turgot had plenty of opportunities for firsthand observation of the poverty and hardships endured by the laboring class and "the habitual state of war between the different parts of our society." Denouncing the pretension of the wealthy that tax exemptions were honorific, he wrote, "It is shameful and odious to take pride in the honor of refusing support and service to one's country."[33] He repeatedly pled with the ministry to lighten the taxes that particularly afflicted the *peuple*, such as the *gabelle*, the *octrois*, and the *corvées*; he protested the "harsh and oppressive" military conscription laws; and he established *ateliers* in Limousin to provide relief during the grain shortage of 1769–1770.[34]

One of the main themes of Maury's and Laharpe's eulogies in 1771 was that Fénelon had believed "that authority no longer exists for its own sake but is accountable for all it does not do for the nation, . . . that if the cries of the destitute are not heeded by the prince they rise to the throne of God," and that as royal tutor it was his duty "to teach the rights of the people to [the] prince" and make him aware of their miserable condition.[35] Even more pointed had been Thomas' eulogy of Marcus Aurelius of the year before, which had contained strong words on the taxation of the impoverished: "The state has no rights against the hardships of the poor; it would be as shameful as it would be barbarous to try to profit from poverty itself and to steal from him who has little to give to him who has everything. Under [Marcus Aurelius] the laborer was respected; the man with no resources but his two hands could enjoy the necessities that his hands had earned for him."[36]

The possible influence of Rousseau in engendering such sentiments must be considered. Condorcet for one felt sympathy and respect for Jean Jacques as a spokesman for *le peuple*, and he believed in an ethical instinct

33. Anne Robert Jacques Turgot to Marie Jean Antoine de Caritat, Marquis de Condorcet, July 16, 1771, in Turgot, *Oeuvres*, ed. Schelle, III, 523, 529; Turgot, "Mémoire sur les municipalités," in Turgot, *Oeuvres*, ed. Daire, II, 521.

34. See Turgot's various official letters of 1771–1773, in Turgot, *Oeuvres*, ed. Schelle, III, 427, 554–57, 606–607, etc.

35. Laharpe, *Eloge de . . . Fénelon*, 17–18; Maury, *Eloge de . . . Fénelon*, 11.

36. Thomas, *Eloge de Marc-Aurèle*, 45. Suppressed by Maupeou, this eulogy could not be published until after the fall of the ministry.

very much like Rousseau's *pitié*. "I believe," he wrote, "that the interest
we have in being just and virtuous is derived from the distress which as
sensitive beings we cannot help feeling from the idea of the suffering of
another sensitive being."[37] This compassion, which under the conditions
of the times a humane thinker could not help feeling for the oppressed,
was the basis, he believed, of the political philosophy held by himself and
his fellow Philosophes—a philosophy whose ethic was founded on the ideas
of justice, humanity, *bienveillance*, and "the original equality of all men."[38]

Like Voltaire, Condorcet protested against the feudal obligations which
were still imposed on peasants and were even being revived. "It will perhaps be said that feudal rights are a more noble form of property. . . .
What is noble about the right to exact from peasants the labor on which
their children's lives depend? . . . Is it noble to tax the bread of the poor?"
Condorcet was not singling out the nobility as a class, for he was equally
bitter against the "bourgeois vanity of possessing an estate and exercising
seignorial rights" and against the government for its discriminatory laws
and taxes, particularly the *corvées*.[39] In reply to Galiani and Necker, his
"laboureur de Picardie" protested,

> We are ignorant because no one has been willing to give us the means
> to learn. . . . We can endure with patience outrageous wrongs against
> which we have no defense, but we are not so brutalized that we do not
> feel them. . . . We detest the laws that brand with a hot iron and send
> to the galleys some poor father of a family without a hundred *écus* to
> his name for having bought some salt not mixed with filth. . . . You
> say we are tempted to consider the rich as "beings of another species"
> and that "the magic of their grandeur inspires us with awe." Ah, sir,
> how far we are from such ideas! We see those pompous rich go by, but
> it is not respect they inspire in us. We know how much less noble are
> the arts that have made them rich than the useful crafts that provide
> us scarcely enough to eat.[40]

37. Marie Jean Antoine de Caritat, Marquis de Condorcet to Anne Robert Jacques
Turgot, December 13, 1773, in Condorcet, *Correspondance inédite de Condorcet et de Turgot*,
148.
   38. Condorcet, *Lettre d'un théologien*, 81–82. On Condorcet's respect for Rousseau, see
ibid., 45–47.
   39. Condorcet, "Réflexions sur les corvées," in Condorcet, *Oeuvres*, XI, 66–67, 31 and
passim; Condorcet, "Sur l'Abolition des corvées," *ibid.*, XI, 87–97.
   40. Condorcet, "Lettre d'un laboureur de Picardie," in Condorcet, *Oeuvres*, XI, 15–
16.

Like his mentor Turgot, Condorcet was keenly aware of the conflicts of class interests. "Do not forget," he told the peasants, "there are very serious men who want you condemned to two weeks of labor without pay, when you have nothing to live on but your wages, for fear that your freedom from this burden may cost them a tax on their excess wealth." His fictional Picard peasant demanded the protection of property laws "against the chicanery and greed of the powerful," laws protecting the peasants' liberty against the slavery of the *corvée*, and laws of justice to "protect our persons and honor against the credit of the rich and the tyranny of petty officials." It would be an error, of course, to give too radical a reading to such words. Condorcet was not, at this time, preaching political democracy or economic equality or the uncompensated abolition of feudal rights, and he had no intention, he said, of "raising vassals up against their lords or arming them against their sovereign."[41] Yet he did identify the problems.

Diderot, who like his former friend Rousseau had known well the pinch of poverty, saw French society "divided into two classes: one very small class of citizens who are rich, and one very large class of citizens who are poor." He was one of the first to point out that for the masses bad working conditions were as great a hardship as lack of money:

> In our society there are many exhausting kinds of work that drain men's strength and shorten their lives, and no increase in wages will make the workers' complaints less frequent or less just. Have you ever thought of how many wretches are afflicted with horrible diseases or die from working in mines or from the manufacture of white lead or from cleaning cesspools? Only sheer brutalization or the terror of utter destitution can drive a man to such work. Ah! Jean Jacques, how badly you pleaded the advantages of the savage over man in society! . . . The Hartz mines conceal in their immense depths thousands of men who hardly ever see the light of day and rarely live beyond thirty years. That is the region where you find women who have outlived a dozen husbands.[42]

Diderot was, however, certainly no proto-Marxist. For him liberty and

---

41. Condorcet, "Sur l'abolition des corvées," *ibid.*, XI, 96; Condorcet, "Lettre d'un laboureur de Picardie," *ibid.*, XI, 18; Condorcet, "Réflexions sur les corvées," *ibid.*, XI, 80–81.

42. Diderot, "Réfutation de . . . L'Homme," in Diderot, *Oeuvres complètes*, II, 415, 430.

the sacred right of property were synonymous, and he saw no conflict between free enterprise and social justice for the laboring class. Inspired by the example of the Netherlands, he envisioned the elimination of poverty under a laissez-faire capitalistic system through the assurance of social and economic mobility by essential guaranties: equal protection under the law; general education, so that "everyone, from the prime minister down to the lowliest peasant, may be able to read, write, and cipher"; equality of professional opportunity; equitable distribution of wealth in proportion to the productivity of the individual; economic security against sickness and old age; free and quick justice for the poor in the courts; and equitable taxation.[43]

Raynal in his *Histoire de deux Indes* gave currency to the still unpublished ideas of his friend Diderot and set them in cosmopolitan dimensions in protesting against the economic servitude of the laboring classes throughout Europe and especially in Germany and Poland. Likewise he denounced slavery in the colonies as contrary to humanity, reason, and justice. Blacks, he insisted, were not naturally inferior to whites but appeared so only because of their enslavement. "[They] are dull-witted because slavery saps all the energy of their minds. They are vicious, but not as vicious as you deserve. They are deceitful, for no man owes truth to his oppressor."[44]

Mercier was equally unrestrained in the rhetoric of his social protest. Of the manifold evils in French society he saw none more reprehensible than the tremendous gap between the wealth of the rich and the destitution of the poor, for the injustice of economic inequality was compounded by the indifference of the affluent, by their exploitation of the defenseless and overworked people, and by their use of the law to consecrate and perpetuate these inequities. "I do not believe," he wrote, "the sewers [of Paris carry] anything more foul than the souls of the rich." In his utopistic *L'An 2440* he envisioned for the France of the future not absolute economic equality but an increase in the real income and the standard of living of the workers such that even the poorest would be assured of economic security.[45]

43. Diderot, *Mémoires pour Catherine II*, 48–49, 63, 64, 129–44, 153, 167; Diderot, "Essai sur les études en Russie," in Diderot, *Oeuvres complètes*, II, 417; Diderot, "Réfutation de . . . L'Homme," in Diderot, *Oeuvres complètes*, II, 417–18, 440.

44. Raynal, *Histoire des deux Indes* (The Hague, 1774), VII, 223, 225, 228–29.

45. [Mercier], *L'An 2440*, 160–61, 158. Mercier's vehemence on this subject was

The Abbé Mably, the sole theoretical communist publishing during these years, was the only philosopher to advocate absolute economic equality. His motivation, however, seems to have been not compassion or indignation but the conclusions he drew from his moral speculations. He came to the belief that the greatest evils afflicting mankind were not material hardships but the unnatural vices of ambition, avarice, and materialism, which sprang from the invention of property. So he dreamed of an ideal society in which all men would enjoy a natural community of goods and live together in virtue and frugal simplicity under the rule of modest magistrates called from their plows to serve their fellow citizens. The inspiration was obviously classical and bucolic. "For my part," Mably wrote, "I am satisfied with virtue and I am not afraid of poverty, for I know that poor citizens are more disposed to respect justice and the law than are the rich. I know that moral purity can achieve great things. With all the wealth in the world the Romans could not defend themselves against a few bands of barbarians."[46] For Mably, and others such as Saint Lambert, poverty seems to have been a philosophic abstraction and a literary myth; it was the modest frugality of Arcadian shepherds, not the grim modern human problem that Diderot saw.

In contrast both to such idyllists and to the compassionate but equally aprioristic humanitarianism of others, Jacques Henri Meister took a realistic, pragmatic line. Like Linguet he attacked the fundamental contradiction in the position of Morellet, Diderot, and others who reconciled pity for the poor with defense of free enterprise by assuming the Physiocratic and utilitarian hypothesis of the compatibility of enlightened self-interest with the welfare of all. In actual fact, Meister said, private and public interests were more often in conflict than in agreement, and to sacrifice the general good to private profit was to negate the essential purpose of society. "To say that the government cannot take the measures necessary to prevent a farmer from setting an exorbitant price on his product without infringing on the rights of liberty and property is the same as saying that the government is unjust if it keeps us from slitting one another's throats." He continued:

If it is true that we are all born free and equal and that we can never

---

echoed and amplified by his imitator Lanjuinais. See Lanjuinais, *Le Monarque accompli*, I, 111–13.

46. Mably, *De la Législation*, I, 21.

legitimately be deprived of these sacred rights, then is not the first consequence that we all have an equal right to live, and that this right would remain wholly imaginary in a society so constituted that any one class of citizens had the power to prevent all others from living on the products of their own labor? The Abbé Morellet says that anyone who is not a landowner or a farmer [*cultivateur*] has no rights. He has no title to his own life; it is a favor which may be granted him or re- fused. How would you answer, sir, a poor day laborer who said to you: "You say I am free. But what is my freedom if I do not have the liberty to live? I work, but I am dying of hunger. My whole day's labor is not enough to provide the food I need. You say you do not have the right to prevent the farmers of my village from making money, yet you dare assert the right to prevent me from staying alive.[47]

Such realistic concern for the problems of the laboring class was far from universal among the Philosophes or other independent thinkers. D'Hol- bach was strong for legal and civil equality, including equal freedom to work, that is, abolition of guild restrictions.[48] But he believed that a man's social, economic, and political status should be in direct proportion to his social utility. If this principle were realized, presumably anyone who was still poor would deserve to be.

Saint Lambert told the story that Helvétius once berated a carter blocking his carriage on a Paris street, and the man replied, "You are right. I am a *coquin* and you are a gentleman, for I am down here in the street and you are up there in your carriage." Helvétius begged the man's for- giveness, gave him six francs, and ordered his servants to finish loading the cart.[49] It was perhaps (as Saint Lambert thought) an indication of Hel- vétius' humaneness that he was ashamed to be caught playing the aris- tocrat, and it is true that Helvétius did see a danger in excessive inequal- ity of wealth that produced conflicts of interest.[50] Yet he was also a wealthy tax farmer who dedicated his *De l'Homme* "to the Catherines and Freder- icks [who] strive to make themselves loved by humanity."

It could be said that Helvétius' six francs, and even Condorcet's and

47. *Correspondance littéraire*, December, 1774 (X, 517–18).
48. [D'Holbach], *Ethocratie*, 151.
49. [Saint Lambert]. "Préface," in Helvétius, *Le Bonheur*, ciii.
50. Helvétius, *De l'Homme*, II, Sections 6 and 8.

Diderot's sincere compassion, came somewhat short of constituting social egalitarianism. It was rather in the independents' views on hereditary aristocracy that a kind of principle of social equality emerged. This was an egalitarianism which proposed the demotion of the aristocracy to the level of the bourgeoisie, but not a classless society. In this position the independents were by no means alone. The Maupeou revolution itself was, of course, essentially anti-aristocratic; the Physiocrats would have replaced the traditional hereditary aristocracy with an agricultural plutocracy; and even the Patriotes were infiltrated by populist radicalism. The intellectual center of gravity of this sort of social egalitarianism, however, was clearly located among the Philosophes and other independent thinkers, and especially among those who maintained the materialistic, utilitarian, and behavioristic doctrine that human worth is not intrinsic but acquired, and that it is to be measured in terms of social utility.

The new history interpreted feudalism as an ancient malignancy from which France still suffered. There was a general acceptance of Delolme's and Robertson's thesis that while the English people had achieved power and liberty by their alliance with the nobles against royal absolutism, the French people since Charlemagne had been caught in the middle of the struggle for dominance between the nobility and the throne, and had alternately or simultaneously suffered the tyranny of both. Thus feudalism and despotism were the twin devils in French history. Diderot said that feudal lords had been "raging beasts that their vassals should have clubbed to death," and D'Holbach called them "a horde of tyrants living in anarchy."[51]

Of course feudalism in the normal modern sense of a form of land tenure in return for military service had ceased to exist in France long before the eighteenth century. Nevertheless the feudal rights and obligations attached to fiefs were still in effect, as were the often indistinguishable seignorial rights and dues. Indeed, under the so-called "feudal reaction" *feudistes* were hard at work resurrecting forgotten rights and even manufacturing new ones for registration in the hated *terriers*. In addition, feudalism could be said to persist in the tax privileges and other rights, powers, and advantages attached to noble status. It was these various as-

51. Diderot, "Fragments échappés du portefeuille d'un philosophe," in Diderot, *Oeuvres complètes*, VI, 450; [D'Holbach], *La Politique naturelle*, I, 203.

pects of French society that the philosophers were attacking under the name of "feudalism" and were stigmatizing, however uncritically, as survivals of medieval feudalism. These attacks were various and manifold—Voltaire's championship of the peasants of Saint Claude, Turgot's *municipalités*, Raynal's call for equitable taxation and the abolition of fiscal privileges, and Des Glanières *Plan*, which proposed a graduated income tax with a supplementary investment tax which would have placed the heaviest burden on the rich and allowed no exemptions for either nobles or clerics.[52]

Feudalism, whether historic or economic, was however only the most flagrant case in point of the prime principle of the social philosophy held by Philosophes and others, that political, economic, or social status should not be hereditary. On this there was little dissent. Even D'Alembert, who carefully qualified his endorsement of the principle of equality, opposed hereditary honors and hereditary nobility.[53] The most forthright and emphatic, however, were Diderot and D'Holbach.

To Diderot it was completely absurd that the nobility were subject to laws different from those that applied to commoners. "Are these people anything more than subjects and citizens? It is right that the nation should recompense them for their services, but not by exclusive privileges or exemptions. All these iniquitous devices are violations of the generality of law and additional burdens on the shoulders of useful and hardworking citizens who do not happen to have titles. Why should we transmit compensations awarded to illustrious men to their degenerate descendants? . . . It is reasonable that honor should mount upward, as it does in China, passing from the living to the dead; but for it to descend from the dead to the living, that is something else again."[54]

---

52. For Raynal's views on taxation, see Raynal, *Histoire des deux Indes* (The Hague, 1774), VII, 227, 241–42, 370, 371, 375. On the general question, see Mackrell, *The Attack on "Feudalism"*.

53. D'Alembert, "Eléments de philosophie," in D'Alembert, *Oeuvres*, I, 220.

54. Diderot, "Essai historique sur la police," in Diderot, *Mémoires pour Catherine II*, 5. This argument against hereditary aristocracy from the Chinese principle of ascending honor was to become a philosophic commonplace. The earliest occurrence I have found is in Diderot's letter to Sophie Volland, September 30, 1760 (Diderot, *Correspondance*, III, 113). He repeated it here and in his "Pages contre un tyran" (1771) (in Diderot, *Oeuvres politiques*, 145), as did D'Holbach in *La Politique naturelle* (I, 201). Benjamin Franklin elaborated an effective and humorous version, first in a letter to his daughter in 1784 and

On this question of inherited status D'Holbach wholly concurred: "Those who have only ancestors have no right to rewards. . . . The man who is useful to his country should be noble in his own right, whoever may have been his ancestors. . . . It is education, not blood, that creates men capable of serving the state."[55] In his *Système social* he made clear, however, that in opposing hereditary honor he was not advocating absolute social equality but rather rational inequality. "Liberty does not consist . . . in a so-called equality between citizens, . . . an illusion worshipped in democratic states."[56] Societies always had been and always should be hierarchies of dependencies and authorities. But the hierarchies should be just and natural. Men inevitably were unequally useful to society because by the operation of material causes they were unequal in talents and powers, and these natural differences in social utility were the only rational, just, and natural bases for differences in status. "Authority and superiority of any sort can be based only on utility, that is, the good done for other men." Social superiority rightly derived, however, from *effective* usefulness, not from mere accumulated wealth or power. ("The superiority of the rich is based on the means their wealth gives them to succor the unfortunate; the miser is not superior to the pauper.") Moreover superior status implied no inequality before the law, no special tax privileges, and no unequal enjoyment of the natural rights of freedom of religion, thought, speech, or press.[57] What D'Holbach was projecting was not properly speaking a class-structured society but rather a complex system of "authorities and dependencies" in which each particular function would devolve naturally to the individual with the appropriate social merit. Rouillé d'Orfeuil's rigid structure of ten uniformed classes categorized by social functions was a perversion of D'Holbach's dynamic and organicistic concept.

Diderot's vision was very similar. "There is between any two individ-

---

later in an essay which was incorporated by the younger Mirabeau into his anti-aristocratic *Considérations sur l'Ordre de Cincinnatus* (1784) and was published in 1790 in the *Journal de la Société de 1789*. See Durand Echeverria, "Franklin's Lost Letter on the Cincinnati," *Bulletin de l'Institut Français de Washington*, n.s., No. 3 (December 1953), 119–26.

55. [D'Holbach], *La Politique naturelle*, I, 204–205. Cf. *ibid.*, I, 123.

56. [D'Holbach], *Système social*, II, 41.

57. *Ibid.*, I, 142; II, 40–41. See also [D'Holbach], *La Politique naturelle*, I, 125; II, 58–105, Discours VI, "De la liberté"; II, 142–43.

uals," he wrote, "natural inequality. There is also conventional inequality, determined by the status an individual holds in society. If merit decides status, such inequality becomes a kind of natural inequality."[58] The only true distinctions were "between ineptitude and talent, industry and sloth, vice and virtue."[59] "Wealth will be legitimately distributed when it is proportionate to the industry and achievements of each man. . . . Such inequality will have no undesirable effects; . . . on the contrary, it will be the basis of public felicity if a way is found to diminish the power of money without debasing wealth. The only way I know to do this is to open up all positions in the state to competition. . . . If the competitors are judged by their morals and their knowledge, if vice is as sure a reason for failure as ignorance, then we shall have only honest and competent men."[60] He imagined for Catherine's edification a scene in which "a man of humble birth but exceptional merit has just been awarded the position for which he has competed." A father draws a lesson for his son:

> "My son, do you know who is First President?"
> "No, papa."
> "It is so-and-so."
> "What! The son of that milliner who comes here with her basket to sell hats to mama?"
> "The very same! What he has become you will become if you work hard. But if you don't work hard, you won't be anything."[61]

Like D'Holbach, Diderot stressed that position meant social responsibility. Economic status entailed the "debt of wealth," the duty of the rich to provide, either by voluntary gifts or through taxes, for at least the minimum necessities of the poor.[62]

This ideal of morally justified inequality attracted many. Mercier predicted that in the France of 2440 the only distinction between men would be "those which naturally result from differences in virtue, genius, and industry," and that the gifted and enlightened rich would devote their wealth to science and public works instead of to depravity and luxury.[63]

58. Diderot, "Observations sur le Nakaz," in Diderot, *Oeuvres politiques*, 366.

59. Diderot, *Mémoires pour Catherine II*, 268.

60. Diderot, "Réfutation de . . . L'Homme," in Diderot, *Oeuvres complètes*, II, 417–18.

61. Diderot, *Mémoires pour Catherine II*, 167–68.

62. Denis Diderot, "Mon Père et moi," in Diderot, *Oeuvres complètes*, IV, 475–82.

63. [Mercier], *L'An 2440*, 312, 158.

Raynal, inspired by the examples of primitive peoples, allowed his enthusiasm to carry him close to real social egalitarianism: "Inequality of status [*inégalité des conditions*], which we believe so necessary for the preservation of society, is in the eyes of the savage the height of madness. He is equally scandalized that in our world one man may possess more property than several others together. . . . The respect we have for titles, for rank, and especially for the hereditary nobility they consider an outrageous insult to humanity."[64]

The importance of all these protests against hereditary status was not merely in specific goals such as abolition of feudal dues, of fiscal and legal discrimination, and of hereditary eligibility for office, but in the enunciated ideal of a fluid, mobile society in which all doors would be open to all and all could compete for status under the same rules. Freedom of opportunity was to be granted to all, including the humblest citizen, as Diderot repeatedly insisted, but it was apparently the lower and middle bourgeoisie that were expected to profit most in the new society.

Once again it seems apparent that the charge that eighteenth-century "liberalism" was a rationale for capitalism needs some qualification. The "right-to-live" thesis of Linguet and Meister certainly ran counter to the principle of free enterprise, and Condorcet's and Diderot's strictures against the exploitation of workers implied something rather different from the free-wheeling capitalism that was to develop in the nineteenth century. The same may be said of Mercier's, Diderot's, and D'Holbach's insistence on the social responsibilities of wealth. What seems to have been foremost in these writers' minds was the urgent need to get rid of the unjust and "unnatural" remnants of feudalism, to alleviate poverty, and to create an open, fluid society with maximum opportunities for the bourgeoisie—and for the lower classes as well if they could take advantage of them. Of these three purposes the abolition of aristocratic privilege was the one that had to be achieved first, and therefore it was given the greatest importance. The dominance of this objective helps to explain the irreconcilable opposition between most of the independents and the Patriotes, however much they might agree on other issues, just as the independents' majority position on absolutism prevented any alliance with royalists, despite hidden affinities between the two parties.

64. Raynal, *Histoire des deux Indes* (The Hague, 1774), VI, 27–28.

CONCLUSION

The four years between the edict of December 1770 and the dissolution of the Maupeou Parlement in November 1774 constituted in the history of France a brief episode during which apparently no important permanent political or social changes occurred. In retrospect we can see that it marked the beginning of a downward curve in the national economy after the growth of the preceding decades, but at the time the alternations of good and bad harvests and the fluctuations of prices seemed merely repetitions of the patterns of the past. There were no significant modifications in social behavior or in social structure. The nation was still nursing its wounds from the Seven Years' War and Louis XV's firm policy was to preserve the existing peace. Despite Terray's temporary achievements there was no decisive reversal of the downward course of the government's finances. Even in the area of politics, after the Maupeou revolution had been liquidated the political structure of France remained essentially the same as before. Yet France emerged from the experience of 1770–1774 a different nation.

The most striking difference was in the way the literate elite were thinking about the political and social problems of their country. In order to understand more clearly what had happened in men's minds we have considered the four years as a single experience, a single moment, and have analyzed it synchronically. The subject matter of intellectual history is of course a continuous process, but it can be made comprehensible only by freezing, so to speak, successive brief segments of time, which when serially described may reveal the true directions of the changes in men's thinking. Each segment must be described as a single moment, yet the occurrence of each moment creates a new situation.

The new situation after the Maupeou revolution was to have revolutionary ideological, political, and social consequences. The patterns of thought of 1770–1774 had possessed a dynamism and momentum which, together with new added forces, were to produce accelerating changes and developments during the following years, to eventuate in the ideologies of 1787–1789, which in turn were to affect in a significant degree the words and actions of the French Revolution. It must be the task of others to demonstrate in detail how the patterns of thought of 1770–1774 became the patterns of thought of 1787–1789, but it may be suggestive to indicate hypothetically and in broad lines how this transformation may have occurred.

A salient characteristic of France in 1770–1774 was the intensified awareness, study, and discussion of social and political problems.[1] This heightened consciousness was immediately occasioned by Maupeou's revolution and the ensuing debate between Patriotes and royalists, but it was directed to every aspect of French society. For many reasons this social and political awareness was destined to increase. As I have shown elsewhere, French popular enthusiasm for the American Revolution was symptomatic of a widespread preoccupation with certain political and social issues.[2] At the same time the great effect of the American Revolution on Frenchmen, and indeed on all Europeans, was, as Robert Palmer has said, to make them feel that they lived in an era of momentous change, and to document, particularly through the publications and discussions of the American constitutions and bills of rights, the mechanics, so to speak, of political change.[3] The American influence probably intensified rather than diminished after the Treaty of Versailles, but from 1783 to 1789 it was overshadowed by events within France, especially by those efforts by the successive ministries to meet the fiscal crisis which occasioned and even invited public discussions of political issues, as in the composition of the *cahiers* for the meeting of the States General.

It must be remembered, however, that during 1770–1774 this political and social consciousness was apparent only in the literate elite—the magistrates of the various courts, officials in the royal government, law-

1. See Mornet, *Les Origines intellectuelles de la Révolution française*, 472–73.
2. Durand Echeverria, *Mirage in the West: A History of the French Image of American Society to 1815* (Princeton, 1957).
3. Palmer, *The Age of Democratic Revolution. The Challenge*, I, 239–82.

yers, Philosophes, and others capable of writing, reading, and discussing the documents we have examined. The Patriotes and royalists (but not the independent thinkers) did attempt to enlist the support of the lower middle and laboring classes; the Patriotes did succeed in 1774 in instigating popular demonstrations; and probably some of the various ideas made their way down to the lower economic and social levels, if only in the form of catchwords like *despotisme*. Yet popular demonstrations for or against the ministry or the parlements were probably still essentially manifestations of the long-standing endemic discontent with economic and social hardships. There is no evidence to indicate that in 1770–1774 the political enlightenment of the elite was paralleled by a similar awakening of the lower classes. This obviously was not to be true later. A significant new development from 1775 to 1793 was the progressive popularization of political and social consciousness.

Another important feature of the thought of the years 1770–1774 was the virtually unanimous feeling, among Patriotes, royalists, and independents alike, that some sort of political "revolution" was both inevitable and necessary. They did not use the word *revolution* in the sense it was to acquire after the French Revolution but rather in the pre-1789 sense of a restructuring of the political constitution either by a nonviolent coup such as the Maupeou revolution itself or by rational agreement. There was of course no consensus on what the nature of this revolution should be. After 1774 this dissatisfaction with a status quo which seemed to be becoming increasingly intolerable continued to be shared by all, and the American example both heightened the expectations and suggested ways by which these expectations might be realized. The reforms envisaged or attempted by Turgot, Necker, and especially Calonne in the fiscal system and in the establishment of provincial assemblies were modest movements toward such a "revolution," while on the other hand the "aristocratic resurgence" was a parallel attempt at a counter "revolution."

A third general characteristic of the thought of the period of the Maupeou revolution was secularism, a secularism which had been increasing during the course of the century and which by 1770 was firmly established as dominant in upper-level public opinion. Though only the Philosophes and other critics of the Catholic Church gave overt expression to antireligious spirit, we have seen that the Maupeou regime itself, despite its political alliance with the clergy, was essentially secular in its philosophy, and we have also noted signs of inroads of secularism in the thinking of some of the Patriotes and Jansenists. As Daniel Mornet said, "The state of mind [*esprit*] which was to prepare for and then demand a profound reform of the state was first of all one hostile to religion. . . . From about 1770 onwards one may say that opinion was in this respect unanimous. . . . The increase in unbelief continued from 1770 to 1787, but all that was essential had been said and the decisive impulse had been given by 1770. During the following years political questions were to dominate men's minds."[4]

From 1770 to 1774 the sole issue on the level of realpolitik was the contest between the parlements and the crown. This struggle enlisted on one side or the other some of the best minds of the time, such as Malesherbes and Voltaire, and involved to various extents Frenchmen of all classes, particularly during the crucial years 1771 and 1774. This was yet one more battle between the forces of aristocracy and absolutism, a contest which had been waged since the Middle Ages and which was to continue through 1788.

On the ideological level this contest instigated elaborations of the theses which had been developed to support these two political theories. But more importantly it stimulated the formulation of a third thesis, the position held by most of those whom we have called the independent thinkers, who not only joined everyone else in believing that the old constitution was obsolete but also rejected the alternative solutions of aristocratic corporatism and monarchical absolutism proposed by the Patriotes and the royalists.

Since eighteenth-century thought was essentially dialectical rather than imaginative, it is not surprising that there were few new basic ideas in this third position. It was in large part a synthesis of the aristocratic thesis and the absolutistic antithesis. The majority of the independents concurred with the absolutists in denying the principle of rule by aristocratic corporations and in proposing a government supported principally by the Third Estate. They agreed also on the rejection of tradition and precedent as guides for the future and on the necessity of creating from scratch a new rational structure of law and government. And they paralleled Lebrun and

4. Mornet, *Les Origines intellectuelles de la Révolution française*, 471–72.

Maupeou in recognizing the problem of the economic condition of the laboring class and the need for a national system of education to train citizens in their civic duties and create an upward flow of talent.

On the other hand most of the independents joined the Patriotes in rejecting absolute monarchism, theocratic government, and statism. They concurred on the principles of the sovereignty of the nation, the contract, government by consent, and constitutional limitations on the royal executive. They agreed also on the basic concept of government by corporations and on the immediate need to reconstitute the national legislature, though of course they envisaged more than the resurrection of the ancient States General. Finally, and most importantly, they affirmed like the Patriotes that the essential purpose of government was to ensure the enjoyment of the rights of life, liberty, and property.

This synthesis was achieved essentially by applying the modernism of the absolutists—the willingness to break completely with the past and to reconstruct the political and social edifice freely and rationally—to the Patriotes' principles of individual rights and the sovereignty of the nation. Yet it presupposed, of course, the whole tradition of Western political thought.

The independents' principal contributions were in the amplification and radicalization of what was already explicit in the theses of the Patriotes and absolutists. They broadened the rights of personal liberty and property to include freedom of the press and freedom of religion. They extended the parlements' and the Jansenists' traditional opposition to transmontane theocracy and ecclesiasticism to a demand for the complete subordination of the clergy and the church to civil authority. And from the crown's long-standing opposition to aristocratic power they moved forward to the concept of a society structured on economic and social function.

Yet this synthesis was more than an amalgamation and development of preexisting ideas, for the dialectic generated a new ideology essentially different from those of aristocracy and absolutism. Perhaps the best term to describe the new position is *democratic*. This is not to say that it was democratic in the modern sense of favoring a universal franchise or social or economic equality, nor was it democratic in the restricted, historical, and scholarly sense used by Montesquieu and still normal in the 1770s.

Rather, *democratic* is to be understood here in the sense used by Robert Palmer and others, signifying opposition to the possession of political power by established, closed, self-perpetuating groups, to the exercise of authority by virtue of inherent right, status, inheritance, or the sanction of history.[5] It is held, however, that this "democratic" opposition—at least in France at this period—was as much against the possession of such power by a monarch and his ministers, as much against *despotisme*, as against rule by aristocratic corporate bodies. It was simultaneously anti-aristocratic and anti-absolutistic. In advocating the delegation of authority by the sovereign nation and the removability of officials it envisaged not only an elected legislature virtually representative of the nation as a whole but also an executive with limited and conditional powers which logically, as Diderot said, should be no less revocable than those granted to the legislators. This ideology produced the variously radical proposals for a constitutional limited monarchy described in Chapter 9.[6]

To explain the democratic third position in 1770–1774 as a synthesis of the aristocratic thesis and the absolutistic antithesis is of course not to imply that aristocracy or monarchical absolutism, either as ideologies or political parties, ceased to exist after 1774. On the contrary, the parliamentary-aristocratic "resurgence" grew in strength from 1774 to 1788, and at the same time the crown continued its efforts to maintain its authority. The two parties continued to dominate the political arena as they had in 1770–1774, and in 1788 they were still accusing each other of trying to establish a royal "despotism" or an "aristocracy of magistrates." Yet the two sides seem to have continued to suffer the philosophic infection they both were said to have experienced in 1770–1774. Both were forced to appeal to the third position. The parliamentary-aristocratic "resurgence" after 1774, though it still stubbornly opposed fiscal reforms, held the support of the Third Estate through 1788 by favoring a form of constitutional monarchy and by championing libertarian principles. On the other hand, the crown was also perforce moving toward a sort of lib-

5. Palmer, *The Age of Democratic Revolution. The Challenge*, I, 4–5.

6. For a recent enlightening examination of the historic fact that the Maupeou revolution "had underlined the need for a restatement of the principles of the political order, a reconstitution of the body politic, and a reconsideration of the traditional theory of representation," see Baker, "French Political Thought at the Accession of Louis XVI," 283 and throughout, 279–303.

ertarianism, for instance in its attempts at fiscal reform, such as the abolition of the *corvée*, and its provisions for different sorts of representative government, first in the proposed provincial assemblies, then in the Assemblée des Notables, and finally in the States General.

Meanwhile the third position apparently continued after 1774 to amass greater support from public opinion. The influence of the American example, besides keeping alive the political consciousness and the expectation of change, also seems to have fueled the fires of third-position thinking, for instance in Mirabeau's *Considérations sur l'Ordre de Cincinnatus*, as later it was to contribute to the constitutional debates over the Declaration of the Rights of Man, unicameralism and bicameralism, and the veto. It would not be in order here to attempt to analyze the relative impacts of the American and British constitutions, the heightened political consciousness, the clash of the aristocratic "resurgence" and the royal ministries, the fiscal crisis, and all the other factors. It seems evident, however, that as France approached 1789 the thinking of the various adherents to the third position rapidly evolved and grew more radical as it increased in potential political power. The eventual triumph came after 1788 with the demise of the parlements, the Tennis Court Oath, the resolutions of August 4, the Declarations of the Rights of Man, and the Constitution of 1791.

This is not to imply that these initial achievements of the French Revolution were designed by the independent thinkers of 1770–1774, for that would be absurd. It does appear, however, a reasonable hypothesis that the ideology of the third position, generated in large part immediately by a synthesis of the contemporary aristocratic and absolutistic theses but derived ultimately from the whole tradition of Western political thought, did provide the point of departure from which the ideologies of the Revolution developed.

To propose such a hypothesis is to stress the view, first, that French eighteenth-century thought was a complex of contradictory yet interrelated and mutually dependent parts, from which no portion, such as the thought of the Philosophes, can be abstracted as an autonomous phenomenon. Was Malesherbes a Patriote or a Philosophe? Voltaire a Philosophe or a royalist? Secondly, this thought, whether reified as a cultural pattern or regarded as the sum of the ideologies of individuals, was in a constant process of dialectical regeneration and transformation. We have only to consider how dated was the libertarianism of the 1770s. If some of its elements seem to have survived into the nineteenth- and twentieth-century liberalism they have done so greatly transmogrified. A secularism that talked of religious toleration as a trap for kings and of salaried priests was not the secularism of today. What most firmly ties this libertarianism to the third quarter of the eighteenth century is the social philosophy on which it rested. It was designed for a basically agricultural economy and was intended primarily to make life safe for the owners of real property, for the large and small agricultural capitalists. The principles of equality before the law, of "democratic" opposition to aristocracy, and of anticlericalism all had as their essential purpose the denial of any other basis of status or power. While this philosophy offered to all Frenchmen negative liberty—equal enjoyment of fundamental rights ensured by the application of the same laws to all—it still restricted positive liberty, the right to govern, to an elite. This elite was identified, it is true, by a new formula, but a formula which was to be erased by the course of events.

Thus the historic importance of the political and social thought generated by the Maupeou revolution seems to lie not in the particular ideas it contained, for all were rapidly to become obsolete in the changing social context, but in the fact that the violent clash of the *thèse parlementaire* and the *thèse royale* stimulated the generation of a new synthesis, which in turn initiated a rapid development of libertarianism—a development which after further quickenings and transformations by the American and French Revolutions and all the other revolutions through which the Atlantic community was to pass during the last quarter of the eighteenth century, eventuated in the democratic liberalism of the nineteenth century.

The industrial revolution, the shift of capital from agriculture to industry, and the creation of urban proletariats were to change, however, the entire context of the problem of liberty. Even Meister's "right to live" was to take on implications in modern society that no eighteenth-century mind could have imagined. This is the reason that key concepts of the liberalism of the following centuries such as protection from the tyranny of the majority and minority rights were totally absent from eighteenth-century libertarianism.

PUBLICATIONS IN SUPPORT OF THE PARLEMENTS, 1770–1775

L'Accomplissement des prophéties, pour servir de suite à l'ouvrage intitulé Le Point de vue; Ecrit intéressant pour la maison de Bourbon. N.p., n.d. [1772]

Acte de protestation de plusieurs membres du bailliage de Caen, contre l'édit de suppression du parlement de Rouen (7 Octobre 1771). N.p., n.d. [1771]

[Aubusson, Pierre Arnaud, Vicomte d']. *Profession de foi politique d'un bon François.* N.p., n.d. [Paris, 1771]

[Augeard, Jacques Mathieu]. *L'Auteur du quatrième supplément à M. de Maupeou.* N.p., n.d. [1772]

[————]. *Correspondance secrète et familière de M. de Maupeou avec M. de Sor***, conseiller du nouveau parlement.* 2 vols. N.p., n.d. [1771]

[————]. *Correspondance secrette et familière de M. de Maupeou avec M. de Sor**, conseiller du nouveau parlement.—Le Maire du palais* [by Athanase Alexandre Clément de Boissy].*—Lettre d'un homme à un autre homme sur l'extinction de l'ancien parlement et la création du nouveau* [by Guy Jean Baptiste Target].*— Remontrances de la Basoche.—La Chancelière, ode* [by Claude Antoine Guyot des Herbiers]. N.p., 1771.

[————]. *Correspondance secrète et familière de M. de Maupeou avec M. de Sor***, conseiller du nouveau parlement.—Suite de la correspondance de M. de Maupeou et de M. Sorhouet.—Oeufs rouges. Première partie. Sorhouet mourant à M. de Maupeou.* 2 vols. N.p., n.d. [1772]

[————]. *Lettre de M. le duc d'Orléans et de M. le duc de Chartres au Roi. Du 28 décembre, 1772.* N.p., n.d. [1773]

[————]. *Mandement de monseigneur l'archevêque de Paris, qui proscrit l'usage des oeufs rouges, à commencer du vendredi dans l'octave de l'Ascension jusqu'à la résurrection des morts exclusivement.* Paris, 1772.

[————]. *Maupeouana ou Correspondance secrette et familière du chancelier Maupeou avec son coeur Sorhouet, membre inamovible de la Cour des Pairs de France. Nouvelle édition sur le manuscrit original (10 mai 1771–25 avril 1772). 2 vols.* N.p., 1773.

[————]. *Oeufs rouges. Première partie. Sorhouet mourant à M. de Maupeou, chancelier de France.* N.p., 1772.

[————]. *Les Oeufus rouges de monsiegneur Sorhouet mourant. A M. de Maupeou, chancelier de France. Du 25 arvil 1772 . . . Première partie.* N.p., n.d. [1772]

Besançon. See Parlement De Besançon.

[Blonde, André]. *Le Parlement justifié par l'Impératrice de Russie, ou Lettre à M ***, dans laquelle on répond aux différents écrits que M. le Ch{ancelier} fait distribuer dans Paris.* N.p., n.d. [1771]

[————]. *Le Parlement justifié par l'Impératrice Reine de Hongrie et par le Roi de Prusse; ou Seconde lettre, dans laquelle on continue à répondre aux écrits de M. le Chancelier.* N.p., 1772.

Bordeaux. See Parlement de Bordeaux.

Bouquet de Monseigneur (4 novembre). N.p., n.d. [1772]

Brancas, Louis Léon Félicité, Duke de, Count de Lauraguais. *Extrait du droit public de la France, par Louis Brancas, comte de Lauraguais. . . .* N.p., 1771.

[————]. *Tableau de la constitution françoise, ou Autorité des rois de France, dans les différens âges de la monarchie.* N.p., 1771.

C'est tout comme chez nous.—Sentence sur la cause du fiscal général, comme étant chargé d'une part, d'être accusateur contre le comte Jean-Frédéric Struensée d'une autre part (25 avril).—Sentence sur la cause (de la nation française) d'une part, accusateur contre (Ch.-Aug.-Nic.-René de Maupeou) d'une autre part (11 juin). N.p., n.d. [1772]

Cinquième suite des affaires du parlement depuis le 3 février jusqu'au 28 mars 1771. N.p., n.d.

[Clément de Boissy, Athanase Alexandre]. *Le Maire du palais.* N.p., 1771.

[————]. *Le Maire du palais.* See [Augeard, Jacques Mathieu], *Correspondance secrette . . . .*

[————(?)]. *Vues pacifiques sur l'état actuel du parlement.* N.p., n.d. [1771]

Copie de la lettre écrite à Mr. le duc d'Orléans par MM les officiers du bailliage de Beaujolois. A Villefranche, ce six mars 1771. N.p., n.d. [1771]

Cours des Aides de Paris. *Arrêt de la Cour des Aides. Du 22 mars 1771.* N.p., n.d. [1771]

————. *Remontrances, arrêts et décrets de la Cour des Aides de Paris . . . au sujet des vexations injustes exercées contre le sieur Guillaume Monnerat.* Paris, n.d. [1770]

————. *Remontrances de la Cour des Aides au Roi.* N.p., n.d. [1771]

————. *Remontrances de la Cour des Aides de Paris, arrêtées le 18 février 1771.* N.p., n.d.

————. *Remontrances de la Cour des Aides de Paris, délibérées dans le mois de janvier 1771. Touchant l'édit de règlement du mois de décembre 1770.* N.p., 1771.

————. *Très-humbles et trés-respectueuses remontrances de la Cour des Aides, arrêtées le 10 avril 1775.* N.p., n.d.

————. *Très-humbles et très-respectueuses remontrances de la Cour des Aydes de Paris sur l'édit de décembre 1770, et l'état actuel du parlement de Paris.* N.p., n.d. [1771]

————. *Très-humbles et très-respectueuses remontrances de la Cour des Aides au Roi, sur l'enlèvement de deux des magistrats du parlement de Bretagne mandés à Compiègne, fait dans la cour du château du Roi, au sortir de l'audience que Sa Majesté venait de leur donner.* N.p., n.d. [1770]

————. *Très-humbles et très-respectueuses remontrances que présentent au Roi notre très-honoré souverain et seigneur, les gens tenant sa Cour des Aides à Paris.* N.p., n.d. [1775]

Critique du palais moderne, par un docteur de Sorbonne. N.p., n.d. [1772]

Les Croniques de la Perse sous Mangogul, avec l'orrigine de la politique actuelle de cet empire. N.p., n.d. [1774]

Les Derniers soupirs du soi-disant parlement de Paris. . . . N.p., 1774.

Détail de la conduite tenue depuis la Saint-Martin 1771, par les avocats du Conseil Supérieur, et par le corps dont ils sont détachés. See *Lettre des habitants de Rouen au corps des avocats* . . . .

[Dorat, Claude Joseph]. *Epître à Thémis, suivie d'un dialogue de Pégase et de Clément, et d'une épître à M. de Champfort.* Amsterdam, n.d.

Les Efforts de la liberté et du patriotisme, contre le despotisme du Sr de Maupeou, chancelier de France, ou Recueil d'écrits patriotiques publiés pour maintenir l'ancien gouvernement françois. 6 vols. London, n.d. [1772–1775]

Les Efforts de la liberté et du patriotisme contre le despotisme du sieur Maupeou, ou Recueil des écrits patriotiques publiés pendant le règne du chancelier Maupeou, pour démontrer l'absurdité du despotisme qu'il voulait établir et pour maintenir dans toute sa splendeur la monarchie française. Ouvrage qui peut servir d'histoire du siècle de Louis XV pendant les années 1770–71–72–73–74. 6 vols. Paris, 1775

Les Efforts du patriotisme, ou Recueil complet des écrits publiés pendant le règne du chancelier Maupeou, pour démontrer l'absurdité du despotisme qu'il vouloit établir, et pour maintenir dans toute sa splendeur la monarchie françoise. Ouvrage qui peut servir à l'histoire du siècle de Louis XV, pendant les années 1770, 1771, 1772, 1773 et 1774. 2 vols. Paris, 1775.

Ego si ab improbis . . . republicam tenere viderem . . . non modo praemis . . . sed ne periculis quidem compulsus . . . ad eorum causam me adjungerem. . . . N.p., n.d. [1773]

L'Esprit de l'arrêt du conseil du 13 avril 1772, sur les liquidations d'offices. N.p., n.d.
   [1772]

*Etat des officiers qui composent le Châtelet de Paris, en exécution de l'édit du mois de mai
   1771.* N.p., n.d.

Les Etrennes supérieures de Normandie pour l'année bissextile 1772. . . . N.p. [Rouen],
   n.d.

*Extraits et arrêtés des parlemens de Paris, Bordeaux, Rouen, etc. sur les lettres patentes
   publiées à Versailles en lit de justice le 27 juin, concernant le duc d'Aiguillon et le
   nommé Audouard.* N.p., n.d.

Les Filets de Monseigneur de Maupeou. N.p., n.d. [1772]

Franches et loyales représentations de la noblesse au Roi. N.p., n.d. [1771]

[Guyot des Herbiers, Claude Antoine], *La Chancelière, ode.* See [Augeard, Jacques
   Mathieu], *Correspondance secrette.* . . .

*Haute messe, célébrée par l'abbé Perchel, conseiller-clerc du ci-devant soi-disant conseil su-
   périeur de Rouen.* N.p., n.d. [1774]

*Journal de ce qui s'est passé à l'occasion du rétablissement du parlement de Toulouse dans
   ses fonctions. Novembre 1774.* N.p., n.d. [1775]

*Journal historique de la révolution opérée dans la constitution de la monarchie françoise,
   par M. de Maupeou, chancelier de France.* Edited by Mathieu François Pidanzat
   de Mairobert. 7 vols. London, 1774–1776.

*Journal historique de la révolution opérée dans la constitution de la monarchie françoise,
   par M. de Maupeou, chancelier de France. Nouvelle édition, revue, corrigée et augmentée.* Edited by Mathieu François Pidanzat de Mairobert. 7 vols. London,
   1776.

*Justification du parlement, ou Observations sur le discours de M. le chancelier, au lit de
   justice du vendredi 7 décembre 1770.* N.p., n.d. [1771]

*Lettre à M ****. conseiller au parlement. Décembre 1774.* Paris, n.d. [1774]

*Lettre à M. D. T. maître des requêtes, par un homme d'honneur et de conscience, à qui
   l'on propose une place dans le nouveau parlement des intrus.* N.p., n.d. [1771]

Lettre à un ami de province sur la liquidation des offices. Paris, le 18 septembre 1771.
   N.p., n.d. [1771]

Lettre à un duc et pair. Utrecht, 1774.

*Lettre aux officiers de justice des provinces sur les dangers du projet de créer des conseils
   souverains dans le ressort du parlement de Paris.* N.p., n.d. [1771]

*Lettre d'un ancien magistrat à un duc et pair sur le discours de M. le chancelier au lit de
   justice du vendredi, 7 décembre 1770.* N.p., n.d. [1771]

*Lettre d'un avocat à un magistrat de ses amis sur le devoir des magistrats par rapport à
   leur secrétaires.* N.p., n.d. [1775]

*Lettre d'un bourgeois de Paris á un provincial, à l'occasion de l'édit de décembre 1771
   {1770}.* N.p., n.d. [1771]

{Deuxième} Lettre d'un bourgeois de Paris à un provincial, sur l'édit de décembre 1770, et ses suites funestes (13 mars 1771). N.p., n.d. [1771]

Lettre d'un François aux victimes d'Ebroïn. N.p., 1771.

Lettre d'un habitant de Rouen, à un de ses amis, qui est à la campagne. N.p., n.d. [1771]

*Lettre de M ***, conseiller au parlement, à M. le comte de ***. (11 février).* N.p., n.d. [1771]

Lettre de M. de Maupeou, chancelier de France, à M. de Miromesnil, garde des sceaux. Roncherolles, 1775.

Lettre des habitants de Rouen au corps des avocats, resté fidèle aux lois et à la province.— Détail de la conduite tenue depuis la Saint-Martin 1771, par les avocats du Conseil Supérieur, et par le corps dont ils sont détachés. N.p., n.d. [1772]

Lettre du sieur Sorhouet au sieur de Maupeou. Septembre 1774. Paris, 1774.

Lettre écrite au nom de la noblesse de France, à chacun des princes séparément. N.p., n.d. [1771]

Lettre ou perspective sur le retour des princes à la Cour. Décembre 1772. N.p., n.d. [1772]

Lettres sur la justice gratuite, ou Doléances d'un plaideur à la veille d'être ruiné par la justice gratuite: et Réponse consolante de son ami, qui sent tous les grands avantages que M. le chancelier nous fait. N.p., 1772.

La Ligue découverte, ou la Nation vengée, lettre d'un Quaker à F. M. A. de V. sur les affaires du temps et l'heureux avènement de Louis XVI au trône. Paris, 1774.

[Le Paige, Louis Adrien (?)]. *Principes de la législation françoise, prouvés par les monuments de l'histoire de cette nation, relatifs, aux affaires du temps.* N.p., 1771.

Malesherbes, Chrétien Guillaume de Lamoignon de. *Discours de M. de Lamoignon de Malesherbes, premier président de la Cour des Aides de Paris, à M. le comte d'Artois, lors du rétablissement de ladite cour dans ses fonctions. Du samedi 12 novembre 1774.—Du lundi 21 novembre 1774.—Discours de M. le premier président de la Cour des Aides au Roi. Du vingt-sept novembre 1774.—Discours à la Reine.* N.p., n.d. [1774]

Manifeste aux Bretons. N.p., 1772.

Manifeste aux Normands. N.p., n.d. [1771]

[Martin de Mariveaux, Jacques Claude]. *L'Ami des loix.* N.p., n.d. [Paris, 1775] 32p.; 8°.

Maupeou tyran sous le règne de Louis le Bien-Aimé. N.p., n.d. [1773]

Maupeouana, ou Recueil complet des écrits patriotiques publiés pendant le règne du chancelier Maupeou. Pour démontrer l'absurdité du despotisme qu'il vouloit établir, et pour maintenir dans toute sa splendeur la monarchie françoise. Ouvrage qui peut servir à l'histoire du siècle de Louis XV, pendant les années 1770, 1771, 1772, 1773, et 1774. 5 vols. Paris, 1775.

Mes Réflexions sur les idées d'un inamovible et compagnie, octobre 1774. Paris, n.d. [1774]

[Mey, Claude]. *Maximes du droit public françois, tirées des capitulaires, des ordonnances du royaume et des autres monumens de l'histoire de France.* 2 vols. N.p., 1772.

[Mey, Claude, *et al.*] *Maximes du droit public françois, tirées des capitulaires, des ordonnances du royaume et des autres monumens de l'histoire de France.* 2nd edition. 2 vols. Amsterdam, 1775.

[Morizot, Martin]. *Inauguration de Pharamond, ou Exposition des loix fondamentales de la monarchie françoise, avec les preuves de leur exécution, perpétuées sous les trois races de nos rois.* N.p., 1772.

Normandie. See Parlement de Normandie.

Nous y pensons; ou Réponse de MM. les avocats de Paris à l'auteur de l'avis: Pensez y bien. N.p., n.d. [1771]

Observations sur l'édit du mois de février 1771, *portant création de conseils supérieurs.* N.p., n.d. [1771]

Observations sur l'incompétence de Messieurs du Conseil, pour la vérification des lois. N.p., n.d. [1771]

Oraison funèbre de très-hauts et très-puissans seigneurs, en leur vivant, les gens tenants les conseils supérieurs de France, prononcée dans la grande salle de l'hôtel-de-ville de C***, le lundi 28 novembre 1774, *à l'occasion de l'enregistrement de l'édit portant rétablissement des parlemens, par M^e D*** avocat en la même ville.* N.p., 1774.

Ormesson de Noyseau, Louis François de Paule Lefèvre d'. *Lettre de M. d'Ormesson au Roi.* N.p., n.d. [1772]

Le Palais moderne. N.p., n.d. [1771]

Paris. See Cour des Aides De Paris.

Parlement de Besançon. *Arresté du parlement de Besançon, du 18 mars* 1771. N.p., n.d. [1771]

Parlement de Bordeaux. *Arrêté de la cour de parlement de Bordeaux. Du mardi 29 janvier* 1771. N.p., n.d. [1771]

Parlement de Normandie. *Arrêté du parlement séant à Rouen, sur l'état actuel du parlement séant à Paris. Du mardi 5 février* 1771. N.p., n.d. [1771]

——. *Lettre du parlement de Normandie au Roi, sur l'état actuel du parlement de Paris. Du 8 février* 1771. N.p., n.d. [1771]

——. *Lettre du parlement de Normandie au Roi, sur l'état actuel du parlement de Paris. Du 26 février* 1771. N.p., n.d. [1771]

——. *Très-humbles et très-respectueuses remontrances du parlement séant à Rouen, au Roi.* N.p., n.d. [Rouen, 1771]

Le Patriote parisien. N.p., n.d. [1774]

[Pidanzat de Mairobert, Mathieu François]. *Anecdotes sur M. la comtesse Du Barri.* London, 1775.

Plan d'une conversation entre un avocat et M. le chancelier. N.p., 1771.

Le Point de vue, ou Lettres de M. le prés. . . . à M. le duc de N. . . . N.p., n.d. [1772]

Principes avoués et défendus par nos pères. Institutions que nous sommes dans l'heureuse impuissance de changer. Lit de justice de 1770, et édit de février 1771. N.p., n.d. [1771]

Protestations des magistrats du parlement de Normandie, rassemblés en temps de vacance par lettre de chachet. N.p., n.d. [1771]

Protestations des Princes du Sang contre l'édit de décembre 1770, les lettres patentes du 23 janvier, l'édit de février 1771, et contre tout ce qui s'en est ensuivi ou pourrait s'ensuivre; signifiées et déposées au greffe du parlement, et lues en présence de MM. du Conseil siégeant au Palais, le 12 avril 1771. N.p., n.d. [Paris, 1771]

Quatrième suite des affaires du parlement. Depuis l'exil jusqu'au premier février 1771. N.p., n.d.

Question: Qui de Nivet ou du conseil supérieur fut plus fatal à la province. . . . N.p., n.d. [1772]

Récit de ce qui a précédé et suivi la rentrée du parlement de Bretagne. Rennes, n.d. [1774]

Récit de ce qui s'est passé à la Chambre des Comptes, Cour des Aydes, Cour de la Monnoye, et au Châtelet de Paris; contenant les arrêts, arrêtés et protestations contre les édits de décembre 1770, les lettres-patentes du 23 janvier, et l'édit de février 1771, et ce qui s'en est suivi, etc. N.p., n.d. [1771]

Récit de ce qui s'est passé à l'occasion du rétablissement du parlement de Toulouse dans ses fonctions, novembre 1774. N.p., n.d.

Récit de ce qui s'est passé au parlement de Besançon sur les édits et lettres patentes des mois de décembre 1770, et janvier et février 1771, et l'état actuel du parlement de Paris. N.p., n.d. [1771]

Récit de ce qui s'est passé au parlement de Dijon, au sujet des édits de décembre 1770, février 1771, et état actuel du parlement de Paris. N.p., n.d. [1771]

Récit de ce qui s'est passé au parlement de Provence, contenant les remontrances et l'arrêt de cette cour sur l'édit de décembre 1770, les lettres patentes du 23 janvier, l'édit de février 1771 et l'état actuel du parlementt de Paris. N.p., n.d. [1771]

Récit de ce qui s'est passé au parlement de Rennes sur les édits de décembre 1770, février 1771, les lettres patentes du 23 janvier, et l'état actuel du parlement de Paris. N.p., n.d. [1771]

Récit de ce qui s'est passé au parlement de Rouen sur l'édit de décembre 1770. Et la situation actuelle du parlement de Paris; contenant l'arrêté, les deux lettres au Roi, et les réponses des Princes du Sang, etc. N.p., n.d. [1771]

Récit de ce qui s'est passé au parlement de Toulouse, sur les édits de décembre 1770, lettres-patentes du 23 janvier 1771, et février même année, et la dispersion du parlement de Paris. N.p., n.d. [1771]

Récit de ce qui s'est passé au sujet de l'édit envoyé au parlement, le 27 novembre 1770.
N.p., n.d.

Récit exact de ce qui s'est passé au sujet du retour de M. le prince de Condé à la Cour.
N.p., n.d. [1772]

Réclamations des bailliages, sièges présidiaux, élections et cours-des-aydes de province, contre les édits de décembre 1770, janvier, février et avril 1771. N.p., n.d. [1771]

Recueil complet, exact et circonstancié de tout ce qui s'est passé au parlement de Paris, au sujet de l'édit portant règlement du mois de décembre 1770, lettres de jussion, lettres de cachet, arrêt du Conseil d'Etat, toutes les remontrances et arrêtés dudit parlement, avec les réponses du Roi, le tout date par date. N.p., n.d.

Recueil de divers arrêtés sur l'état actuel du parlement de Paris. N.p., n.d. [1771]

Recueil de pièces en forme de journal, touchant les affaires du parlement de Paris. N.p., n.d. [1771]

Recueil de toutes les pièces concernant les affaires du tems. N.p., 1771. Contains both pieces in support of the parlements and pieces in support of the Maupeou revolution.

Recueil des réclamations, remontrances, lettres, arrêts, arrêtés, protestations des parlemens, cours des aides, chambres des comptes, bailliages, présidiaux, élections au sujet de l'édit de décembre 1770, de l'érection des conseils supérieurs, de la suppression des parlemens, etc. . . . avec un abrégé historique des principaux faits relatifs à la suppression du parlement de Paris et de tous les parlemens du royaume. 2 vols. London, 1773.

Réflexions générales sur le système projetté par le Maire du Palais, pour changer la constitution de l'état. N.p., 1771.

Réflexions succinctes sur ce qui s'est passé au parlement de Paris depuis le mois de décembre 1770. N.p., n.d.

Réflexions sur ce qui s'est passé à Besançon le 5 et 6 août 1771. N.p., n.d.

Réflexions sur les affaires présentes. N.p., n.d. [1771]

Réponse au citoyen qui a publié ses réflexions. N.p., n.d. [1771]

Réponse aux trois articles de l'édit enregistré au lit de justice du 7 décembre 1770. N.p., n.d. [1771]

Réponse d'un François à un magistrat exilé, sur la liquidation des offices. N.p., n.d. [1771]

Représentations du bailliage de Langres, et lettre des officiers de celui de Villefranche, etc. N.p., n.d. [1771]

(Requête de la noblesse de Normandie, en octobre 1772, contre la suppression du parlement et des états de la province, commençant par ces mots:) Au Roi: Sire, la nécessité de la réclamation personnelle de vos nobles et fidèles sujets de Normandie. . . . N.p., n.d. [1772]

Rouen, Parlement de. See Parlement de Normandie.

[Saige, Guillaume]. *Catéchisme du citoyen, ou Elémens du droit public français, par demandes et par réponses.* Geneva [Bordeaux], 1775.

[————]. *Catéchisme du citoyen, ou Elémens du droit public français, par demandes et par réponses.* N.p., 1788.

Second recueil de divers arrêtés et lettres au Roi de différens parlemens du royaume sur l'état actuel du parlement de Paris. N.p., 1771.

Seconde suite des opérations du parlement depuis le 18 janvier 1771. jusqu'à l'exil total de cette compagnie. N.p., n.d.

Séguier, Antoine Louis. *Discours de Me Antoine-Louis Séguier, avocat-général, prononcé au lit de justice, tenu par le Roi au château de Versailles, le samedi treize avril 1771.* N.p., n.d. [1771]

Sentence sur la cause (de la nation française) d'une part, accusateur contre (Ch.-Aug.-Nic.-René de Maupeou) d'une autre part (11 juin). See *C'est tout comme chez nous.*

Sentence sur la cause du fiscal général, comme étant chargé d'une part, d'être accusateur contre le comte Jean-Frédéric Struensée d'une autre part (25 avril). See *C'est tout comme chez nous.*

Suite de réclamations des bailliages, sièges présidiaux, élections et cours des aydes de province, contre les édits de décembre 1770, janvier, février et avril 1771. N.p., n.d.

Suite des opérations du parlement. N.p., n.d.

Suplement aux Etrennes-Supérieurs de Normandie, pour servir de mémoire à M. le chancelier, sur son projet de métamorphose des Conseils de Rouen et Bayeaux en un parlement. Amsterdam, n.d. [1772]

Supplément à la Gazette de France, October 18, 1771–May 22, 1773.

Supplément à la Gazette de France, article de Normandie. N.p., n.d. [1771]

Tableau des monumens qui constatent l'origine du parlement de Bretagne, et qui démontrent l'impossibilité de la suppression. N.p., 1772.

Target, Guy Jean Baptiste. *Discours prononcés en la Grand'Chambre, par M. Target, avocat, le 28 novembre 1774, à la rentrée du parlement.* N.p., n.d. [1774]

[————]. *Lettre d'un homme à un autre homme, sur l'extinction de l'ancien parlement, et la création du nouveau.* N.p., n.d. [1771]

[————]. *Lettre d'un homme à un autre homme sur l'extinction de l'ancien parlement, et la création du nouveau.* See [Augeard, Jacques Mathieu], *Correspondance secrette. . . .*

[————]. *Lettres d'un homme à un autre homme sur les affaires du temps.* N.p., n.d. [1771]

[————]. *Réflexions sur la destitution de l'universalité des offices du parlement de Paris par voie de suppression.* N.p., n.d. [1771]

[Thévenot de Morande, Charles]. *Le Gazetier cuirassé, ou Anecdotes scandaleuses de la Cour de France.* N.p., 1771.

[————]. *Mélange confus sur des matières fort claires, par l'auteur du Gazetier cuirassé.* N.p., n.d.

[————]. *Le Philosophe cynique, pour servir de suite aux Anecdotes scandaleuses de la Cour de France.* N.p., n.d. [1771]

Titres de la province de Normandie, au Chartre des Normands. N.p., n.d. [1771]

Troisième recueil de diverses pièces de différens parlemens du royaume sur l'état actuel des affaires du parlement de Paris. N.p., 1771.

Troisième suite des affaires du parlement, contenant la lettre de MM. les présidens; la liste générale des exilés, et les lieux de leur exil. N.p., n.d.

PUBLICATIONS IN SUPPORT OF THE MAUPEOU REVOLUTION,
1771–1774

A l'auteur de la Correspondance entre M. le chancelier et M. de Sorhouet. N.p., n.d. [1771]

Ah! Les Grands Sots! ou Réflexions de F. M. A. D. V. [François Marie Arouet de Voltaire] *décrotteur, sur les affaires du temps.* N.p., n.d. [1771]

Apparition du cardinal Alberoni. N.p., n.d. [1771]

Arrest du conseil d'en haut contre les compagnies souveraines. Du 8 juillet 1661. Extrait des registres du Conseil d'Estat. N.p., 1771.

Arrêté des bons François contre la protestation faite sous le nom des Princes du Sang. N.p., n.d. [1771]

Au public abusé: Messieurs, entendons-nous. N.p., n.d. [1771]

Aventures du Colisée, et le dernier mot sur les affaires du temps. N.p., n.d. [1771]

Avis aux dames. N.p., n.d. [1771]

Les Bons Citoyens, ou Lettres des sénatographes, écrites par des gens respectables. Rouen, 1771.

[Bouquet, Pierre]. *Lettres provinciales, ou Examen impartiale de l'origine, de la constitution, et des révolutions de la monarchie françoise, par un avocat de province à un avocat de Paris.* The Hague, 1772.

[————]. *Tableau historique, généalogique et chronologique des trois cours souveraines de France.* The Hague, 1772.

Bouquet poissard, ou Dispute de deux marchandes de bouquets, sur les affaires présentes. N.p., 1771.

Le Code des François. Recueil de toutes les pièces intéressantes publiées en France, relativement aux troubles des parlemens, avec des observations critiques et historiques, des pièces nouvelles et une table raisonnée. 2 vols. Brussels, 1771.

Le Confiteor d'un ci-devant avocat, qui n'étoit pas du commun. N.p., n.d. [1771]

[Mary, Abbé (?)]. *Considérations sur l'édit de décembre 1770.* N.p., n.d. [1771]

Le De Profundis de la Cour des Aydes. N.p., n.d. [1771]

Délibération du Sénéchal de Toulouse, du lundi 27 mai 1771. N.p., n.d. [1771]

Des droits de la province de Bretagne, relativement à l'administration de la justice. N.p., n.d. [1771]

Dialogue entre un officier françois qui revient de Corse, et son neveu, ci-devant conseiller au parlement de Paris, exilé dans une petite ville. N.p., n.d.

Discours de M. le premier président de la Chambre des Communes du Caffé de Dubuisson, successeur de Procope, sur les affaires actuelles de l'état. . . . N.p., n.d. [1771]

Discours de M. Séguier, avocat général, prononcé au lit de justice du samedi 13 avril 1771. Nouvelle édition, revue et corrigée. N.p., n.d.

Entretien d'un ancien magistrat et d'un abbé, sur le discours de M. Séguier, au lit de justice du 13 avril 1771. N.p., n.d.

Entretien d'un militaire et d'un avocat sur les affaires présentes. N.p., n.d.

Examen analytique et raisonné d'un écrit qui a pour titre: Protestations des Princes du Sang. N.p., n.d. [1771]

Extrait d'une lettre en date de Londres, du 3 mai 1771. N.p., n.d. [1771] 8 p.; 8°. Erroneously attributed to Voltaire.

Extrait du livre intitulé: Angliae notitia, ou l'Etat présent de l'Angleterre, par Jean Chamberlayne; de la trente-cinquième édition. Londres, 1748. N.p., n.d.

Le Fin mot de l'affaire. N.p., n.d. [1771] 31 p.; 8°.

La Folie de bien des gens dans les affaires du temps. N.p., n.d. [1771] Erroneously attributed to Voltaire.

Idées d'un patriote. N.p., n.d. [1771]

Ils reviendront; ils ne reviendront pas; ou le Pour et le contre. N.p., n.d.

Itératives remontrances du Grenier à Sel de Paris, présentées par les juges du Grenier eux-mêmes. N.p., n.d.

[Lebrun, Charles François]. *Lettre de l'auteur des Observations sur les Protestations des Princes, à M. Dupaty, avocat général de Bordeaux.* N.p., n.d.

[————]. *Observations sur l'écrit intitulé: Protestations des Princes.* N.p., n.d. [1771]

[————]. *Remontrances d'un citoyen aux parlemens de France.* N.p., 1771.

Lettre à nosseigneurs du parlement de Paris. N.p., n.d.

Lettre d'un ancien magistrat de province à son fils, sur la Lettre d'un ancien magistrat à un duc et pair, au sujet de l'édit de décembre 1770. N.p., n.d.

Lettre d'un avocat de Paris, aux magistrats du parlement de Rouen, au sujet de l'arrêt de cette cour du 15 avril 1771. N.p., n.d. [1771]

Lettre d'un jurisconsulte français à un publiciste allemand, sur une question de droit public. London, 1771.

Lettre d'un officier du régiment de *** à Monsieur de ***, son frère, conseiller au parle-

ment de ***. See *No. XXIII. Pièces contenues dans la présente brochure.* . . .

Lettre de M. C.*** à M. de St****, à Rouen. Servant de réponse à la Lettre du parlement de Normandie au Roy, en date du 8 février, sur l'état actuel du parlement de Paris. N.p., n.d. [1771]

Lettre de M. D. L. V. avocat au parlement de Paris, à M . . . ci-devant président du même parlement. N.p., n.d. [1771]

Lettre de Saint Louis aux Princes du Sang. N.p., n.d.

Lettre écrite à M ***, président du parlement de Rouen, par un membre d'un présidial dans le ressort de ce parlement. N.p., n.d.

Lettre LXVᵉ du tome VII. de l'Espion turc, à son ami Binet Golon. N.p., n.d. [1771]

Lettres américaines sur les parlemens. 1770 et 1771. N.p., n.d. [1771]

Le Limonadier du Palais, Essai critique et raisonné d'un maître limonadier du Palais, sur les essences et les épices du ci-devant parlement, ouvrage utile à ceux qui étudient la médecine. N.p., n.d.

Mémoire sur le droit des pairs de France d'être jugés par leurs pairs. N.p., 1771.

Menippe ressuscité, ou l'Assemblée tumultueuse. A Veredicta, chez les frères hardis et sincères, au Repentir. 16000. N.p., n.d.

Monumens précieux de la sagesse et de la fermeté de nos rois, pour le maintien de leur autorité. N.p., 1771.

[Moreau, Jacob Nicolas]. *Leçons de morale, de politique et de droit public, puisées dans l'histoire de notre monarchie, ou Nouveau plan d'étude de l'histoire de France, rédigé par les ordres et d'après les vues de Monseigneur le Dauphin, pour l'instruction des princes ses enfants.* Versailles, 1773.

Le Mot d'un militaire: Prenez et lisez. N.p., n.d.

No. XXIII. Pièces contenues dans la présente brochure. L'Equivoque. . . . *Lettre d'un officier du régiment de *** à Monsieur de ***, son frère, conseiller au parlement de ***.* . . . N.p., n.d. [1771]

Nouveau catéchisme françois. N.p., n.d.

Nouvelles réflexions d'un citoyen sur l'édit de décembre 1770. N.p., n.d.

Observations d'un ancien magistrat. N.p., n.d. [1771]

Ode sur la rentrée du parlement de Paris. N.p., n.d.

L'Ombre secourable, ou l'Apparition salutaire à messieurs les avocats de Paris, sur l'édit de création des cent avocats. N.p., nd.

Pensez-y bien, ou Avis à MM. les avocats de Paris. N.p., n.d.

Preuves de la mauvaise conduite du parlement de Paris. N.p., n.d.

Protestations et arrêté des dames. Contre l'édit de 1770, le lit de justice du 13 avril 1771, et tout ce qui a précédé et suivi. N.p., n.d.

La Raison gagne. N.p., 1771.

Raisons pour désirer une réforme dans l'administration de la justice. N.p., n.d. [1771] 14 p,; 8°. Erroneously attributed to Voltaire.

Recherches sur les Etats Généraux. N.p., n.d.

Recueil de toutes les pièces concernant les affaires du tems. N.p., 1771. Contains both pieces in support of the Maupeou revolution and pieces in support of the parlements.

Réflexions d'un citoyen sur l'édit de décembre 1770. N.p., n.d.

Réflexions d'un vieux patriote sur les affaires présentes. N.p., n.d. [1771]

Réflexions nationales. N.p., n.d. [1771]

Réponse à la Lettre d'un magistrat à un duc et pair, sur le discours de M. le chancelier au lit de justice le 7 décembre 1770. N.p., n.d. [1771]

Réponse au citoyen qui a publié ses Réflexions. Seconde édition avec des observations. N.p., n.d. A reply to *Réponse au citoyen qui a publié ses Réflexions.*

Réponse au libelle intitulé: Le Parlement justifié. N.p., n.d. [1771]

Réponse de H. le Grand, aux remontrances des parlemens. N.p., n.d.

[Saint Pierre, de]. *Discours d'un pair de France à l'Assemblée des Pairs, sur l'édit de règlement de décembre 1770.* N.p., n.d.

Le Songe d'un jeune Parisien. N.p., n.d.

La Tête leur tourne. N.p., n.d. [1771]

Très-humbles et très-respectueuses remontrances de la communauté des clercs du Palais, dite la Bazoche, au Roi. N.p., n.d. [1771]

Très-humbles et très-respectueuses remontrances des écoliers de l'université de Paris, fille aînée du Roi. N.p., n.d.

[Villette, Charles, Marquis de]. *Le Coup de peigne du maître perruquier, ou Nouvel entretien du maître perruquier avec sa femme.* N.p., n.d.

[———]. *Lettre du maître perruquier à M. le procureur général, concernant les magistrats de Rouen et les dames de Paris. A Paris, le 29 avril 1771.* N.p., n.d. [1771]

[———]. *Réflexions d'un maître perruquier sur les affaires de l'état.* N.p., n.d.

[———]. *Le Soufflet du maître perruquier à sa femme.* N.p., n.d.

Visions et révélations d'un ci-devant magistrat. N.p., n.d.

[Voltaire, François Marie Arouet de]. *Avis important d'un gentilhomme à toute la noblesse du royaume.* N.p., n.d. [Geneva, 1771]

[———]. *L'Equivoque.* N.p., n.d. [Paris (?), 1771]

[———]. *L'Equivoque.* See *No. XXIII. Pièces contenues dans la présente brochure.*

. . .

[———]. *Fragment d'une lettre écrite de Genève 19 mars 1771, par un bourgeois de cette ville, à un bourgeois de L*** [Lyon]. Geneva, 1771.

[———]. *Lettre d'un jeune abbé.* N.p., n.d. [Geneva (?), 1771]

[———]. *Les Peuples aux parlements.* N.p., n.d. [Geneva (?), 1771]

[———]. *Les Peuples aux parlements. Seconde édition, corrigée et augmentée.* N.p., n.d. [Geneva (?), 1771]

[————]. *Réponse aux Remontrances de la Cour des Aides, par un membre des nouveaux conseils souverains.* N.p., n.d. [Geneva (?), 1771]

[————]. *Sentiments des six conseils établis par le Roi, et de tous les bons citoyens.* N.p., n.d. [Paris, 1771]

[————]. *Très-humbles et très-respectueuses remontrances du Grenier à Sel.* N.p., n.d. [Geneva, 1771]

OTHER PRIMARY SOURCES

[Abeille, Louis Paul]. *Principes sur la liberté du commerce des grains.* Amsterdam, 1768.

Albertas, Jean Baptiste, Marquis de. "'Journal de nouvelles' formé par le Marquis d'Albertas, premier président du parlement de Provence (1770–1783)." MS, Bibliothèque Nationale, N.A. 4386–4392.

Alembert, Jean Le Rond d'. *Corrrespondance inédite de d'Alembert avec Cramer, Lesage, Clairaut, Turgot, Castillon, Béguelin, etc.* Edited by Charles Henry. Rome, 1886.

————. *Oeuvres de d'Alembert.* 5 vols. Paris, 1821–1822.

[————]. *Sur la destruction des Jésuites, par un auteur désintéressé.* N.p., 1765.

Allonville, Armand François, Count de. *Mémoires secrets, de 1770 à 1830.* 6 vols. Paris, 1838–1845.

Almanach des muses. 1765–[1833]. 69 vols. Paris, 1766–1833.

Augeard, Jacques Mathieu. *Mémoires secrets de J.-M. Augeard, secrétaire des commandements de la reine Marie-Antoinette (1760 à 1800), documents inédits.* Edited by Evariste Bavoux. Paris, 1866.

Avertissement de l'Assemblée Générale du Clergé de France, tenue à Paris, par permission du Roi, en 1775, aux fidèles de ce royaume, sur les avantages de la religion chrétienne, et les effets pernicieux de l'incrédulité. Paris, 1775.

[Barbeu-Dubourg, Jacques]. *Petit code de la raison humaine: ou Exposition succincte de ce que la raison dicte à tous les hommes.* London, 1773.

[Baudeau, Nicholas]. *Avis au peuple sur l'impôt forcé qui se percevoit dans les halles et marchés sur tous les bleds et toutes les farines. . . .* N.p., 1774.

[————]. *Avis au peuple de Paris sur la Caisse de Poissi.* N.p., 1774.

————. "Chronique secrète de Paris sous le règne de Louis XVI." *Revue retrospective,* III (1834), 29–96, 262–96, 375–414.

[————]. *Lettres et mémoires à un magistrat du parlement de Paris, sur l'arrêt du conseil du 13 septembre 1774.* N.p., n.d.

[————]. *Lettres historiques sur l'état actuel de la Pologne et sur l'origine de ses malheurs.—Avis économiques aux citoyens éclairés de la république de Pologne sur la manière de percevoir le revenu public.* Amsterdam, 1772.

[————]. *Mémoire sur les corvées, servant de réplique à leurs apologistes*. N.p., 1775.

[————]. *Première introduction à la philosophie économique, ou Analyse des états policés. Par un disciple de l'Ami des Hommes*. Paris, 1771.

————. *Questions proposées par M. l'abbé Baudeau à Monsieur Richard Des Glanières sur son Plan d'impositions, soi-disant économiques*. N.p., n.d. [1774]

Beaumarchais, Pierre Augustin Caron de. *Mémoires de Beaumarchais dans l'affaire Goezman, 1773–1774*. N.p., 1974.

Beaurieu, Gaspard Guillard de. *L'Elève de la nature*. New edition. 3 vols. Amsterdam, 1771.

Besenval, Pierre Victor, Baron de. *Mémoires de M. le Baron de Besenval . . . écrits par lui-même, imprimés sur son manuscrit original . . . sur la Cour, les ministres, et les règnes de Louis XV et Louis XVI et sur les événements du temps, précédés d'une notice sur la vie de l'auteur*. 4 vols. Paris, 1805.

Bigot de Sainte Croix. *Essai sur la liberté du commerce et de l'industrie*. Edited by Nicolas Baudeau. Amsterdam, 1775.

Boesnier de L'Orme, Paul. *De l'esprit du gouvernement économique*. Paris, 1775.

[Boncerf, Pierre François]. *Les Inconvénients des droits féodaux*. N.p., n.d. [1776]

Catherine II, Empress of Russia. *Instruction de Sa Majesté Impériale Catherine II, pour la commission chargée de dresser le projet d'un nouveau code de loix*. Saint Petersburg, 1769.

[Cerfvol, Chevalier de (?)]. *Du Droit du souverain sur les biens fonds du clergé et des moines, et de l'usage qu'il peut faire de ces biens pour le bonheur des citoyens*. Naples, n.d. [Rouen, 1770]

Chansonnier historique du XVIIIᵉ siècle. (Recueil Clairambault-Maurepas). Edited by E. Raunié. 10 vols. Paris, 1879–1884.

Chastellux, François Jean, Marquis de. *De la félicité publique; ou Considérations sur le sort des hommes dans les différentes époques de l'histoire*. 2 vols. Amsterdam, 1772.

Choiseul-Stainville, Etienne François, Duke de. *Mémoires du duc de Choiseul, 1719–1785*. Edited by Fernand Calmettes. Paris, 1904.

[Clément, Jean Marie Bernard]. *Boileau à M. de Voltaire*. N.p., 1772.

————. *Première (—Neuvième) Lettre à Monsieur de Voltaire, où l'on examine sa politique littéraire, et l'influence qu'il a eu sur l'esprit, le goût et les moeurs de son siècle*. 3 vols. The Hague, 1773–1776.

Collé, Charles. *Journal historique ou Mémoires critiques et littéraires sur les ouvrages dramatiques et sur les événements les plus memorables depuis 1748 jusqu'en 1772 inclusivement*. 3 vols. Paris, 1807.

Condillac, Etienne Bonnot de. *Le Commerce et le gouvernement considérés relativement l'ún à l'autre. Ouvrage élémentaire par M. l'abbé de Condillac*. Amsterdam, 1776.

Condorcet, Marie Jean Antoine de Caritat, Marquis de. *Correspondance inédite de Condorcet et de Turgot, 1770–1779.* Edited by Charles Henry. Paris, 1883.

————. "Un Fragment inédit de Condorcet." Edited by Léon Cahen. *La Révolution française,* XLII (1902), 115–31.

[————]. *L'Influence de la révolution de l'Amérique sur les opinions et la législation de l'Europe.* Amsterdam, 1786.

[————]. "L'Influence de la révolution de l'Amérique sur les opinions et la législation de l'Europe." In Filippo Mazzei. *Recherches historiques et politiques sur les Etats-Unis de l'Amérique septentrionale.* Colle [Paris], 1788, IV, 237–83.

[————]. *Lettre d'un théologien à l'auteur du "Dictionnaire des trois siècles."* Berlin, 1774.

————. "Une Lettre de Condorcet à Diderot sur le parlement." *Révolution française, Revue d'histoire moderne et contemporaine,* LXV (1913), 365–66.

[————]. *Lettres sur le commerce des grains.* Paris, 1774.

————. *Oeuvres.* Edited by A. Condorcet O'Connor and F. Arago. 12 vols. Paris, 1847–1849.

————. *Vie de Turgot.* London, 1786.

[Coquereau, Jean Baptiste Louis]. *Mémoires de l'abbé Terrai, contrôleur général des finances, avec une relation de l'émeute arrivée à Paris en 1775, et suivis de quatorze lettres d'un actionnaire de la Compagnie des Indes.* London, 1776.

Correspondance littéraire, philosophique, et critique, par Grimm, Diderot, Raynal, Meister, etc. Edited by Maurice Tourneux. 16 vols. Paris, 1877–1882.

Cour des Aides de Paris. *Mémoires pour servir à l'histoire du droit public de la France en matières d'impôts, ou Recueil de ce qui s'est passé de plus intéressant à la Cour des Aides, depuis 1756 jusqu'au mois de juin 1775; avec une table générale des matières.* Brussels, 1779.

Croÿ, Emmanuel, Duke de. *Journal inédit du duc de Croÿ, publié d'après le manuscrit autographe conservé à la bibliothèque de l'Institut.* Edited by the Vicomte de Grouchy and Paul Cottin. 4 vols. Paris, 1906–1907.

[Delisle de Sales, Jean Claude Izouarde, called]. *Paradoxes par un citoyen.* Amsterdam, 1772.

Delolme, Jean Louis. *Constitution de l'Angleterre.* Amsterdam, 1771.

[Des Glanières, Richard]. *Plan d'imposition économique et d'administration des finances, présenté à Monseigneur Turgot, ministre et contrôleur général des finances.* Paris, 1774.

Les Devoirs de l'homme, ou Abrégé de la science du salut, et de celle de l'économie politique. Par un curé du diocèse de Soissons. Paris, 1771.

Dickinson, John. *Lettres d'un fermier de Pensylvanie, aux habitans de l'Amérique septentrionale.* Translated by Jacques Barbeu-Dubourg. Amsterdam, 1769.

Diderot, Denis. *Correspondance.* Edited by Georges Roth. 16 vols. Paris. 1955–1970.

————. *Diderot et Catherine II.* Edited by Maurice Tourneux. Paris, 1899.

————. *Lettres à Sophie Volland.* Edited by André Babelon. 3 vols. Paris, 1930.

————. *Mémoires pour Catherine II.* Edited by Paul Vernière. Paris, 1966.

————. *Observations sur l'Instruction de Sa Majesté Impériale aux députés pour la confection des lois.* Edited by Paul Ledieu. Paris, 1921.

————. *Oeuvres complètes.* Edited by J. Assézat and M. Tourneux. 20 vols. Paris, 1875–1877.

————. *Oeuvres philosophiques.* Edited by Paul Vernière. Paris, 1956.

————. *Oeuvres politiques.* Edited by Paul Vernière. Paris, 1963.

————. *Oeuvres romanesques.* Edited by Henri Bénac. Paris, 1951.

————. "Rêveries à l'occasion de la révolution de Suède." In Herbert Dieckmann, "Diderot, Grimm et Raynal: Les Contributions de Diderot à la 'Correspondance littéraire' et à l''Histoire des deux Indes.'" *Revue d'histoire littéraire de la France.* LI (1951), 417–40.

[Du Buat-Nançay, Louis Gabriel, Count]. *Eléments de la politique, ou Recherches des vrais principes de l'économie sociale.* 6 vols. London, 1773.

[————]. *Les Maximes du gouvernement monarchique, pour servir de suite aux "Eléments de la politique" par le même auteur.* 4 vols. London, 1778.

[————]. *Les Origines, ou l'Ancien gouvernement de la France, de l'Allemagne et de l'Italie: Ouvrage historique, où l'on voit, dans leur origine, la royauté et ses attributs, la nation et ses différentes classes, les fiefs et le vasselage. . . . .* 4 vols. The Hague, 1757.

Du Deffand, Marie Anne de Vichy-Chamrond, Marquise. *Correspondance complète de Mme Du Deffand avec la duchesse de Choiseul, l'abbé Barthélemy et M. Craufort. . . .* New edition. 3 vols. Paris, 1866–1877.

————. *Lettres de la marquise Du Deffand à Horace Walpole (1766–1780).* Edited by Mrs. Paget Toynbee. London, 1912.

Du Pont de Nemours, Pierre Samuel. *Carls Friedrichs von Badens brieflicher Verkehr mit Mirabeau und Du Pont.* Edited by Carl Knies. 2 vols. Heidelberg, 1892.

————. *De l'origine et des progrès d'une science nouvelle.* London, 1768.

————. *Mémoires sur la vie et les ouvrages de M. Turgot.* Philadelphia, 1782.

————. *Table raisonnée des principes de l'économie politique.* Carlsruhe, 1773.

Encyclopédie, ou Dictionnaire raisonné des sciences, des arts et des métiers, par une société de gens de lettres. Mis en ordre et publié par M. Diderot . . . et quant à la partie mathématique par M. d'Alembert. Paris, 1751–1765.

Ephémérides du citoyen ou Bibliothèque raisonnée des sciences morales et politiques, 1767–1771, 1776.

Epinay, Louise F. P. Tardieu d'Esclavelles, Marquise d'. *Mémoires et correspondance.* . . . 3 vols. Paris, 1818.

———. *La Signora d'Epinay et l'abate Galiani: Lettere inedite,* 1769–1772. Edited by F. Nicolini. Bari, 1929.

Essuile, Jean François Barandiéry Montmayeur, Count de. *Traité politique et économique des communes, ou Observations sur l'agriculture, sur l'origine, la destination et l'état actuel des biens communs.* Paris, 1770.

La Ferme de Pensilvanie. Les Avantages de la vertu. Plan d'instruction pour le peuple; avec quelques observations sur la liberté du commerce des grains. Philadelphia [Paris], 1775.

Friedrich II, King of Prussia. *Examen de l'essai sur les préjugés.* London, 1770.

———. *Oeuvres.* 31 vols. Berlin, 1846–1857.

———. *Oeuvres posthumes de Frédéric II, Roi de Prusse.* 2nd ed. 15 vols. Berlin, 1788.

Galiani, Ferdinando. *L'Abbé Galiani. Sa Correspondance avec Madame d'Epinay, Madame Necker, Madame Geoffrin, etc.* . . . Edited by Lucien Perey and Gaston Maugras. 2 vols. Paris, 1881.

———. *L'Abbé Galiani. Sa Correspondance.* . . . Edited by Lucien Perey and Gaston Maugras. 3rd ed. Paris, 1890.

———. *Dialogues sur le commerce des blés.* London, 1770.

———. *Lettres de l'abbé Galiani à Madame d'Epinay.* Edited by E. Asse. Paris, 1882.

———. *La Signora d'Epinay et l'abate Galiani: Lettere inedite (1769–1772).* Edited by F. Nicolini. Bari, 1929.

Gazette d'agriculture, commerce, arts et finances, 1774.

Gazette de Cologne, 1773.

Geffroy, Auguste, ed. *Gustave III et la Cour de France.* 2nd ed. 2 vols. Paris, 1867.

———, ed. *Notices et extraits des manuscrits concernant l'histoire ou la littérature de la France qui sont conservés dans les bibliothèques ou archives de Suède, Danemark, et Norvège.* Paris, 1855.

Georgel, Jean François. *Mémoires pour servir à l'histoire des événements de la fin du XVIIIᵉ siècle.* 2nd ed. 6 vols. Paris, 1820.

Gleichen, Carl Heinrich, Baron von. *Souvenirs de Charles-Henri, baron de Gleichen, précédés d'une notice par M. Paul Grimblot.* Paris, 1868.

[Götzman, Louis Valentin de] *Analyse de l'ouvrage ayant pour titre: Questions de droit public sur une matière très intéressante, avec pièces justificatives.* Amsterdam, 1770.

[———]. *Essais historiques sur le sacre et couronnement des rois de France, les minorités et les régences, précédés d'un discours sur la succession à la couronne.* . . . Paris, 1775.

[————]. *La Jurisprudence du Grand Conseil examiné dans les maximes du royaume, ouvrage précieux contenant l'histoire de l'Inquisition en France. . . .* 2 vols. Avignon, 1775.

[————]. *Questions de droit public sur une matière très intéressante.* Amsterdam, 1770.

[Guibert, Jacques Antoine Hippolyte, Count de]. *Essai général de tactique, précédé d'un discours sur l'état actuel de la politique et de la science militaire en Europe, avec le plan d'un ouvrage intitulé: La France politique et militaire.* London, 1772.

Hardy, Siméon Prosper. "Journal." MS, Bibliothèque Nationale, 13733.

————. *"Mes Loisirs," Journal d'événements tels qu'ils parviennent à ma connaissance, 1764–1789. . . .* Edited by Maurice Tourneux and Maurice Vitrac. Paris, 1912.

Helvétius, Claude Adrien. *Le Bonheur, poème, en six chants. Avec des fragments de quelques épîtres. Ouvrages posthumes de M. Helvétius.* Preface by Jean François de Saint Lambert. London, 1772.

————. *De l'homme, de ses facultés intellectuelles, et de son éducation, ouvrage posthume de M. Helvétius. . . .* 2 vols. London, 1773.

[Holbach, Paul Henri Dietrich, Baron d']. *Le Bon Sens, ou les Idées naturelles opposées aux idées surnaturelles.* London, 1772.

[————]. *Ethocratie, ou le Gouvernement fondé sur la morale.* Amsterdam, 1776.

[————]. *La Morale universelle, ou les Devoirs de l'homme fondés sur la nature.* 3 vols. Amsterdam, 1776.

[————]. *La Politique naturelle, ou Discours sur les vrais principes du gouvernement. Par un ancien magistrat.* 2 vols. London [Amsterdam], 1773.

[————]. *Système de la nature, ou Des lois du monde physique et du monde moral. Par M. Mirabaud.* 2 vols. London, 1770.

[————]. *Système social. Ou Principes naturels de la morale et de la politique. Avec un examen de l'influence du gouvernement sur les moeurs. . . .* London [Amsterdam], 1773.

Holland, Georg Jonathan von. *Réflexions philosophiques sur le "Système de la nature."* London, 1773.

Journal d'agriculture, du commerce et des finances, 1771, 1774.

Journal de politique et de littérature, Brussels, 1774.

Journal politique, ou Gazette des gazettes, 1773.

Laharpe, Jean François de. *Correspondance littéraire, adressée à Son Altesse Impériale Mgr. le Grand Duc, aujourd'hui Empereur de Russie . . . Depuis 1774 jusqu'à 1789.* 6 vols. Paris, 1801–1807.

————. *Eloge de François de Salignac de La Motte-Fénelon . . . Discours qui a remporté le prix de l'Académie Françoise en 1771, par M. de La Harpe.* Paris, 1771.

Lanjuinais, Joseph. *Le Monarque accompli, ou Prodiges de bonté, de savoir et de sagesse*

*qui font l'éloge de Sa Majesté Impériale Joseph II, et qui rendent cet auguste mo-
narque si précieux à l'humanité, discutés au tribunal de la raison et de l'équité, par
Mr. de Lanjuinais, Principal du Collège de Moudon.* . . . 3 vols. Lausanne, 1774.

Le Blanc de Guillet, Antoine Blanc, called. *Les Druides, tragédie. Représentée pour
la première fois sur le Théâtre Français le 7 mars 1772.* Saint Petersburg, 1783.

Lebrun, Charles François. *Opinions, rapports, et choix d'écrits politiques.* . . . Paris,
1829.

[Le Paige, Louis Adrien]. *Lettres historiques sur les fonctions essentielles du Parlement,
sur le droit des pairs, et sur les loix fondamentales du royaume.* 2 vols. Amsterdam, 1753–1754.

[Le Roy, Charles Georges]. *Réflexions sur la jalousie, pour servir de commentaire aux
derniers ouvrages de M. de Voltaire.* Amsterdam, 1772.

[Le Seure]. *Testament politique de M. de Silhouette.* N.p., 1772.

Lespinasse, Julie Jeanne Eléonore de. *Correspondance entre Mlle. de Lespinasse et le
comte de Guibert.* Edited by the Count de Villeneuve-Guibert. Paris, 1906.

————. *Lettres.* . . . Edited by Eugène Asse. Paris, 1876.

————. *Lettres inédites . . . à Condorcet, à d'Alembert, à Guibert, au comte de Cril-
lon.* . . . Edited by Charles Henry. Paris, 1887.

Le Trosne, Guillaume François. *De l'intérêt social par rapport à la valeur, à la circulation, à l'industrie et au commerce intérieur et extérieur.* Paris, 1777.

————. *De l'ordre social, ouvrage suivi d'un traité élémentaire sur la valeur, l'argent,
la circulation, l'industrie et le commerce intérieur et extérieur.* Paris, 1777.

*Lettre d'un gentilhomme du diocèse d'Apt à M. ****.* N.p., n.d. [1773]

"Lettres de M. R** à M. M**, concernant ce qui s'est passé d'intéressant à la
Cour, depuis la maladie et la mort de Louis XV, jusqu'au rétablissement du
parlement de Paris." *Mélanges publiés par la Société des Bibliophiles Français.*
Paris, 1826. Vol. IV, Pt. 3, pp. 1–135.

Lévis, Gaston Pierre Marc, Duke de. *Souvenirs et portraits, 1780–1789.* Nouvelle
édition. Paris, 1815.

Liger, René. *Lettres critiques et dissertation sur le prêt de commerce, par M. Liger, prêtre,
licencié ès loix.* Caen, 1774.

[Linguet, Simon Nicolas Henri]. *La Cacomonade: Histoire politique et morale, traduite de l'allemand du docteur Pangloss, par le docteur lui-même depuis son retour de
Constantinople.* Cologne, 1766.

————. *Canaux navigables, ou Développement des avantages qui résulteraient de l'exécution de plusieurs projets en ce genre pour la Picardie, l'Artois, la Bourgogne, la
Champagne, la Bretagne, et toute la France en général. Avec l'examen de quelques-
unes des raisons qui s'y opposent, etc.* Amsterdam, 1769.

[————]. *Considérations politiques et philosophiques sur les affaires présentes du nord
et particulièrement sur celles de Pologne.* London, 1773.

————. *Dissertation sur le bled et le pain, par M. Linguet, avec la réfutation de M. Tissot, D.M.* Neuchâtel, 1779.

————. *Du pain et du bled.* London, 1774.

————. *Du plus heureux gouvernement, ou Parallèle des constitutions politiques de l'Asie avec celles de l'Europe; servant d'introduction à la "Théorie des loix civiles."* 2 vols. London, 1774.

[————]. *Essai philosophique sur le monachisme, par Mr. L.* Paris, 1775.

[————]. *Le Fanatisme des philosophes.* London, 1764.

[————]. *Lettre à l'auteur des "Observations sur le commerce des grains."* Amsterdam, 1775.

————. "Lettre de M. Linguet [à l'abbé Roubaud]." *Journal de politique et de littérature,* November 15, December 5 and 15, 1774.

[————]. *Lettres sur la "Théorie des loix civiles, etc." Où l'on examine, entr'autres choses, s'il est bien vrai que les Anglois soient libres, et que les François doivent, ou imiter leurs opérations, ou porter envie à leur gouvernement.* . . . Amsterdam, 1770.

————. *Observations sur l'imprimé intitulé, "Réponse des Etats de Bretagne au Mémoire du duc d'Aiguillon."* Paris, 1771.

————. *Réponse aux docteurs modernes, ou Apologie pour l'auteur de la "Théorie des loix" et des "Lettres sur cette théorie." Avec la réfutation du système des philosophes économistes par Simon-Nicolas-Henri Linguet.* 2 vols. N.p., 1771.

[————]. *Théorie des loix civiles, ou Principes fondamentaux de la société.* . . . 2 vols. London, 1767.

————. *Théorie des lois civiles.* Rev. ed. 3 vols. London, 1774.

[————]. *Théorie du libelle, ou l'Art de calomnier avec fruit. Dialogue philosophique, pour servir de supplément à la "Théorie du paradoxe."* Amsterdam [Paris], 1775.

Longchamp, Sébastien G., and Jean Louis Wagnière. *Mémoires sur Voltaire et sur ses ouvrages par Longchamp et Wagnière, ses secrétaires.* 2 vols. Paris, 1826.

Mably, Gabriel Bonnot de. *Collection complète des oeuvres.* 15 vols. Paris, An III.

————. *De la législation, ou Principes des lois.* 2 vols. Amsterdam [Paris], 1776.

————. *Du gouvernement et des loix de Pologne.* London, 1781.

————. *Observations sur l'histoire de France.* 2 vols. Geneva, 1765.

————. *Observations sur l'histoire de France . . . Nouvelle édition, continuée jusqu'au règne de Louis XIV et précédée de l'Eloge historique de l'auteur par l'abbé Brizard.* 3 vols. Kehl, 1788.

[Mably, Gabriel Bonnot de (?), and Count Michel Wielhorski (?)]. *Manifeste de la république confédérée de Pologne, du 15 novembre 1769. Traduit du polonais.* N.p. [Paris], 1771.

Marie Antoinette. *Correspondance secrète entre Marie Thérèse et le comte de Mercy-Argenteau, avec les lettres de Marie Thérèse et de Marie Antoinette.* Edited by Alfred d'Arneth and M. A. Geffroy. 2nd ed. 3 vols. Paris, 1875.

Marin, François Louis Claude. "Gazette à la main, de Marin, 1768–1772." MS, Bibliothèque de la Ville de Paris.

————. Letters. MS, Bibliothèque Nationale, Fr. 12901.

Marmontel, Jean François. *Lettre de M. de Marmontel à M. *** sur la cérémonie du sacre de Louis XVI. Reims, le 11 juin 1775.* N.p., n.d.

————. *Mémoires.* Edited by Maurice Tourneux. 3 vols. Paris, 1891.

Massillon, Jean Baptiste. *Sermons de M. Massillon. . . .* Paris, 1768.

Maupeou, René Nicolas Charles Augustin de. "Compte rendu de son administration (1768–1774)." MS, Bibliothèque Nationale, 6570–6572.

————. Letters. MS, Bibliothèque National, Fr. 12901.

Maurepas, Jean Frédéric Phélypeaux, Count de. *Mémoires du comte de Maurepas.* 3rd ed. Paris, 1792.

Maury, Jean Siffrein, Cardinal. *Eloge de François de Salignac de La Motte-Fénelon. Discours qui a obtenu l'accessit.* Paris, 1771.

Mémoires authentiques de madame la comtesse Du Barri, maîtresse de Louis XV, Roi de France. Extraits d'un manuscrit que possède madame la duchesse de Villeroy. Par le chevalier Fr. N. Traduits de l'anglois. London, 1775.

Mémoires secrets pour servir à l'histoire de la république des lettres en France, depuis 1762 jusqu'à nos jours. Edited by Louis Petit de Bachaumont *et al.* 36 vols. London, 1777–1789.

[Mercier, Louis Sébastien]. *L'An deux mille quatre cent quarante. Rêve s'il en fût jamais.* London, 1771.

————. *L'An deux mille quatre cent quarante. Rêve s'il en fût jamais.* N.p., 1787.

[————]. *Jean Hennuyer, évêque de Lisieux, drame en trois actes.* London, 1772.

Mercier de La Rivière, Pierre François Joachim Henri. *De l'instruction publique, ou Considérations morales et politiques sur la nécessité, la nature et la source de cette instruction, ouvrage demandé pour le Roi de Suède.* Stockholm, 1775.

————. *L'Intérêt général de l'état, ou la Liberté du commerce des blés démontrée conforme au droit naturel, au droit public de la France, aux lois fondamentales du royaume, à l'intérêt commun du souverain et de ses sujets dans tous les temps, avec la réfutation d'un nouveau système publié en forme de Dialogues sur le commerce des blés.* Amsterdam, 1770.

[Métra, François, ed.]. *Correspondance secrète, politique et littéraire, ou Mémoires pour servir à l'histoire des cours, des sociétés et de la littérature en France depuis la mort de Louis XV.* 18 vols. London, 1787–1790.

Mirabeau, Honoré Gabriel Riqueti, Count de. *Considérations sur l'Ordre de Cincinnatus, ou Imitation d'un pamphlet anglo-américain.* London, 1784.

[————]. *Essai sur le despotisme.* London [Neuchâtel], 1775.

Mirabeau, Victor Riqueti, Marquis de. *L'Ami des hommes, ou Traité de la population.* 6 vols. Avignon, 1756–1758.

————. *Carls Friedrichs von Badens brieflicher Verkehr mit Mirabeau und Du Pont.* Edited by Carl Knies. 2 vols. Heidelberg, 1892.

[————]. *Les Economiques, par L. D. H.* Amsterdam, 1769.

[————]. *Leçons oeconomiques, par L. D. H.* Amsterdam, 1770.

[————]. *Lettres sur la législation; ou l'Ordre légal, dépravé, rétabli et perpétué. Par L. D. H.* 3 vols. Berne, 1775.

[————]. *La Science, ou les Droits et les devoirs de l'homme, par L. D. H. . . . augmenté d'un Dialogue entre Mrs de P. et L. D. H.* Lausanne, 1774.

————. *Supplément à la théorie de l'impôt.* The Hague, 1776.

Miromesnil, Armand Thomas Hue de. *Correspondance politique et administrative.* Edited by P. Le Verdier. 5 vols. Rouen, 1899–1903.

————. "Lettres sur l'état de la magistrature en l'année 1772." MS, Bibliothèque Nationale, F.F. 10986.

Montesquieu, Charles Louis de Secondat, Baron de La Brède et de. *Oeuvres complètes.* Edited by André Masson. 3 vols. Paris, 1950–1955.

Moreau, Jacob Nicolas. *Mes souvenirs.* 2 vols. Paris, 1898–1901.

————. *Principes de morale, de politique et de droit public, puisés dans l'histoire de notre monarchie, ou Discours sur l'histoire de France, dédiés au Roi.* 21 vols. Paris, 1777–1789.

Morellet, André. *Lettres à Lord Shelburne . . . 1772–1803.* Edited by Lord E. Fitzmaurice. Paris, 1898.

————. *Mémoires inédites de l'abbé Morellet de l'Académie Française, sur le dix-huitième siècle et sur la Révolution.* 2 vols. Paris, 1821.

[————]. *Réflexions sur les avantages de la liberté d'écrire et d'imprimer sur les matières de l'administration, écrites en 1764 à l'occasion de la déclaration du Roi du 28 mars de la même année, qui fait défense d'imprimer, débiter aucuns écrits, ouvrages, ou projets concernant la réforme ou administration des finances, etc. Par M. L'A. M.* London, 1775.

[————]. *Réfutation de l'ouvrage qui a pour titre "Dialogues sur le commerce des bleds."* London, 1770.

[————]. *Réponse sérieuse à M. L** par l'auteur de la "Théorie du paradoxe."* Amsterdam [Paris], 1775.

[————]. *Théorie du paradoxe.* Amsterdam [Paris], 1775.

[Morizot, Martin]. *Le Sacre royal, ou les Droits de la nation françoise, reconnus et confirmés par cette cérémonie.* 2 vols. Amsterdam, 1776 [1775].

Necker, Jacques. *Eloge de Jean-Baptiste Colbert, discours qui a remporté le prix de l'Académie Françoise, en 1773.* Paris, 1773.

————. *Sur la législation et le commerce des grains.* 2 vols. Paris, 1775.

Nouvelles Ephémérides économiques, ou Bibliothèque raisonnée de l' histoire, de la morale et de la politique, Paris, 1774–1776.

Procès-Verbal de l'Assemblée Générale du Clergé. Paris, 1772.

Procès-Verbal de l'Assemblée-Générale extraordinaire du Clergé de France, tenue à Paris, au Couvent des Grands-Augustins. Monsieur l'abbé Du Lau, Agent-Général, Secrétaire de l'Assemblée, et nommé à l'Archevêché d'Arles. Paris, 1775.

Raynal, Guillaume Thomas François. *Histoire philosophique et politique des établissemens et du commerce des Européens dans les deux Indes.* 6 vols. Amsterdam, 1770 [1772].

————. *Histoire philosophique et politique des établissemens et du commerce des Européens dans les deux Indes.* 7 vols. The Hague, 1774.

————. *Histoire philosophique et politique des établissements et du commerce des Européens dans les deux Indes.* 10 vols. Geneva, 1781.

Récit abrégé de ce qui a précédé et suivi le lit de justice. N.p., n.d. [1774]

Recueil général des anciennes lois françaises depuis l'an 420 jusqu'à la révolution de 1789. Edited by François André Isambert *et al.* 29 vols. Paris, 1821–1833.

Regnaud, Pierre Etienne. "Histoire des événemens arrivés en France depuis le mois de septembre 1770 concernans les parlemens et les changemens dans l'administration de la justice et dans les loix du royaume." MS, Bibliothèque Nationale, F.F. 13733–13735.

Les Remontrances du parlement de Paris au 18ᵉ siècle. Edited by Jules Flammermont. 3 vols. Paris, 1888–1898.

Robertson, William. *L'Histoire du règne de l'Empereur Charles-Quint, précédée d'un tableau des progrès de la société en Europe . . . par M. Robertson . . . ouvrage traduit de l'anglois.* 6 vols. Amsterdam, 1771.

Rothney, John, ed. *The Brittany Affaire and the Crisis of the Ancien Regime.* New York, 1969.

Roubaud, Pierre Joseph André. *Histoire générale de l'Asie, de l'Afrique et de l'Amérique.* 15 vols. Paris, 1770–1775.

[————]. *Recréations économiques, ou Lettres de l'auteur des "Représentations aux magistrats." A M. le chevalier Zanobi, principal interlocuteur des "Dialogues sur le commerce des blés."* Amsterdam, 1770.

[————]. *Représentations aux magistrats, contenant l'exposition raisonnée des faits relatifs à la liberté du commerce des grains, et les résultats respectifs des règlemens et de la liberté.* N.p., 1769.

[Rouillé d'Orfeuil, Augustin]. *L'Alambic des loix, ou Observations de l'Ami des François sur l'homme et sur les loix.* Hispaan, 1773.

[————]. *L'Alambic moral, ou Analyse raisonnée de tout ce qui a rapport à l'homme. Par l'Ami des François.* Maroc, 1773.

[————]. *L'Ami des François.* Constantinople, 1771.

Rousseau, Jean Jacques. *Correspondance générale de J.-J. Rousseau.* Edited by Théophile Dufour [and Pierre Paul Plan]. 20 vols. Paris, 1924–1934.

———. *Oeuvres complètes.* Pléiade edition. Edited by Bernard Gagnebin and Marcel Raymond. 4 vols. Paris, 1959–1969.

———. *The Political Writings of Jean Jacques Rousseau.* Edited by C. E. Vaughan. 2 vols. Cambridge, England, 1915.

Ségur, Louis Philippe, Count de. *Mémoires, souvenirs, et anecdotes.* 3 vols. Paris, 1827.

Soulavie, Jean Louis Giraud. *Mémoires historiques et politiques du règne de Louis XVI depuis son mariage jusqu'à sa mort.* 6 vols. Paris, 1801.

Thomas, Antoine Léonard. *Eloge de Marc-Aurèle.* Amsterdam, 1775.

Turgot, Anne Robert Jacques, Baron de L'Aulne. *Correspondance inédite de Condorcet et de Turgot, 1770–1779.* Edited by Charles Henry. Paris, 1883.

———. *Oeuvres de Turgot.* Edited by Eugène Daire. 2 vols. Paris, 1844.

———. *Oeuvres de Turgot et documents le concernant.* Edited by Gustave Schelle. 5 vols. Paris, 1913–1923.

Véri, Joseph Alphonse de. *Journal de l'abbé de Véri.* Edited by the Baron Jehan de Witte. 2 vols. Paris, 1928–1930.

[Voltaire, François Marie Arouet de]. *Au Roi en son conseil. Pour les sujets du Roi qui réclament la liberté de la France. Contre des moines Bénédictins devenus chanoines de Saint Claude en Franche-Comté.* N.p., n.d. [Geneva, 1770]

[———]. *Collection des mémoires présentés au Conseil du Roi par les habitants du Mont-Jura et le chapitre de S. Claude, avec l'arrêt rendu par ce tribunal.* N.p., 1772.

———. *Voltaire's Correspondence.* Edited by Theodore Besterman. 107 vols. Geneva, 1953–1965.

[———]. *Epître à Henri IV sur l'avènement de Louis XVI.* Paris, 1774.

[———]. *Histoire du parlement de Paris par Mr. l'abbé Big.* 2 vols. Amsterdam, 1769.

[———]. *Lettre d'un ecclésiastique sur le prétendu rétablissement des Jésuites dans Paris, 20 mars, 1774.* N.p., n.d. [Geneva, 1774]

———. *Les Lois de Minos, ou Astérie, tragédie en cinq actes, par M. de Voltaire. Prix 30 sols.* Geneva, 1773.

[———]. *Les Loix de Minos, tragédie. Avec les notes de Morza, et plusieurs pièces curieuses détachées.* N.p. [Geneva], 1773.

[———]. *La Méprise d'Arras.* Lausanne, 1771.

[———]. *Nouvelle requête au Roi en son conseil par les habitants de Longchaumois, Morez, Morbier, Bellefontaine, les Rousses et Bois-d'Amont, etc. en Franche-Comté.* N.p., n.d. [1770]

———. *Oeuvres complètes de Voltaire.* Edited by Louis Molland. 52 vols. Paris, 1877–1885.

[————]. *Questions sur l'Encyclopédie.* 9 vols. N.p. [Geneva], 1770–1772.

[————]. *Requête à tous les magistrats du royaume, composée par trois avocats d'un parlement.* N.p. [Geneva], 1769.

[————]. *Sermon du papa Nicolas Charisteski, prononcé dans l'église de Sainte-Tole-ranski, village de Lithuanie, le jour de sainte Epiphanie.* N.p., n.d. [Geneva, 1771]

[————]. *La Voix du curé sur le procès des serfs du Mont Jura.* N.p., n.d. [Geneva, 1772]

Walpole, Horace. *Horace Walpole's Correspondence with Madame Du Deffand and Wiart.* Edited by Wilmarth S. Lewis and W. H. Smith. 6 vols. New Haven, 1939.

SELECTED SECONDARY SOURCES

Albert, François, and Albert Bayet, eds. *Les Ecrivains politiques du XVIIIe siècle: Extraits, avec une introduction et notes.* Paris, 1904.

Allison, John M. *Lamoignon de Malesherbes, Defender and Reformer of the French Monarchy.* New Haven, 1938.

Ameline, Léon. *L'Idée de la souveraineté d'après les écrivains français du XVIIIe siècle.* Paris, 1904.

Amiable, Louis. *La Franc-Maçonnerie et la magistrature en France à la veille de la Révolution.* Aix, 1894.

Amiable, Louis, and J. C. Colfavru. *La Franc-Maçonnerie en France depuis 1725. (Exposé historique et doctrinale). Discours prononcés, le 16 juillet 1889, en séance du Congrès Maçonnique Internationale.* Paris, 1890.

Antoine, Michel. *Le Conseil du Roi sous le règne de Louis XV.* Geneva, 1970.

————. "Le Discours de la Flagellation (3 mars 1766)." In *Recueil de travaux of-fert à M. Clovis Brunel.* Paris, 1955.

Baker, Keith Michael. *Condorcet: From Natural Philosophy to Social Mathematics.* Chicago, 1975.

————. "French Political Thought at the Accession of Louis XVI." *Journal of Modern History,* L (1978), 279–303.

————. "A Script for a French Revolution: The Political Consciousness of the Abbé Mably." *Eighteenth-Century Studies,* XIV (1981), 235–63.

Barber, Elinor G. *The Bourgeoisie in Eighteenth-Century France.* Princeton, 1955.

Barni, Jules Romain. *Histoire des idées morales et politiques en France au XVIIIe siècle.* 2 vols. Paris, 1865–1867.

Becker, Carl L. *The Heavenly City of the Eighteenth-Century Philosophers.* New Haven, 1932.

Belin, Jean Paul. *Le Mouvement philosophique de 1748 à 1789: Etude sur la diffusion des idées des philosophes à Paris d'après les documents concernant l'histoire de la librairie*. Paris, 1913.

Berlin, Isaiah. *Two Concepts of Liberty: An Inaugural Lecture Delivered Before the University of Oxford on 31 October, 1958*. Oxford, 1958.

Bickart, Roger. *Les Parlements et la notion de souveraineté nationale au XVIIIe siècle*. Paris, 1932.

Biek, Paul H. *A Judgment of the Old Regime*. New York, 1944.

Bluche, François. *Les Magistrats du parlement de Paris au 18e siècle, 1715–1771*. Paris, 1960.

———. *L'Origine des magistrats du parlement de Paris au 18e siècle (1715–1771): Dictionnaire généalogique*. Paris, 1956.

———. *La Vie quotidienne de la noblesse française au 18e siècle*. Paris, 1973.

Bosher, John Francis. *French Finances 1770–1795: From Business to Bureaucracy*. Cambridge, England, 1971.

Brumfitt, J. H. *Voltaire Historian*. Oxford, 1958.

Cahen, Léon. "Idée de lutte de classe au 18e siècle." *Revue de synthèse historique*, XII (1906), 44–56.

———. "Le Pacte de famine et les spéculations sur les blés." *Revue historique*, 51e année, CLII (1926), 32–42.

———. *Les Querelles religeuses et parlementaires sous Louis XV*. Paris, 1913.

Carcasonne, Elie. *Montesquieu et le problème de la constitution française au XVIIIe siècle*. Paris, 1927.

Carné, Louis Joseph Marie, Count de. *Les Etats de Bretagne et l'administration de cette province jusqu'en 1789, par le comte de Carné*. 2nd ed. 2 vols. Paris, 1875.

Carré, Henri. *La Chalotais et le duc d'Aiguillon*. Poitiers, 1893.

———. "Turgot et le rappel des parlements." *Institut de France. Académie des Sciences Morales et Politiques. Séances et travaux*, LVIII (1902), 442–58.

Carré, Henri Pierre Marie Frédéric. *La Noblesse de France et l'opinion publique au 18e siècle*. Paris, 1920.

Cassirer, Ernst. *The Philosophy of the Enlightenment*. Boston, 1955.

Caussy, Fernand. *Voltaire, seigneur de villlage*. Paris, 1912.

Cavanaugh, Gerald J. "Turgot: The Rejection of Enlightened Despotism." *French Historical Studies*, VI (1969), 30–58.

Church, William F. "The Decline of the French Jurists as Political Theorists, 1660–1789." *French Historical Studies*, V (1967), 1–40.

Cobban, Alfred. *Aspects of the French Revolution*. New York, 1968.

———. *Old Régime and Revolution, 1715–1799*. London, 1968.

Colombet, Albert. *Les Parlementaires bourguignons à la fin du XVIIIe siècle*. 2nd ed. Dijon, 1937.

Crocker, Lester G. *An Age of Crisis: Man and World in Eighteenth-Century French Thought.* Baltimore, 1959.

————. *Nature and Culture: Ethical Thought in the French Enlightenment.* Baltimore, 1963.

Cruppi, Jean. *Un Avocat journaliste au 18ᵉ siècle, Linguet.* Paris, 1895.

Dakin, Douglas. *Turgot and the Ancien Régime in France.* London, 1939.

Dedieu, Joseph. *Histoire politique des Protestants français, 1715–1794.* 2 vols. Paris, 1925.

Desnoiresterres, Gustave Le Brisoys. *Voltaire et la société au XVIIIᵉ siècle.* 8 vols. Paris, 1867–1876.

Dieckman, Herbert. "Diderot, Grimm et Raynal: Les Contributions de Diderot à la 'Correspondance littéraire' et à l''Histoire des deux Indes.'" *Revue d'histoire littéraire de la France,* LI (1951), 417–40.

————. "*L'Encyclopédie* et le Fonds Vandeul." *Revue d'histoire littéraire de la France,* LI (1951), 318–32.

Doyle, William O. *The Parlement of Bordeaux and the End of the Old Regime, 1771–1790.* London, 1974.

————. "The Parlements of France and the Breakdown of the Old Régime, 1771–1788." *French Historical Studies,* VI (1970), 415–58.

Echeverria, Durand. "Franklin's Lost Letter on the Cincinnati." *Bulletin de l'Institut Français de Washington,* n.s., No. 3 (December, 1953), 119–26.

————. *Mirage in the West: A History of the French Image of American Society to 1815.* Princeton, 1957.

————. "The Pre-Revolutionary Influence of Rousseau's *Contrat Social.*" *Journal of the History of Ideas,* XXXIII (1972), 543–60.

————. "Roubaud and the Theory of American Degeneration." *French American Review,* III (1950), 24–33.

————. "Some Unknown Eighteenth-Century Editions of Voltaire's Political Pamphlets of 1771." *Studies on Voltaire and the Eighteenth Century,* CXXVII (1974), 61–64.

Egret, Jean. "L'Aristocratie parlementaire française à la fin de l'ancien régime." *Revue historique,* CCVIII (1952), 1–14.

————. *Louis XV et l'opposition parlementaire, 1715–1774.* Paris, 1970.

————. "Malesherbes, premier président de la Cour des Aides (1750–1775)." *Revue d'histoire moderne et contemporaine,* III (1956), 97–119.

————. "L'Opposition aristocratique, en France, au XVIIIᵉ siècle." *Information historique,* November–December, 1949, pp. 181–86.

————. *Le Parlement de Dauphiné et les affaires publiques dans la deuxième moitié du XVIIIᵉ siècle.* 2 vols. Grenoble, 1942.

————. *La Pré-révolution française (1787–1788)*. Paris, 1962.

————. "Le Procès des Jésuites devant les parlements de France (1761–1770)." *Revue historique*, CCIV (1950), 1–27.

Faguet, Emile. *La Politique comparée de Montesquieu, Rousseau et Voltaire*. Paris, 1902.

————. "La Politique de Voltaire." *Revue des cours et conférences*, 10ᵉ année, 1ère série (November 21, 1901), 49–57.

Faÿ, Bernard. *La Franc-Maçonnerie et la révolution intellectuelle au XVIIIᵉ siècle*. Paris, 1935.

Felice, Guillaume de. *Histoire des Protestants en France*. 6th ed. Toulouse, 1895.

Feugère, Anatole. *Un Précurseur de la Révolution, l'abbé Raynal (1713–1796); documents inédits*. Angoulême, 1922.

Flammermont, Jules Gustave. *La Chancelier Maupeou et les parlements*. Paris, 1883.

Ford, Franklin Lewis. *Robe and Sword: The Regrouping of the French Aristocracy after Louis XIV*. Cambridge, Mass., 1953.

Garrett, Clarke W. "The *Moniteur* of 1788." *French Historical Studies*, V (1968), 263–73.

Gay, Peter. *The Enlightenment: An Interpretation*. 2 vols. New York, 1966–1969.

————. *Voltaire's Politics: The Poet as Realist*. Princeton, 1959.

Gazier, Augustin Louis. *Histoire générale du mouvement janséniste depuis ses origines jusqu'à nos jours*. 2 vols. Paris, 1922.

Giesey, Ralph E. *The Juristic Basis of Dynastic Right to the French Throne*. Philadelphia, 1961.

Girard, René. *L'Abbé Terray et la liberté du commerce des grains, 1769–1774*. Paris, 1924.

Glasson, Ernest Désiré. *Histoire du droit et des institutions de la France*. 8 vols. Paris, 1887–1903.

————. *Le Parlement de Paris: Son rôle politique depuis le règne de Charles VII jusqu'à la Révolution*. 2 vols. Paris, 1901.

Godechot, Jacques Léon. "Le Contrat social et la révolution occidentale de 1762 à 1789." In *Etudes sur le Contrat social de Jean-Jacques Rousseau. Journées d'études sur le Contrat social. Dijon, 1962*. Paris, 1964.

————. *La Grande Nation: L'Expansion révolutionnaire de la France dans le monde de 1789 à 1799. Ouvrage publié avec le concours du Centre National de la Recherche Scientifique*. 2 vols. Paris, 1956.

————. *Les Révolutions, 1770–1799*. 2nd ed. Paris 1965.

Grimsley, Ronald. *Jean d'Alembert, 1717–1783*. Oxford, 1963.

Grosclaude, Pierre. *Malesherbes, témoin et interprète de son temps*. Paris, n.d.

Guerrier, Vladimir Ivanovich. *L'Abbé Mably, moraliste et politique: Etude sur la doc-*

trine morale du jacobinisme puritain et sur le développement de l'esprit républicain au 18ᵉ siècle. Vieweg, 1932.

Havens, George R. *The Age of Ideas: From Reaction to Revolution in Eighteenth-Century France.* New York, 1965.

Hazard, Paul. *La Pensée européenne au XVIIIᵉ siècle, de Montesquieu à Lessing.* 2 vols. Paris, 1946.

Hinton, Normand Howard. *Political Semantics: A Case Study.* Hanover, 1941.

Hudson, David Carl. "In Defense of Reform: French Government Propaganda During the Maupeou Crisis." *French Historical Studies,* VIII (1973), 51–76.

————. "Maupeou and the Parlements: A Study in Propaganda and Politics." Ph.D. dissertation, Columbia University, 1967.

Hugues, Edmond. *Les Synodes du désert: Actes et règlements des synodes nationaux et provinciaux tenus au désert de France, de l'an 1715 à l'an 1793.* 3 vols. Paris, 1885–1886.

Jallut, Maurice. *Histoire constitutionelle de la France.* 2 vols. Paris, 1956–1958.

Kaplan, Steven L. *Bread, Politics, and Political Economy in the Reign of Louis XV.* 2 vols. The Hague, 1976.

Knies, Carl, ed. *Carls Friedrichs von Badens brieflicher Verkehr mit Mirabeau und Du Pont.* 2 vols. Heidelberg, 1892.

Kors, Alan Charles. *D'Holbach's Coterie: An Enlightenment in Paris.* Princeton, 1976.

Kozminski, Léon. *Voltaire financier.* Paris, 1929.

Krauss, Michael. *The Atlantic Civilization: Eighteenth-Century Origins.* Ithaca, 1949.

Kreiger, Leonard. *An Essay on the Theory of Enlightened Despotism.* Chicago, 1975.

Kreiser, B. Robert. *Miracles, Convulsions, and Ecclesiastical Politics in Early Eighteenth-Century Paris.* Princeton, 1978.

Ladd, Everett C., Jr. "Helvétius and D'Holbach: 'La Moralisation de la Politique.'" *Journal of the History of Ideas,* XXIII (1962), 221–38.

Laski, Harold J. *The Rise of Liberalism: The Philosophy of a Business Civilization.* New York, 1936.

Le Bihan, Alain. *Francs-Maçons parisiens du Grand Orient de France (fin du XVIIIᵉ siècle).* Paris, 1966.

————. *Loges et chapitres de la Grande Loge et du Grand Orient de France (2ᵉ moitié du XVIIIᵉ siècle).* Paris, 1967.

Lefebvre, Georges. *The Coming of the French Revolution.* Translated by Robert R. Palmer. Princeton, 1947.

————. *La Révolution française.* Paris, 1951.

Le Griel, Jacques. *Le Chancelier Maupeou et la magistrature française à la fin de l'ancien régime. Le Conseil Supérieur de Clermont-Ferrand, 1771–1774.* Paris, 1908.

Lemaire, André. *Les Lois fondamentales de la monarchie française d'après les théoriciens de l'ancien régime.* Paris 1907.

Le Moy, A. *Le Parlement de Bretagne et le pouvoir royal au XVIIIᵉ siècle.* Paris, 1909.

Levasseur, Emile. *Histoire des classes ouvrières et de l'industrie en France avant 1789.* 2 vols. Paris, 1900–1901.

Levy, Darline Gay. *The Ideas and Careers of Simon-Nicolas-Henri Linguet: A Study in Eighteenth-Century French Politics.* Urbana, 1980.

Lichtenberger, André. *Le Socialisme au XVIIIᵉ siècle: Etude sur les idées socialistes dans les écrivains français au XVIIIᵉ siècle avant la Révolution.* Paris, 1895.

Lion, Henri. "Essai sur les oeuvres politiques et morales du baron d'Holbach." *Annales révolutionnaires,* XIV (1922), 89–98, 265–80, 441–63.

———. "L'Ethocratie de d'Holbach." *Annales révolutionnaires,* XV (1923), 378–96.

———. "Les Idées politiques et morales de d'Holbach." *Annales historiques de la Révolution française,* I (1924), 356–70.

———. "La Morale universelle de d'Holbach." *Annales historiques de la Révolution française,* I (1924), 42–63.

———. "La Politique naturelle de d'Holbach." *Annales révolutionnaires,* XV (1923), 209–19.

Lough, John. *The Contributors to the "Encyclopédie."* London, 1973.

———. "The 'Encyclopédie' and the Remonstrances of the Paris Parlement." *Modern Language Review,* LVI (1961), 393–95.

———. *The Encyclopédie in Eighteenth-Century England and Other Studies.* Newcastle-upon-Tyne, 1970.

———. *Essays on the Encyclopédie of Diderot and D'Alembert.* London, 1968.

———. "The Problem of the Unsigned Articles in the *Encyclopédie.*" *Studies on Voltaire and the Eighteenth Century,* XXXII (1965), 327–90.

McDonald, Joan. *Rousseau and the French Revolution, 1762–1791.* London, 1965.

Mackrell, J. Q. C. *The Attack on "Feudalism" in Eighteenth-Century France.* London, 1973.

Maffey, Aldo. *Il Pensiero politico de Mably.* Turin, 1968.

Marion, Marcel. *La Bretagne et le duc d'Aiguillon, 1753–1770.* Paris, 1898.

———. *Dictionnaire des institutions de la France aux XVIIᵉ et XVIIIᵉ siècles.* Paris, 1923.

———. *Histoire financière de la France depuis 1715.* 6 vols. Paris, 1914–1931.

Martin, Basil Kingsley. *French Liberal Thought in the Eighteenth Century: A Study of Political Ideas from Bayle to Condorcet.* 2nd ed. London, 1954.

Martin, Gaston. *La Franc-Maçonnerie française et la préparation de la Révolution.* 2nd ed. Paris, 1926.

————. *Manuel d'histoire de la Franc-Maçonnerie française.* Paris, 1929.

Martin, Paul. *Les Idées de Turgot sur la décentralisation administrative.* Paris, 1917.

Mathiez, A. "Les Doctrines politiques des Physiocrates." *Annales historiques de la Révolution française,* XIII (1936), 193–203.

Maugras, Gaston. *La Duchesse de Choiseul et le patriarche de Ferney.* Paris, 1889.

Maupeou, Jacques, Vicomte de. *Le Chancelier Maupeou.* Paris, 1942.

Mornet, Daniel. "Les Enseignements des bibliothèques privées (1750–1780)." *Revue d'histoire littéraire de la France,* 17ᵉ année (1910), 449–96.

————. *Les Origines intellectuelles de la Révolution française, 1715–1787.* Paris, 1933.

Oestreicher, Jean. *La Pensée politique et économique de Diderot.* Vincennes, 1936.

Palmer, Robert R. *The Age of Democratic Revolution: A Political History of Europe and America, 1760–1800.* 2 vols. Princeton, 1959, 1964.

Palmer, Robert R., and Jacques L. Godechot. "Le Problème de l'Atlantique du XVIIIᵉ au XXᵉ siècle." In *Relazioni del X Congresso Internazionale di Scienze Storiche, Roma 4–11 Settembre 1955.* Florence, 1955.

Pappas, John Nicolas. *Voltaire and D'Alembert.* Bloomington, 1962.

Payne, Harry C. *The Philosophes and the People.* New Haven, 1976.

Peignot, Gabriel. *Dictionnaire des livres condamnés.* Paris, 1806.

Pocquet du Haut Jussé, Barthélémy Ambroise Marie. *Le Pouvoir absolu et l'esprit provincial: Le Duc d'Aiguillon et La Chalotais.* 3 vols. Paris, 1900.

Poland, Burdette C. *French Protestantism and the French Revolution: A Study in Church and State, Thought and Religion, 1685–1815.* Princeton, 1957.

Préclin, Edmond, and Eugène Jarry. *Les Luttes politiques et doctrinales au XVIIᵉ et XVIIIᵉ siècles.* 2 vols. Paris, 1955–1956.

Priouret, Roger A. *La Franc-Maçonnerie sous les lys.* Paris, 1953.

Proust, Jacques. *Diderot et l'Encyclopédie.* Paris, 1962.

————. *L'Encyclopédie.* Paris, 1965.

————. "Pour servir à une édition critique de *La Lettre sur le commerce de la librairie.*" *Diderot Studies* (Geneva, 1961), III, 321–45.

Renaudet, Augustin. *Etudes sur l'histoire intérieure de la France de 1715 à 1789.* 2 vols. Paris, 1946.

Rocquain, Félix. *L'Esprit révolutionnaire avant la Révolution, 1715–1789.* Paris, 1878.

Schwab, Richard N. "The Diderot Problem: The Starred Articles and the Question of Attribution in the *Encyclopédie.*" *Eighteenth-Century Studies,* II (1969), 240–85, 370–438.

Schwab, Richard N., Walter E. Rex, and John Lough. *Inventory of Diderot's Encyclopédie.* Vol. LXXX of *Studies on Voltaire and the Eighteenth Century.* Geneva, 1971.

Sée, Henri Eugène. "La Doctrine politique des parlements." *Revue historique de droit français et étanger*, 4th series, 3rd year (1924), 287–306.

———. *L'Evolution de la pensée politique en France au XVIIIᵉ siècle*. Paris, 1925.

———. *La France économique et sociale au XVIIIᵉ siècle*. Paris, 1925.

———. "Les Idées politiques de Voltaire." *Revue historique*, XCVIII (1908), 254–93.

———. *Les Idées politiques en France au XVIIIᵉ siècle*. Paris, 1920.

Shennan, J. H. *The Parlement of Paris*. Ithaca, 1968.

Sydenham, Michael John. *The French Revolution*. New York, 1965.

Tate, Robert S., Jr. *Petit de Bachaumont: His Circle and the Mémoires secrets*. Vol. LXV of *Studies on Voltaire and the Eighteenth Century*. Geneva, 1968.

Taveneaux, René. *Jansénisme et politique*. Paris, 1965.

Taylor, Samuel S. B. "Rousseau's Contemporary Reputation in France." *Studies on Voltaire and the Eighteenth Century*, XVII (1963), 1545–74.

Tocqueville, Alexis Charles Henri Maurice Clérel de. *L'Ancien Régime et la Révolution*. Edited by J. P. Mayer. Paris, 1952.

———. *De la démocratie en Amérique: Les Grands thèmes*. Edited by J. P. Mayer. Paris, 1968.

Van Kley, Dale. "Church, State, and the Ideological Origins of the French Revolution: The Debate over the General Assembly of the Gallican Clergy in 1765." *Journal of Modern History*, LI (1979), 629–66.

———. *The Jansenists and the Expulsion of the Jesuits from France, 1757–1765*. New Haven, 1975.

Vartanian, Aram. *Diderot and Descartes: A Study of Scientific Naturalism in the Enlightenment*. Princeton, 1953.

Vaughan, Charles Edwyn. *Studies in the History of Political Philosophy Before and After Rousseau*. Manchester, 1925.

Villiers, Robert. *L'Organisation du parlement de Paris et des conseils supérieurs d'après la réforme de Maupeou (1771–1774)*. Paris, 1937.

Vyverberg, Henry. *Historical Pessimism in the French Enlightenment*. Cambridge, Mass., 1958.

———. "Limits of Nonconformity in the Enlightenment: The Case of Simon-Nicolas-Henri Linguet." *French Historical Studies*, VI (1970), 474–91.

Wade, Ira O. *The Intellectual Origins of the French Enlightenment*. Princeton, 1971.

Welch, Oliver John Grindor. *Mirabeau: A Study of a Democratic Monarchist*. London, 1951.

Weulersse, Georges. *Les Manuscrits économiques de F. Quesnay et du marquis de Mirabeau aux Archives Nationales*. Paris, 1910.

———. *Le Mouvement physiocratique en France, de 1756 à 1770*. Paris, 1910.

————. *La Physiocratie à la fin du règne de Louis XV,* ˙*1770–1774*. Paris, 1959.
————. *La Physiocratie sous les ministères de Turgot et de Necker, 1774–1781*. Paris, 1950.
Whitfield, Ernest A. *Gabriel Bonnot de Mably. With an Introduction by Professor Harold J. Laski*. London, 1930.
Wickwar, William Hardy. *Baron d'Holbach: A Prelude to the French Revolution*. London, 1935.
Wilson, Arthur M. *Diderot*. New York, 1972.
————. "Why Did the Political Theory of the Encyclopedists Not Prevail? A Suggestion." *French Historical Studies*, I (1960), 283–94.
Wolpe, Hans. *Raynal et sa machine de guerre: L'Histoire des deux Indes et ses perfectionnements*. Stanford, 1957.

INDEX

Absolutism: affirmed by Edict of Dec. 1770, pp. 16–17; and Patriote constitution, 78–83; of royalists, 125–35, 139–46; paternalistic, 139–42, 157; and Voltaire, 155–60, 168; enlightened, 79–80, 155–60, 168, 219–20, 226–27; and Linguet, 172–74; and Physiocrats, 191–97, 213; opposed by independents, 221–28, 245; theocratic, 276, 278–81; monarchical, 300, 302–303. *See also* Bureaucratic despotism; Divine right; Legal despotism; *Thèse royale*

Académie des Jeux Floraux, 273

Académie Française, 26, 58

Aiguillon, F. A., Duke d', 13–14, 30, 96–97

Albertas, J. B., Marquis d', 26

Alembert, J. L. d': and Patriotes, 59; and freedom of press, 114, 254; on absolutism, 224, 227; on Maupeou, 234–25; on parlements, 234–35; on restoration of parlements, 234–35; pessimism of, 242–43; on liberty, 249; on equality, 257; on law, 257; on freedom of religion, 275; on aristocracy, 292; mentioned, 258

Argenson, M. R., Marquis d', 126

Aristocracy: and Patriotes, 48–50; and Patriote constitution, 84; and royalists, 135–39; and Voltaire, 160–61; and Physiocrats, 197; and independents, 291–93, 295. *See also* Equality; *Noblesse d'épée; Noblesse de robe*; Status

Arrêts de défense, 2

Assemblée du Clergé (1772), 273, 274

Assemblée du Clergé (1775), 273, 274, 281

Aubusson, P. A., Vicomte d', 40, 43, 67–68, 109, 114–15

Augeard, J. M.: *Correspondance secrète*, 23, 42; as Patriote propagandist, 40, 41–42; *A. M. Jacques Verges*, 59–60; as Patriote, 74; on States General, 86; on powers of parlements, 88–89; on power of taxation, 92; on freedom of person, 110

Auxerre, College de, 46, 113

Bachaumont, L. P. de, 54–55

Barbier, E. J. F., 8

Baudeau, Nicolas, 180, 185, 187, 195, 197, 204, 207–208

Beaumarchais, P. A. C. de, 23, 42

Beauvau, Prince de, 58

Beccaria, C. B., Marquis de, 258

Berlin, Isaiah, 105

Besenval, P. V., Baron de, 27–28

Blanchard, 110

Blonde, André: as Patriote propagandist, 40, 42, 43; and Patriote constitution, 66; on divine right, 81; on States General, 86; on judicial tenure, 96; on law, 97, 99; on freedom of religion, 116; on positive and negative liberty, 117; and revolution, 120

Boesnier de L'Orme, Paul, 185, 186, 206, 207, 210, 211, 212